From Silence to Voice

From Silence to Voice

The Rise of Maori Literature

Paola Della Valle

To my father, who enclosed the north and south seas in his eyes, and all the world inside.

Published by Oratia Books, Oratia Media Ltd, 783 West Coast Road, Oratia, Auckland 0604, New Zealand (www.oratia.co.nz).

ISBN 978-0-947506-41-4

First published 2010 by Libro International
Reprinted 2014
This edition 2017 by Oratia Books

Editors: Peter Dowling, Sam Hill

Printed in New Zealand and the UK

CONTENTS

Introduction

The rise of Maori writing in English in the 1970s, part of the so-called Maori Renaissance, was a milestone in the young literature of Aotearoa/New Zealand. It marked a shift of perspective in its officially monocultural and Anglocentric society, offering the point of view of the indigenous people of the country, and involved the appropriation of the written word by an oral culture, which had been subjected to and 'othered' by the production of Western texts dealing with Maori up to the mid-twentieth century.

This study explores the passage from silence to voice in the literary representation of Maori — from the role as objects of external representations to becoming agents of self-representation — and then records the modulation of the Maori voice up to the New Millennium through the production of two major Maori writers: Patricia Grace and Witi Ihimaera. The arguments of the book are positioned in the conceptual space of postcolonial theory, but the analysis of texts rooted in a non-Western tradition requires a localised perspective, which takes into account different cultural (and even ontological) premises to avoid the trap of unconsciously Eurocentric criticism. The approach employed will therefore be an 'indigenised reading', which is, in Eva Rask Knudsen's words, 'the outsider's attempt to read with an understanding of the indigenous perspective'.

Part One ('The Maori Silence') focuses on the control of the means of communication as a key feature of the colonial enterprise in New Zealand and on the use of literary texts as the ideological weapons of imperial power in the nineteenth and early twentieth centuries. The considerable number of essays and literary texts referring to Maori or including them as characters provided a system of representations of Maoriness functional to the colonial discourse. It affirmed and defined the colonisers' self-identity, fixed Maori stereotypes and acted as a justification of the colonial enterprise. The appearance of Maori characters in Katherine Mansfield's and Frank Sargeson's fiction reflects a development in the treatment of Maori figures in literature, insofar as indigenous characters seem to be used to criticise those aspects of New Zealand provincial society the writers dislike. Sargeson in particular criticised materialism and Puritanism, and his emphasis on an ecologically friendly attitude and the advocacy for a return to the primacy of imagination over cold rationality indirectly draws on the Maori vision. This view is also shared by Roderick Finlayson in his fierce attack on Western capitalism. Finlayson is the first Pakeha author that acknowledges Maori as the other soul of the country, conveying the disorientation of a race that is risking the loss of its identity and roots. Unlike previous Pakeha writers, Finlayson underscores the malaise of Maori people, not to foresee their demise but to urge a remedy and, further, to embrace their view as a model to follow. Another Pakeha writer showed, some years later, a deeper insight into Maori culture and preoccupations: Noel Hilliard. Part One also includes a chapter on Janet Frame and the influence that the Maori holistic vision exerted on her writing, which has an emphasis on a reality that is not limited to the visible and on mythology as the basis of any history or story.

Part Two ('The Maori Voice') starts with a close reading of Grace's and Ihimaera's early fiction, the so-called 'pastoral tradition' of the 1970s — probably the most important phase in their careers because it was aimed at the recovery of the foundational traits of Maori identity and formed the basis of a literary aesthetic — and continues with the analysis of their politically committed works of the 1980s. Due to the writers' copious subsequent production, the study proceeds by applying a thematic approach to a selection of major texts so as to focalise recurring preoccupations and issues. These include asserting a different notion of history from the dominant rationalist approach; appropriating and remodelling the Western literary canon and the language of the imperial centre; affirming the environmental imperative inherent in the Maori holistic vision; redefining foundational Maori values, such as the extended family, in the light of the present; and finally, their opening up to international influences and foreign genres. In Grace's *Tu* the Maori Battalion's Italian campaign during the Second World War contributes to sharpening the awareness of Maori rights and strengthening their racial self-esteem, two factors that will be of crucial importance for their self-determination at home in the years to come. Italian melodrama, American cinematography and global television broadcasting have had an important impact on Ihimaera's fiction, informing the content and aesthetics of some of his works. Altogether the development of Grace's and Ihimaera's fiction in the last 40 years testifies to Maori people's rejection of a concept of identity as a pristine pre-colonial self to be retrieved, and affirms it as a narrative that needs to be retold in order to be vital and face the challenges of modernity.

To conclude, a few lines about the orthographic choices made in the book. The words 'Maori' and 'Pakeha' have always been capitalised, whether they appear as nouns or adjectives, according to Maori preference. The Maori form of plural without the final 's' has been retained (i.e. one Maori/one Pakeha, two Maori/two Pakeha). The Anglo-Saxon possessive case has not been employed with these two terms, in order to avoid their Anglicisation, and the corresponding adjective has been used instead. For practical reasons the use of a macron to indicate long vowels has also been omitted. However, the words included in quotations may follow different orthographic rules and are reported exactly as they appear in the sources. Finally, the double Maori and Pakeha name of the country (Aotearoa/New Zealand) has been applied when discussing the country's recent bicultural past but not for earlier references, and when the country name functions as an adjective, I have preferred the shorter 'New Zealand' only.

Acknowledgements

My warmest thanks to my tutors Prof. Paolo Bertinetti and Prof. Pietro Deandrea, for their precious help and encouragement in my research; to Prof. Donatella Abbate Badin, Prof. Carmen Concilio, Prof. Claudio Gorlier and Prof. Ruth Henderson for conversation and information; to my publisher Peter Dowling and editor Sam Hill for their invaluable advice and careful supervision; and to my inspirational sources, Patricia Grace and Witi Ihimaera.

PART 1

The Maori Silence

Maori in Colonial Literature

Colonialism reshaped existing structures of human knowledge. No branch of learning was left untouched by the colonial experience. The process was somewhat like the functioning of ideology itself, simultaneously a misrepresentation of reality and its reordering. Like ideology, it arose from 'material circumstances' and was 'material in its effect'. – Ania Loomba[1]

Power and knowledge directly imply one another ... there is no power relation without the correlative constitution of a field of knowledge, nor any knowledge that does not presuppose and constitute at the same time power relations. – Michel Foucault[2]

Defining the 'other': the text as ideological discourse

The notion of ideology — the interaction between power and knowledge — is central to the colonial discourse. Ania Loomba explores the development of this key concept of postcolonial thinking in *Colonialism/Postcolonialism*, showing its passage from mere reflection of the economic reality (Marx) into the broader domain of 'discourse' (Foucault, Said).[3] In *The German Ideology* (1846) Marx and Engels describe ideology as the 'false consciousness' that disguises people's real relationship to their world. It is, in other words, a distorted vision of the reality (superstructure), produced by capitalism (the economic base), aimed at defending the interests of the dominant social classes and obscuring the oppressed classes' perception of their real state and exploitation. While recognising the importance of ideology, Marx's determinist perspective still asserts the supremacy of the material/economic world over ideas, since it locates the driving force of historical development within the capitalist system and its contradictions, which will necessarily lead to the proletariat's revolution.

Italian communist Antonio Gramsci first questioned the supremacy of the economic base over ideas, and viewed ideologies as something more than just an effect of material reality. In his attempt to understand the failure of the proletariat's revolution in Western Europe, Gramsci focused on the reasons that make people absorb the ideology of the dominant classes and identify with it. His formulation of the concept of 'hegemony' is crucial to postcolonial studies: hegemony is effected through a combination of 'coercion and consent', an idea that recalls Machiavelli's suggestion that power can be achieved through 'force and fraud'. It implies manipulation and indoctrination but also plays upon the common sense of people, which Gramsci views as a contradictory amalgam of ideas, prejudices and intuitions that constitute the practical everyday consciousness of human beings.[4] The Gramscian notion of hegemony has been used by postcolonial scholars to probe how colonial regimes achieved domination by creating partial consent. It also shows how ideology can actually mould material reality, an idea developed by Marxist philosopher Louis Althusser and his student Michel Foucault.

Althusser reformulated the concept of ideology, granting it a certain autonomy from the capitalist mode of production.[5] Ideology became a transhistorical, 'organic' element of any society, the essential function of which is to 'form' and 'equip' individuals to 'respond to their conditions of existence'.[6] It is basically a 'system of representations' in and through which the human subject defines itself: 'Ideology does not represent the world to the individual but represents the individual in their world'.[7] By conceptualising ideology in a sense that is akin to the broader domain of consciousness and by underlying its contribution to the process of subject-formation, Althusser moved a considerable distance from Marx's view. He also developed Gramsci's theory about hegemony, arguing that in modern capitalist societies coercion is achieved by the repressive state apparatuses (RSAs) such as the police, the army, law courts, and state functionaries, while consent is enforced by the ideological state apparatuses (ISAs) such as the church, the family, the media, the trade unions, and above all the education system.[8] This idea will be relevant in the study of colonial systems.

Althusser's concept of ideology was later transformed by Foucault into the notion of 'discourse'. Foucault's historical research into psychiatry, medicine, criminology and sexuality led him to believe that the human subject is not a free entity, but is always defined from the outside as the object of a certain discourse. Discourse is 'an archive-like body of texts and a self-regulating system for the production of ideas about a designated object or field of objects'.[9] It is the conceptual territory in which knowledge is formed and produced and is the field within which language itself is defined. It is rooted in human practices, institutions and actions that vary according to different eras. By studying, in particular, the development of some systems of exclusion (for example, mental hospitals and prisons) and their engagement with the definition of what is true or false, normal or abnormal, he contended that knowledge about the human subject is never objective but always contingent. Foucault's position is a critique of humanism — that is, the belief in the existence of universal truths or natural ideas about the human race — and of its faith in human nature. It also denies the objectivity of human sciences. A discourse is governed by its systematic rules rather than by a sovereign subject. The conclusions are that:

1. The subject's agency is contingent on the rules and systematic relations that constitute a discourse.
2. The subject is necessarily subjectified, that is, 'subject to' an external code or 'order of discourse'.
3. Knowledge and power are mutually dependent and constitutive of each other.[10]

Although Foucault's analysis of the modern cultural order has been charged with Eurocentrism, inasmuch as he did not consider the relevance of the colonial expansion on the Western power/knowledge systems,[11] his research into the modalities that constitute 'otherness' as a category functional to power is crucial for postcolonial studies and was a major influence on Edward Said. In his foundational work *Orientalism*, Said employed Foucault's notion of discourse to demonstrate how the huge body of Western representations of the Orient — from scientific theories to commonsense notions, from pictorial images to literary images — was functional to the imperial power and helped organise a conceptual territory that justified and promoted colonial expansion. Unlike Foucault, who explored social institutions, texts and practices, Said focused in particular on literary or cultural texts to show how ideas can shape the human perception of reality and be an instrument of power as effective as the military, political and economic apparatuses.[12]

This discussion of the development of 'ideology' underscores the growing relevance attributed by Western thinking to the concept of knowledge, in its broadest sense, for the constitution of any system of power. Said re-elaborated Marxist and poststructuralist thought in a form that applied to the colonial experience. It is no accident that he included both Gramsci and Foucault among his inspirational sources,[13] while he synthesised the Western assumptions on the other, quoting Marx's sentence: 'They cannot represent themselves; they must be represented', in which 'they' refers both to the oppressed and the colonised people.[14] The two major points made by Said in *Orientalism* are:

1. Western representations of the Orient are always self-reflecting and self-confirming — that is, by defining the other the Western mind constructs a powerful and superior self-identity.
2. Texts and ideas always have material effectiveness.

Although he does not directly deal with indigenous resistance, these points are crucial in the context of a settler colony like New Zealand, inhabited by two distinct ethnic groups: the indigenous Maori population, whose culture was oral, and the dominant Western — basically British — settlers.

As argued by Ashcroft, Griffiths and Tiffin in *The Empire Writes Back*, the control over the means of communication is the key feature of any colonial enterprise.[15] An interesting example they give is Tzvetan Todorov's analysis of Cortez' successful campaign against the Aztecs of Central America.[16] Todorov's contention is that the Spanish and Aztec cultures were based on two incommensurable forms of communication. In the oral Aztec culture, based on a ritual and cyclic interpretation of reality, there was no place for the arrival of Cortez:

> Aztec communication is between man and the world, because knowledge always proceeds from a reality that is already fixed, ordered and given. On the other hand European communication is between man and man.[17]

For the Aztec Emperor Montezuma, the most plausible explanation for the conquistadores' arrival was that they were gods. Faced with the inexplicable, the only recourse of the oral system was silence. Cortez took advantage of this silence and filled it with his own discourse. All his actions were designed to control what the others 'knew' about him, for example, he took care to bury horses killed in battles to maintain the impression that they were supernatural. Cortez's success lay exactly in his ability to control the means of communication.

'Silence' was also the inevitable reaction by Maori to colonisation. The encounter between indigenous and European cultures in New Zealand, at the end of the eighteenth century, was one between two antithetical ways of communication. Maori life was bound up in a unified vision in which every aspect was related to the other: art, religion, war, myth, story-telling, food gathering, love-making, death — all were integrated parts of a single picture.[18] It was the ordered, cyclical, 'paradigmatic' world of the oral word. The invasion of Western rationality and technology disrupted a pre-existing economic and social system as well as epistemological and ontological categories.

A clear example, which can be reconnected to Foucault's notion that language and the subject are always defined by a certain 'discourse' of inclusion/exclusion, is the evolution of the word 'Maori'. Prior to European arrival, Maori had no concept of nationhood or race, and did not define themselves as 'Maori'. They were divided into iwi (tribes) and hapu (subtribes) and their identity was determined by the name of the founder of the iwi or hapu they belonged to, preceded by the prefix 'Ngati' (descendants of), as well as by the place where they lived. As Michael King notices, 'the first question they would be asked by strangers was not who they were, but where they were from.'[19] This means, first of all, that they knew who they were — that is, each person could retrace a recognisable identity similar to his/her own in every stranger. Second, it reflects how their subjectivity was formed within a 'discourse' that stressed the importance of the past and origins, and the bond with a specific land. According to the Maori notion of history, 'the past is not behind, it is before us, a long line of ancestors to whom we are accountable and with whom we have an implicit contract.'[20] Furthermore in Maori culture land does not belong to people, rather people belong to the land. Each person has the inalienable right to have a turangawaewae (a place to stand), because everyone has a particular ancestry that connects him/her to a specific land. Turangawaewae is the place from which the people receive their standing or identity.[21] In pre-European society, the term 'Maori' simply meant 'normal' or 'usual', as in tangata Maori (an ordinary person). The perception of their own identity and their subject- formation changed completely when the Pakeha (the foreigner, the alien) arrived and imposed a different 'discourse'.

The intrusion of the 'syntagmatic' world of the written word into the Maori oral culture was one of the most powerful weapons of the Pakeha. As argued by Ashcroft et al., 'the presence or absence of writing is possibly the most important element in the colonial situation. Writing does not merely introduce a communicative instrument, but also involves an entirely different and intrusive orientation to knowledge and interpretation'[22] — that is, a completely different 'discourse'. The Treaty of Waitangi, signed by the British Crown and the chiefs of most (but not all) tribes in 1840, is an example. The effects of this foundational 'text' of New Zealand history on the indigenous population are still the subject of historical claims between Maori tribes and the New Zealand government. Although the Treaty was translated into te Reo (the Maori language), it could not be fully understood by the members of a culture who did not share the same concepts, vocabulary, political or legal structures — in particular the notion of sovereignty.[23] The result was a widespread disillusionment among Maori signatories, which led to the New Zealand Wars and the birth of the Kingitanga movement in the mid-1850s.[24]

Controlling the means of communication was also enacted through the production of a great amount of non-fictional works on Maori (ethnological and anthropological surveys, histories, institutional reports, essays, pamphlets, collections of myths and legends and so on), and literary works referring to Maori or including them as characters (in poetry, novels and short stories). This considerable body of texts provided a system of representations of 'Maoriness' functional to the colonial discourse. While the distinction between Maori/normal and Pakeha/foreign was the comprehensible and natural reaction of an isolated paradigmatic world to the intrusion of the colonisers, the European search for the definition of the other in written texts, as Said suggested, is an artificial construct aimed at affirming the colonisers' superior self-identity and justifying their colonial enterprise. Maori dissatisfaction with the Treaty of Waitangi led to numerous clashes and acts of warfare between them and Pakeha. But Maori people had few weapons to use in the subtler 'textual' war. The written texts developed a set of binary oppositions (colonisers/colonised, white/black, self/other, civilised/uncivilised, Maori language/English language), which basically represented Maori as inferior beings, savages, cannibals, lazy and cunning, either children to be guided or bloodthirsty enemies to be exterminated.

Missionaries promoted literacy among Maori mainly as part of a programme to convert them to Christianity. As Jane McRae illustrates, 'once an orthography was available, the mission schools taught classes in Maori, a practice that was brought to a close by government policies requiring that the medium of instruction in schools be both English and Maori (from 1847) and from 1867 onwards, English only.'[25] Literacy, therefore, was a means to impose first the religion then the language of the colonisers on the colonised. The 'textual attack' was double: from the outside, by the huge amount of European writing on Maori; and from the inside, by an educational system dedicated to silencing and erasing Maori identity and language.

Postcolonial theorist Homi Bhabha has criticised Said's *Orientalism* for giving an image of colonialism as all powerful, ignoring how it was forged relationally.[26] He posits 'liminality' and 'hybridity' as necessary attributes of the colonial condition, creating an in-between cultural space where both colonisers and colonised develop unstable split-identities, and are dependent on each other. 'The colonial presence is always ambivalent,' says Bhabha, 'split between its appearance as original and authoritative, and its articulation as repetition and difference'.[27] This organic ambivalence carries the seeds of resistance insofar as colonial authority is unable to replicate itself perfectly, that is to say, it necessarily produces cracks within which a counter-discourse can rise. A site of Maori resistance — a chink in the 'armour' of colonial authority — originated in the production of texts. The struggle for the survival of Maori identity and culture was paradoxically fostered by writing, by the very tool that had been used to silence them. This reached a climax in the 1960s when Maori writers started publishing works in English, using the means (the written word), the language (English) and the literary structures (poetry, short stories and novels) of the colonisers to subvert their dominant discourse.

It was an important act of appropriation and self-determination, and was followed by many others in the political and social arenas. A petition of 40,000 signatories calling for the official recognition of the Maori language and its compulsory teaching in the school system was presented to the minister of education on 14 September 1972,[28] and it led, in the early 1980s, to the establishment of kohanga reo (language nests), preschools where only Maori is spoken,[29] and kura kaupapa Maori, primary schools providing all teaching in Maori within a framework of Maori culture and values. In 1987, Maori was recognised as an official New Zealand language, along with English. The subversion of Eurocentric discourse implied an autochthonous representation of the self, in other words, the building of a new system of representations through literature. As Ihimaera forcefully said, 'Literature is language. Maori literature is Maori politics. For Maori, literature, whether in English or in Maori, is a Waitangi issue, a Treaty issue, a sovereignty issue.'[30] The recovery of a Maori subjectivity within the dominant discourse was enacted with the same weapons previously used by the colonisers to suppress it.

Forming the Western discourse: the control of literacy and the media in nineteenth-century New Zealand

Although writing was not part of the Maori cultural legacy, their culture can be defined, as Eva Rask Knudsen suggests, as non-literate rather than illiterate or preliterate. This means that they were 'trained readers'[31] not of books but of

9

their own cultural texts, for example the carvings in their wharenui (ancestral or meeting houses) or oral storytelling. Ancestors of the Maori came by canoe from East Polynesia to the land they called Aotearoa, 'the land of the long white cloud', some time after 800 AD. Following the patterns of Polynesian heritage, they produced a rich and complex oral tradition concerning all aspects of their life including tribal history, sacred rituals and secular etiquette, and customary skills and practices. The main genres of composition were waiata (sung poetry), whakapapa (genealogy), whakataukī (sayings), kōrero (narratives) and karakia (prayers and incantations).[32]

Each genre was used on particular occasions and for particular purposes. As illustrated by Margaret Orbell, waiata were generally laments or complaints sung publicly, on a marae [33] or elsewhere, to express the poet's feelings, convey a message and arouse emotions in the listener. There were waiata tangi (weeping songs) or laments for the dead used in funerals, and waiata aroha (songs of love and longing) or waiata whaiāipo (sweetheart songs), composed by women and dealing with love. Waiata aroha and whaiāipo could be also adapted by men to use in oratory: if a chief wanted another leader to be his political ally, for example, he could use, in the course of his speech, a certain waiata aroha with the words modified in such a way as to identify himself with the woman poet and the desired ally with her distant lover.[34]

Migration myths and tribal history generally took the form of whakapapa, represented visually in the carvings and decorations of the meeting houses and recited as part of the protocol in official meetings. The mana[35] of a chief relied greatly on his ability to speak, to show knowledge of tribal history and to construct ornate speech by quoting whakataukī, reciting kōrero or singing waiata. The karakia were recited by tohunga (priests) in sacred ceremonies and rituals. Although the primary record of the oral tradition lay in people's memories and was preserved by regular use, it was prompted by a multiplicity of 'texts' that constituted and surrounded the Maori world: names given to places and the landscape (mountains, rivers, bays); carvings and panels of ancestral houses; patterns of weaving and other crafts; speeches given on the marae; and rituals on any special occasion. It was a paradigmatic world wherein everything was connected.

A Maori orthography was created in the early 1800s, and as literacy spread rapidly among the indigenous people their cultural, social and cognitive structures were profoundly changed. Maori used writing for practical purposes (letters, minutes or genealogies)[36] rather than as a means to express their culture, which remained mainly oral. The transcription of Maori oral tradition, as well as most of what was published in Maori or in English about the indigenous culture and literature up to 1900, was produced by Pakeha. This can be explained by cultural conventions. In the traditional Maori view, knowledge is a private matter: it is tapu (sacred) and should remain within the tribe. Most Maori manuscripts are known to have been buried with their authors.[37] Throughout the nineteenth century the majority of publications in Maori were produced by church and state bodies.[38] They included religious books, newspapers promoting the diffusion of Christianity, and information about European civilisations. Government presses featured transcriptions of Maori oral literature and, in addition, direct translations of a selection of texts that could help the understanding of European culture. Interestingly, two of the texts chosen were *The Life and Adventures of Robinson Crusoe* and *The Pilgrim's Progress*.

If the diffusion of Bunyan's work in 1854 is clearly a supplement of the Christian indoctrination fostered by local churches, the Maori translation of Defoe's novel cannot be seen but as a covert promotion of imperial discourse. What the two books have in common is the ability of their authors to convey an implicit didactic message with immediacy, realism and vividness. Although *The Pilgrim's Progress* deals with the archetypal Christian theme of man's life as a journey from the City of Destruction to Salvation and Heaven, Bunyan was able to render spiritual experience in concrete and homely terms, which makes him a predecessor of the eighteenth-century English novelists.[39] Both texts represent Calvinist ethics that are at the foundation of capitalist society and of its outcome, colonialism.

The Maori version of *Robinson Crusoe* was published in 1852 under the authority of Sir George Grey, twice governor of New Zealand (1845–53 and 1861–68) and premier from 1877 to 1879.[40] Whether a 'great dictator and Maori-tamer', in Sinclair's words,[41] or an administrator who dealt with Maori matters 'with considerable skill and a strong sense of justice', as described by King,[42] he is definitely a very clear example of a leader who knew the importance of the means of communication in the exercise of power. Grey was sent to New Zealand to settle the explosive situation that emerged in the years that followed the signing of the Treaty of Waitangi. Several clashes had occurred in the Nelson/Wellington areas and in the Far North from 1843 to 1845 in what can be defined as the first period of the New Zealand Wars. Using both arms and diplomatic agreements, Grey re-established peace for over a decade. He ensured that the terms of the Treaty were observed, restored the Crown monopoly on Maori land purchases despite the opposition of private speculators, and granted to the British government large areas in the North Island (roughly 1.2 million hectares) and almost the entire South Island (about 12 million hectares).[43] As Sinclair states, 'under Grey a method of negotiating land purchases was developed which was *nicely grafted on to Maori custom* and which for some years worked well and fairly' [my emphasis].[44] This method consisted of hui (official meetings) for the discussion of land sales, which recognised the communal nature of tribal ownership and allowed participation by all parties interested in the negotiations. The government bought huge areas of land for sixpence or a shilling an acre and sold it to the settlers for ten shillings or a pound, effectively 'robbing the Maori ostensibly in order to save them from being swindled by settlers.'[45]

In pre-European times Maori had no individual private property in land, nor was there any system of alienating tribal land. Grey's 'efficient' method consisted in 'grafting' the Western notion of land sale onto the traditional institution of the hui: he created a 'false consciousness' (in Marxist terms) among Maori by bringing a strange concept into a territory that was recognisable and apparently safe for them. He exercised his power on Maori subjects by letting them believe that they were not losing theirs in order to create consent. Grey exercised 'hegemony' in the Gramscian way, infiltrating new notions into Maori thinking and manipulating it.

When the Europeans arrived in the late eighteenth century, the population of Maori was around 100,000.[46] In 1830 there were 300 Europeans living in the whole of New Zealand. By 1840 there were about 2000 and by 1860 the European population had surpassed that of the Maori for the first time. Previously, European settlement had taken place on Maori terms, with Maori in control of the process. Now Maori began to realise that their race, culture and mana would be entirely erased if steps were not taken to preserve them. As King notices, the 'Maori oratory of these years began to employ proverbs about the power of saltwater to contaminate freshwater'.[47] This led to the birth of the Maori King Movement (Kingitanga), to the rise of messianic sects and renewed hostilities (the Waikato War or Second Period of the New Zealand Wars). It was in this decade that the word 'Maori' came to be commonly used by Polynesians of New Zealand to describe themselves.[48]

Besides playing on Maori customs, common sense and everyday practices, Grey understood the importance of literary texts to diffuse the dominant discourse. As already mentioned, he promoted the translation of *Robinson Crusoe*, a key text of British colonialism, which was distributed widely as an official government publication in an effort to contribute to Maori literacy. Lani Kavika Hunter has analysed the Maori translation of Defoe's novel and compared it to the original version in English.[49] Firstly, she underscores that a thousand copies of the text were printed and quickly distributed to a Maori population estimated at eighty thousand, which suggests a reading rate of at least one copy for every eighty Maori subjects —

a significant number, if one thinks that the book would probably be passed around and also read to as well as read by Maori.[50] Secondly, Hunter notes that although the Maori version is shorter by about half and does not include many of Crusoe's diary entries and inventories, it still permits a reader to grasp the details of the core relationship between Crusoe and Friday. Finally, the names of the protagonists were transliterated into Maori (Robinson Crusoe becomes 'Ropitini Kuruho' and Friday is 'Paraire'),[51] to allow a closer identification between readers and characters. The subtitle 'A Story of a Pakeha Ancestor of Olden Times' ('Written by the Author Himself' in the English version) not only contributes to presenting the story in a non-fictional mode but also applies the Maori notion of respect for their ancestors.

Hunter proceeds with a close comparison of the 'submission scene', revealing among other smaller discrepancies one marked difference between the two versions. In the original edition, after Crusoe rescues Friday from his cannibal pursuers the latter demonstrates his gratitude by 'laying himself down' and setting Crusoe's foot upon his head to express his willingness to serve him forever. In the Maori translation, on the contrary, it is Kuruho/Crusoe himself who places his foot on Paraire/Friday's head and rests it there, thus giving a forceful visual representation of his power. After this act of unconditional domination the Maori text adds several lines wholly absent in Defoe's original: a declaration of 'eternal love' or aroha uttered by Kuruho/Crusoe to Paraire/Friday. Like Grey in the exploitation of the traditional hui system, the translator draws the Maori reader into a familiar territory, as already offered in the subtitle. Aroha means 'caring'; it is the concept of love in its widest sense including respect, concern, hospitality and the process of giving. Aroha is given freely: it does not take account of personal cost, but considers only what is beneficial to others.[52] In ancient times it was the bond between people belonging to the same tribe or to allied tribes. While affirming his supremacy over Paraire/Friday, Kuruho/Crusoe transforms himself into a naturally superior and benevolent protector, who must be respected and loved as a tribesman or brother of Paraire/Friday (and of the Maori readers).

Grey learned the Maori language and persuaded Maori authorities to commit their legends and traditions to writing, some of which he subsequently published. His *Polynesian Mythology* (London, 1855) has been reprinted many times and has had a wide readership. It is a collection of cosmogonic and migration myths, which was preceded by two versions in Maori, written by Grey himself: *Ko nga Moteatea me nga Hakirara o nga Maori* (Wellington, 1853) and *Ko nga Mahinga a nga Tupuna* (London, 1854). These collections were the result of his collaboration with the Arawa chief Te Rangikaheke. The two men started working together in 1849, not in the government offices but in a special whare tuhituhi (writing house).[53] Te Rangikaheke produced three manuscripts, one for Grey, the other two addressed to the people of 'Hawaiki'.[54] To publish the 1853 and 1854 editions, Grey drew on the narratives and genealogies of the three manuscripts. *Polynesian Mythology* is the English translation of the 1854 version.

In *Maori Oral Literature as Seen by a Classicist*, Agathe Thornton first compares the three manuscripts by Te Rangikaheke, which she calls the Grey Book (for Grey), Hawaii 1 and Hawaii 2 (for the people of Hawaiki), then Grey's subsequent dealings with them. Major distinctions between the Grey and Hawaii Books derive from the different audience they addressed. As the Hawaii Books are addressed to people who would have expert knowledge about ancient traditional stories, they are 'as authentic a piece of oral tradition as we can hope for, both in content and in form.'[55] In the Grey Book, on the contrary, Te Rangikaheke is concerned with leading Sir Grey to an understanding of the traditions of his people:

> What in the Hawaii Book[s] goes without saying, and would be understood by any Maori versed in the traditional forms of his literature, is here analysed for the sake of the Pākehā.[56]

The art of narrative is less important in the Grey Book. Connections between the narrative and the 'sayings', whether cosmogonic or proverbial, are explained. Many rhetorical devices typical of a full oral narrative — the use of repeated words to build up to a climax, the symmetry and balance of the parts, parallelisms, formulaic passages and direct speech — are limited or omitted. The sequence of events narrated is more chronological than in the Hawaii Books, which include many 'appositional expansions'. The appositional style (from 'ap-positing' or adding bit by bit to the initial statement) is typical of storytelling and common in Homeric literature. It reflects the Maori notion of time, according to which the past lies in front and the future behind. Therefore we move into the future with our eyes in the past.[57] The attitude to time that underlies the appositional mode of storytelling gives pre-eminence to the past over the present. The difference in attitude and style between the books demonstrates that Te Rangikaheke had adapted himself to the needs of his friend Grey, and was more concerned in satisfying his will than in following the traditional philosophy of his own culture. This itself could be interpreted as an example of aroha, an act of giving that does not take account of personal cost but considers only what is beneficial to the other.

As to Grey's treatment of the manuscripts, Thornton says that the 1853 Wellington edition is basically structured on the Grey Book with the addition of an appendix including an account of the demigod Maui's exploits (only present in Hawaii 1) and the narrative of the Arawa's migration myths of Hawaii 2 (much more detailed than the corresponding one in the Grey Book). In the 1854 London edition and its 1855 subsequent English translation, Grey eliminates the appendix and adapts its two narratives inside the text, rearranging them in a chronological order more suitable to a Western understanding and notion of time. In reporting Maui's exploits Grey also makes some adaptations. In Te Rangikaheke's manuscript Maui fights twice with the Great Night Woman Hinenuitepo: the first time he goes to see her and fetch fire, since all the cooking fires are out; the second time he wants to kill her and defeat death for ever, but is himself killed. These two episodes are a 'doublet', which is a form of oral storytelling frequently used by Homer also.[58] Grey used a different source for the fire episode, in which the demigod fights with another goddess, Mauika, thus breaking the doublet. In addition he censored the physical attributes of Hinenuitepo, who in the original text has fire coming out of her vulva in accordance with the early Maori idea that fire resides in a woman's sexual organ.[59] Thornton's comment on Grey's adaptations of the Maui myth reveals the disappointment of a philologist before an apocryphal text: 'It is a great pity that most New Zealanders, both Maori and Pakeha, only know that magnificent story in this mutilated form.'[60]

Grey and other Pakeha scholars in the nineteenth century contributed to the collection and publication of Maori oral traditions. Some may have been driven by a genuine interest in the heritage of the people who shared their country. Others, like Grey, probably saw this task as part of a larger political design that implied learning about the subjects' culture as a necessary duty of a good administrator. Whether in good faith or not, what emerges from Thornton's essay is the superimposition of the Western canon and world view on to indigenous cultural forms. Moreover, while on one hand Pakeha were collecting Maori myths, on the other they were promoting literacy in English, which became the only language taught in schools from 1867. The suspicion arises that, in the colonisers' mind, what was being collected was just the remains of a 'dying race' to be put in the glass case of some museum, a topic treated by much literature written by Pakeha, as will be seen in the next section.[61]

Maori in colonial novels and short stories

Until well into the twentieth century the New Zealand novel remained a derivative form within the European canon, due to the fact that books were mainly published in Great Britain for a British public and that most novelists were not professional writers. As argued by Lawrence Jones,[62] the novel was basically a pre-made 'container' built on imported Victorian conventions, to be filled with local ingredients, characters or facts. The short story was the favoured genre in New Zealand and was considered to be the literary form where, in Wevers' words, 'the preoccupations of the colonial and postcolonial literature have worked themselves out'.[63] The reason is both practical and rooted in the nature of the genre itself. Short stories were published in local magazines and addressed to a local public, so were meant to reflect the specificity of a regional context in an unmediated way. Moreover the short story does not require the complexity of plot and characterisation of a novel, features that make it particularly suitable to express the problems or concerns arising, for instance, in a settler culture that is not yet stable.

One of the first collections of verse and prose, published in 1864 with the evocative title *Literary Foundlings*, includes a story showing the rise of the quest for identity that characterises colonial fiction. In 'A Tale I Heard in the Bush', two men travelling in the Australian bush give a tentative definition of 'colonial self' as different from the 'British self', epitomised by a third character (the typical newcomer or 'New Chum'). They describe the latter 'a gentleman in the drawing-room ... not gentleman enough in the bush [because] only when the polish is off you can see the real fibre',[64] a statement implying that some of the values of the imperial centre were being questioned and redefined in the colonial periphery. If the white settler affirms masculinity and toughness as values, as opposed to the sophistication of the 'New Chum', he cannot but simultaneously assert his deep moral and cultural bond with his mother country, especially when confronted with the other that is, the Maori, in the new land.

The settler is therefore located in an in-between space, as Bhabha contended, a limbo where existential and cognitive co-ordinates must be affirmed and reviewed at the same time. This ambiguous situation and the anxiety it causes are reflected in the ambivalent attitude of colonial novelists and short-story writers towards Maori: 'hostile and patronising' at the same time.[65] The short story may prove more flexible than the novel in exploring European New Zealand's search for identity, but the resulting representation of Maori is similar in short and long fictions alike, and is always functional to the dominant discourse.

In colonial novels Maori are present in three major thematic contexts: 'ethnographic' works (centred on their habits and customs), war accounts and melodramatic romances. Their treatment varies from an 'exterminate the brutes' philosophy,[66] especially in novels dealing with the New Zealand Wars and the land question — such as H.B. Stoney's *Taranaki: A Tale of the War* (1861), Joshua Henry Kirby's *Henry Ancrum: A Tale of the Last War in New Zealand* (1872) and John Featon's *The Last of the Waikatos: A Sensational Tale of the Province of Auckland* (1873) — to views that are more critical towards the Pakeha appropriation of land and see it as the cause of the conflict. Interestingly, the latter belong to works from writers mostly not of British origin, including Jules Verne's *A Voyage Round the World: New Zealand* (1877), Sygurd Wiśniowski's *Tikera or Children of the Queen of Oceania* (published in Polish in 1877, but not translated to English until 1972) and Joseph Spillmann's *Love Your Enemies: A Tale of the Maori Insurrections in New Zealand* (translated from German in 1895). Jones underlines the frequent ambivalence of many writers, who on one hand sense that Maori were fighting for their own land and admire them for their courage, but on the other see their defeat as necessary for the realisation of the pioneers' pastoral dream, that is, the inevitable transformation of a hostile land into a paradise shaped as the British 'home'. Influenced by the theory of 'social Darwinism', which held that indigenous populations would decline to extinction due to the 'fatal impact' with the biological and cultural superiority of white races,[67] most writers believed that Maori were doomed to succumb to the stronger civilising energies of their European colonisers.

The representation of the Maori male as a formidable warrior has become a major identity trait in the collective imagery, both in Aotearoa/New Zealand and abroad. However, given the mass of early Pakeha writing promoting the idea and obsessively focusing on Maori warfare and internecine tribal conflicts, it could be also viewed as a deliberate strategy underlying the colonial philosophy. Even in ethnographic novels, such as Capt. J.C. Johnstone's *Maoria: A Sketch of the Manners and Customs of the Aboriginal Inhabitants of New Zealand* (1874), wider space is devoted to the description of war strategies, weapons and the building of hill fortifications than to Maori cultural, agricultural or fishing practices, as if 'the love of war' was the centre of their existence.[68] In such a context the white man's military intervention is legitimated as it brings order and rationality to a chaotic, lawless primitive world.

Hunter underlines how the identity of the first European New Zealanders was permeated by a sense of 'lack' and 'inadequacy', implicit in their condition of exile from the mother country[69] and, therefore, the aggressive textuality of early Pakeha writings, especially accounts of war, conceals an urgent need to affirm their own prowess. By setting up a 'worthy' but ultimately 'inferior' opponent, Pakeha men were able "'to acquire" for themselves a powerful masculine identity, not merely as good fighters but as better fighters belonging to a better race of men.'[70] This also explains the double attitude that most writers had towards Maori, who were given both positive and negative attributes. They are contradictorily described as proud, brave and honourable but also wicked, vicious and cruel. Significantly, among the more than 40 texts Hunter has analysed there are no accounts of Maori 'warriors' defeating Pakeha 'warriors'.[71]

The war-loving Maori is a frequent topos in short stories too, as can be seen in 'The Blind Eye of the Law', 'The Utu of the Ngati-Toa' (utu means revenge), 'About Te Kooti's Massacre', 'The Courting of Te Rahu', and 'A White Wahine', all included in A.A. Grace's *Tales of a Dying Race* (1901). In its preface Grace describes Maori as a people who lived in a state of 'tribal communism' and 'had brought their communism and their methods of warfare to a ripe perfection'. He says that in times of peace they had enjoyed an 'Arcadian existence', nevertheless underscoring an innate thirst for fighting:[72]

> When the white man arrived, he found the islands rent from end to end by internecine wars; but instead of seeing in him their common enemy, against whom it was expedient for them to unite, the Maoris welcomed the *pakeha*, because he could supply them with powder and shot with which to exterminate each other. This they almost accomplished, and now the assimilation of a civilization they do not understand is finishing the work. In spite of the sincerest efforts of a paternal Government, it is the sad belief of those who know the race best, that the Maoris are doomed to be extinguished or absorbed. Therefore I have named this book 'Tales of a Dying Race.'[73]

It is difficult to understand how an 'Arcadian existence' and a perfect 'tribal communism' could co-exist with an innate love of warfare. A.A. Grace's point of view, which confirms Hunter's theory, is of the white coloniser who does not want to admit the responsibility of Western colonisation in dismantling a system that had successfully lasted for centuries, and in promoting a *divide et impera* philosophy functional to the imperial power. As previously explained, Maori lived and thrived under a tribal system that provided them with an ancestry-based identity. The necessity to unite under a common Maori king and fight against the 'common enemy' did arise, but only after Maori realised what British rule had deprived them of. The King Movement was its result, but by that time it was too late and Maori had become a minority in their own land.

Among colonial novels, the melodramatic romance is the most widespread mode and also the one in which the figure of the Maori is most frequently employed. The 'Maori romance' was so successful that it rose to the position of an autonomous genre and was even parodied by R. Ward in 1894 in his *Supplejack: A Romance of Maoridom*.[74] Loomba analyses the construction of the female indigenous subject in colonial literature, pinpointing some common stereotypes that cut across regional productions. The identification between land and woman can be traced in the traditional iconography, which depicts the continents of Africa and America as naked women to possess, and Asia as a richly clad woman to seduce.[75] Oceania, too, was feminised in the representations of eighteenth-century European explorers (Wallis, De Bougainville and Cook) and of later writers and painters (Melville,

Loti and Gauguin) as a utopian sexual paradise for male Europeans. The label of 'South Seas' alone — given to all the Pacific region by Europeans — is evocative of a romantic and idealised Arcadia. As argued by Michelle Keown, the image of indigenous women freely offering their sexual favours to European male visitors became a metonym for a land that offered itself to European colonisation.[76]

Loomba summarises the most common representations of the indigenous female subject in three main models:

1. She voluntarily submits to the white coloniser, renouncing her riches and her culture (an example is the Native American Pocahontas).
2. She is saved from the barbarity of native men, as in the texts dealing with the rite of Indian widow burning or sati, and is grateful to her rescuers.
3. She becomes an example of Amazonian or deviant femininity, where female volition, desire and agency are pushed to the limits of the civilised world.[77]

These contradictory representations are basically grounded on the projections of the Western male's desires concerning gender-based relations and sexuality. In the first and second case they convey the idealised feminine behaviour of submission and devotion to men, worthy of being emulated by English women; in the third case we find a projection of his forbidden sexual desires and fears that could not find expression in the morally strict Victorian society, and a view of the colonial frontier as a place open to transgression. The treatment of the indigenous female subject reflects the traditional alignment of the sexes in a hierarchical order according to the 'dominant male /submitted female' pattern, but can similarly be seen as a promotion of colonial discourse. The colonial rhetoric (and also scientific writing) has often drawn analogies between sex and race, suggesting an equivalence between the 'lower' gender of the human species (the female) and the 'lower' type of the human race (for example, the black).[78]

The treatment of the Maori woman in colonial novels mirrors the above-mentioned categories individuated by Loomba. Perhaps the best representation of Maori womanhood is the beautiful and passionate Hinemoa, who swims across the cold water of Lake Rotorua to her lover Tutanekai, in contravention of her family's ban on the relationship.[79] Her story, one of the most popular Maori legends, was first collected and published by Grey. In his version Hinemoa becomes the symbol of the natural woman: virginal but passionate, energetic but submissive. She is an archetype of primeval femininity and a model for Western women to follow.

The figure of the young Maori woman, often of noble origin, who becomes a temptation for the white male and an example of unconditional love is common. She turns from an object of desire into an object of conquest. Yet, as explained by Hunter, the destiny of the Maori heroine, after being conquered by the white male, is often tragic. If there is a good ending, then the heroine is taken to England, like the Native American Pocahontas, and anglicised:

> One often finds the female figure 'discarded' by the text either by arranging for her to die in an accident or commit suicide, or by sending her 'back to her tribe'.… If she is not then discarded, her identity is reconfigured as virtually non-Maori.[80]

Examples of tragic love between a Pakeha man and a Maori woman are found in Robert. H. Scott's *Ngamihi: or, The Maori Chief's Daughter; A Tale of the War in New Zealand* (1895) and Rolf Boldrewood's *'War to the Knife'; or, Tangata Maori* (1899), where noble Maori heroines die for their Pakeha lovers. In Robert Whitworth's *Hine-Ra; or, The Maori Scout: A Romance of the New Zealand War* (1887), the chief's daughter marries the hero but then spends five years with him in England to become thoroughly anglicised. The female characters who are depicted as transgressive are eliminated too, like the helplessly passionate Atareta in A.A. Grace's *Atareta: The Belle of Kainga* (1896), or the aggressive Amazonian warrior Ena in George Wilson's *Ena; or, The Ancient Maori* (1874), both of whom end up committing suicide.

Hunter draws up a balance of over 40 novels she consulted.[81] Twelve of them include depictions of 'pure' and 'half-caste' Maori female figures as principal characters. Eight of these figures are killed off, two are obliged to return to their tribes, while the remaining two marry their European lovers but are 'exported', that is, removed from their sociocultural settings to live somewhere else. Unsurprisingly there are no love stories described between Maori men and Pakeha women in these texts, as if the dominance of the white man over the white woman was given for granted, or to exorcise the spectre of miscegenation.[82]

What emerges from Hunter's accurate study of colonial novels is the constant search for an affirmation of European identity. Maori subjects both male and female are ultimately presented as defeated characters. The Maori male is elevated as a warrior but then defeated in the battlefield and therefore 'feminised' by a stronger and superior Pakeha male opponent; the Maori female, if not deviant, is idealised as a model to follow, but then rejected or turned into a European. Both representations are functional to a discourse aimed at compensating for the lack of a stable settler identity and to confirm the idea of a 'dying race' that must succumb, whether by natural selection or by assimilation, to the European.

Romance is also the prevalent mode in the 28 tales that compose A.A. Grace 's *Tales of a Dying Race*. They can be divided into two types: those between

Pakeha men and Maori women, such as 'Reremoa and the Pearly Nautilus', 'Told in the Puia' (hot spring) and 'Why Castelard took to the Blanket'; and those between Maori men and Maori women. As in the novels, love between a Maori man and a white woman is never contemplated. Maori heroines in the first type appear seductive, passionate and enterprising. They fall in love almost at first sight and comply with all their beloved's wishes, following the first pattern of indigenous feminine representation: the 'natural' woman and archetype of primeval femininity. But these love stories are tinged with darkness because 'the man who has once fallen under the spell of Maoridom, and has learnt to love its ways, comes back no more to civilization, but eschews the dwellings of the pakeha.'[83] Even in the idealised world of romance the fear of being assimilated into the other is present. In the elaborated context of the novel, which requires a resolution, this fear was exorcised by the death of the Maori heroine or her conversion to Pakeha ways. In the short story it is alluded to and unresolved, nevertheless it casts a shadow on the real possibility of successful inter-racial relationships and acts as a warning against them.

The only truly successful romances in *Tales of a Dying Race* are those with lovers who are both Maori. They are generally idealised and set in an indefinite time. The structure is that of the fairy tale, where the hero must undergo a trial to conquer his beloved, demonstrating courage or cleverness. In 'Patopato and the Water Nymphs' the hero rescues the heroine from drowning; in 'Putangitangi and the Maero' (fabulous monster) and in 'The Ngarara' (reptile) he kills the terrible monster that keeps her prisoner; while in 'Big Piha and Little Piha' he demonstrates his superiority over another suitor to win her love. Relegating successful love stories only to Maori couples suggests the Western diffidence about inter-racial relationships. The fairytale setting creates the temporal distance that allows Grace to trace a clear divide between an Arcadian Maori past and their contemporary reality of war. Only the white man's 'civilising' intervention would end the conflict.

The coloniser's anxiety about identity is also reflected in the treatment of the Pakeha-Maori[84] figure, the white settler who, by living or working with Maori, has taken up their ways and manners and lost touch with his culture of origin. If the settler's life is always characterised by a sense of dislocation, the Pakeha-Maori is seen as somebody who has crossed an ultimate border, stepping into a forbidden territory from which there is no return. He has been 'Maorified' and has become an outcast in 'civilised' society. In Grace's stories this character is, one way or another, doomed to perish, such as Bagshaw in 'King Potatau's Powder-Maker'. Two other Pakeha-Maori share the same tragic destiny as Bagshaw: Felton, in 'Under the Greenwood Tree' and Layard in 'The Skipper of the *Good Intent*'.

Maori were commonly associated with a world of irrationality, dominated not only by emotions and instincts — as in romances and war tales — but also by supernatural events and magical practices. They are depicted as superstitious, devoted to sorcery and prey to believe in any sort of apparition or fabulous monsters. This association defines a border between two different modes of knowledge and increases the distance between a familiar and ordered world, where reason and empiricism prevail, and the inexplicable world of the other that is imaginative and unpredictable, mysterious and dangerous. The supernatural motif expresses the settler's anxiety about losing his supremacy over an unknown reality that he wants to control and reshape according to his own rational certainties and knowledge. It convinces him of the rightness of his role as a light-giver and justifies his intervention with either arms or evangelical Christianity.

It also acts as a warning, however, because contact with this world is dangerous and can lead to madness. 'The Disappearance of Letham Crouch' (1901), by Chas. Owen, is a perfect example.[85] A missionary wants to convert a tribe of Maori and engages in a battle with superstition and heathen beliefs. He accepts a role as their new tohunga, but ends up being converted to Maoridom. He turns 'sunken and wild', develops a fanatical attitude and vanishes only to reappear as a Maori 'stripped for dancing'. By becoming a Maori tohunga, the preacher has crossed the boundary between rationality and irrationality: he is in the territory of the other. The character of Letham Crouch anticipates Joseph Conrad's Kurtz by a year.[86] Like him, the missionary has crossed the border between the known and the unknown. He has stepped into the 'heart of darkness', falling inevitably into insanity.

'Under the Greenwood Tree' includes another episode of madness connected to the supernatural motif. Like many colonial short stories, it is structured as a yarn told from a 'domestic' place (in this case, a camp set up for the night in the bush) and concerns something unfamiliar, frightening and inexplicable. Two Pakeha and a Maori have been recruited to capture a madman, Pannifer, who wanders about the bush terrorising people and setting fires. The first yarn is that of Pannifer's madness. The other is of the Pakeha-Maori, prompted apparently by a material detail but actually evoked by the topic of Pannifer's madness. Felton, too, is defined a 'lunatic' for his Maorification and subsequent tragic death in his village.

Both Pannifer and Felton belong to the bush, with its frightening noises, its association with the supernatural and Maori. At a certain point Pannifer appears as a ghost. The party chases him away by throwing a burning stick in his face. But the next day they find his corpse in an advanced state of putrefaction. The real Maori of the hunting party, Karepa, is no threat since he has been 'civilised'. He represents the typical comical figure of 'Pakehafied Maori': jovial, child-like, speaking hilarious pidgin English. In sum, 'Under the Greenwood Tree' is one of the stories that best reflects the complex and contradictory relationship between the settler, a strange new land and its indigenous population.

As for the character of Karepa, the way to exorcise the fear of the Maori other and his /her irrational world is to turn him/her into a comical figure and deconstruct his/her world according to European rational categories. Grace applies this method in 'The Tohunga and the Taniwha', where a Pakeha sailor saves a Maori girl from her arranged wedding to an old and respected tohunga by devising the apparition of a monster, a taniwha (whose skin, says Grace ironically, was made of tarpaulin), who kidnaps the girl and scares to death both the ridiculed old priest and the whole tribe. In 'The Tohunga and the Wai Tapu' another tohunga, who is jealous of the popularity of a Christian priest and wants to discover the secret of his incantations and rituals, is ridiculed and punished. He creeps into the priest's house to steal some holy water (wai tapu), which he believes must have virtues and powers unknown to him, and performs the ritual of baptism on himself. Unfortunately he takes a bowl of sulphuric acid by mistake, and burns an everlasting cross on his forehead.

Maori who adapt themselves to Pakeha ways are ridiculed in several collections. A.A. Grace began this tradition with *Hone Tiki Dialogues* (1910), twelve sketches that first appeared in journals and are centred on a 'mythical character in a dented bowler hat [who] philosophises shrewdly and ineptly on Pakeha customs.'[87] As Pearson notes, others continued in this vein. *Letters from Private Henare Tikitanu* (1917) and its sequel *Corporal Tikitanu* (1918) by V.C. Fussell depict a 'typical Maori soldier' from the Waikato area: semi-literate, simple-minded to the point of stupidity, who writes home in mongrel English. Finally, Pat Lawlor's *Maori Tales* (1927) is a sort of jest-book about 'cunning, simple old Hori', expressing himself in the usual pidgin English.[88]

Another comical representation of the Maori depicts him/her as a child-figure towards whom the Pakeha must show indulgence. An example is Blanche Baughan's 'Pipi on the Prowl'.[89] Pipi, an old 'mummy-like' Maori, roams about every time she can elude the control of her respectable granddaughter, the Pakeha coachman's wife. Like a child in search of adventure, she picks up any interesting object she finds on her way so that it can be bartered in exchange for some tobacco. The story tells of Pipi's encounter with a young Pakeha woman and all her cunning efforts to exchange the pumpkin she has just found for some of the woman's garments. She ends up getting only two cigarettes and a shilling. The young woman's attitude is that of a patronising good-willed Pakeha, who likes the Maori, laughs indulgently at the crone's tricks and easily neutralises them. The real age of the characters turns to a 'racial age': the adult Pakeha is supposed to lead the Maori child by the hand.

What emerges from the analysed texts is the constant use of Maori as a projection of Pakeha anxiety and fears (in war tales or the supernatural mode), of their repressed desires (in romances) and of the ways to exorcise them (in comedy). A further topos is the employment of the indigenous figure to criticise those aspects of Pakeha culture that the authors dislike — their vices (especially drinking and gambling), Puritanism or materialism. This appears as a local variant of the Romantic theory of the 'noble savage'. An example is William Baucke's 'A Quaint Friendship',[90] narrating the meeting between the author, an old Maori woman, and her debauched grandson. The dignified grandmother embodies the traditional values of early Maori while the boy symbolises the modern Maori generation who has absorbed every Western evil. She condemns her ill-mannered grandson, yet also loves the boy since he represents the future of her people. The narrator cannot but sympathise with her, though his overall attitude is imbued with condescending sentimentalism.

The temptation to find within Maori virtues that are missing in Pakeha, to paraphrase Pearson,[91] appears markedly in one of Katherine Mansfield's stories, 'How Pearl Button Was Kidnapped'.[92] Pearl is a neat, blonde little girl, wearing an impeccable pinafore with frills and living in an elegant residential area. Told from the child's perspective, the story narrates how she follows two 'dark women', dressed in bright colours, to their home. The women and their community are depicted with colourful and lively images. Everyone is cheerful and kind to Pearl, as if she were a precious and delicate flower. Mansfield stresses Pearl's new sensorial perceptions, as if she had lived in a silent, cold colourless world all her life. She is allowed to wear her curls loose, get her clothes dirty, walk barefoot on the beach and paddle freely in the shallow water: 'Pearl had never been happy like this before.'[93] She never feels sad, frightened or homesick. This holiday from the strict code of a puritanical childhood ends when 'little men in blue coats' come to take her back home.

Details that Mansfield uses to describe the two 'dark women' and their community suggest they are undoubtedly Maori, but they are never explicitly identified as such.[94] Interestingly, when the story appeared British readers presumed Pearl had been kidnapped by gypsies.[95] The omission allows readers to approach Maori without preconceptions and to feel the humanity, warmth and colour of their world as opposed to the cold, grey world of Pakeha convention. Mansfield's dislike of puritanical, provincial New Zealand was shown in her self-imposed exile to Europe. As Pearson notes, referring to the pages of her *Journal* written in 1908 while she was travelling around New Zealand before leaving for England, Mansfield was fascinated by Maori as the embodiment of qualities she could not find in her fellow Pakeha citizens: a heroic and noble society as opposed to a materialistic and puritanical one. Her contact with or direct knowledge of Maori culture was, in reality, minimal, and the attraction was in fact to the myth of the 'true' noble savage, untainted by European civilisation. She 'found nothing of interest'[96] in Maori who spoke English and dressed in Western attire.

Although Mansfield's treatment of Maori is no doubt original, it reveals more about the writer, her will to deconstruct her culture of origin and stigmatise what she dislikes about it, than about Maori themselves. From the first colonial fictions to Mansfield, then, Pakeha representations of Maori have undergone substantial changes, but they are still instrumentally employed, in this case to affirm a private vision instead of the dominant public one. We have to wait for Sargeson and especially Finlayson for a more articulate and sensitive view.

2 Frank Sargeson and Roderick Finlayson

Frank Sargeson (1903–1982) and Roderick Finlayson (1904–1992) belong to the generation that is generally considered as the makers of modern New Zealand literature, including, among others, Allen Curnow, A.R.D. Fairburn, Denis Glover, Charles Brasch and John Mulgan. Sargeson and Finlayson are the masters of the short story in this age group, although the latter appears as a secondary figure, notable mainly for his realistic and sympathetic view of Maori life.[1] Sargeson was amply celebrated as the founding father of New Zealand national literature and praised for his faithful rendition of the local idiom as well as his remarkable social fresco of the country in the period between the two world wars. His work has been viewed as an exemplary model of realist and socially committed literature, then rediscovered in symbolist/existentialist terms, and recently reinterpreted in the light of his difficult condition as a closeted homosexual in a homophobic, puritanical society. Finlayson, on the other hand, has not only been given little critical attention but has even been forgotten, as is the case in E.H. McCormick's 1940 history *Letters and Art in New Zealand*, which omits him completely. It was Sargeson himself who prompted McCormick to correct the omission, which he did some time later, including a full account in his *New Zealand Literature: A Survey* (1959). Second only to D'Arcy Cresswell, Sargeson was the intellectual who most supported and encouraged Finlayson's career as a writer. A subtle bond seems to connect the most prominent figure of New Zealand national literature to the man with 'a modest and unassertive temperament', in Dennis McEldowney's words,[2] who elected Maori as the subject matter of most of his writing.

Sargeson's appreciation of Finlayson's writings was certainly due to some shared ideas. Both writers show a fierce distaste for the social and economic conventions of their time enforced by the Western capitalist system in its provincial, antipodean version. They both held that economic liberalism and industrialism have violated the core values of humanity, and consider man's proximity to nature (also intended in a modern environmentalist sense) as a principle Western civilisation ought to recover. Incidentally, they both experienced a life close to nature on the farms of their respective uncles: Oakley Sargeson and Arthur Wilson. They also share a sensitive view of Maori, grounded in their recognition in Maori culture of a code of values and attitudes underestimated or vanished in the Western world: the systemic understanding of nature, that is, the respect for the mutual interdependence of all forms of life; the importance of affective bonds within the family group and between human beings in general; the primacy of imagination over rationality in the understanding of reality; and a more relaxed attitude towards the body and sexuality. But while Sargeson mainly focused on the effects of materialism and Puritanism on the white subject, relegating Maori to minor characters and merely alluding to their view as a possible counter-discourse to the devastating power of the dominant ethic, Finlayson devoted a consistent part of his production to the representation of Maori culture, its beauty, and its decline as a result of the overwhelming thrust of Western civilisation. Suspicion arises that this prevalent topic turned out to be a considerable drawback for him and the cause of his being neglected, underestimated and pushed to the margins of the new movement rising in the 1930s.

If that decade marked the beginning of a national literature, it basically identified with the voice and the preoccupations of the New Zealand white male subject. As argued by Kai Jensen, the emerging group of male writers criticised most previous literature, especially women's literature, as too flowery, sentimental, socially naïve and derivative. In their view all this had to be replaced by a more masculine mode of writing based on factual reality rather than subjective emotions, on the representation of the ordinary working-class man's life and its hardships, and on a down-to-earth language devoid of intellectualism.[3] The new movement rose in the heyday of Marxism in New Zealand and all of its members were one way or another committed to socialist or communist ideals. They published their works in the left-wing magazine *Tomorrow* and claimed that literature should deal with urgent social issues in a language accessible to all. Jensen underlines how writers themselves wanted to be seen not as intellectuals but as 'makers' or 'craftsmen', defining their writing as manual work or 'handiwork'. They displayed practical skills and the same interest in do-it-yourself work as the working man. The emerging prototype of New Zealand man encompassed the essence of what was true and vital in the colonial spirit, as opposed to the sophistication of his European counterpart. The reviews and criticism produced by these writers created a gendered polarisation between good and bad writing according to their taste: the former was 'masculine', 'tough', 'strong', 'robust', 'muscular' and 'vigorous', while the latter was 'effeminate', 'weak', 'slack', 'womanish' and 'feeble'. But there was a homophobic vein too, as one statement by Fairburn shows:

> It is a long time since a really robust love lyric was produced by any of our celebrity poets. Most of the love-songs that have been written during the past two decades suggest either impotence or homosexuality.[4]

The advent of a masculine tradition and the strengthening of a New Zealand (male) identity coincided with the rise of a new mode of writing and specific concerns that did not entail a particular interest in Maori culture or destiny (with the notable exception of Finlayson). The birth of a national literature, basically defined as a Pakeha nationalist male literature, was grounded therefore on an extremely contradictory basis: its writers were leftist, progressive and socially aware but also sexist, homophobic and virtually indifferent to indigenous issues. As in the colonial period they asserted the preoccupations of the European male New Zealander over and against the 'lower' gender (the female) and the 'lower' race (Maori). Finlayson and Sargeson, however, stand out from the group: Finlayson for his anti-conformist focus on Maori life; Sargeson for the wide range of issues he raised directly or indirectly, including his complex condition as father of the movement and closet homosexual, and his perceptive intuitions on Maori culture. He escapes any easy labelling or categorisation.

Reading Sargeson from a Maori perspective

Sargeson was welcomed by critics as 'a hard new realist for a hard new era'.[5] Many of his earliest and best-known stories, set mostly during the Great Depression, include white itinerant labourers or job hunters, often unemployed, seldom married and frequently without any apparent family connections. They are depicted either in their lonely condition as seasonal workers, in isolated farms or the bush, or against a desolate background of cities inhabited by materialist and unimaginative bourgeois, such as the narrator's uncle in 'Conversation with My Uncle'. Sargeson dismantles the pioneers' faith in the 'New Zealand

Dream', showing the immanent void of a puritanical bourgeois society built on imported values that have lost their roots and deepest sense. James K. Baxter noted that the country described by Sargeson is one where 'the prevalent philosophy is an amalgam of liberalism and broken-down Protestantism. Ethics remain ... though faith has departed.'[6] In this dislocated, arid spiritual world, too narrow and too empty at the same time, economic success is reached only by a few and always at the expense of their emotional and imaginative life. Humanity's emotional needs are underestimated or neglected, and sacrificed to the principles of respectability and economic fulfilment.

Families, far from being foundational elements of the society, appear as broken structures unable to offer any warmth or protection, as epitomised by the dull picture of parenthood in 'A Good Boy'. Hardly any images of happy marriages or good parental/filial relationships appear. The gap between generations and the sexes is tinged with sombre colours. What emerges is the picture of a disrupted society made up of lonely atoms, single threads that cannot be harmoniously woven into a texture. Women in particular do not come off well in Sargeson's pages, 'repeatedly serving as shadowy agents of temptation, torture, punishment, and revenge'.[7] An example is Mrs Crump in 'The Making of a New Zealander', the type of indefatigably bossy country wife who wears the trousers in the household, reversing traditional gender roles, so much so that her husband is depicted doing crochet by the fire; and Mrs Parker in 'The Hole that Jack Dug', the model of an urbanised, sophisticated wife picking on her husband since he cannot afford to buy her modern domestic appliances or a car. Another mean motherly figure is found in 'They Gave her a Rise'. Here, Mrs Bowman puts the logic of profit before her daughter's personal safety by pushing the latter back to work in an ammunition factory after the explosion that killed two of her friends.

The only escape or consolation in a reality connoted by a prevalent claustrophobia seems to be the bond of male friendship or mateship between the waifs and strays of Western civilisation, which seems to confirm the sexist attitude of the masculine tradition. A few women are spared Sargeson's criticism, but they generally do not conform to the dominant ethic: a minority, he seems to suggest, in the New Zealand society that his works depict. In 'Chaucerian' the narrator, brought up in the Unitarian Church, seems quite happy with the wife he has chosen, a woman whose mind is 'a good deal more independent than [his]',[8] although he met her in a disreputable pub. The reference to Chaucer's *Canterbury Tales* in the title, due to the similarity the narrator finds between the pub and that described in the prologue of Chaucer's poem (set at the London Tabard Inn), could also allude to the satire of the Roman Church that emerges in Chaucer's poem. Another intelligent and emancipated woman is Marge Hayes in *I Saw in My Dream*, who is also very critical of the church after reading anti-clerical writer James Joyce, and is ready to leave her claustrophobic provincial town to start a new life abroad.

In the 1950s and 1960s, critics perceived that labelling Sargeson as a social or realist writer would not fully represent the extent of his work. His fiction appears as a deep investigation into human motives and behaviour, evoking larger symbolic meanings. Therefore they stressed the importance of repetition, his insistence on detail, short, suggestive sentences and suspended or incomplete textures. All this contributed to the creation of what Sargeson himself had called the 'third dimension', that is, 'a process in which the reader must participate in order "to make sense" of the fiction, in order, indeed, to "make" the narrative'.[9] Sargeson's dialogues are particularly evocative of the 'third dimension' and through the inarticulate utterances of his laconic social outcasts, who express themselves in a vernacular idiom unequivocally reproducing the rhythms and vocabulary of New Zealand English, he is able to make silence eloquent. As Dan Davin underlined, Sargeson's characters (such as Bill, the protagonist of the novella 'That Summer') are not 'incapable of feeling, but they are incapable of being articulate about a feeling'.[10] On the contrary, those who can articulate their language seem to have no emotions or ideas to convey, like the uncle of 'Conversation with My Uncle' who 'can't suppose'. The act of communication, therefore, becomes a central subject suggesting how there can be 'talking with no communicating and communicating with no talking',[11] and revealing that his characters' isolation is not only geographical or physical but most of all spiritual and existential. Sargeson's view went beyond the borders of New Zealand and connected him to some major movements and figures of twentieth-century culture such as French existentialism, Albert Camus, Franz Kafka[12] and the great Victorian social critics — Carlyle, Ruskin and Arnold.

Sargeson's concept of mateship certainly has homosexual undertones, but it was never made explicit in his fictions, nor was Sargeson's sexual orientation in his autobiographical writings.[13] Up until recently critics had always avoided this topic, not only because it was an embarrassing subject in pre-liberation days, but also due to Sargeson's prominent role in national literature and the masculinist tradition. It was Michael King's biography *Frank Sargeson: A Life* (1995) that definitively unveiled the writer's sexual orientation and established that his withdrawal from the public life of a lawyer and his change of name (from Norris Frank Davey to Frank Sargeson) was a result of homosexual activity (in 1929 he was arrested during a sexual encounter with an older man and charged with a two years' suspended sentence). As Jensen remarks, 'Sargeson's life was shaped by alienation as a homosexual from his family and society'.[14] King's work therefore urged a new reading of Sargeson's fiction, a different approach that took into account the central importance to his writing of his closeted sexuality and the complexity of his role in New Zealand literary history. His attack on marriage and the conventional family, for example, must have been largely affected by his personal experience.

After his exposure to public scandal, Sargeson was disowned by his own family and retreated to his uncle's King Country farm. Oakley Sargeson (his uncle, hence the writer's new surname) is depicted as a simple but perceptive man, whose relaxed approach to life was free from the puritanical hypocrisy and obsession with material success of the urban middle class (and of his father). On the farm Sargeson discovered manual work, a life in harmony with the land and seasons, and rough but satisfying male friendship.[15] Mateship is for Sargeson 'the only ethical value' that remains in a world where 'tenderness is not the rule but the exception',[16] wrote Winston Rhodes in the late sixties. In the light of what we know today, it likewise appears as the only possible source of affection and sexual love. His third-dimension technique can be read as a necessary strategy to circumvent homophobic censure, and the untold side of his laconic characters can be interpreted as what could not be openly said or even thought. Having to make a virtue of necessity, Sargeson played 'a game of hide and seek' (also the title of one of his novellas), in Jensen's words, enacting gay desire but at the same time denying it.[17]

Sargeson's treatment of Maori has received little critical attention so far, probably due to the scant reference to Maori culture in his works. For example, his collection of 46 short stories published as *The Stories of Frank Sargeson* in 1973, which spans almost 40 years of writing, includes only one story with Maori as explicit protagonists: 'White Man's Burden'. But there are so many allusions in the remaining stories to an approach to life that is alternative to the Western one, that readers could hypothesise an indirect reference to the Maori view and the influence of Maori culture on him. Sargeson's reliance on the untold rather than the explicitly told, the so-called third dimension, could be at work in this sense too. Unlike Finlayson, who had a direct knowledge of Maori culture, Sargeson might not have dared to step openly into a world he was not thoroughly familiar with, but he nevertheless perceived it as having retained most of the values he affirmed. If the third-dimension technique requires the reader to participate, to make sense of the fiction, this hypothesis cannot be excluded and a reading of Sargeson from a Maori perspective can be attempted. Furthermore, in *I Saw in My Dream* (1949) we find another of his few explicit treatments of Maori characters, and this goes in the same direction as the hints found in his short stories. I will start exploring some of the short stories that evoke Maori principles and views and will later analyse the novel *I Saw in My Dream*.

In 'White Man's Burden' (1936)[18] a man travelling up north stops for the night at an isolated pub. The clientele is made up of rough labourers and farmhands — loud, heavy drinkers and chain smokers — mostly Maori. The traveller, probably an itinerant labourer himself narrating in the first person, describes the surrounding land in bleak terms, voicing the disillusionment with the pastoral dream common to many lower-class Pakeha during the 1930s Depression. The context is that of a colonial tale, with the typical demarcation between in/domestic/safe/known and out/bush/dangerous/unknown. The threat, however, comes not only from a hostile land outside but is inside too and, unlike colonial stories, it is not personified in Maori. The real troublemakers are the few white chaps who 'were rough, rougher than the Maoris' (21), as the protagonist comments. The girl who relieves the barman confirms it:

> She told me the Maoris were good customers, and when they'd spent all their money they didn't want you to let them go on drinking on credit like the Europeans. And another thing, they *did* have a sense of refinement. Why, some evenings when a few *pakehas* she could name were down it wasn't safe for her to put her head outside the front door. (22)

The narrator is a man from the south and has not met many Maori before.[19] Being one of Sargeson's uncouth and inarticulate characters, he cannot draw conclusions from what he is witnessing and can instead simply observe and report what he sees. The reader must 'make the narrative'. He notices that the Maori are better mannered than the Pakeha. One of them, in particular, speaks very well and the barman adds that he 'wrote the best hand he'd ever seen' (21), since he was going to be a parson. Another tells him he spends all his wages at the races and has a Pakeha girlfriend in town, who is very nice but 'too dear' for him. They offer him drinks, sing American songs and dance the foxtrot. Sargeson's story highlights the contradictory results of European colonisation on indigenous people, who have been assimilated into the habits of Western civilisation as well as into all its evils. Yet if the Maori appear as a bunch of loud underdogs, their Pakeha counterparts are much worse and carry the potential for threat and tension in the story. While showing Maori and Pakeha alike as victims of the system, Sargeson seems to suggest that Maori have not completely lost their centre and in fact remain within the boundaries of reciprocal respect. The narrator does not investigate where this centre lies, but the reader may assume it is found in the bond with their origin, values and culture that, however flimsy, exists nevertheless: it is a bond that white workers, pushed to the margins of a system where only few can succeed, have lost in the inhospitable land of 'yellow clay' and 'starved hills' that is their 'home' (20).

The ending also requires the reader to complete it. After retiring into his shed for the night, the narrator cannot stop thinking about the Maori. He hardly knew anything about them before that night, apart from 'the press photos of the Arawas turning out for Lord what's his name and the pictures in the Art Gallery' (22), and he once read a couple of books by a man 'called Elsdon Best'.[20] The narrator voices the average Pakeha attitude towards Maori — namely his view of them as an exotic attraction or as a dying race doomed to extinction, whose remains are to be kept in a museum or in the pages of a book. His bewilderment, however, signals he has perceived something disconcerting in the scene he has witnessed. The only comment the man can formulate is a stock sentence that sounds ironic to the reader's ear, especially if connected to Kipling's famous poem in the title: 'Gosh, there is a great day coming for Abyssinia when civilisation gets properly going there' (22). The remark, separated from the body of the text by double spacing as if it were a *vox populi* commonplace, gives the story an epigrammatic close, a cliché on colonisation that has been subverted by the narrative.

Reading some of Sargeson's stories now, after the rise of Maori literature in the 1970s, allows us to see them in a different light from times past. Some of their recurrent themes have striking affinities with those later explored by Maori writers. A story like 'An Attempt at an Explanation' (1937), for example, celebrates a holistic view of the world that is completely alien to Western thinking. A hard-working single mother cannot afford to buy her son some food. After trying unsuccessfully to pawn the family Bible, mother and son sit on a park bench alone and miserable. When the boy starts crying, the mother thinks it is because he is hungry. But the narrating voice of the boy explains that he was actually moved by the deep perception of the interdependence of all forms of life he can feel in that unfortunate situation, and from which he is excluded:

> I know I wasn't crying because of myself personally. I think it was
> because for the first time in my life I understood how different
> sorts of things are all connected up together. I thought of the way
> my silkworms ate the mulberry leaves that I gave them, and the
> way the lice had crouched down and held on tight to my hand
> when I tried to shake them off. And there, right in front of me,

the birds were looking for food, and the worms that themselves wanted something to eat were being eaten by the blackbirds. And there came into my heart a pity for all living things that were hungry and needed food. (65–66)

This story contrasts with 'An Affair of the Heart' (1936), presenting another single mother, Mrs Crawley, living in a 'tumble-down bach' (46) by the sea with her children. The narrator, a Pakeha boy who always spends his Christmas holidays in the bay, gets to know them year after year and learns that the family lives on the pipi (molluscs), mussels and pine cones they collect in flax kits and sell, and on the vegetables grown in their little garden. The boy never mentions that they are Maori, but the detail of the pipi, the flax kit and the fact they also grow kumara seem to prove their Maori origin. The viewpoint is again that of a child who cannot fully understand the terrible condition of the family's poverty and even envies them because they live all year round in a place he associates with his holidays. He is also surprised by Mrs Crawley's warm and overprotective feelings towards Joe, the smallest and skinniest of the children and her only son, because 'in our family we never showed our feelings much' (46).

The two stories depict contrasting conditions of extreme poverty in a Pakeha and a Maori family who are at the bottom of the society and victims of an unfair system. The Maori family is not sentimentalised but portrayed in all the bleakness of their makeshift hut and ragged, second-hand clothes. Yet being still part of the wider natural texture ensures them the food that the Pakeha family cannot get in their 'civilised' state of lonely atoms within a fragmented reality. In 'An Attempt at an Explanation', neither the unsellable Bible nor the minister of their Methodist church, described while strolling in the park and admiring the flowers, can heal the fracture between man and nature, the individual and the divine, or between human beings. Here, as in 'Chaucerian' and in *I Saw in My Dream*, Christian religion (in all its persuasions) is held up as an empty normative code devoid of its original spiritual message and in collusion with the economic forces at work in a liberal, capitalist state.

A holistic view of reality is common to indigenous peoples throughout the world and has formed the basis of their unconditional support for ecological and social justice movements. As environmentalist Paul Hawken underlines, the indigenous viewpoint blurs the division between ecology and human rights, environmentalism and justice, seeing them as two sides of the same dilemma because 'the way we harm the earth affects all people and how we treat one another is reflected in how we treat the earth.'[21] Hawken argues that while it is normal for indigenous people to accept a systemic understanding of nature, this proves difficult for Europeans because of theocratic dogma and the dominant economic system. Sargeson's lifestyle makes him a forerunner of environmentalist thinking. After his reconnection with nature on his uncle's farm, he spent most of his life living in a bach at Takapuna combining writing and agriculture, and selling produce to supplement his meagre income. He was also a keen supporter of organic gardening.[22] Jensen reads the combination of 'closeness to the land' and 'writing' celebrated in the masculinist tradition as a way to revive the pioneering spirit in which the true New Zealand identity resides: 'These writers could claim an authority grounded in the soil'.[23] Such an interpretation, however, seems to limit the extent of Sargeson's view. The pioneering spirit, it must be remembered, was not always good or ethically correct and also comprised acts of injustice and fraud, abuse of the land and violation of indigenous rights to gain ownership of that soil on which nationalist writers claimed their authority was grounded. Conversely, Sargeson's nearness to the land, as testified in his writing and modest lifestyle, goes beyond the praise of an arguable 'pioneering spirit' to embrace the belief that nature informs ideas and truth. His closeness to the land is therefore a natural and social philosophy very similar to the Maori vision, encompassing the environment, religious beliefs, social relationships, ethical principles and economic practices as parts of the same whole. This also entails a different approach to primary affections, the body and sexuality — viewed in their naturalness and spontaneity — and the primacy of imagination over the rigidity of rational categorisations.

'Gods Live in Woods' (1943) is one of the stories that best explores the meaning of 'closeness to the land' for Sargeson, linking it to the notion of imaginative wisdom as opposed to the rigidity of rationalism. Roy visits his Uncle Henry, living alone on the farm he has broken in from the heavy bush country. The story presents two different points of view: on one hand verbose and theoretical young Roy, who tells how he has joined a 'Rationalist' group and turned his back on religion or any sort of spiritual approach to the reality; on the other Henry, who embodies the point of view of the old taciturn farmer who has acquired practical knowledge on the land. He certainly epitomises the pioneering spirit of the white settler who tamed the land to build his personal pastoral dream, but at the same time he seems to question it constantly; his laconic remarks reveal his doubts about an exploitative approach to the environment. Sargeson again leaves the reader to complete and make sense of Henry's thoughts, as this dialogue shows:

> Roy wanted to know, didn't he feel like cutting the bush out?
> No, Henry said. I've done enough of that.
> Why? Roy said. Wouldn't it pay?
> Oh yes, Henry said, there'd be money in it all right.

And they started climbing again and it wasn't long before they
came out of the bush without having gone through very much
of it. (232)

Henry looks knowingly at the slips that scar the soil he has cleared
from the bush, and the clean water of the creek coming from the bush and
flowing into the turbid lower one. He also mentions a flood that carried away
the fence the winter before. Landslides, one consequence of deforestation,
become a recurrent image in Sargeson's fiction, symbolising the blind
Western notion of development as well as moral/spiritual blindness. Henry's
attitude epitomises the notion of 'agriculture' as 'culture', of 'knowledge'
as 'observational science', very similar to the indigenous approach based,
in Hawken's words, on 'a kind of applied science that has guided people's
relationship with the land and its resources',[24] and evidenced by his refusal
to cut out any more trees. At the end, Roy gets lost in the bush after trying
to muster a sheep from the bottom of a gully, despite Henry's advice to let it
go. When he comes back late at night scared and bleeding, his clothes filthy
and torn, he has experienced the bush as a natural and spiritual force and
to exorcise his fears he takes refuge in his rationalist approach — his new
religion — suggesting that all the bush should be got rid of. But the reader
perceives that Henry knows better than that.

'Letter to a Friend' (1944) explores the same themes, juxtaposing Paul, a
17-year-old man with 'a talent for the abstract' (238), and the older first-person
narrator. The two men are guests in the same hotel and the story basically tells of
their walk along the ocean beach. Paul's desire to become a priest and his reading of
Poe's tales are prompted by his philosophical interest in the problem of evil, but his
abstract speculations on the difficulty of separating philosophy from religion have
completely numbed his imagination, his sensory perceptions and his appreciation
of what is immediately around him: the cicada that flies onto the narrator's arm,
the black-backed gulls landing on the beach and the pipi collected by the narrator.
It is worth remarking that the triumph of sensory perceptions is exemplified by
the scene showing the two men eating pipi grilled on hot stones with gusto and
with no regard for formalities, in contrast to the stiffness of the dinner later at the
hotel where the boy's father eats chunks of raw carrots with knife and fork. The two
scenes provide opposing representations of food and food consumption creating a
'gastronomic polarisation'[25]: on one hand the relish in gathering simple food directly
from the sea, on the other the sophistication and formality of a gastronomic culture
that produces food for profit and mass consumption. They prefigure a different
attitude to food recorded in Patricia Grace's novel *Mutuwhenua*.

Farming and imagination, agriculture and culture are likewise linked in 'A Man of Good Will' (1941), where the anti-conformist protagonist leaves his job in a draper's shop (equated with being in jail or in a cage at the zoo) to grow organic tomatoes in his small garden. He rejects all sorts of chemical aids — quick manure or poisonous spray against caterpillars — and feels creative pleasure in doing his work, so much so that in a period of overproduction he refuses to bury half his crop in accordance with the other farmers' scheme to keep the prices of tomatoes up. Instead he piles them up in a heap, forming a beautiful pyramid: a work of art, his creation, necessarily destined to rot. Finally, the unrelenting advance of urban development and the loss of man's imaginative power overlap in 'Just Trespassing Thanks' (1964), featuring an old suburban recluse, Edward Corrie, who prefers to remain indoors immersed in his poetry to avoid seeing what 'many abstract forces' (272), together with bulldozers and builders, have done around his 'ancient two-room cottage' (272). Interestingly, Sargeson uses the term 'abstract', as in 'Letter to a Friend', to indicate man's stultifying, rational detachment from practical knowledge, and the adjective 'ancient' to endow his small cottage with a dignity from the past. Edward's senses are so offended by the sight of tarmac and cement and by the fumes coming from the nearby motorway that he seldom goes out and always wears dark sunglasses. Edward's dismay is similar to the bewilderment of a Maori elder in Grace's 'Journey' at the concrete jungle he sees in the Wellington area, as the following passages from 'Journey' and from 'Just Trespassing Thanks' demonstrate:

> Funny people these pakehas, had to chop up everything. Couldn't talk to a hill or a tree these people, couldn't give the trees or the hills a name and make them special and leave them. Couldn't go round, only through. Couldn't give life, only death. (Grace)[26]

> While he was putting his feet up he glanced out the window, where the countryside had been replaced by cement and tarmac: wilderness was perhaps the appropriate name for what had once been woodland — and hardly the right kind of breeding-ground for a race of deities. (Sargeson, 274)

While denouncing the uncontrolled development enforced by white society in the name of progress, both writers connect it with the loss of a spiritual connection with nature, underlined by the animistic approach of Maori in Grace's passage, and by Edward's definition of the urbanised area as 'wilderness' unsuitable to gods in

Sargeson. The trespassers, however, are not only the cement and tarmac invading Edward's house, but also a group of young people wanted by the police — two Pakeha and one of Polynesian origin — who are using his house as a temporary shelter. A subtle link is activated between the man and the three fugitives as they are poets. Poetry becomes the means to open channels of communication between different generations and races, to recreate a communal space or 'a country of the imagination' (282) alternative to the dominating rationalist and economic logic, where 'deities' can be repaid 'by token money' (283). Imagination is seen therefore not only as a refuge but also as a subversive weapon, embodied by the young poets on the run from the law who defy the system.

Importantly, the Polynesian is described as having 'a grinning good nature which radiated a comprehensive warmth' (280). As in the stories previously examined, Sargeson's use of Maori references to the indigenous world is never casual, but knowingly connected to the world of imagination, affections and closeness to nature. Uncle Henry in 'Gods Live in Woods' goes mustering with Roy carrying his food in his pikau (bag) and mentions weta and taipo (insects and goblins). The narrator in 'Letter to a Friend' collects pipi like the (supposed) Maori family in 'An Affair of the Heart'. Even Karl, the protagonist of 'An International Occasion' (1969), who organises a collective Sunday dinner to recreate some semblance of warmth and human relationships among the misfits living in his lodging house, has a face marked by 'age-and-weather tattooings' that recall the 'art of moko' (323).

Every theme already identified in Sargeson's stories is explored more explicitly in his novel *I Saw in My Dream* (1949), a Bildungsroman clearly indebted to Joyce's *A Portrait of the Artist as a Young Man*. The first part, which appeared separately in 1945 under the title *When the Wind Blows*, recounts the childhood and adolescence of its protagonist, Henry Griffiths, Sargeson's alter-ego. Trapped in the paralysing grip of a respectable, well-off family and puritanical life, he slowly realises (like Joyce's Stephen) that 'when the soul of a man is born in this country there are nets flung at it to hold it back from flight.'[27] It is no accident that after a life of deprivation marked by fruitless attempts to reconcile his desires and his duties, his sensual/sensuous instincts and the religious/moral attitudes he has been nurtured in, Henry collapses. His illness, together with an acquired awareness of the hollowness of his parents' assumptions, will lead him to escape, metaphorically, from his mental prison and physically from his family's house. Part One, replete with images of enclosure — from the reassuring bed of his childhood, where he was 'snug as a bug in a rug',[28] to the evermore claustrophobic spaces of his school, house and office — ends with Henry lying naked on the grass in the sun. This liberating act is the intimation of escape narrated in Part Two. Except for the Maori names for two insect species, weta and huhu (44), related to the natural world of the bush, and a type of crayfish, the koura (82), there are no other Maori references in Part One. Interestingly, the word 'koura' is mentioned in the last page within one of the many italicised interior monologues of the book, and associated to the best holiday Henry has ever had with his family in the countryside, in a relaxed atmosphere of communion with nature. This seems to foreshadow his encounter with the Maori community later in the novel.

Part Two is the account of Henry's experience as a farm hand in some remote unidentified place in the North Island and of the development of his self-consciousness. Maori become a real presence and are treated in a complex symbolic way here, interwoven with the protagonist's own growth. Henry's 'metamorphosis' is soon announced by an interior monologue:

> *Why am I oh why am I here in the cold and the dark? Cold bed rolling over to the sun, cold embryo waiting to be born. Why am I waiamihea.* (85)

The image of the 'cold embryo' in a cold bed, as opposed to the reassuring bed of childhood, symbolises the price of his emancipation: the 'experience' that must necessarily follow 'innocence'. This is merely the first of many parallels the novel draws, according to a contrapuntal method that shows the connections between different events as complementary to each other. The word 'waiamihea' — a contraction of 'why am I here', seemingly said in a state of drowsiness — posits the direction of his quest and will appear again on the Maori neighbours' gate, apparently as a Maori word. The beginning of Henry's transformation is further marked by his choice of a new name (Dave Spencer), recalling Sargeson's own change of name.

The story tells of farming families living in the same valley: the Macgregors, on whose farm Dave works with Johnny, another labourer; the Poruas, the Andersons, the Daleys and other minor characters. All are Pakeha except for Rangi and Eileen Porua and their relatives. It is a brand new dimension for Dave, marked by the rhythms of the land and animal breeding. Such a pastoral atmosphere, however, is far from idyllic. It is a tough reality where gossip, racial prejudice and cramping religious creeds dominate. While Part One illustrates the destruction of Henry/Dave's values, culminating in his symbolic death (the illness) and resurrection (the final epiphany), Part Two is the phase of reconstruction. This occurs through a process of learning and self-knowledge, which involves the recognition of old and new models. His role of 'new chum' in this context differs from previous colonial fictions.

Dave is not ridiculed to elevate pioneers' rustic virtues, but acts as an external observer of a 'waiting world' (90) that needs to be explored, decoded and reconnected to his own new awareness. This is symbolised by his watching the outside reality through a hole between the boards of his shack — an act reiterated many times — and by his frequent role of listener to other people's stories, intimate recollections or angry outbursts, as the following statement shows: 'There isn't a thing I can say or do about it, Dave was telling himself. I just have to stay here and listen' (158). The old models are represented by the Macgregors, the new ones by the Poruas.

The parallel between the Macgregors and Dave's parents is clear. The climate in their house is as repressive and claustrophobic as back home, the only difference being that, in this uncouth environment, it is less subtly imposed and more explicitly, even violently, externalised. Their son Cedric — an elusive presence in the novel, who never appears in person but is often referred to — escaped like Dave, and his spirit haunts him. While trying to uncover the mystery behind Cedric's disappearance, Dave relives his own experience. The Poruas, on the other hand, represent a new mode of being, alternative to the Western one. First of all Dave notices their nearness to the land, as exemplified by Mrs Porua's and Mrs Macgregor's different reactions to the late frost, unexpectedly occurring well into December:

> You get the frost this morning? She [Mrs Porua] asked
> Yes, they had got the frost.
> Late frost, eh? No good. She pointed over where the earliest potatoes were just coming through. They get nipped all right, but O.K. they come again — though lucky it didn't come any later on by golly, because then it do them in. (99)

> Look! She [Mrs Macgregor] shouted, and pointed to the ground.
> God did all that. He sent the seeds, and then He sent the rain to make them grow, and now He's sent the frost to kill them.
> And they say there's a God!
> God! God! (87)

While Mrs Porua, in her broken English, accepts adverse natural events and is ready to look on the bright side, Mrs Macgregor's religious creed collapses whenever she feels God is not allied with her, which shows the broken-down religious attitude of a society where, as mentioned, ethics remain although faith has departed. Throughout the novel the reader perceives the distance that Western people have created between themselves and nature, conceived merely as a source of economic exploitation. If the land does not comply with their interest, it becomes an enemy. Even Mr Anderson, the most open-minded and reflective of all the farmers, who lives in a comfortable house with his refined English wife, cannot but voice his uneasiness and dislocation:

> That's the trouble, Mr Anderson said. The season round these parts is too short. You can get a frost at any time up to Christmas, and then again about the middle of February if you're unlucky.... Jack says it's our home but sometimes it'll strike you a different way. As if the white man never should have tried to settle it at all — though it might be all right for a few maoris living along the rivers. They'd make it a good enough home, granted. But for the white man he's only got it on a sort of lease ... (128)

Although his point of view coincides with that of any white farmer trying to make the most of his land, Anderson is the only one who discerns the real problem. Like Uncle Henry in 'Gods Live in Woods' he admires Maori wisdom and perceives a core of rightness in their way of relating to the land. He also realises how the white man's presumption to dominate nature is dangerous. An example is his account of how one day, when he had run out of rope, some Maori made one simply by cutting some flax from a field (208). Another is Anderson's remark on the big 'slip' that has blocked a track — 'that's what happens once you've got rid of the bush on this sort of country' (117) — that foreshadows the disastrous landslide that buries the Macgregors' house at the end, killing both of them. The environmental theme is a constant in the story. Not only does it anticipate crucial contemporary issues, it also endorses a philosophy of nature that will become a major concern of Maori writers and their political/environmental battles, such as those seen in Ihimaera's *The Whale Rider* or in Grace's *Potiki and Dogside Story*. Throughout the novel we learn that the white man has tamed the bush, felling trees, burning hill slopes and promoting intensive agriculture. Maori subsistence farming is criticised by Pakeha, typified by the following passage:

> Wally said that if he was Mr Anderson he'd never let the tarpots inside the shed with their lousy sheep.[29]
> Don't be hard Wally, Jack said. After all, it used to be their country.
> Huh! Wally said. Used to be. Is, you mean. Look at the country Rangi's sitting on. Half the bush is still there, and the rest bloody rubbish with the ragwort blowing over on to our land. Why shouldn't I have a bit of that country and make something out of it? (112)

The future worldwide dominance of global surplus production, as opposed to indigenous local subsistence economies, had been tellingly foreseen by Sargeson in a dialogue between Johnny and Dave where they comment on the long shopping list given them by the Macgregors (including rice, barley, lentils, sugar, tea, cocoa, coconut raisins, dates, currants, curry, ginger, caraway seeds, lemon peel, prunes, bacon, salt and flour), and wonder why they need so many things beyond all that is offered by the land (102–103).

The Poruas and the other minor Maori characters show 'a deep respect for the social instincts which they have preserved' and have kept 'their humanity intact.'[30] The relaxed atmosphere of their Christmas party — their insistence on inviting Dave to share their homebrew, their playing, singing and dancing, the mixing together of people of all ages, the disregard of formalities — underscores the persistence of strong family and social bonds as well as openness to communality. The scene differs remarkably from the other two Christmas celebrations described in the novel, which are marked by suffocating claustrophobia (at the Macgregors') and an empty display of social formalities (at the Andersons'). *I Saw in My Dream* differs from Sargeson's stories in the variety of characters, narrative technique and language, but it still demonstrates his concern about the difficulty of communicating. Although characters are able to articulate their thoughts and feelings, even to the point of paroxysm, like Mrs Macgregor, their channels of communication seem to be obstructed by obsessions (the Macgregors) or frozen by incompatible expectations of life (the Andersons). The image of the Porua family on the merry-go-round at the country fair — Rangi and Eileen on horses, each with one of their little boys riding in front, and their little girl in the dragon by herself — symbolises a harmonious whole that never appears in Sargeson's Pakeha families.

If the enclosure/escape dichotomy is one of the main themes of the novel, the Maori view represents a possible direction for the escape. Every image of enclosure in the book is connected to the puritanical world Dave has dissected and finally overcome. In Part One, when Dave is still in its grip, he locks his colleague Molly in the strongroom of their office to prevent her from socialising with the 'bad men' working outside on the scaffolding. In Part Two Johnny tells Dave he was sent to borstal when he was 15 for having sex with a girl of the same age. The Macgregors try to shut their son in a cave in order to bring him back to the path of righteousness. The ultimate image of enclosure is that of the Macgregors buried under the landslide. On the contrary, the other is not frightening, but offers a different viewpoint of reality that helps amend one's own. It represents openness and the existence of other possibilities, and helps man find an answer to the question 'Why am I here?' ('waiamihea'). The presence of the same word on the Poruas' gate is unexplained and sounds like a joke but, in a paradigmatic world, it represents the human race's ultimate question.

Cedric's escape is directly related to the Maori community as well. He and Rangi became best friends and he was influenced by the Maori philosophy of life. He discovered a different perception of his adolescent body when he lay naked on the beach with a half-caste girl. 'They didn't do anything at all' says Johnny, watching them, waiting to intervene in case 'they started to do anything' (165). 'They only sat there and talked and threw stones in the water. And then they both had a lie-down on their backs'. When his parents attempt to stop Cedric from visiting the Poruas, he spends his days in the bush. Cedric had no ambitions in his parents' eyes, he was a good-for-nothing, so they decide to lock him up in a cave to teach him a lesson and turn him into a good boy. Dave learns about it from Johnny, who helped Mr Macgregor prepare the prison and promised to keep the secret. In the end, Cedric is not locked up and instead disappears just before the plan is to be carried out. Nobody knows where Cedric is, but the reader understands he is still in touch with the Poruas and the Maori community. When Dave approaches the Poruas' house on the night of the Christmas party, Rangi's cousin Jerry welcomes him and calls out 'Cedric', then corrects himself.

Sargeson's inclusion of Maori in *I Saw in My Dream* presents a textual complexity unprecedented in New Zealand long fiction. His treatment is not merely instrumental and raises some crucial issues of Maori life and culture. He presents every possible Pakeha attitudes to Maori: Mrs Macgregor's self-righteousness, especially concerning Maori moral views and sexuality;[31] Mrs Daley's racial prejudice and sense of superiority;[32] Mrs Anderson's sophisticated philanthropy; the Brennans' (Mrs Anderson's guests) interest in the Maori as exotic attractions;[33] the white labourers' antagonism towards Maori over the possession and use of land.[34] Nevertheless we also find the search for a Maori point of view and an attempt to let them speak from their own perspective. Sargeson again employs the third-dimension technique used for the urban outcasts of his short stories. Unlike the Pakeha verbosity (especially of Johnny, Mrs Macgregor and Mr Anderson), the few dialogues of the Maori characters are short, semi-articulate and contain many silences, but they succeed in expressing a whole world beyond, to the reader and protagonist alike.

When Dave goes back to his family in Part Three, a brief section that acts as a synthesis after the previous thesis and antithesis, he is a changed person who 'knows': he has observed, listened and felt so now he can *be*. This new awareness has been reached not by fearing the other but by learning from them, by experiencing the possibility of being other than one is. In his perceptive and sensitive appreciation of Maori culture, Sargeson's view was shared by Finlayson, albeit in a different mode and style.

Learning from the Maori view: Finlayson's critique of Western capitalism

Roderick Finlayson's collection of short stories *Brown Man's Burden* (1938)[35] provides a new and direct insight into the Maori world. In his foreword the author explains his reasons for writing exclusively about Maori life. He denounces the dispossession of Maori enacted by Europeans, nevertheless finding that the indigenous people are 'still more truly of the land than we who have dispossessed them'. He asserts that 'the identity with the soil' is the 'pride and birth-right of the native', a major issue that will become a crucial political theme in later Maori writing. Like Sargeson in 'Just Trespassing Thanks', he equates 'closeness to nature' with 'poetic justice' that is also 'God's justice', that is to say he envisages the necessity of a return to a life appealing to spiritual and imaginative powers and looks to Maori culture as a model to follow. Furthermore he identifies 'modern materialism' and 'scientific barbarism' as the forces that have nearly annihilated indigenous culture and concludes:

> The author himself belongs to the remnant of a race not defeated in battle, but more surely defeated by an alien and material society, which may explain in part, why he loves his brother of the 'Iwi Maori'.[36]

The foreword acts as a manifesto of Finlayson's thoughts, but to have a full picture of the theoretical framework encompassing the collection and more generally his writing, it must be read alongside his essay published in 1940, *Our Life in This Land*. In this pamphlet Finlayson deals only marginally with Maori and launches a vocal attack on the spread of industrialism, the consumer society and capitalism in New Zealand and around the world. In outlining the history of the country, he points out its increasing decline due to the loss of that 'salutary contact with nature'[37] that had been guaranteed by its isolation during the Pioneering period, and before its entry into a capitalist economy and the global market. Finlayson never mentions the word 'globalisation' yet his analysis anticipates the coming of a uniform world dominated by the same economic logic and devoid of local specificity and cultural individuality.

Focusing on New Zealand, he stigmatises the rise of mass production and intensive agriculture to satisfy the demand of an import-export based economy.

He criticises the consequent shift of the population from the countryside towards the four main shipping ports and contends that the abolition of provinces and the centralisation of the government have created an artificial community devoid of social cohesion, which in turn is made to conform to the needs and tastes of the wider global village. He denounces the system's encouragement of ruthless competition instead of co-operation, its making work a senseless drudgery, culture a mere distraction and leisure pure emptiness of body or mind. The attendant mechanisation of humankind has, he argues, turned people into dissociated beings who perceive the physical as alien to the spiritual and nature as simply a matter for ungodly exploitation. The false abstractions of science and rationalism have only served to encourage a dogmatic faith in progress: materialist science is the new god. Finlayson questions a notion of progress and civilisation grounded on material achievements, efficiency and the possession of technological items; envisages wars and mass migrations as a result of the unfair distribution of wealth in the world; denounces the media as responsible for the perpetuation of our follies; and finally predicts an environmental crisis:

> Efficiency is a delusion. Nature is not and never was efficient in the sense our experts mean. But men once knew how to ally their efforts with Nature, and that knowledge is not lost. Sooner or later we shall be greatly humbled and compelled to reverence Nature once more; that is Nature as the divine harmony of God and the physical world. (20, OL)

Although these assertions may seem dogmatic and polemic, as Finlayson himself admits in his preface, from the present viewpoint his prognostications are at the centre of today's debate among economists, social philosophers and environmentalists. In his introduction to *Brown Man's Burden and later stories* (1973), Bill Pearson underlines that Finlayson's achievement has been 'to address himself repeatedly to a problem that is important in every part of the world that has been touched by the industrial revolutions, old and new'. His stories are also acknowledged to have 'renewed relevance during the current reaction against the ethos of success and materialism'.[38] The relevance Pearson saw in the decade following the 1968 cultural revolution is even more evident today, in a present reality confronted by an economic world crisis and the threat of environmental disaster, both of which question Western capitalism as a viable system for the future and urge a reconsideration of its practices.

Finlayson's position toward Maori, as stated in the foreword to *Brown Man's Burden* and confirmed by his criticism of Western thought in *Our Life in This Land*, is not just a reformulation of the 'noble savage' theme, nor does he simply try to find in Maori the virtues missing in Pakeha (as we saw in Baucke and Mansfield, for instance).

He genuinely supports the Maori vision insofar as it encompasses core values inextricably linked to retrieving the truest sense of humanity as well as to ensure our very survival. His view is similar to that expressed by environmentalist Paul Hawken in the chapter 'Indigene' of *Blessed Unrest* (2007), his history of the environmental movement. Hawken reverses British historian Hugh Trevor-Roper's point, made in 1965, that the function of native cultures 'is to show to the present an image of the past from which by history it has escaped.'[39] Hawken contends instead that 'indigenous cultures may show us an image of a future by which we can escape our present. If a culture does not become like us, it may not be a failure but a gift to what is now an uncertain future.'[40] Similarly, Serge Latouche, the French economist renowned for *décroissance* (literally 'degrowth') — a theory that rejects the progressivist growth economics of capitalism, advocating the passage to a post-capitalist society based on economic downscaling and social conviviality — looks to traditional societies of the South and to indigenous peoples for inspirational models of sustainable economies, of harmonic reciprocity between the human race and the biosphere and between human beings.[41]

Finlayson's choice to write mostly about Maori is therefore programmatic and political, and must be reconnected to a precise set of beliefs he put into practice in his writing as well as in his modest lifestyle. Pearson defined Finlayson's childhood as 'rich', 'warm in affection and international in outlook'.[42] His biography of the writer outlines a life characterised by openness to other cultures and races, affectionate family bonds and long-lasting friendships, and by an utter disregard for professional advancement (as an architect), fame (as a writer) or economic success. In his youth he came to know three Maori families living on Maori land at Pukehina, near the farm where his uncle was employed and where he spent his childhood summers. He became intimate with one of them in particular and established a long-lasting friendship. He also had a chance to witness the life of landless Maori working in the flax swamp from Pukehina to Maketu, and later in life was deeply struck by the news of the violent deaths of some of the young Maori men he had known. All this offered him first-hand knowledge of Maori life and culture that he used in his writings. Other long-lasting bonds accompanied Finlayson's life: first of all, his friendship with poet D'Arcy Cresswell, famous for his attack on utilitarianism, his religious attitude to nature and his advocacy for the reunion of intellect with intuition through poetry (an idea we found in Sargeson as well). Cresswell introduced him to Sargeson and to the small press publisher Ron Holloway. Sargeson encouraged Finlayson's writing throughout his life, while Holloway was to be his publisher for 50 years. The importance of his family must also be mentioned, not only that of his origin but also the one he formed with wife Ruth Taylor — a young woman he met in Raratonga and who like him was open to other cultures — including his six children and numerous grandchildren.

Finlayson's life is relevant insofar as it emphasises his unconditioned embrace, in theory and in practice, of a philosophy of life grounded on a profound respect for nature and all human beings (independent of their race and culture) and favouring the family and emotional bonds over commercial partnerships, co-operation over competition, imagination and closeness to the land over the ethics of consumer economics and material success. These are tenets of Maori culture too, which explains his deep focus on them, and these are also the principles underlying much of present environmental and economic debate (Hawken and Latouche among others), which Finlayson (like Cresswell and, indirectly, Sargeson) anticipated. As mentioned earlier, the current debate focuses on rejecting a 'growth for growth's sake' economic model and instead promotes the idea that we need to reduce our use of natural resources that are not infinite. It advocates a re-localisation of economies across the planet to create 'integrated, self-sufficient and materially responsible societies' free of the domination of progressivist growth economics,[43] and it underlines the need to fill the affective voids caused by the logic of consumerism and productivity by acknowledging the importance of convivial relationships among human beings. The same themes form a thread through Finlayson's works: in his fictions about Maori, and in the later texts exploring Pakeha society.

Finlayson celebrates the core principles underlying Maori culture in his foreword to *Brown Man's Burden*. His stories do not fall into easy sentimentalism, but offer a realistic representation of the rural Maori of his time that becomes more sombre in his next work *Sweet Beulah Land* (1942), which deals with urbanised Maori. His characters cannot be truly defined as individuals insofar as they are not fully developed and only sketched, but they present a complexity that makes them something more than simple stereotypes. They express all the problems, expectations and disappointments of people who have had to adapt to a completely different world view and come to terms with a value system that has superseded their own. As Wevers notices, 'Finlayson's stories do not sentimentalise the Maori, nor do they represent the Maori as less complex or ambiguous than the Pakeha.' Though Finlayson's Maori are 'comic, tragic, cheerful, drunken, dying, polluted, and corrupted, characterized by the muddled ambiguities of a colonized existence, the stories *affirm* a culture whose loss brings deprivation and caricature and absence to those Maori who reject or forget it'[44] (my emphasis). The traditional values of Maori culture are also affirmed, although indirectly, in Finlayson's stories about Pakeha society, as was the case for Sargeson.

Before analysing some of Finlayson's works we should acknowledge another major influence on him, by two Italian writers from Sicily, namely Giovanni Verga (1840–1922) and Luigi Pirandello (1867–1936). In *Beginnings*, Finlayson states he was extremely impressed by D.H. Lawrence's translations of Verga's collections *Vita dei campi* (1880) and *Novelle rusticane* (1883), the former published under the title of one of its stories *Cavalleria Rusticana* (1928) and the latter as *Little Novels of Sicily* (1928).[45] These stories deal mainly with agricultural labourers, property owners and tenant farmers in late nineteenth-century Sicily, after its incorporation into the new Kingdom of Italy in 1861. Verga had first welcomed this event, which promised to guarantee administrative efficiency and economic development to a land that had been immutable for centuries, preserving ancient traditions as well as an essentially feudal economic and social system. Italian unification, however, could not erase the enormous differences between the north of the country — open to the surge of European capitalism and eager to promote industrial development under the thrust of the rising middle class — and the rural, 'backward' south. Verga's view changed after he broke away from the provincial milieu of his native Catania and pursued a professional career as a writer in the foremost literary and artistic centres of the kingdom: first Florence, the political and cultural capital at the time,[46] then Milan, the commercial and financial capital, where he lived for about 20 years. The mood of disillusionment that followed the attainment of the great Romantic political ideal of Italian unification, together with his contact with the 'centre' of modernity, offered him a new perspective on the 'periphery'. The advent of the new administrative system had proved a failure in the Sicilian context, merely creating new forms of oppression, clientage and privileges, augmenting the poverty of the lower classes (hence the mass emigration of peasants from the south of Italy to the US, Argentina and Australia in the early 1900s) and broadening the chasm between north and south. The ephemeral values of the rising capitalist society he saw at work in Milan increased his diffidence towards a notion of progress basically coinciding with the cult of activism and the disregard of affections and human relationships. All this aroused Verga's profound pessimism and regret for what had been lost from pre-capitalist economies, and prompted a re-evaluation of his Sicilian heritage, epitomised in the two collections later translated by Lawrence.[47] Although living in completely different contexts and times, Verga and Finlayson seem to share the same distaste for the dominant system.

Vita nei campi and *Novelle rusticane* were written in a completely different mode from Verga's previous works. Embracing the *verismo* movement, the Italian equivalent of French naturalism, Verga turned to the dry, impersonal unsentimental style that struck Lawrence and Finlayson so much. He let his characters speak out and unfold without any intervention of the narrator. The narrative and its implications were to be conveyed through dialogue, which assumed a new importance in the overall structure of his works. He also adopted a new prose style, *prosa dialogata* or free indirect style, which allowed the narrator to identify completely with the point of view and language of his characters. Verga's stories portray an immutable world outside time, paradigmatic and holistic, caught between history and myth. It is a reality dominated by natural laws, the rhythm of seasons, fatalism and resignation, rituals and traditions, and anchored to archaic values: the centrality of the family, the importance of one's home, the dignity of every job however humble, attachment to the land, the devotion to Catholic precepts, and festivals imbued with the flavour of pagan natural rituals. His protagonists are simple peasants who are essentially good at heart but have to struggle against misfortune, poverty, sickness and prejudice. Despite their humble origins Verga endows them with the moral stature of epic heroes carved in stone, acting according to ancient codes of honour, following their spontaneous passions and stoically accepting their fate or death. As Lawrence stated, 'Verga's people are always people in the purest sense of the word. They are not intellectual, but then neither was Hector nor Ulysses intellectual.... He had a passion for the most naïve, the most unsophisticated manifestation of human nature.'[48] There is no idealisation of rural life, seen in all its hardships and drudgery, nor does Verga express any opinion on the social justice of the situations he depicts, but the naivety, good nature and uncompromising attitude of his characters stand out as values even though they may lead them to their destruction.

His masterpiece is *Malavoglia* (*The House by the Medlar Tree*, 1881), the first of the cycle of five veristic novels meant to investigate the human condition from the lower classes through the bourgeoisie up to the aristocracy and the politicians. In the preface Verga envisages progress as a 'flood', a powerful 'current' sweeping people along. It creates false virtues and values, setting people in search of material well-being and inducing new desires, prompting a yearning for a better life even when they are already happy and well off. Being a blind, overwhelming force it overtakes the weak and weary, leaving them by the wayside. But even the victors of today will be defeated sooner or later, as evinced by the title he gave to the overall cycle: *I vinti* (The Defeated Ones).[49] As Verga explains in 'Caprice' from *Cavalleria Rusticana*, all one can do is follow 'the ideal of the oyster', in other words, cling tenaciously to the rock onto which fortune decreed one should fall: the metaphor recalls the image of the lice crouching down and holding on tight, used by Sargeson to represent the struggle for survival in 'An Attempt at an Explanation'.

Finlayson said that he recognised similarities between the Maori and Verga's Sicilians: 'the same poverty, hardship and ill-health, the same upflaring of passions and sudden violence, the feuds and the festivals. They were enduring people sustained by similar fatalism, dignity, arrogance even.'[50] Like Lawrence, Finlayson was attracted to Verga because his characters 'are too unsuspicious, not sufficiently armed and ready to do battle with the greedy and the sophisticated. When they do strike, they destroy themselves too.'[51] As Pearson notes, this could account for the numerous bad endings in Finlayson's Maori stories, but in *Beginnings* Finlayson says that his endings were mostly inspired by experience, that is, by the unfortunate deaths of many of his Maori friends 'of disease, of suicide or other violence, of makutu, of insanity'.[52]

If Verga's impersonal prose and human types were an inspirational source to Finlayson, the Italian's tone is definitely more austere and sombre than the New Zealander's, which often verges on a comic, or rather, humouristic approach. Here we find the other major Italian influence on Finlayson, Luigi Pirandello's *Novelle per un anno*. In his essay *L'umorismo* (1908), Pirandello explores the concept of 'humourism' that informs his vast production of short stories, novels and plays, defining it as 'il sentimento del contrario' (the feeling of the opposite). He offers a sample of the humouristic process in action by proposing the image of an old woman with dyed and pomaded hair, dressed up in youthful clothes and excessively made up. She is exactly the contrary of what a proper lady should be and cannot but arouse laughter in the viewers. This is what Pirandello calls 'l'avvertimento del contrario' (the awareness of the opposite), which is the basis of comedy, but if viewers realise that her ridiculous attire and outlook are not due to vanity — that she does not even feel pleasure in masquerading like that but is somehow forced to do it, perhaps because she is afraid of losing the love of her younger husband — then they can laugh at her no longer. The altered perception produces a feeling of sympathy based on understanding rather than on surface impressions: 'the feeling of the opposite'.[53] As Fiora A. Bassanese explains:

> reflection fosters compassion and responds to what is universally human by weighing existential factors and their impact on the individual. Humour is predicated on this shift in the viewer's perception of existence. The humourist burrows to discover the masked reality.[54]

Pirandello distinguishes comedy from humour. The former never moves beyond the realisation of the opposite and remains at the level of awareness. On the contrary:

> humourists are neither detached nor condescending toward their created world. They can concurrently perceive the duality of tragicomedy and the serious underpinnings of a funny situation or character because they have gone beyond mere awareness to the heart of the matter.[55]

Pirandello adds that a humouristic disposition can be determined by an innate or inherited melancholy, by scepticism or pessimism fostered by one's studies, or by sad events experienced in one's life.[56] Following this view, we can interpret Finlayson's humouristic disposition as the result of the close contact with the Maori communities he had in his youth and his dismay at the tragic lot of most of them. His humourism is therefore predicated on understanding and sympathy, not on mockery or a sense of superiority.

Verga's and Pirandello's teachings deeply informed Finlayson's representation of Maori. His approach is unmediated and unobtrusive. Like Verga, he allows the characters to speak out and expose all their frailty and contradictions. There is something epic in their fatalism, pursuing dreams that are doomed to collapse or falling victim to pride or passions. In 'The Wedding Gift' from *Brown Man's Burden*, a young bridegroom uses the gun given to him by prophetic old Uncle Kapi in an unpredictable way, not to take revenge on his best friend Rua, who has eloped with his bride on their wedding day, but to kill himself. In 'New Year', from the same collection, gang leader Peta is sent to prison for using an iron bar to hit a rival who is harassing his sister. The police can extract no information from Maori witnesses, who cover up for him maintaining it was an accident. It is Peta himself who lets them know the truth, boasting about his deed before the judge and openly challenging Pakeha authority: 'He stuck to his story of how he'd done it on purpose, as if he was proud of acting like a young Maori blood instead of like a law-abiding Pakeha' (27, BMB). By doing so, he is sentenced to three years' hard labour and subsequently perishes in prison from tuberculosis, a Pakeha-introduced disease. Young cowherd Rui's dream to go to sea as a sailor in 'Rui's Ship' (published in *Bulletin* in 1947) seems to come true when he finally finds the wreck of a boat swamped by the beach. But the boat will only provide him with a fatal splinter in his arm that will cause his death and, bitterly, his sailing to Hawaiki (the ancestral afterworld). If Pearson detects an element of literary parentage between Rui and the boy who herded horses in Verga's 'Jeli the Herdsman',[57] there is also a striking similarity between the widow Paku in 'The Swamp The Sea The Sky' (from *In Georgina's Shady Garden*) and the protagonist of Verga's 'La Lupa'. Both are frowned upon by the other women for their unconventional behaviour and ostracised by their communities; both are depicted as disquieting, eerie figures, possessed by an insatiable spirit, gifted with lean erotic bodies and great hungering eyes ('she had merely to look at them with her great evil eyes, to have them running after her skirts', in Verga; 'hungry somber eyes' which 'ate men up', in Finlayson)[58]; and both cast a spell on the men they lay those eyes upon, causing their fatal ruin.

What strikes today's reader, however, is how Finlayson's themes foreshadow most of the core concerns of Maori writers from the 1970s onwards: the widening generational gap; the decay of Maori traditions under the thrust of dominant Western culture; the importance of the land and Maori language for the survival of Maori identity; the hybridisation of young Maori falling prey to criminality in the cities; and the clash between Pakeha and Maori in urban settings. As mentioned in the editor's note to his last collection *In Georgina's Shady Garden* (1988), 'now that fifty years have passed, Rod Finlayson is coming into his own. But it was he who wrote of Maori and Pakeha and the importance of conserving the land, fifty years before there was a band-wagon for protesters to jump on.'

The generation gap, the elders' dignity and nostalgia for the past, and the degradation of Maori culture are explored in 'On Top of the Hill' and 'The Totara Tree', both from *Brown Man's Burden*. 'On Top of the Hill' is based on the juxtaposition of father and son, who represent opposite views of life. Tamarua is happy in his old shack and with the little he gets from his small piece of land on the hillside; young Peta, who tried but failed to make it in the Pakeha urban world, is frustrated and angry, which is also the reason why he defies the judge in the sequel story 'New Year', mentioned above. Unable to succeed in the Pakeha world, he can neither stay on his father's land: Peta has been hybridised and become 'un-Maorilike'. He ends up joining the widespread Maori rural proletariat, working as a flax-cutter. In 'New Year' he joins a gang and dies in prison. If we read Finlayson's characters in Verga's terms, Tamarua has followed 'the ideal of the oyster' and has survived, while Peta, fatally attracted by progress and overtaken by its flood, has joined the list of the 'defeated ones'.

In 'The Totara Tree' the gulf between generations is analysed within a community, depicted through the different viewpoints of its members. This technique, often used by Finlayson, allows him to describe them as individuals in relation to their community, according to Maori culture. A Power Board Inspector wants to cut down a totara that stands in the way of the new power line being set up in the valley. The totara is the birth-tree[59] of an old woman, Taranga, who protests against the felling by climbing up the tree and refusing to move. Taranga's gesture is taken very seriously by old Uncle Tuna, who still believes in tapu (sacredness), but quite humorously by all the younger people living in the village. Their commitment to Taranga's cause turns into a big feast with a lot of drinking, laughing and boasting about their future deeds. Finally a fire breaks out, burning one of the houses. Uncle Tuna is the only one who does not participate in the binge, but watches in disgust at that 'senseless generation' working 'their own destruction' (45, BMB). After rescuing Taranga from the fire, they discover she has been dead for some time. Following Uncle Tuna's advice they bury her beneath the tree and, since the area is turned into a burial site, it cannot be desecrated and the tree is saved. Finlayson uses a humouristic approach (in Pirandello's terms) to the serious problem of younger generations' fatal attraction to Western progress (the children fingering the inspector's big car or young Panapa's admiration for the ten thousand volts carried by the power lines) and their consequent corruption by it (drinking and mocking traditions) to see what lies behind their contradictory actions and sympathise with them. Uncle Tuna's disapproving remark 'Can't the Pakeha bear the sight of one single tree without reaching for his axe?' (41, BMB) conveys the same concern for the environment as the Maori elder of Grace's 'Journey' and Edward Corrie, the poetic Pakeha outcast of Sargeson's 'Just Trespassing Thanks'.

'Sweet Beulah Land', the story that provides the title to Finlayson's second collection, gives a more sombre picture of a community organising a feast for the sale of communal land 'in the name of Pakeha progress — and on the Government's terms' (90, BML). The point of view shifts continuously between characters, envisaging a fragmented reality: old Matiu fiercely opposes the sale, but is ignored; young Turi rejoices at the thought of ready money he will be able to squander in city life; Makeri is puzzled but unable to take a clear stand; Penny Watene perceives their defeat but is also flattered by the governor's speech; Pakeha authorities display their best political rhetoric to pursue their objectives; reporters move hungrily around to catch the sensational news of the day; a tall Pakeha, supposedly a priest or a government emissary, doles out tracts entitled *Sweet Beulah Land*.

The story, loosely based on the hui arranged at Waitangi in 1934 by Maori to celebrate the restoration of the house where the Treaty of Waitangi was signed in 1840, evokes the gradual loss of Maori land after the treaty. While its title ironically alludes to the promised land ensured to the faithful in the Book of Isaiah, its content shows 'the faithful' actually being deprived of their own land. As in 'The Totara Tree' the carnival turns into a mockery of traditions, a muddle of people eating, drinking, flirting, playing old-time warriors and yelling the words 'ake, ake, ake' (an excerpt from a haka affirming defiance to the Pakeha) in front of the movie camera. The story most effectively explores all the means used by the dominant power to impose itself: a commercial agreement apparently favourable to Maori but which in fact determines their ruin, religious indoctrination (the tracts), and the flowery rhetoric of politicians helped by the power of the media (all of which can be seen as ideological texts or weapons). The story ends with the symbolic image of Makeri 'crying happily' (90, BML) in a corner of the hall, an oxymoron that comes to epitomise Maori people as a whole. Finlayson cannot but lay a satirical seal on the scene by alluding to the real value of the *Sweet Beulah Land* tracts: handy little pamphlets to have in one's pocket, since a dysentery-like disease is spreading among the crowd.

The consequences of selling communal land are explored in other stories in the same collection, dealing with tragic destinies of landless urban Maori. Three major aspects arise: the uprooting and moral degradation of the young in the city, usually Auckland; their premature aging due to a debauched life and lack of expectations; and their recourse to humble farming jobs in the market gardens of another minority in the country, the Chinese. In 'Pakapoo' Turi visits his old friend Penny Watene in Auckland. Unemployed, skinny and sick, Penny lives in an unhealthy, crumbling house in the slums stealing money from his 14-year-old sister, whom he has taken out of school and employed in a boarding house. He is only 26 but looks like an old man, with no plans or expectations in life beyond gambling, to the extent that he does not stop to wonder where his sister's gold bracelet and pink silk stockings come from and, like a pimp, steals her bracelet to gamble on the new Chinese game, Pakapoo.

Poverty and degradation also characterise the two protagonists of 'Tara Does a Job', who both work in Chinese market gardens. Patu, who 'looked old at twenty-nine' (98, BML), shares a shack with a Maori family, while Tara lives in master Yang's stable. One night Patu overhears the girls of the family thrilled about their rendezvous with well-off Chinese men who can pay for the amusements they want. Later on Tara calls up drunk and confides the dirty job he has done that night in exchange for a few bottles: he has helped another Maori girl to get rid of her unwanted baby, drowning the 'kitten' in the river. The story ends with Tara wanting to attack his master Yang, either for revenge or to expiate his guilt. According to Maori tradition, abortion is forbidden because it goes against the mauri (life principle), as Finlayson explained in a letter to the *New Zealand Listener* (9 July 1973),[60] which makes Tara's crime even more hideous. Other Maori working in Chinese gardens appear in 'They All Go Home to Die', in which Ah Koo takes pity on Lena and her father because he is sick and longing for his home. He feels close to them because he perceives their deracination, as if they were immigrants as well: '"You and me sick men," Ah Koo said to Poto. "You and me poor men. Never mind. Let us be friends while we can."' (104, BML). As in the previous story, Finlayson indirectly alludes to the condition of landless Maori as poor foreign immigrants in their own country. This is similarly underlined in a later story, 'Great Times Ahead' (*NZ Listener*, 1973), when mixed-race protagonist recalls a visit to Auckland in his youth and his puzzlement at seeing the first urban Maori he ever met, sadly waiting outside the Land Court:

'Why are they waiting here then, Dad? Are they waiting to die?' I asked.
'Much the same,' Dad said. 'They are losing their land,' he told me. 'Come on, or we'll miss the ferry.'

I didn't see how people could lose their land. Land was something under your feet, there it was, and you stood on it. But I did know what losing is like. I'd just lost my mum. And losing makes the one who loses feels like lost. So then I knew why they looked sad and hopeless and lost. (129, BML)

In this passage Finlayson defines the notion of 'land' in the Maori way, as turangawaewae or an inalienable place of belonging. It is a right that has, however, been denied, and which leads Maori to their spiritual and physical death. The loss of the land and of Maori language are the deepest wounds to Maori identity, as evidenced in 'Another Kind of Life' (*Arena*, 1971). The narrator, a Maori bus driver living in Auckland, feels desolate on the day he pays a visit to an uncle in his kainga (village), which has become an unrecognisable holiday destination. The two men do not even manage to meet because the uncle, who has sold his land, now works in a factory. The feeling of deracination increases when the protagonist hears two men speaking Maori, a language that is alien to him since he was raised speaking only English:

I am ashamed that I cannot speak my people's language, that I cannot even understand, and it makes me mad. It is because of what the Pakeha did to my father, and to all the other kids' fathers, when they were youngsters. My father told me the teacher strapped him when he was a little boy going to school the first time, and how could he know better. The teacher strapped him, a little Maori boy, for speaking Maori, and then he made him wash out his mouth with soap and water, wash the dirty Maori off his tongue. So my father stopped speaking the Maori. And I never learn. (125–26, BML)

The loss of the Maori idiom, a result of the repressive school system aimed to create a uniformly English-speaking country, is directly connected to death by the discomforted narrator at the end of the story when he comments that only a tangi can 'bring us city horis back to the heart of our people now' (126, BML).

Maori who assimilate into Pakeha life fare no better, but are overtaken by the 'flood of progress', in Verga's terms. Johnny Wairua's attempts to develop his hot spring and mudhole near Rotorua into a thermal spa, in 'Johnny Wairua's Wonderland' (*Bulletin*, 1947), only result in depriving him of his land, now declared a national reserve, and turn him into a waged undertaker with a metal badge and white peaked cap. In 'Like the Pakeha' (*Bulletin*, 1949), the Maori interpreter Tom Walker and his Europeanised wife Lizzie become victims of consumerism in their spotless house devoid of life and love. Their attempt to be accepted in the Pakeha neighbourhood resolves into an exclusion from both worlds, and Tom's symbolic gesture of repeatedly washing his hands exemplifies his will to get rid of his Maori identity while not having acquired a new one. The hilarious scene of Maori relatives from Wairoa pa invading their house to help Lizzie during her breakdown recalls the clash of Maori and Pakeha lifestyles evoked in many later Maori fictions.[61] What strikes most in the Walkers' lifestyle is the absence of affection and family warmth, reminiscent of Sargeson's dreary families. Lizzie, in particular, completely dismisses the Maori attitude to life, death and illness. She does not want more than one child so as to maintain their material standard of living. Her participation in a tangi at the pa is brief and formal, and she confronts illness in solitude. Lizzie epitomises a sad, uncritical abdication of Maori identity.

Although unsentimental, Finlayson's picture of Maori is not hopeless. Wevers' contention that he is treating the Maori as a dying race, as A.A. Grace before him, is questionable.[62] Undoubtedly Finlayson denounces the deracination of a people who risk losing their roots and that live in a liminal space between tradition and modernity, nevertheless he underscores the malaise of the Maori race not to decree its death but to urge a remedy. This attitude is confirmed by his short stories depicting the impact of Western values on Pakeha, and in the novel *Tidal Creek* (1948) that celebrates the life of a Pakeha man whose attitudes and principles are close to those of the Maori.

His last collection, *In Georgina's Shady Garden*, published in 1988 but including stories written over a span of 40 years, deploys a gallery of Pakeha characters who are, one way or another, professionally or existentially frustrated, imaginatively inhibited and sexually repressed. They appear perceptively numbed, unable to solve their tensions and inexorably destined to disaster or failure. Those who are trapped in the cult of respectability and materialism act as persecutory agents of the unconventional or imaginative ones, enforcing an inquisitorial control on their morality. Human relationships become struggles for supremacy and are characterised by diffidence and distrust due to miscommunication, enclosure and rigidity, or lack of perception. Marriage is the tomb of love and imagination in 'A Nice Little Nest of Eggs' (1947) and 'The Girl at the Golden Gate' (1948), where dull asexual wives act as strict normative agents, leading their repressed husbands to seek affection elsewhere, only to be fooled by those women. In 'Jesus Loves Me' (1975) an ebullient working-class girl with artistic ambitions and a liberated attitude towards sex is ostracised by the other women in her office, but, beyond mere appearances, proves mature and morally honest. The optician's assistant of 'You Little Witch' (1978), who has renounced an emotional relationship and passively accepts a dreary life with his twin sister, escapes into a world of dreams and loses touch with reality. The only imaginative act he can make is misinterpreted and punished. The clumsy attempts of a shy young coalman to court a customer's niece in 'Fuels for the Fires of Love' (1952) are misread, causing him to lose his job. In 'Flowers and Fruit' (1982) the hypochondriac Weston, indulged by a mother-like elderly wife, vents his frustration on the inhabitants and flowers of the island where he has been appointed fruit inspector, projecting his destructive instincts on them.

All of these stories seem to portray unnatural lives subdued by a rigid external code that dehumanises what is most properly human, as evidenced by the sterility of the Rookers and the Westons, which becomes a symbol of spiritual dryness. One scene in 'A Nice Little Nest of Eggs' exemplifies this view, showing Mrs Rooker's reaction to Rosie, the indigent girl she has employed as housemaid to comply with the vicar's request:

> 'Oh! That girl,' Mrs Rooker whispered hoarsely to Mr Rooker as she watched Rosie out in the yard hanging clothes on the line. 'Do you see her limbs? She's only fifteen. And look at her bust!' Almost as though to say that Rosie was to blame for it — that something ought to be done about it.
> 'Well, it's nature, ain't it?' said Mr Rooker. 'Girls grow that way, don't they?' (5, GSG)

In *Tidal Creek* (1948), on the contrary, Finlayson celebrates the life of a self-contented Pakeha man in tune with himself, other humans and nature. Its protagonist, Uncle Ted, was inspired by Finlayson's Uncle Arthur. In his introduction to the 1979 edition, Dennis McEldowney mentions that in the confident surge of post-war development *Tidal Creek* seemed 'an exercise in nostalgia rather than a message for the future, a conclusion reached by a scholar as late as 1971.' But he adds: 'I doubt whether this can be asserted as confidently now. At least, if Finlayson is looking backwards for guidance, many are now doing the same; and many more have an uneasy feeling that perhaps they ought to be.'[63] Thirty years later this comment appears even more incisive with reference to a global system that has increasingly affirmed values such as 'quantity' instead of 'quality', 'goods' instead of 'the Good', 'well-having' instead of 'well-being', in Latouche's terms.[64] Drawing from Finlayson's own words, McEldowney also underscores that the writer viewed Uncle Ted as a Pakeha embodiment of Maori values that Pakeha should retrieve:

> 'Although Uncle Ted is caught up in the increasing industrialisation of farming', Finlayson says, 'he is still steeped (some would say sunk) in peasant tradition; witness his frugal living and finding of pleasures on his land rather than treating his work as drudgery to be relieved by "holidays". Consider too his childish antics and glee in making use of what others would discard as rubbish or waste. Then there are the remnants of rituals (once agriculture was governed by a series, or seasons, of rituals), which we see in his ritual shaving and his regard for beasts and implements. Uncle Ted's attitudes are more akin to those of the Maori. Today Uncle Ted would say that agriculture is indeed sunk! Wholesale use of poisonous chemicals and fuel-consuming machines, overlarge and overstocked holdings, failure to cultivate crops for normally dry summers, Uncle Ted would declare to be the most ruinous and laziest use of land that ever was!' (12, TC)[65]

Uncle Ted has all that he needs on his little farm. His philosophy of life is unfolded in dialogues with nephew Jake, who pays him two visits in seven years. The author here juxtaposes two different viewpoints according to a model we already found in Sargeson's 'Gods Live in Woods', namely the restless enthusiasm for technology, progress and the urban life of youth versus the self-contented wisdom of a mature man acquired from contact with the land. Uncle Ted's notion of time is based on quality rather than quantity. It is punctuated by daily or seasonal tasks that don't turn humdrum since they are varied and carried out according to his own rhythm. He is not subjugated by time but takes his time in doing things: 'You don't want to go at it like you got no time on earth.... There's whips of time. What's a man's life but whips of time. You just want to go steady at things and enjoy doing a little all the time, you see?' (90, TC). He is curious, gets involved in all that surrounds him (people, animals and objects alike), enjoys repairing broken things that can be reused, and takes pleasure in finding solutions to problems that arise. He is what today we would describe as ecologically conscious. The episode of the old rusty tractor of American make, which Jake and Ted find dumped in a field, is meaningful. Their dialogue contrasts a progressive, environmentally careless attitude with a conservative, environmentally aware attitude. Jake underlines the benefits that tractors can bring to agriculture — relieving a worker's fatigue, speeding up work and reducing the cost of crops — and calls his uncle 'old-fashioned' and 'out of date'. Uncle Ted highlights their drawbacks, objecting to them — these days he would enlarge this objection to appliances like computers, cell phones, and television sets — because they are not easily recyclable ('What's a man to do with them things that won't rot?' [91, TC]) and utilise energy that is not renewable and must be imported ('Old-fashioned, eh?' says Uncle Ted. 'Here's another thing — can you graze a tractor, eh? Don't they burn benzene or oil or something from the devil knows where?' [92, TC]). In the same episode, faced with a dead sheep, Jake considers it unusable while Ted applies the indigenous view that nothing must be wasted: 'We can get wool and hide and fat from her, and we'll bury her carcase where it'll help manure the ground' (93, TC). Finally, while Jake expresses his faith that scientists will be able to find solutions for waste treatment, Uncle Ted expresses his distrust of omnipotent science:

> 'But you're out of date,' says Jake. 'Science will alter that kind of messing about anyway.'
> 'Let them try,' Uncle Ted says. 'Just let them scientists try to get away with it. Nobody can get away from the proper use of God's creatures without coming a cropper.' (93–94, TC)

In his ungrammatical English, Uncle Ted criticises one of the founding pillars of European universalism: scientific universalism, to use Immanuel Wallerstein's words. The rise of science to universal truth and as the only reliable instrument of knowledge has been one of the means to legitimise Western supremacy, relegating other modes of knowledge, especially those of indigenous or Third World peoples, to the debased sphere of emotional, artistic or religious prejudice.[66] Uncle Ted's attitude, on the contrary, epitomises the notion of agriculture as culture, of knowledge as observational science, an approach similar to the indigenous one that is not exploitative or speculative but co-operative with the land and its resources. His easy life in harmony with nature contrasts with Jake's uneasiness (like Sargeson's Roy in 'Gods live in Woods'), such as when he finds himself alone on a track in the middle of the bush. He feels the same fear as the first white settlers, for whom the bush was too uncanny, rationally uncontrollable and therefore dangerous, and his reaction cannot but be supportive of the settlers' deforestation: 'No wonder the pioneers burnt the bush. Jake remembers old settlers speaking of such experiences. Bush fright, they reckoned' (80, TC). Jake's rational attitude makes him turn nature into an enemy to eliminate, into an inexplicable other to subdue through the control of reason. Yet its clearing, in turn, produces other fears and nightmares, as evidenced by Mr Moss, an English neighbour living in an old pioneering homestead, who is obsessed by the clay slips behind his house. As in *I Saw in My*

Dream, landslides become the symbol of nature revolting against man's abuse:

> 'Now whenever I try to take a nap I *see* those blasted hills with
> my eyes shut. If there were sheep on them I might count sheep,
> but you know, I've caught myself counting those bally clay slips
> instead. If I close my eyes I can see every one. It's nightmarish.
> They're driving me crazy. Every summer and every winter there
> are more of them.' (83, TC)

Finlayson attempted to write a sequel to *Tidal Creek* in which an older and wiser Jake begins to recognise the force of Uncle Ted's view, but he never finished.[67] Some Maori characters appear in the book, but they are not really developed. Rua conforms to the stereotype of 'lovable rogue', in McEldowney's terms,[68] while the account of the prophet Monday Wiremu is a story within the story and was later included in the 1973 edition of *Brown Man's Burden*. The focus of Finlayson's attention is Uncle Ted, a Pakeha deeply indebted to the Maori world, so much so that he embraces the Maori belief that at his death his soul will go to North Cape, where all dead souls depart to reach Hawaiki (118 and 152, TC): on that day only will he leave Tidal Creek.

Finlayson's attack on the capitalist system and distrust of the Western notion of progress, his account of their effects on Pakeha and Maori, his well-grounded knowledge and respect of Maori culture make him a coherent, anti-conformist figure in New Zealand literature. He was able to envisage the crisis of Western models and to express a new insight into indigenous issues well ahead of his time. Between him and the rise of Maori writers in the 1970s only one Pakeha writer, Noel Hilliard, would be able to explore Maori concerns with the same sympathy and shrewdness.

3 Janet Frame and Noel Hilliard

A 'way of seeing': Janet Frame and the Maori vision

If realism is the rule characterising New Zealand literature in most of the twentieth century, both in the novel and in short stories, Janet Frame is an exception. The territory of her writing is the world of imagination, where dream and fantasy merge into memory and experience, and the evocation of mood replaces any coherent sequence of events. Frame stresses the importance of the point of view, the relativity of meanings and the power of language to recreate a reality that is never limited to the visible or tangible, but goes beyond the factual and the objective. Her characters, often children and the so-called mentally ill, are others insofar as they live in a world where, in Rhodes' words, 'the borderline between fact and fantasy is not clearly marked nor, to the irritation of unimaginative and sober-minded adults, even recognised'.[1]

In his essay on Frame's collection *The Lagoon and Other Stories*, Rhodes states that she possessed 'that inward eye which is the bliss as well as the bane of solitude'.[2] Her way of seeing was 'a double vision', caught between the outward and the inner eye. This double vision is typical of childhood and of schizophrenia, the disease she was wrongly diagnosed with by a young psychology teacher and that led her to be institutionalised. It is the gift of poets, who by combining outward and inner views are able to rewrite the real, revealing unknown links between things and new meanings in words. As Frame said to Elizabeth Alley, what really interested her was to find 'what is beyond the real, the invisible beyond the real'.[3] It is also a Maori perspective 'informed by the holistic frameworks of the real as well as the unreal',[4] in Ihimaera's words, suspended between two worlds: reality and myth, fact and imagination.

In an interview with Claudio Gorlier for the Italian newspaper *La Stampa*,[5] Frame directly underlined her debt to the mythical vision of Maori, which Gorlier identifies with her use of words as magic tokens, transcending the ordinary world and uncovering a larger space and time. The influence of Maori culture is clearly expressed in the opening of *To the Is-Land*, the first volume of her *An Autobiography* (1989):

1 In the Second Place

From the first place of liquid darkness, within the second place of air and light, I set down the following record with its *mixture of fact and truths and memories of truths* and its direction always toward the Third Place, where the starting point is myth.

2 Toward the Is-Land

The *Ancestors* — who were they, *the myth and the reality?* As a child, I used to boast that the Frames 'came over with William of Orange'. I have since learned that this may have been so, for Frame is a version of Fleming, Flamand, from the Flemish weavers who settled in the lowlands of Scotland in the fourteenth century. I strengthen *the reality or the myth* of those *ancestors* each time I recall that Grandma Frame began working in a Paisley cotton mill when she was eight years old; that her daughters Polly, Isy, Maggie spent their working lives as dressmakers and in their leisure produced exquisite embroidery, knitting, tatting, crochet; and that her son George Samuel, my father, had a range of skills that included embroidery (or 'fancy-work', as it was known), rug making, leatherwork, painting in oils on canvas and on velvet....

There were the *ancestors*, then, given as *mythical possessions* — your great-grandmother, your great-grandfather, did this, was this, lived and died there and there — and the living parents, accumulating memories we had not shared. (my emphases)[6]

Frame opens her autobiography questioning the truth of fact (her record is defined as a mixture of fact *and* truths) and establishing myth as the starting point of her origins. She underscores the limits of reality, which necessarily needs to be completed by or included in myth, to be true. The primacy of factual reality over fiction and myth is therefore subverted. Frame continues listing names and deeds of her ancestors, following the practice of Maori whakapapa or genealogy, which connects humans to the gods. Her incipit sounds like an actual quotation from Maori mythology, according to which the beginnings of all things are traced back to Te Kore (the Void) and Te Po (the Night.) This was the original condition in which humans, animals and plants lived, enclosed in the tight embrace of their primeval parents Rangi (the Sky) and Papa (the Earth). Only by pushing them apart did their children see the light, and the world began. The notion of history (personal or collective) as necessarily inclusive of myth is a central tenet of Maori culture, found in much contemporary Maori fiction, and includes the recitation of whakapapa as part of the education of the young (for example, in Ihimaera's *The Matriarch*), or the connection of the fictional story that is about to be told to myth through genealogy, as in the foreword to Ihimaera's *Tangi*.

More generally, it is Frame's urge to find the 'invisible beyond the real' that testifies to her indebtedness to Maori culture, that is, her search for a communication between humanity and the world that is typical of paradigmatic cultures. By erasing the border between fact and fiction even in her own autobiography, she underlines her disbelief in the possible existence of a reality outside imagination, as she highlighted in her interview with Alley:

> Well, I am always in fictional mode, and autobiography is found fiction. I look at everything from the point of view of fiction, and so it wasn't a change to be writing autobiography except the autobiography was more restrictive because it was based in fact, and I wanted to make an honest record of my life. But I was still bound by the choice of words and the shaping of the book, and that is similar to when one is writing fiction. I think that in writing there's no feeling of returning to or leaving a definite form, *it's all in the same country, and within view of one's imaginative home* so to speak, or in the same town. (my emphasis)[7]

An example of overlapping of fact and fiction, reality and myth is found in Frame's treatment of the grandmother figure in *Owls Do Cry* (1961) and *An Autobiography*. In *Owls Do Cry*, Frame uses the image of her own real grandma to depict the Withers children's grandmother. The comparison between the following two excerpts — one from the novel, the other from the autobiography — shows both the writer's creative process and the interconnection of fact and fiction in life and literature. To understand the first excerpt, the reader must be aware that the Withers children are from a Pakeha family and the description is from their point of view:

> Their grandmother was a negress who had long ago been a slave with her long black dress and fuzzy hair and oily skin, in the Southern States of America. She sang often of her home,
> – Carry me back to ole Virginny ....
> And now that she is dead she will have returned to Virginny and be walking through the cotton fields, with the sun shining on her frizzy hair that is like a ball of black cotton to be danced on or thistledown that birds take for living in if their world be black. (From *Owls Do Cry*)[8]

> It was while Mother was busy with the new baby that Grandma Frame, who lived with us, became my companion and friend.... Her skin was dark, her black hair frizzy, and although she talked Scottish, the songs she sang were of the American Deep South. She'd be going silently about the house when suddenly her voice would come out in a singing that filled me with the kind of feeling I learned much later to identify as sadness. 'Carry me back to ole Virginny...' ... I assumed that Grandma Frame was African and had been a slave in America, that her real home was Virginny, where she longed to return; for you see I knew about slaves.
> The book that everyone was talking about in our house was *Uncle Tom's Cabin* by Harriet Beecher Stowe, and I was being called Topsy because my hair was frizzy. (From *An Autobiography*)[9]

From the slaves of *Uncle Tom's Cabin*, to Frame's assumption that her grandma was African, to the Withers children's belief that their grandmother was a negress: it is a passage from fiction to fact and back to fiction, but in this process the real and the imaginary continuously overlap. For the young Frame, *Uncle Tom's Cabin*'s fictional slaves were real. Her real grandmother is associated with them and turned into an African fictional character. In *Owls Do Cry* this process is reproduced without any mediation on the part of the writer: the children's grandmother is a 'negress' and has gone back to Virginia after death.

The disruption of conventional temporal and spatial co-ordinates, a tenet of Maori literature, is found in most of Frame's fiction. In *The Lagoon and Other Stories* (1951) she drew widely on her childhood, reinventing people and places. But, as Rhodes underscores, her memories and evocations are not just 'confined to a way of seeing that originates in an exceptionally vivid imagination. They also reproduce the timeless experience of the age of innocence to which Blake's lines have special relevance: "To see a World in a grain of sand/And Heaven in a flower,/ Hold Infinity in the palm of your hand/And Eternity in an hour."[10] In her reminiscences and character sketches Frame seeks the true spirit of childhood, embodied in its visionary power and its trespass of conventionally accepted boundaries of here and there, present and past, real and fantastic. This is symbolised by the lagoon itself, in the eponymous story, a space suspended between land and sea, which can be seen just as 'a stretch of dirty grey sand shaded with dark pools of sea-water'[11], but it is also the place where generations of children played, found unexpected treasures and animals, made sand castles and told stories ('you be Father I'll be Mother and we'll live here and catch crabs and tiddlers for ever' [8]), oblivious of all but an eternal present. The repetition of this sentence at the end as a close to the story underlines the circularity of time and the expansion of the present into past and future.

Jeanne Delbaere-Garant has pinpointed the 'essential undividedness of the universe' that a story like 'The Lagoon' suggests, as evidenced in its opening passage, where "'*faces in the water*" [meet] clouds and rushes and octopus in the dark pools of sea-water left behind on the land':[12]

> There is a bridge over the lagoon where you may look down into the little pools and see your image tangled up with sea-water and rushes and bits of clouds. And sometimes at night there is an under-water moon, dim and secret. (7)

In his essay 'Maori Life and Literature: A Sensory Perception', Ihimaera gives this definition of himself: 'I have therefore been sometimes a writer, something more of a Maori, but I have inherited a time and a space greater than both.'[13] This holistic view applies to Frame, too. She wanders in a wider space and time, looking for secret bonds among things, connecting objects with their Platonic ideas. In her fiction, the power to connect things to the whole is not only a gift of children but also of the 'mentally insane', equated with 'seers' or 'people of vision'.[14] In *Faces in the Water*, Istina Mavet laments she cannot tell the difference between apparently distant things, because '[she] knew only the similarity that grew with it; the difference dispersed in the air and withered, leaving the fruit of similarity, like a catkin that reveals the hazelnut'.[15] The mentally ill come to symbolise those who do not conform, who don't fit in a reality dominated by monological inflections of identity and the principle of rationality that treats imagination as a dangerous infection. As Delbaere-Garant suggests, psychiatric hospitals become a metaphor for a totalitarian society 'in which those who do not conform are forced back to "normality" by means of the most brutal treatments',[16] such as electroconvulsive therapy or leucotomy. Interestingly, Istina Mavet describes her rehabilitation in hospital in terms of a colonisation of the mind, effected by the exchange of glass beads for other valuable goods, as in pioneering times, and calls her institutionalisation a process of 'civilisation': 'I was not yet *civilised*; I traded my safety for the *glass beads* of fantasy' (5, my emphases).

Diversity becomes a value for Frame: the ability to see deeper 'into the life of things', in Blakean terms. Far from unawareness, it is equated with too much awareness, which needs a special language and real communication to be conveyed. That's why in *Scented Gardens for the Blind* Erlene takes refuge in silence, since 'there was nothing to say and no words to say it'.[17] In *Owls Do Cry* Teresa, totally committed to the ethos of materialism and supporting the idea of lobotomy for her sister Daphne (the diverse), cannot but express herself in the unimaginative, dull language recorded in her diary. Diversity was also celebrated by Sargeson with his waifs and strays of society, who are capable of deep feelings but cannot convey them because language has been emptied of its emotional valence. Diversity is celebrated in a similar way by Patricia Grace in *The Sky People*, exploring the lives of those who live at the margins, because they are 'connected to the sky in their mind'. As Grace argues, 'they are apart from ordinary people through their imagination, their spirituality, or their socialization, and so may not be quite so fixed to the earthly and practical things.'[18] Frame, Sargeson and Grace explore the territory of 'otherness' in all its multifaceted aspects of non-conformity. Their characters, different because they are interpreted through the alphabet and grammar of a spiritual/physical/ cultural colonisation, are locked up in systems of exclusion or pushed up to the margins in communities of 'others' like them. While Sargeson uses his third dimension technique to visualise silence, both Frame and Grace often apply shifts in points of view, which allow them to enter the minds of their characters to offer multiple perspectives of reality and a language appropriate to their personal world. Shifting viewpoints are physically visualised in the division of chapters or sections conveying the single voice of one character (for example, in *Scented Gardens for the Blind* or the second part of *Owls Do Cry* and in Grace's *Potiki* and *Baby No-Eyes*), a technique that challenges a monolithic notion of identity, narrative and reality.

In *Scented Gardens for the Blind* another character can be reconnected to the Maori view: Edward, Erlene's father. He has devoted the past 11 years of his life to tracing the genealogy of the Strangs, people completely strange to him and remote in space and time. His project seems at first to be urged by a noble purpose: preserving the memory of the human race through the chronicle of a family that 'had persisted over the centuries in spite of war, disease, and other catastrophes which have visited humankind' (62). But his attempt to defend memory from the erosion of time, similar to the keeping of a whakapapa, turns into a cold theoretical work. Edward is more at ease with the dead than with the living. He is incapable of having relationships of any sort and cannot deal with people in flesh and blood (for example, the living Strangs that he gets to know). Close contact with human beings (even on a bus) irritates him, and his chronicle of the past in the service of the future implies the paradoxical abandonment of his own family in the present. His effort to preserve the memory of the human race ends up being a sterile recording of data and files to be kept in a museum, devoid of sense and emotional attachment. If Frame draws on the Maori vision to highlight the importance of memory, origins and ancestors for the definition of identity, Edward's genealogy is a rationalist imitation, fake as the false tears watering his eyes throughout the story.

The importance of memory and the overlapping of history and myth, fact and imagination, are central also to *The Carpathians* (1988). The novel focuses on one of the many 'desperate searches'[19] of the protagonist Mattina Brecon, a wealthy American philanthropist whose passion is to know the truth about the lives of people and places. She becomes absorbed 'in the power of the distance of time as well as of space' (19), in particular after the scientific discovery of the Gravity Star that opens up a new prospect of the usual perception of distance and closeness. What the narrator calls the 'Gravity Star' refers to a real fact: the discovery of 'a galaxy that appears to be both relatively close and seven billion light years away ... the paradox is interpreted as being caused by the focussing of light from a distant quasar (starlike object) by the gravity of an intervening galaxy'.[20] Mattina does not share her American compatriots' faith in progress and impulse towards the future. She is scared by the power of forgetfulness, by the possibility that any knowledge can be affected by distance (of time and space) and be lost, and poses the question of the importance of memory:

> As a New Yorker, Mattina was not one of the many who believed that in spite of the love they gave to their city, the city had failed them. Many of her friends were leaving to live elsewhere — in Vermont, New Hampshire, Long Island, Connecticut, and further afield, and as soon as they had gone, they appeared, to Mattina, to have lost the knowledge of being in New York City, as if elsewhere had given them the taste of the seed of their forgetting.... How might distance affect her and her family, she wondered. And her bond with her city and her country? (19)

One day Mattina learns about the legend of the Memory Flower in a tourist brochure and promptly leaves New York for Puamahara, New Zealand. As the narrator claims, her quest contains 'the longing for the "unchangeable certainty of truth"' (14), which is the domain of myth.

Unlike the Gravity Star, the legend of the Memory Flower was invented by Frame and shaped in the form of a Maori myth[21], according to which a young woman was chosen by gods to release the memory of her land by tasting the ripe fruit of a bush tree: 'Where Eve tasted her and Adam's tomorrow, the woman of Maharawhenua tasted the yesterday within the tomorrow' (11). For many years she had no other function than that of a story teller, recounting the ancestral memory to her people, until one day she vanished and in her place 'a tree grew with one blossom named, then, the Memory Flower from which, it is said, fruit invisible to most eyes from time to time may grow' (11). The fictional Maori origin of the legend is supported by the choice of names. 'Puamahara', which is the name of both the flower and the town, is formed by pua (flower) and mahara (memory), hence the Flower of Memory or Memory Flower. The region around Puamahara is named 'Maharawhenua': whenua means land but also placenta. According to the holistic Maori vision, land and placenta are nurturing shells for man, so 'Maharawhenua' is literally the Memory of the Land[22] as well as a memory of human origins. As presented by Frame, the legend includes another tenet of Maori philosophy: the inexorable bond between past, present and future. The Western thrust towards the future, symbolised by Adam and Eve's transgression of tasting tomorrow with the apple, is substituted for the knowledge of the past as a necessary passage to the future.

Mattina thought she would find in Puamahara 'the land memory growing in the air, so to speak, with everyone certain as could be of the knowledge of the programme of time, learning the language of the memory, like the computer language, to include the geography, history, creating the future ...' (60). As Isabella Maria Zoppi notices, she was 'in search of the essence of existence'.[23] She wanted to find out the principle lying behind the survival of the human race, like Edward in *Scented Gardens for the Blind*. Actually, her two months' anthropological investigation into the inhabitants of Kowhai Street, Puamahara, results in the picture of a displaced group of people, each characterised by some want or inconvenience, who become specimens of the 'marginalised side of New Zealand population'.[24] None of her neighbours seems to have captured the aura of the fabled Memory Flower. They are all strangers to the place and to one another, passengers in transit. To them the legend is nothing more than a tourist attraction. Their ordinary life is apparently grounded in the real and in the present but, unknowingly, they continuously affirm their disorientation or displacement, the lack of an encompassing past that is a lack of future and undermines their notion of the present and the real too. They are no different from Mattina's American friends, with their inclination to oblivion.

Ed Shannon, a computer dealer who is learning to fly on a simulator, claims that flying in 'Reality Mode' is 'more real than real' (110). But when his son Pete notices that Ed also plays the murderer in a computer game, he soon underlines that this is just a game and therefore unreal. His wife Renée, who is looking forward to moving to Auckland because 'that's the place to live like New York', admits their deracination with her comment on the value of legends:

> They don't often break into our *real* life…. We're only now beginning to look closely at the place we're living in. The Maoris have been looking at it for centuries and their legends have long ago crept in out of the cold to be part of their lives. And now we are looking. You have to look at something, I suppose, besides your homes, furniture and gardens. (111)

Sergeant-Major Hercus Millow, a retired war veteran, spends his days gardening and looking through the binoculars at the details of the mountains, 'changing unattainable distances to palpable closeness' (64). He moved to Puamahara after his wife's death and cannot get used to its landscape with no river, no sea and the mountains too far away. He mentions his place of origin, the 'Hutt down the Coast', as if it were a marvellous or mythical place, but when asked to describe it he just says: 'Mostly industrial now. With a river that floods from its normal piddling size.' (39). His life is suspended between an idealised land of origin and the artificially constructed place where he is living. His will to redesign his reality is applied to time as well as space, the memories of his war experience having widely superseded the reality of the present. George Coker is 93 years old and 'alone in the world' except for his roses. All his children and relatives have deserted him apart from one daughter. Coker's detailed description of his world — furniture, crockery, relics from the past — contrasts with the image of the goods displayed in his yard for auction after his death. To Mattina it seems that in Kowhai Street 'the memory tree might be hung not with flowers but with items of household furnishing' (99). His properties are not given to keep memory, but sold to erase it.

Joseph and Gloria James, the piano tuners, remember the time when New Zealand was a 'piano country' (71) and settlers brought their pianos and sheets of music as a bond with 'Home' and completion to their dream of success in the new land. They also tell Mattina about their adolescent daughter Decima, suffering from autism, who has never spoken and is therefore an unknown and unknowing reality to them: 'She's lost to us, she could be thousands of miles away, in the Andes or the Carpathians, or she could be in your home town, New York City, for all the signs she gives that she's here and she knows us.... She's one person alone in her own country' (106–107). Hene and Hare Hanuere, the only Maori neighbours, run the local dairy but are planning to move to the country. The separation from their origins has resulted in the loss of their language, as Hene explains: 'It's the younger generation that are speaking Maori. I'm learning you know, it's not so easy when you've been brought up Pakeha, but it's coming back. The trouble is it's been away so long.' (26). A touch of magic realism is given to the story by Dinny Wheatstone, an apparently mad woman who defines herself 'an imposter novelist', and plays the part of modern Cassandra, foreseeing Mattina's destiny in her writing. Her imposture comes from her core of being, 'because there's nothing else there. Your central being never develops a self. That's not a disadvantage entirely, though you do have to fight for your point of view, almost as if you were dead' (44). Dinny is a non-entity who has no point of view and is therefore all points of view. She symbolises the condition of the modern novelist.

The residents of Kowhai Street have no sense of belonging, no organic past, no fixed identities. They are not so different from the autistic girl Decima, insofar as each of them lives in the margins, isolated in his or her own country, and 'almost on the outskirts of verbal, mutual exchange', to use Zoppi's words.[25] Puamahara becomes the symbol of modern civilisation, suffering from the loss of common bonds, of ancestral memory and values, and of the words to express them. The image of the Carpathians is repeatedly used in the novel as a 'metonymy for remoteness and alienation',[26] an unknown place that is all places and no place.

Following a surrealist mode, the novel finally describes the Gravity Star exerting its influence on Kowhai Street, for the first time in the world. Mattina perceives it around her as a 'breathing presence that had broken through the fabric of time and space, an ancient distant presence that was new and close by.' (115). Thinking about its possible consequences, she wonders: 'How would the residents of Kowhai Street survive within the new order of thought, in the world of the Gravity Star? How could they find the new words when they may not realise they had lost the old?' (121). The climax is reached one night. All of a sudden the residents find themselves in a 'momentary now' that is centuries old (126) and enter 'the time of coexistence of dream and reality' (131). It is like an overwhelming tidal wave, a flood of worlds and meanings that makes them completely lose their capacity for verbalising their own world and meanings. The question arising is: have they ever had a world or meanings of their own? They are swept away like trees with shallow roots. Not only do they lose human speech, but their aspect becomes non-human too. Symbolically they come to represent the condition of death-in-life:

> The families of Kowhai Street stood at their gates or in their
> driveway, screaming and shrieking; ... The sounds were primitive,
> like the first cries of those who had never known or spoken words
> but whose urgency to communicate becomes a mixture of isolated
> syllables, vowels, consonants; ... It was not entirely the cries that
> brought a renewed feeling of horror: it was the faces, the bodies,
> the clothes of the people of Kowhai Street.... Everyone's clothes
> appeared to be in shreds as if each person had been attacked. (126)

The flood is symbolised by a rain of letters, falling on them: apostrophes, notes of music, letters of the alphabets of all languages.

> The people of Kowhai Street had experienced the disaster of
> unbeing, unknowing, that accompanies death and is thought by
> man to mark the beginning of a new kind of being and thought
> and language that, in life, is inconceivable, unknowable. The
> people of Kowhai Street, still alive, were now unintelligible
> creatures with all the spoken and written language of the world
> fallen as rain about them. The only judgement likely to be made
> about them, should their plight be discovered, was a diagnosis of
> mass hysteria or insanity. They were alive, yet on the other side of
> the barrier of knowing and being. (129)

The only two people who are spared transformation on the night the Gravity Star shines are Mattina and Dinny Wheatstone. The reasons can only be hypothesised: Mattina is a foreigner and an external observer; Dinny is a writer, a prophetess already living in the world of imagination and can therefore bear the weight of eternity. Both of them had believed in the existence of the Memory Flower. In the morning, from her hiding place, Mattina sees stretcher bearers, cleaners, and household removers coming to erase the memory of what happened, until Kowhai Street is a sort of immense tombstone. The Kowhai Street residents are removed, cancelled, forever disappeared; yet Kowhai Street had already been turned into a cemetery by its lack of memory, as shown by Mattina's first impression on her arrival: 'If you walk in mid-afternoon through the streets of Puamahara you might suppose you walk through a neatly kept cemetery where the graves are more spacious than usual' (15).

Mattina herself is naturally destined to disappear, as all human beings are, but in the months preceding her death for an inoperable cancer she will narrate the story to her husband Jake, a writer with writer's block, offering him the material for his unwritten second novel. It is their son John Henry, however, who will collect Mattina's story and make it into a fictional work. In the end Mattina has become the 'Housekeeper of Ancient Springtime', a memory collector like the girl in the legend. Mattina's emphasis on the importance of memory as the necessary condition for survival is synthesised by Jake, on his visit to empty Kowhai Street after Mattina's death:

> She had talked of memory not as a comfortable parcel of episodes to carry in one's mind, and taste now and then, but as a naked link, a point, diamond-size, seed-size, coded in a code of the world, of the human race; a passionately retained deliberate focus on all creatures and their worlds to ensure their survival. (171–72)

The Carpathians is the book that probably best exemplifies the influence of the mythical Maori vision on Frame. The importance of ancestral memory as a necessary condition of identity is a major tenet of Maori culture, as is the notion of survival through narration and language, which for the Maori was accomplished by the oral transmission of knowledge whereas for Frame it includes both the spoken and written word. Mattina's story is saved before being made into a novel when it is told and retold from mouth to mouth, in the ancient way. Maori influence is also evident in Frame's implied criticism of the disregard for old people among Pakeha. In Maori culture the elders are revered as preservers of tribal lore, which they hand down to younger generations. As anthropologist Anne Salmond reports in her study on Maori ceremonial gatherings:

> Often at a *hui* [gathering] in a quiet moment the elders sit around telling stories, explaining chants and practising them together, and the *hui* itself is by far the best school for its own rituals.... The elders are revered as keepers of these traditional treasures, and every time one of the old experts dies, he is mourned as irreplaceable.... There are now weekly programmes in Maori on the radio, where elders of different areas discuss local traditions, explain their chants and *marae* etiquette; and university archives have substantial collections of field and interview tapes of Maori verbal art.[27]

Puamahara 'has more than the usual number of homes and hospitals for the aged' (13), where they are locked up like the 'mentally ill'. All the elders in the novel are lonely figures, deserted by their relatives, lost in memories they cannot hand down and repositories of a language that will die with them. The general indifference towards them can be seen as a disregard for heritage and a cause of the residents' disconnection. Madge McMurtrie, who is dying of cancer, cannot communicate with her grandniece as the words she uses — paddocks, keepsake, creek — are outdated: 'I speak the language of another age.' (30). Connie Grant, just arrived from England after being widowed, is not allowed to live with her son's family: 'They don't want a grandmother. I'm so lonely, so lonely. My husband dead, my house gone, the furniture too, and now I am in another country where no-one wants me' (92). George Coker is deserted by his children and his personal effects put up for auction after his death. Hercus Millow is mostly alone and lost in his war memories.

Finally, a central point of Mattina's quest is her visit to the Maori village where the Hanueres are planning to move in their attempt to retrieve their identity and language. In their communal life — the preparation of hangi, the mix of generations, the sharing of common spaces — and in their closeness to nature, she seems to find the answers to her questions: 'Mattina felt the presence of a yesterday's silence that brought a hunger to the back of her throat: a world-hunger' (85–86). In particular the conversation with village matriarch Rua opens up a new level of consciousness about what lies at the core of language, and of its deepest meanings and values:

> 'Can you tell me something about flax weaving?'
> Rua smiled. 'First,' she said, 'you must know flax. I know flax and flax knows me. You understand the sort of knowing I mean?'
> 'I do', Mattina said, with rising excitement at the recognition that here was *her* kind of knowing; and that of the James family; and Hercus Millow; and of the others in Kowhai Street; the knowing that included but was not dependent on the Memory Flower or the Gravity Star; that by itself could banish distance, nearness, weight, lightness, up, down, today, yesterday, tomorrow.
> Without binoculars, cameras.
> Without the Memory Flower, the Gravity Star. (86)

As Zoppi suggests, 'the old Maori flax could be the true Memory Flower, the origin of which was forgotten a long time ago'[28] or, more simply, the symbol of a deeply rooted knowledge, described by and preserved in language. This is the kind of knowledge Mattina is questing for, which comes into close contact with a primal self and provides an organic approach to one's history. It needs to be passed on through language in order to survive, therefore necessarily becoming a story. This kind of knowledge is at the core of Frame's concerns. In the erasure of borders between myth and history, word and fact, dreamtime and reality, her narrative aims at reproducing a holistic view of the world akin to that of Maori.

Delving deeper: Noel Hilliard's fiction

Noel Hilliard's first work, *Maori Girl*, aroused a lot of controversy when it appeared in 1960. Critics did not receive Hilliard's social realist mode favourably, considering it to be an unfashionable revival of the literature of the thirties. Besides, it was the first novel openly treating the topic of race relations and depicting Maori as 'members of contemporary society and fellow citizens', as Hilliard himself mentioned in an interview with Peter Beatson.[29] Lawrence Jones has written that Hilliard's realism belongs to the literature of 'protest' rather than 'accommodation', concentrating 'on the individual in relation to social forces' and implying 'a criticism of social and political systems.'[30] In his study of Hilliard's short stories, Jones associates him with the American social realism of authors such as John Steinbeck, John Doss Passos, Henry Roth and Richard Wright. This was a realism aiming at a democratisation of literature by extending its subject matter to include those who had previously been neglected or considered unworthy of literary dignity. Like them, Hilliard wanted to give the point of view from the fringes of the society, guiding readers towards a sympathetic understanding and denouncing a social malaise.

Hilliard continues Sargeson's realistic tradition, but his choice of characters and topics is more radical. First, his wide exploration of contemporary Maori life and issues is unprecedented in New Zealand literature, with the exception of Finlayson. Second, he broadens his boundaries to include 'unseemly' categories such as prostitutes ('Girl on a Corner', 'Anita's Eyes', 'At Angelo's' and 'Send Somebody Nice'), hippies ('The Dropout'), gays and lesbians ('The Telegram' and 'Corrective Trainings'), and displaced young delinquents ('Absconder' and 'The Girl from Kaeo').[31] As to Hilliard's possible 'literary descent' from Finlayson, some similarities and differences must be noted. Both of them openly point to the socioeconomic system as the main cause of social and racial marginalisation. Hilliard criticised both Christianity and Freudian analysis for their focus on individuals' flaws and their search for either a spiritual remedy or therapy to make them fit into society: 'It is society which has shaped them the way they are, so it is a social solution that you must seek.' He concluded that if the individual does not fit in it may be the society, not the individual, that must be changed.[32] Hilliard's working-class origins and militancy in the Labour and Communist parties certainly affected his thinking. Finlayson, however, never went beyond the limited extent of the short story, parable or sketch, with the attendant impossibility of developing his characters fully. Moreover, his choice to embrace a humouristic approach (in Pirandello's sense) put some distance between him and his subject matter. On the contrary, Hilliard's realist mode allowed him a wider range of tones and greater dramatic impact. His employment of long fiction enabled him to probe deeper into his Maori characters, providing the resolution that was missing in Finlayson. Particularly relevant is the tetralogy formed by the novels *Maori Girl*, *Power of Joy* (1965), *Maori Woman* (1974) and *The Glory and the Dream* (1978), following the separate lives of a Maori woman and a Pakeha man who finally get to know each other and marry. The tetralogy basically juxtaposes two different world views and, by analysing an inter-racial marriage, provides a recipe for the inevitable cultural gap.

Maori Girl explores the rural childhood of Netta Samuel against a background of poverty, but also of warm affection, close communal relationships and shared values. The pull of city life makes its appearance in Netta's adolescence as part of a social thrust towards economic independence, modernity and emancipation from old models. Netta represents the 'amphibious' Maori youth striding two worlds that will be the subject of much literature written by Maori, their condition epitomised in the novel by the contrast between the Samuel children and their grandmother. Granny is the symbol of all that young generations have lost: 'She remains bold and confident, lacking everything the *pakeha* expects of the Maori'.[33] Netta is not allowed to speak Maori at school. Maori words are equated with 'swear words' and their use is punished with caning. This attitude is somehow encouraged by her parents, who speak Maori to each other but English to the children: 'Dad's view was that since they would have to make their way in a *pakeha* world they must know English well or forever bear the brand of "straight from the bush"' (34, MG). But it is fiercely opposed by her grandmother, who approves of using English only in conversation with Pakeha, underlining the importance of maintaining their Maori identity, customs and rituals, and lamenting that the young generations are building a future country inhabited by two races 'the *pakeha pakehas*, and the Maori *pakehas*' (35, MG).

Netta was born at the beginning of the Depression (12, MG) and belongs to the generation that saw major advancements in modern technology: electric power accessible to everybody, the movies, the radio, records. Hilliard explores the effects of progress on the Samuel children, who end up being irresistibly attracted by it. Interestingly, he not only denounces the loss of Maori culture but also alludes to an hypothesis that its survival will necessarily pass through a recovery and renewal of tradition:

> Their love and respect for her [Granny] are strong enough to make them feel renegades at every compromise. Yet they know that they cannot inherit, and they cannot develop within themselves, whatever it is that makes Granny what she is; they cannot understand all that she understands, know the old ways as

she does, the songs and stories, the genealogies, the great names of the past; .... They looked around her, past her, and felt a certain shame at the sight of radios, gramophone records, sheet-music, ukuleles — symbols of cultural surrender. But they knew that the inevitable had to be adjusted to, that they could not isolate themselves from the present or future. The best they could do was to assimilate as much of the new as they could while preserving what was most important of the past. (37–38, MG)

In this passage Hilliard shrewdly anticipates a tenet underlying the Maori Renaissance: the idea that the rebirth of Maori culture necessarily presupposes 'forms of rupture and renewal' rather than 'continuity' with the past, in Chris Prentice's words.[34] The point is that 'rebirth is not a return to some mythically past moment, but always into a context that shapes that to which it gives birth.'[35] Hilliard questions the usefulness of a nativist approach, and finds the resolution Finlayson was seeking.

If renewal is important, however, it is the persistence within Netta of what is most valuable in her culture, acquired through her upbringing in a warm and caring family, that shelters her from the dangers and temptations of the city and prevents her fall into the same degraded life as other Maori girls around her, like Myra, Minnie and her old school friend Grace, or into delinquency like the protagonists of 'The Girl from Kaeo' or 'Corrective Training'. Hilliard makes the same point as Grace in *Cousins* — that a solid cultural as well as emotional upbringing empowers Maori people, reinforcing their self-esteem and enabling them to succeed in the Pakeha world in their own terms, without being overwhelmed by Western models. The end of the novel seems to contradict this reading, envisaging a bleak future for Netta, who loses her job and is abandoned by her previously caring Pakeha boyfriend, Arthur, when he discovers that the baby she is expecting is not his. Netta's story, however, must be seen within the larger context of the tetralogy.

In *Maori Girl*, Hilliard denounces widespread Maori racial discrimination in the fifties, as shown by Netta's difficulty in renting a room or finding a job in Wellington. In Beatson's interview, Hilliard confirms that all this was real and not invented (he remembers accommodation notices saying 'Europeans only' and states he still has a photograph of a bar sign saying 'Native women will not be served in this hotel'), asserting his notion of literature as an act of political denunciation.[36] The same theme is dealt with in 'Young Gent., Quiet, Refined', where the landlady does not rent the room to Sonny because he is Maori, but then lets it to Sonny's brother Tom, because he looks European.

The story of Paul Bennett in *Power of Joy* can be defined as a revisitation of what Jones ironically defines as 'that New Zealand perennial, growing up in a puritanical small town',[37] amply explored by Sargeson. Despite the novel's reiteration of an overused topos, its novelty lies in the fact that it indirectly contrasts Netta's Maori upbringing in *Maori Girl*. It also explains Paul's reasons for choosing a Maori instead of a Pakeha for his wife, contrary to his parents' will, in its sequel *Maori Woman*. While referring only marginally to Maori, the book depicts the gap between two seemingly irreconcilable world views and delineates a deep criticism of the dominant model in its juxtaposition to the implied Maori one. Unlike the Griffiths in Sargeson's *I Saw in My Dream*, the Bennetts are not bourgeois but are a working-class family, living in a railway construction village. Nevertheless, we find the same puritanical enclosure, disrupted communication and repressed emotional life. If Paul's father shows signs of an emotional and imaginative sensibility, he seems to be a minor influence on his son, overwhelmed by his wife's conformity. Paul's mother has the most profound impact, with her materialism, respect of formalities, phobic attitude to sex and the body, and conditional love: a cultural baggage that he totally rejects, but that nonetheless will unconsciously emerge in his married life, narrated in the fourth volume of the tetralogy. Paul takes refuge in an intense and solitary immersion in nature, epitomised by his continual climbing in trees, as though he needs to put some distance between himself and the human world on the ground. Here he sharpens his sensory perceptions and develops a rich inner life, a profound sense of communion with nature, and an understanding of the interconnection of all living things, as shown in the following passage that recalls Sargeson's 'An Attempt at an Explanation':

> The grasses here were of a strong and vigorous hue. Here he could see together the beginning and the end of the life-process. It seemed to him that nothing really dies, it merely changes its form and undergoes rejuvenation, or despairing of one form transfers its living energies to another....
>
> He was a part of every living thing, because it had life and he did too: every leaf, every blade of grass, every insect....
>
> He would live in harmony with all creatures, all things. The world he had discovered from treetops might merge into the world of people and perhaps one day he would find the key to we few, we band of brothers.[38]

This holistic perception of nature is one of the major forces that brings Netta and Paul together, emphasised in their picnic at the lake from the first part of *The Glory and the Dream:*

'I love this,' she said.

'Better than hanging over a washtub?'

'Too right.' She put her hands behind her head. 'Up here makes me think of home.'

What did it make him think of? Not of home; not of being little again. Those were not good to think about. Yet he was happy, as happy as he'd ever been as a kid, out on the hills or in the bush or along the riverbank, on his own .... Now he was not on his own, never would be again, yet he was just as happy; happier probably, since he was not now trying to escape.[39]

The passage manifests several differences between Netta and Paul. She identifies nature with her origins, and her holistic view includes humanity and the environment. For Paul, conversely, nature is an escape from his family and seems to exclude human/social relations. Their marriage therefore enables him to share the blessing of nature with somebody else. The shift from childhood to adulthood in *Power of Joy* is marked by Paul's growing awareness that he must go beyond his solipsistic isolation and face the complexities of social life. Although his disappointing school experience shows him, once more, the repressive and conformist nature of social institutions and the difficulty of relationships, he realises that his 'self-centredness [would] drain his vitality' and that the only 'dynamic release' would be to confront the hard reality of social life and reach out to his fellow human beings (320, PJ). The fact that he is instinctively driven towards a Maori girl, however, suggests a refusal of dominant models.

In *Maori Woman* Paul and Netta, who had already met casually in the previous novel, get to know each other and finally fall in love. Most of the book, however, is devoted to the relationship between Netta and her ex-partner Jason, a problematic young Maori man she hung on to, despite his violent and selfish temperament, after the lacerating decision to give her baby away for adoption. Netta's moral and cultural dilemma of having alienated her own daughter from herself and her heritage continues in *The Glory and the Dream*, when she finally discloses it to Paul. Jason needs Netta too, as a normative identity figure after being in jail under the ignominious (and unjust) charge of rape. Jason epitomises the displaced Maori living in an in-between state. Incapable of coming to terms with his hybridity and filling his emotional and cultural void, he hungers for traditional authority, wisdom and guidance yet at the same time continually challenges them, the attraction of modernity and easy money being too strong. Jason's contradictory feelings are exemplified in his equation between 'coming home' (to his village) and 'going back to prison', because in both of them 'your life was run for you' (266, MW). His poor educational background makes him inadequate in the Pakeha world too, and his frustration breaks into violence or pathetic self-pity. He is doomed to fail in both the Maori and Pakeha worlds, as shown by his final assault on Netta and Paul, which leads him to prison again.

Another viewpoint on race relations in *Maori Woman* is offered by Mr Rushbury, Netta's Pakeha boss at the clothing factory. His unexpressed infatuation for Netta, articulated by his stream of consciousness, aligns with the nineteenth-century myth of Polynesian women as erotic objects, open to free sexual pleasure and naturally uninhibited, as mentioned in chapter one. The gradual (mental) disclosure of Rushbury's desires — repressed by his dull childless marriage and inflated by his imaginary constructions — offers a half-humorous picture of implications of this myth, grounded as it was on the projection of forbidden fantasies and a sense of white men's superiority, as evidenced in the following passage:

> What was the peculiar and compelling fascination this girl had for him? She was young — so young, so desirable; what a thrill to make love to a body like that! She was Maori — and the knowledge that she was *different* would add piquancy; he would sample the pleasures of miscegenation, break that particular taboo, miserable and absurd in one way but a good taboo in that it added zest and exhilaration. To make such a contact socially acceptable would drain it of its joy.[40]

The love between Paul and Netta feeds off the reciprocal perception of the other as somebody who can love without preconceptions, and the belief that they like each other just as they are (or, maybe, because they are as they are). They also feel they can give one another what they have been deprived of: Paul, by his own family; Netta, by her previous unfortunate relationships and, more generally, by the social restraints of Pakeha society.

Paul is an unconventional Pakeha who has critically analysed and rejected the emotional void of his parents' life and their narrow-mindedness on matters concerning the body and sexuality. Two episodes in *Power of Joy* allude to Paul's slow withdrawal from his family's normative model. When a Maori boy, Anzac, refuses to take an unjust punishment from the teacher and is expelled from school, Paul envies him: 'Anzac was lucky. He would go home to the Maori shearers' shacks and his mother would tell him not to worry and kiss him and stroke his hair, and there would be the singing in the evening after work and the quiet musical talk, like telling secrets' (79, PJ). Then when Paul swims with his Maori girlfriend Huia at the pool, both naked, he feels no shame or guilt and instead, '[h]e had a vision from the memory of the race of a man and a woman walking hand in hand, naked and without shame: as they once were and might have been but could be no more' (190, PJ). Paul seems to follow the same direction as Sargeson's Henry Griffith. These episodes are a prelude to his falling in love with Netta in the sequel. During Paul's visit to his parents' place to announce his wedding in *Maori Woman*, the sight of the abandoned mill village gives him a pungent sense of death. The dismantled mill, the derelict village, the bare hills once covered by the bush and now scarred by slips (a frequent symbol also in Sargeson and Finlayson): all add to the image of the devastation left by Western civilisation. Yet an unfinished meeting house, clearly deserted for years, stands not far away, as another reminder of death. The two desolated sites, epitomising natural and Maori cultural death, infuse Paul with a strong desire to foster the 'Spirit of Life' through his union with Netta:

> And he was here. Perhaps something of the essence of the place [the meeting house] had entered into him too, without knowing. He and Netta together would do something to carry forward the Spirit of Life. It made no difference that he was of another tradition and belief: the Spirit of Life made no distinction between patterns of thought, colours of flesh. (200, MW)

To Paul, his union with Netta therefore appears as an exchange of cultural and natural values aimed at renewal and life. The futile and mean objections of Paul's parents to his marriage, and the feeling that their home is alien to him, reinforce his conviction to move off the path they have traced.

Netta, on the other hand, can rely on a rich emotional background that she treasures, demonstrated by her feeling at home with her family, in her parallel visit to announce the wedding, and by her spontaneous approach to sexuality that is devoid of any sense of moral dirtiness or sinfulness. She is also aware, however, that she cannot go back to her old life any more and must come to terms with her amphibious self. Paul represents a man who, as a non-conforming Pakeha, can therefore appreciate and understand her. They seem to complement one another.

Netta and Paul's marital life does not always live up to their respective expectations in *The Glory and the Dream*. Their different views are orchestrated in counterpoint, through long dialectical exchanges in which each character exposes his or her thoughts. Despite an excess of didacticism, the book succeeds in depicting culturally relevant differences that emerge in Maori literature too, in particular notions of time, money and ownership, family and communality, education, rationality and imagination, and spirituality. Paul's cultural baggage seems gradually to re-emerge, even certain aspects he did not like about himself: 'In his failure to change her he felt keenly his failure to change himself' (129, GD). His preoccupation with the future — saving and planning — are counterpointed with her 'not to worry' philosophy. For Netta, the quality (not the quantity) of time is important, 'living and not just staying alive' (85, GD). She thinks Paul's projection into the future makes him 'discontented with the present' (240, GD) and that money is made to be spent on useful or concrete things, not accumulated. For Paul the family is made of two people, for Netta it is made of relations, 'not only the ones living now but all the other ones way back' (91, GD). Paul has formal relationships with his friends and is jealous of Netta's spontaneous conviviality. He tends to rationalise everything, while she has an intuitive approach to people and knowledge. Paul's knowledge is bookish while Netta's is practical and experiential. He is an atheist, believing in individual man not in religious institutions, which he views as instruments to avoid making personal choices and delegate responsibilities. She is religious and thinks that church service is 'a feeling' (93, GD). Paul is left-wing and politicised; Netta is apolitical, drawing her beliefs from her cultural heritage.

Although Netta's convictions are apolitical her views seem much more radical than Paul's. Her lack of a sense of ownership, her focus on communality and reciprocity both between human beings and between the human race and nature, and her emphasis on the quality of life that makes up for the quantity of money you can earn, take her in a direction diametrically opposed to Western notions of progress and development. In chapter nine we will see that Grace's *Potiki* and *Dogside Story* question the validity of progress, indirectly asserting post-development ideas (to which Latouche's theory, mentioned in chapter two, belongs). Paul's holistic view is biased by his individualism and Western attitude to progress. His attempts to explain to Netta 'the need to give more thought to money' (129, GD) are also culturally determined, since he finds a justification even in ancient Greece, where people 'used to bury a coin with the dead so they could pay Charon to take them over the Styx' (129, GD). The difference he traces between his job at the paper mill and Netta's work at home, 'one producing surplus value for profit' the other 'creating use value' (130, DG), still operates within the same logic, although he may side with the proletariat rather than the bourgeois. Socialism advocates a redistribution of profit but does not question the way profit is produced, nor does it change our exploitative approach to natural resources.

Interestingly, the contrapuntal method used by Hilliard enables the characters to probe apparently irreconcilable dichotomies and deconstruct them to see the possible good underlying them. If sometimes there appear to be generalisations that do not apply to all Pakeha or Maori, they tend to give an overall idea of contrasting cultural views that can be either integrated or at least accepted, as in Paul's final re-evaluation of Netta's notion of time[41] and Netta's act of presenting Paul with an 'object' — a book — absolutely alien to her but relevant to him: *The Meditations of Marcus Aurelius* (241, GD).

The Glory and the Dream is divided into four parts, each representing a stage of Paul and Netta's relationship. Part One is the idyll of beginnings (summer), Part Two the start of tensions (autumn), Part Three the apex of crisis (winter) and Part Four reconciliation and rebirth (spring). The evolution of their relationship emphasises certain aspects that are typical of the larger dynamics of Pakeha-Maori relations. Paul is self-centred and overly rational, inquisitive and sincerely convinced of being right on many matters, which he asserts dialectically. Despite his non-conformity to the Pakeha norm, his culturally dominant view leads him to a judgmental and 'offensive' attitude, demanding that Netta account for her thinking, feeling or being. On the contrary, Netta's behaviour is by and large co-operative and 'defensive', nevertheless the solidity of her own cultural values enables her to resist and counter-attack. In one of their dialectical confrontations she describes his behaviour as an attempt to colonise her:

> It looks different to me. You've always got to be the boss. Is it just pakeha, or is it being a man? Let me just be myself. Don't try to make me be like you. Then we'll get along fine. But don't try to colonize me. You do it all the time. (126, GD)

From the expectations of pre-marital times in *Maori Woman* to the reality of everyday life in *The Glory and the Dream*, the tone changes and the contrasts increase. Yet the final message of the book is optimistic, envisaging the possibility of working one's way through differences. The solution that emerges in the dialogical structure of the book lies in effective communication, as Netta underlines: "'Having a chat," she said. "Not a discussion or an argument. We hardly ever seem to have a chat. And that's what I like'" (239, GD). Hilliard's emphasis on integration — which is different to assimilation — or accepting what is really important for the other culture and cannot be integrated, is important. We find this view in Maori writers too, in Grace's *Mutuwhenua* for example, in which the central idea is that personal and cultural nourishment contributes to the reinforcement of identity and helps the minority culture to affirm its values or renegotiate them on its own terms.

As we have seen, most of Hilliard's short stories have a strong political intent. Some, however, are descriptive and even documentary, giving voice to his profound knowledge of Maoritanga. The Bubby and Paikea stories from *A Piece of Land*, for instance, depict the life of a community through representative moments (a wedding, a tangi, a fishing day), showing 'how family, community, the land, the seasons, and the basic forces of life and death shape the lives of the Maori'.[42] Another is 'The Tree', from *Send Somebody Nice*, which is likewise interesting for its notion of renewal within the assertion of traditional values. A centenarian matai tree must be felled to make space for the new community centre and because its root system is stopping the installation of sewerage pipes for a new block of houses. The village agrees to what is considered a necessity, but when the elders see that neither a bulldozer nor chain-saws can manage to uproot the big matai, they perceive something wrong: in their view, a child of Tane[43] is resisting death and struggling for its life. Later, in the meeting house, they express their feelings in ornate korero to the community. The point made by the elders is not that the matai must be saved at all costs — many trees have been turned into canoes, houses and objects useful for man's survival — but that the mauri ora (life principle) immanent in all beings deserves respect. The tree is fighting for its dignity, because 'it is the living record of all our days and nights together in this place'.[44] It must be thanked for the service given to people, for being cover to them in storms and shade from the sun, and shelter from wind and rain. The elders always refer to the matai tree as a personal 'she', as though it were an ancestor. They decide that the old ways must be followed, that the communication between man and tree must be resumed, as in the old days when 'we never knew what it was to be alone or unwanted. To us all things were the children of the Sky Father and the Earth Mother as we ourselves are.'[45] The quotation underlines the paradigmatic Maori vision of the world.

Before dawn the tree felling starts, preceded by ancient rituals: chants, invocations, prayers to Tane. The elders are wearing traditional garments and have reverted to their old stone axes. The first chip from the tree is burnt as an offering to the gods. In the second fire, lit with other chips and sawdust, the elders cook potatoes to feed Tane and themselves. Then they light a third fire inside the gap of the trunk. The work proceeds with the deepening of the scarf[46] and a new burn.

The theme and rituals described by Hilliard recall those illustrated by Agate Thornton in her analysis of an ancient song included in the collection *Nga Moteatea*, edited by Apirana Ngata and Pei Te Hurinui Jones.[47] The song implicitly refers to Rata's myth recounting how he felled the same tree several times to build a canoe, yet the tree always stood upright again the next morning.

Rata soon understood he would not succeed in fashioning his canoe unless he first gained permission from the god Tane. Thornton explains some passages of the song with reference to felling rituals, including the burning of the first chip accompanied by a chant to reconcile Tane to the sacrifice of one of his children; and the custom of lighting a fire in the scarf cut by an adze into the tree. All the rituals hinted at in the ancient song correspond to those illustrated by Hilliard. The whole village is present when the tree is finally pulled down using flax ropes and accompany its death with chants, as in a solemn tangi of an ancestor.

The story offers a solution on the same theme dealt with in Finlayson's 'Totara Tree'. While claiming the right of Maori to assert their values, it does not exclude them from progress but implies a notion of progress on their own terms. Maori people are not against technological advancement *tout court*. What is necessary to or can improve life must be welcomed. However, respect for the spirit of life implies an approach opposed to the Western belief that the earth is just matter for exploitation. Viewing trees as ancestors presupposes their safeguard and worship as a norm, their destruction as the exception.

The vastness and complexity of Hilliard's work concerning Maori issues and culture, as well as his commitment to their cause, heralds a new attitude in Pakeha literature towards the destiny of the indigenous minority of New Zealand. After having been written about for over a century, the time was right for Maori to make their own voices heard.

PART 2

The Maori Voice

The Rise of Maori Literature

New Zealand, it is plain, has no future as a watered-down tasteless Britain of the South. It is as a genuinely Pacific society of mixed blood, mediating between east and west, that we may hope for its emergence in time to come with gifts of its own to offer the world. — Landfall, editorial, June 1953 [1]

It's not sticking to the old ways that's important ... but it's being us, using all the new knowledge our way. Everything new belongs to us too. — Patricia Grace [2]

Postcolonial Aotearoa/New Zealand and the Maori Renaissance: the building of a nation

Postcolonial studies have been concerned with both colonial discourse analysis and the legacies of colonialism in the numerous areas of the world that were affected by imperialist expansion and have now achieved political autonomy as independent national states. Critics have foregrounded patterns of similarity and crossovers in the colonial and postcolonial condition, especially in relation to notions of identity, liminality and hybridity, mimicry, resistance, and the complex relationship between the metropolitan centre and the colonial periphery. But imperial power was necessarily inflected according to the particularities of each territory — with its specific geographical, historical, racial and social background — and prompted different local responses. Being that postcolonialism is a 'portmanteau word', in Stephen Slemon's words, 'an umbrella thrown up over many heads, against a great deal of rain',[3] it necessarily needs to be reconsidered in regional or local terms. This chapter will explore the specificity of colonialism and postcolonialism in Aotearoa/New Zealand, demonstrating how postcolonial issues can be found only recently in its literature, and mainly in connection with the rise of Maori self-determination and writing.

Firstly, the concept of the postcolonial condition varies considerably between invaded colonies such as India or Nigeria, and settler colonies such as Canada, Australia or New Zealand.[4] In invaded colonies, postcoloniality applies in the same way to all the population, which is widely indigenous. In settler colonies, white settler Canadians, Australians and New Zealanders must be differently located within postcolonialism from, respectively, First Nations or Métis people, Aborigines and Maori. Having been dispossessed of their land, the indigenous populations of Canada, Australia and New Zealand appear under a condition of political colonialism in their own postcolonial country. As Ralph Crane notes in his essay on the postcolonial literatures of Australia and New Zealand, 'in neither country has the colonising power left or in any real fashion relinquished the power acquired by invasion.'[5] This can, of course, be extended to Canada, too. Secondly, the relationship between centre and periphery has been extremely different from one settler colony to another. Crane argues that the centre/periphery dichotomy has been much stronger in Australia than in New Zealand; while in the former the many convicts and dispossessed settlers bore little love for the British centre, in the latter 'the free settlers who made up the majority of its early European population had less cause to reject the Anglocentric hegemony that had fed rather than starved them.'[6] Pakeha New Zealanders chose to keep the umbilical cord intact and maintained a tight bond with 'mother England' for a long time. The architecture of the first towns (Christchurch and Dunedin in particular), the economic and administrative systems, the social organisation: all should comply to the pre-ordained model of Englishness that was to be followed unquestioningly, even in a new and remote land. Newness was too daunting and rejected in favour of conformity.

New Zealanders' reluctance to detach from the metropolitan centre is illustrated by their delay in ratifying the Statute of Westminster, which gave the country complete autonomy in foreign as well as domestic affairs. Most of the other dominions had ratified it in 1931, however, New Zealand waited until 25 November 1947.[7] Hunter notes what she considers the strangely contradictory category occupied by Aotearoa/New Zealand today, as an 'Independent State of the British Monarchy' after having been a colony until 1907 and a dominion of Great Britain for a further 40 years. She argues that New Zealand has achieved a 'distinct and separate constitutional identity but not a "national" one,'[8] supporting her argument by referring to an article by political commentator Colin James published in the *New Zealand Herald* in 2002 and significantly entitled: 'Making a nation is still eluding us'. Referring to historian James Belich's revisionist theories, James agrees with him that New Zealand identity at the turn of the millennium was still an elusive concept:

> Down to earth from the initial expansionist boom, we settled for being a tribe of Britain, displaced geographically but not socially, culturally or economically.... Then from the 1960s, says Belich, Britain forced independence on us. Now it is a commonplace that when this lost tribe of Britain seeks distinctiveness to show the world, it turns to Maori — but finds a people whose leaders have grown disconcertingly confident of their identity and their place here.... Britain did push us out. And we resisted. We delayed formalising full self-government until 1947. We hung on for dear life to all we could keep of the butter, cheese and lamb trade with Britain after it joined Europe in 1973....
>
> All of that drove us to trade elsewhere and, in part, contributed to a disastrous slump in our terms of trade — our earning power in the world — by more than one-third from the mid-1960s to the mid-70s.... Belich is right that this *lost tribe of Great Britain* has not forged an identity. That is partly because the assertion of independence resembled an adolescent flounce. And it is partly because, in shucking the convenient British monoculture, we discovered that two deeply different cultures inhabit this place. So we aren't a nation.[9]

James openly admits that the renewed strength of Maori is disconcerting for Pakeha, whose identity has been undermined by the cut of the privileged bond with 'mother England'. The cut he is referring to is the UK's gradual withdrawal from its previous economic agreements with the ex-Commonwealth dominions and its entry into the European Economic Community in 1973,[10] which in turn compelled New Zealand to redesign its economy and look for new markets in Australia and Asia. The article basically pictures the country until the early 1970s not as a post-colony but as a neo-colony, a term coined by the first president of independent Ghana, Kwame Nkrumah. 'The essence of neo-colonialism', wrote

Nkrumah, 'is that the State which is subject to it is, in theory, independent and has all the outward trappings of international sovereignty. In reality its economic system and thus its political policy is directed from the outside.'[11]

The 1970s period in which Britain's actions forced economic independence on New Zealand coincided with the beginning of the so-called Maori Renaissance movement. A growing sense of self-determination among Maori and the break with Britain marked a turning point in the country's dominant monoculture, urging increasing numbers of Pakeha beyond the cultural elite to come to terms with their still derivative identity and realise that their country was indeed made of two cultures. If Pakeha wanted to build a nation, they needed to relate to Aotearoa/New Zealand as a South Pacific country, rather than develop into a 'watered-down tasteless Britain of the South', as the *Landfall* editorialist prefigured in the epigraph.

Prior to the 1960s, the sense of liminality and hybridity that dominate other postcolonial literatures applies to New Zealand writing only to a very limited extent. Liminality relates to an in-between or interstitial space where cultural change occurs. and goes hand in hand with hybridity — that is, the creation of transcultural forms.[12] Before the 1950s and the great migration of Maori to the cities, however, contact between European and Maori cultures was limited. Apart from a few writers like Finlayson and, marginally, Sargeson, Pakeha writing mainly reflected the needs and anxieties of a European monoculture, whose primacy was unquestioned and that paradoxically wanted to keep a tight bond with the centre while struggling to define its own identity. Even nationalist writers of the masculine tradition were essentially Anglocentric, as Crane argues, 'borrowing many of their ideas from the centre they were supposedly rejecting, as their identification with the poets of the Pylon School — principally W.H. Auden, Cecil Day-Lewis, Louis MacNeice, and Stephen Spender — illustrates.'[13] For this reason these writers do not truly address postcolonial issues.

Examples of mimicry in New Zealand can be found only in Pakeha writing, which imitates British literature. Since Maori culture was non-literate, however, there was not the literary mimicking of the imperial power that occurred in India, for example.[14] The centre/periphery dichotomy also needs to be revised in a settler colony like early New Zealand so as more closely to examine an additional layer of the outer periphery that arose between the white settler and the indigenous population. As contended by Crane:

> the historical situation in the settler colonies has meant that the center, rather than becoming the ex-colonial power, has been absorbed into the periphery, pushing the indigenous peoples, the Aborigines and the Maori, into what is effectively an outer

periphery .... While it may be convincingly argued that white Australian writers and Pakeha writers in New Zealand do write back to the center, they do so from the privileged position of the settler, whereas indigenous writers are frequently not writing back to the absent (British) center so much as writing back to this (sic) present and dominant 'settler cultures' which have maintained a Eurocentric perspective at the expense of a deliberately muted indigenous one.[15]

Postcoloniality in New Zealand, therefore, can be talked about only from the 1960s onwards when the first Maori voices appeared, writing back to a centre located in their own land, challenging mainstream literature and expressing a different point of view on reality. Maori writing in English is necessarily a hybrid literature, which moulds the genres of the Western canon and the language of the colonisers into new forms, reflecting the influence of the Maori oral tradition, the pace and rhythm of the Maori language, and a different sensibility. It is also a vehicle to pose the political stances of a marginalised group, an act of resistance to hegemonic discourse, and a defence of cultural identity that cannot be interpreted in essentialist or nativist terms.

Critical debate has widely explored the ambiguities underlying modes of resistance to colonial power that employ a reverse-discourse, for example a nativist/essentialist approach. A typical example is the construction of an idealised Black race and African past made by the African and Caribbean liberation/ national movements in the 1960s and 1970s and their claims to ancestral purity and monolithic notions of identity. Such a counter-discourse, according to postcolonial critics, runs the risk of being trapped in the same dichotomies it means to oppose.[16] As Benita Parry has summarised, criticism of nativist/essentialist views is grounded on the notion that 'a simple inversion perpetuates the coloniser/ colonised opposition within the terms defined by colonial discourse, remaining complicit with its assumptions by retaining undifferentiated identity categories, and failing to contest the conventions of that system of knowledge it supposedly challenges.'[17] Moreover, in some contexts 'the mythologising of the beginnings' can serve the purpose of reactionary forces. Quoting Rashmi Bhatnagar, Parry underlines that in India 'the search for the source of Hindu identity in Vedic times has almost invariably led to a loss of commitment to our contemporary plural/ secular identity.'[18] Yet Parry questions the idea that nativism has necessarily 'a fixed retrograde valency'[19] and, before articulating her defence of Liberation theorists Aimé Césaire and Frantz Fanon, she makes a distinction between 'the empowering effects of constructing a coherent identity or of cherishing and defending against calumniation altered and mutable indigenous forms' and 'the hopeless attempt to locate and revive pristine pre-colonial cultures.'[20] Parry therefore recognises the empowering valency of a coherent identity that draws on its cultural and ethnic heritage and the political necessity of maintaining the idea of oppositionality.

Stuart Hall's valorisation of the notion of cultural identity follows a similar line, as underscored by Parry. Hall applies this concept to the context of the Caribbean, affirming that the retention of cultural traits from Africa — in religion, folk customs, music and dance — helped its people survive the trauma of slavery. The African diasporas of the New World would not have found their place in modern history without 'the symbolic return to Africa',[21] but he is also conscious of the colonial subject as a product of multiple constitutions and presents identity as a question of representation and narrative:

> Questions of identity are always questions about representation. They are always questions about the invention, not simply the discovery of tradition. They are always exercises in selective memory and they almost always involve the silence of something in order to allow something else to speak.[22]

Consequently, identity is subject to changes and dependent on negotiations with historical circumstances: 'Identity is not only a story, a narrative which we tell ourselves about ourselves, it is stories which change with historical circumstances.'[23] Hall's conclusion is that 'identities for the twenty-first century do not lie in taking old identities literally, but in using the enormously rich and complex cultural heritages to which history has made them heir.'[24]

Hall and Parry make many important points that can be applied to the New Zealand context. First, the struggle to preserve cultural identity is seen by Maori as an act of survival as well. The traumatic experience of colonial conquest, dislocation and slavery suffered by the Caribbean people is analogous to that inflicted on Maori by European domination, testified by the biblical imagery employed by the messianic movements of the nineteenth and twentieth centuries that identified the Maori with the Israelites — an enslaved people forced into exile — and the colonisers with the Egyptian Pharaoh. Then cultural identity is a creative act that presupposes not so much the definition of an essential self, but rather the redefinition of the self in contact with the other: an 'imaginative rediscovery', in Hall's words, which takes into account historical circumstances, but also imposes '"an imaginary coherence" on the experience of dispersal and fragmentation, and acknowledges that the other side is only rupture and discontinuity.'[25] The Maori Renaissance was animated exactly by this spirit of 'imaginative rediscovery and coherence', which enabled Maori to see their political stances as legitimate and their view of human experience as a viable alternative to the hegemonic view. It did not cherish a return to a pristine essentialist past, rather a reconsideration of the present that values their heritage and takes into account their own narrative of historical circumstances.

The Maori Renaissance of the 1970s marked a flowering of Maori cultural and artistic expression. It was indeed the beginning of an imaginative rediscovery through the arts. Actually, the very first published Maori writer in English was a woman: J.C. Sturm, whose stories 'The Old Coat' and 'For All the Saints' appeared in the periodicals *Numbers 1* in 1954, and *Te Ao Hou* in 1955. The bilingual quarterly *Te Ao Hou/The New World*, issued by the Maori Affairs Department from 1952 to 1976, was a propulsive force in the promotion of Maori culture and included transcriptions of traditional literary forms and new writing in English. As Jane McRae relates, the material offered in Maori varied from tribal stories, sayings, songs, incantations and legendary tales to biographies of famous ancestors, local stories and reports on contemporary events.[26] But the periodical was also open to literary forms of European origin, such as short stories and poems, in English and Maori. Many of the best-known Maori writers started out publishing in *Te Ao Hou*, such as Hone Tuwhare and Patricia Grace.

The 1950s and 1960s were a period of experimentation in expressing 'new truths' in 'new forms'[27] — the condition of being Maori in the present, in the new (for Maori) written word. This is how Powhiri Wharemarama Rika-Heke describes Maori writing in those years:

> Almost universally we spoke of the experience of leaving our rural land and, inherent in this, our culture, for the cities. They [the stories and poems] were invocations of loss, filled with regret, nostalgia, and resignation which did not threaten anybody.[28]

Although Maori literary works started appearing in periodicals, Hone Tuwhare was the only Maori writer to have a book published: his collection of poems, *No Ordinary Sun*, appeared in 1964. Ihimaera and Long ironically note the classic tale of the writer who, when asked by a publisher 'Who will read your books?', responded that Maori would. The publisher's reply was: 'But Maoris don't read books.'[29] Nevertheless the Maori reading public increased in the 1970s, a fact that cannot be disconnected from a growing awareness of their rights and their political struggle for sovereignty. The main issues at stake were land claims and preserving the language. As highlighted by Mark Williams, 'what distinguishes features of the Maori Renaissance from the previous movements is the support it has found among Maori people generally and the range of forms it has found for its expression.'[30] The Maori Renaissance cannot be divorced from its political and historical context and must be seen as a continuation of the Maori nationalist movements that date back to the mid-nineteenth century.

Maori made their voices heard in marches, demonstrations, petitions and occupations. The Land March, launched by Whina (late Dame Whina) Cooper in 1975, brought Maori from the far north down to Wellington to give Parliament the message: 'Not one acre more!' That year the government established the Waitangi Tribunal to deliberate and rule on alleged breaches of the Treaty of Waitangi. The tribunal's powers were increased further in 1985, when it was empowered to look at all possible breaches back to 1840, the year the treaty was signed. Since then, it has become the focus of Maori resource claims.[31] Two of the most famous protests in the 1970s were the campaigns urging the return to Maori ownership of Raglan Golf Course, near Hamilton, and Bastion Point in Auckland. Furthermore, the 1972 petition of 40,000 signatories calling for the official recognition of the Maori language and its compulsory teaching in the school system was the catalyst for the establishment, in 1981, of kohanga reo — preschool language immersion classes — and kura kaupapa Maori primary schools, which provide a curriculum based on the study of Maori language, tradition and culture.[32] Maori was finally recognised as an official New Zealand language, along with English, in 1987.[33]

The 1970s also saw the recognition of a growing number of artists. They include the painters Ralph Hotere and Robyn Kahukiwa; dramatists Harry Dansey — the first Maori published playwright with *Te Raukura: The Feathers of the Albatross* in 1972 — and Rowley Habib (Rore Hapipi); traditional weavers like Rangimoana Hetet; film-makers like Barry Barclay and Merata Mita; poets Hone Tuwhare and Apirana Taylor; and, finally, fiction writers such as Witi Ihimaera and Patricia Grace. The blossoming of Maori arts embodied the need to voice political stances and offer an autonomous representation of the self. The fight for self-determination was also a textual fight that provided, for the first time, an autochthonous body of texts to challenge dominant discourse.

The first collection of Maori writing in English, *Contemporary Maori Writing*, was edited by Margaret Orbell and appeared in 1970. It included short stories and poems. Witi Ihimaera was the first Maori writer to publish a collection of short stories, *Pounamu, Pounamu*, in 1972 and a novel, *Tangi*, in 1973. Patricia Grace was the first Maori woman to publish a book, *Waiariki and Other Stories*, in 1975. These texts, and those that increasingly appeared in the following years, are really 'the big story' in New Zealand literature, as Fergus Barrowman signals,[34] marking radical changes in the literary as well as social domain. They opposed any monocentric view on reality and showed the potential of alternative values. They rewrote history, challenging the dominant version, and counter-colonised the genres of the Western canon and the English language. They redefined the position of Maori in relation to Pakeha and, by doing so, forced Pakeha to do the same, underpinning the importance of literary texts as ideological discourses. In 1986 two historical novels on the New Zealand Wars appeared: Witi Ihimaera's *The Matriarch* and Maurice Shadbolt's *Season of the Jew*, the first of a trilogy that includes *Monday's Warriors* (1990) and *The House of Strife* (1993). If Ihimaera's work is an account of the wars from a Maori perspective, Shadbolt's revisionist Pakeha version suggests a remarkable change of perspective too. Both authors challenge a monolithic notion of history in favour of seeing history as a story, subject to a point of view.

The voice of Maori, silenced for over a century, has prompted a redefinition of New Zealand as Aotearoa/New Zealand, from neo-colony to post-colony.

A sense of purpose: the rediscovery of Maoritanga[35] through writing in Patricia Grace and Witi Ihimaera

Although Patricia Grace and Witi Ihimaera come from different backgrounds the impulse that prompted their writing is similar. Grace grew up in an urban environment in Wellington and attended a Catholic convent school. She was born in 1937 to a Pakeha mother of Irish descent, and to a Maori father of Ngati Toa, Ngati Raukawa and Te Ati Awa descent.[36] As she said in an interview with Sue Kedgley, her Pakeha upbringing in town was complemented and counterbalanced by the summer holidays and weekends spent with her father's whanau (family) on their ancestral land in Plimmerton, where she lives at present. That warm communal environment and its closeness to nature left a deep mark in her personality:

> I always knew as I grew up that I lived in two distinct worlds....
> There was the world of the city and going to school in a convent
> .... Then there was the world of my father's family, living amongst
> my relatives in the country in a Maori way of life.... I loved doing
> physical things, playing on the beach and in the bush, being with
> all my cousins and relatives and joining everything they did.[37]

She felt quite isolated at primary school, being the only Maori girl. At secondary school she remembers only one other Maori girl. Teachers had low expectations of her intellectual abilities because she was Maori, and she often heard disparaging comments by other children about her people. But being

Maori was positively reinforced in her family and that made her competitive and willing to prove herself:

> [My parents] never put any limitations on me and encouraged me
> to believe that I could do anything.... I wanted to do everything
> better than the next person.[38]

Although they did not speak Maori in the whanau, nor learn much about their ancestry, their way of life was traditional in the sense that they shared the true communal spirit of a Maori extended family:

> We learned about our immediate relationships to each other —
> who we were related to and how. We ate traditional food and
> behaved in a traditional way towards each other. We had our own
> way of celebrating events or mourning the dead.[39]

Her father's family had been close to the city for some years, and Maori language was not used except for few items of vocabulary. Even the older people did not speak it in front of the children, thinking it was better for young generations and their future to learn proper English.[40] Books in English were the only texts Grace had at school, with topics that had no relevance to her:

> We would be told to write about a day at the seaside or a walk
> in the forest, and because I never connected the seaside with the
> beach or the forest with the bush, I used to write about what I had
> picked up in books about the seaside with little striped tents and
> people wearing bathing costumes.[41]

This example of mimicry was one of Grace's first writing experiences. Interestingly, in another interview with Thomas T. Tausky she explains that although she did enjoy writing, she never considered writing an option for her because she had never read anything by a living New Zealand writer at school: 'I didn't even know that writers existed in New Zealand in the present time. I thought they were all dead and in another country.'[42] Grace later clarified that she had read some of Katherine Mansfield's work at school, but it was so removed from her in time and social class that she could never identify with it. The first great literary impact on her was Sargeson's short stories, which she read at 18 while attending Teachers' Training College. For the first time she could locate New Zealand characters, settings and a language that related to her. In terms of influence on her writing, however, she signals a second-generation New Zealander of Dalmatian origin, Amelia Batistich. Belonging to a minority group herself, Batistich showed Grace the possibility of a narrative outside New

Zealand mainstream literature, transmitting to her a confidence in the value of her own themes and preoccupations.[43] If Pakeha writers had to find their way by shaking off British models, the burden on Maori was double: shaking off both British and Pakeha. Living in an 'outer periphery', Maori had a longer way to go to find their own centre in writing.

While working as a teacher and raising her own children Grace joined a Penwomen's writing club, and started writing short stories, one or two a year, drawing mainly on her childhood memories and events of her past that had never been able to find a space on paper. Grace's first impulse to write originated from an inner voice that had been silent for a long time or was required to mimic models and experiences other to her. Combined with her growing dissatisfaction with the way Maori were represented in literature by non-Maori writers, this urged her 'to show others who they were', to use the words of a character of her story 'Parade'. The evolution from her first collection *Waiariki* through her first novel *Mutuwhenua* (1978) to her second collection *The Dream Sleepers* (1980) is marked by the gradual rise of a 'Maori consciousness', as she explains:

> When I had my first opportunity to put together a collection I knew that I wanted to write about Maori people who hadn't ever been written about. It was an instinctive feeling. Even before Maori consciousness had really surfaced. By the time my next set of short stories, *The Dream Sleepers*, came out I was more concerned with the issues facing my people and I wanted to make statements about what was happening in society. So they are more political.[44]

If Grace was an urban Maori who learned about her roots by going back to the communal life of her father's wider family, Witi Ihimaera's path was in many ways the opposite. He grew up in a rural environment and was encouraged by his loving and supportive parents to achieve university qualification and 'make it' in the Pakeha world. Grace moved from the Pakeha city world to the natural and communal one of her father's whanau, whereas Ihimaera moved from a rural Maori community into the Pakeha world. What they have in common is that they rediscovered and explored their Maoritanga through writing.

Born in 1944 in Gisborne on the East Coast of the North Island, Ihimaera is the eldest of eight children. He traced his whakapapa, according to Maori traditional customs, during a lecture at the Turnbull Library, mentioning his links with Te Aitanga-a-Mahaki, Rongowhakaata and Ngati Kahungunu through his father, and Ngati Porou through his mother's line. He is also a descendent of Wi Pere, who took the Eastern Maori seat in Parliament in 1883.[45] Ihimaera grew up first in the suburbs of Gisborne, then on a country farm. Like the boy in 'One

Summer Morning' from *Pounamu, Pounamu*, he had to milk the cows in the morning before going to school.[46] In their monograph, Corballis and Garrett mention other biographical facts that left a mark on the writer such as his close relationship with his grandparents, in particular the two grandmothers, and with a great-aunt, Nanny Mini, who inspired the character of Nanny Miro in 'A Game of Cards' and lived in the village of Waituhi, the literary setting of many of his works. The character of Riripeti in *The Matriarch* was inspired by his paternal grandmother, Teria Pere, and the shearing gangs in *Bulibasha* were drawn from his father's seasonal jobs as a farm-worker and shearer.

As was the case for Grace, Ihimaera's parents supported and encouraged him to go on with his studies, overcoming the scepticism of teachers who had low expectations of him. After obtaining his School Certificate, Ihimaera spent a year at the Mormon College at Tuhikaramea, Hamilton, where he pursued his love of music. Then he attended Gisborne Boys' High School and completed his University Entrance. He enrolled at the University of Auckland, dropped out, worked as a journalist with the *Gisborne Herald* and as a postman before transferring to the Savings Bank division of the Post Office in Wellington and enrolling part-time at the University of Victoria, where he finally graduated in 1971.[47] He worked as a diplomat for the Ministry of Foreign Affairs and later became a professor in the English Department at the University of Auckland.

Many of Ihimaera's characters live, to use Pearson's words, in an 'amphibious state'[48] between Waituhi and Wellington, which directly reflects Ihimaera's personal experience. After interrupting his studies at Auckland and feeling discouraged with his university work — Grace often describes the lack of motivation in Maori students dealing with learning programmes that have little relevance to their own life experiences — Ihimaera went back to Gisborne but felt an outsider there as well, since the path he had taken was different from those of all his Maori relations and acquaintances.[49] The kaupapa or purpose underlying Ihimaera's early writing was the urge to retrace the path that had moved him away from his cultural and spiritual roots. He wanted to recover and celebrate the heritage, rural and communal, from which he had detached himself and offer it to all urbanised Maori like him.

Both Grace and Ihimaera write out of their personal experience, yet what happened to them exemplifies the condition of most Maori in the fifties and sixties. In those years the number of Maori dropouts was extremely high and comparatively few managed to obtain university degrees or high school qualifications. As Umelo Ojinmah highlights, quoting from J.B. Beston, the Maori migration from rural and agricultural-based communities to urban areas that began in the 1950s led to 'an inversion in the ratio of rural to urban Maori and an attendant cultural discontinuity.'[50] This rapid shift caused an identity crisis and threatened the system of values of a whole culture. Early Maori works in English, part of the so-called pastoral tradition,[51] aimed at recovering Maori cultural identity, that is, at giving 'an imaginary coherence on the experience of dispersal and fragmentation', in Hall's words. As Ihimaera explains, 'they were for Maori people, trying to interpret their lives within rural settlements in New Zealand for them, and the race relations component in those stories was not very high.'[52]

They depict the spirit of Maoritanga, exemplified in the traditional concepts of whanaungatanga (kinship and family responsibilities) and manaakitanga (reciprocal assistance to one another),[53] in the bond with the land and the belief in its spiritual nature, in the respect of ancestors, and in the basic concept of aroha. They place in the foreground what is at risk, or has been lost, as a consequence of urbanisation and deculturation. This phase includes Ihimaera's *Pounamu, Pounamu, Tangi* and *Whanau* (1974), and Grace's *Waiariki* and *Mutuwhenua*. But later on, as Ihimaera says, having 'interpreted sufficiently ourselves to ourselves [it was] time for us to interpret ourselves to the Pakeha.'[54] Like Grace, his works gradually became more politicised, focused on the relationship between Maori and Pakeha and aimed at representing the Maori stance in relation to present issues, especially land issues. For Ihimaera this process got underway in *The New Net Goes Fishing* (1977), and for Grace with *The Dream Sleepers*. Whether nostalgic and lyrical or more politicised, however, all their works are committed to the Maori cause and animated by a 'great sense of purpose'.[55]

From an 'outside-in' approach to an 'indigenised' reading: critical views of Ihimaera's and Grace's early writing

Maori writing uses the English language and is articulated through Western literary genres, yet it is grounded on premises that do not belong to the scope and forms of the European canon. What clearly appears from Ihimaera's and Grace's writings is a Maori point of view, expressed in a language noticeably different from British or New Zealand English, and in a new form. The two authors embody the necessarily hybrid condition of Polynesian New Zealanders striding two worlds, producing works that could never have been written by a Pakeha. The critical reaction to them testifies to the novelty of their writing.

Prominent Pakeha scholars analysing Ihimaera's works, while expressing appreciation for his literary skill, nevertheless needed to frame them within British or European literary/cultural categories. In his effort to defend *Pounamu, Pounamu* from charges of sentimentality and excessive softness, Pearson compares it to an early Charlie Chaplin film, contending that a proper reading of it requires 'an effort of humility to respond to simplicity' similar to that required for the reading of Blake's *Songs of Innocence*.[56] Blake's images of innocence and experience are used again by Corballis and Garrett to exemplify first the different perspectives presented in *Pounamu, Pounamu* and *The New Net Goes Fishing*, then Tama's rediscovery of Maoritanga and the responsibilities it entails in *Tangi*.[57] Corballis and Garrett define Tama's gradual incorporation of his personal experience into Maori myth as a process from 'paradise lost' to 'paradise regained'.[58] Ihimaera's skill in interweaving past and present strands of narrative raises an analogy with Arthur Miller's *Death of a Salesman*, and the character of Mattie Jones in *Whanau* becomes 'a personification of the idea of Maoriness, a sort of Cathleen ni Houlihan (the traditional personification of Ireland), whose sad condition reflects the state of her people.'[59] These parallels reflect the critics' effort to translate something new and other into a familiar lexis rather than really apply to the texts examined. While Ihimaera was conjugating his texts according to a Maori view, critics were trying to inflect them back according to Western categories.

Another remarkable example is the perplexed reaction of critics towards stories dealing with supernatural or extraordinary events. Corballis and Garrett contend that 'The Makutu on Mrs Jones' in *Pounamu, Pounamu* essentially deals with a 'sex game' played between Mrs Jones and Mr Hohepa and misinterpreted as a makutu (spell) by a child whose naivety does not allow him a full vision of the events. They support their argument by mentioning a long tradition of stories narrated through children's eyes (including Henry James' *What Maisie Knew*) and find further evidence in Mrs Jones' lost handkerchief protruding from Mr Hohepa's pocket (the tohunga who is supposed to have cast the spell on her by using an object belonging to his 'victim'). According to them the handkerchief evokes another well-known love-story, that of Othello and Desdemona.[60] This realist reading implies a rejection of events that cannot be ascribed to a Western rational view, underestimating Maori beliefs and the supernatural flavour that pervades the story.

Ihimaera tells about another supernatural event in 'The Greenstone Patu', from the collection *The New Net Goes Fishing*. An ancient patu (traditional short club) belonging to the narrator's family, once lost by the passage from generation to generation, is, after a long search, finally retraced by Auntie Hiraina and found to be in the possession of a Maori woman unrelated to the family. When Aunt Hiraina and the narrator pay a visit to the woman, showing evidence that the patu belongs to them, she refuses to return it. The object signals its presence as a sort of vision, swimming in the air towards its legitimate owners and crying out its name. Cracking sounds come from the cabinet where it is locked, as if a living being were imprisoned there, until Aunt Hiraina punches through the glass and frees it. The story conveys a traditional tenet of Maori philosophy: the sacredness of man-made objects, which are not regarded as inanimate, as Europeans would regard a bowl or spade.[61] As Terence Barrow argues:

> In Maori belief all things had a kind of soul — the wairua. Most things — men, manufactured objects, land, and indeed all nature — had a spiritual 'essence' called *mana*. This vital inner force, which has been likened to electricity, could be drained away by improper contacts.[62]

The 'Greenstone Patu' is among the least successful stories of the collection, according to Corballis and Garrett.[63] In another essay, Corballis refers to it as 'a curious story which probably smacks rather too strongly of *Star Wars* for most Pakeha tastes'.[64] Pearson looks desperately for a rational explanation, resorting to 'an optical illusion' and to a parallel with the Old English poem *The Dream of the Rood*, in which the cross sails through the air and tells the story of the crucifixion. His puzzlement is explained in his addition to the essay when it was later republished:

> Since I wrote this essay I have learnt that there is a belief, widely held by older people though not freely revealed, that a greenstone weapon, once it has been prayed over with karakia and curses, can take on occult powers and might move of its own volition and swim through water to return to its owners.
>
> Clearly I have missed something in my response to 'The Greenstone Patu' .... The question is raised, however, of the extent to which a Western literary tradition, which requires of the reader no more than a willing suspension of disbelief in its tales of the supernatural, can accommodate the more deeply held occult beliefs of another culture.[65]

Pearson's baffled response and apologetic clarification show that Maori authors like Ihimaera use the Western canon to express their own concerns and beliefs, changing conventional rules and modulating them according to an aesthetic vision alien to European modes and tradition. Even the general label of 'magic realism', often applied to South American and some postcolonial literatures, appears as a superimposed category and external to the Maori world. As Fergus Barrowman underlines, 'fiction by a Maori writer poses formal challenges to critical orthodoxies'. The example he mentions is 'the insistence that readers take the supernatural elements as *literally* true — not as a literary device in the way a writer like Angela Carter makes use of European fairytales.'[66] Taking magic, premonitory dreams, personifications of natural events or objects as literally true presupposes a different inflection of the world, a change of perspective. Respected Maori scholar Ranginui Walker argues that the continual search for parallels or labels clouds the understanding of the real meaning of, for instance, Maori religious beliefs.[67]

Two early articles on Grace's fiction reveal Pakeha critics' uneasiness with Maori writing. John Beston shows an ambiguous patronising attitude, swinging from a flattering stance in favour of Maori as 'the best educated of the native people in the South Pacific'[68] to a celebration of the New Zealand democratic system, which ultimately appears as the only agent in the rise of Maori consciousness:

> Although the Maori have not enjoyed the material benefits of New
> Zealand society on equal terms with the Pakeha (the Whites), they
> have not been excluded from the mainstream of that society to
> the extent that the native peoples have been in Australia or Papua
> New Guinea. Consequently, the Maori have more *confidence* and
> *pride* in themselves than other Pacific peoples surrounded by an
> overwhelming White society, and the Maori writers are much
> more concerned with establishing what constitutes the *essence* of
> their identity as a people.[69] (my emphases)

Beston's statement implicitly allows no agency to Maori, because all their qualities (good education, pride and confidence) apparently stem from the Pakeha system. Moreover, instead of decoding how the 'Maori essence' is inflected in Grace's text, he contradictorily focuses on her (supposed) attempts to reconcile the Maori and the Pakeha world, attributing to her a search for general universalising features and repeatedly stressing her will to ingratiate herself with the Pakeha audience, which ultimately constitute the majority of her reading public.[70] Beston contradicts himself when dealing with the 'strong anthropomorphic strain in Maori thinking'[71] that he recognises in Grace's works. He mentions the slippers, to which the woman in 'Between Earth and Sky' speaks, as an example of a typical Maori attitude, but he is unable fully to understand the importance of the greenstone patu in *Mutuwhenua*, which in his view becomes merely an object that the characters have a 'feeling of appropriateness and respect' towards.[72] The novel's complex protagonist, Linda, is reduced to a 'universalised' figure who is only occasionally Maori. His final judgement is that 'Grace's attempt to establish her [Linda's] common humanity tends to drain her, not only of her Maori identity, but of any strong individuality.'[73]

What is striking in this article is how Beston cannot read most of the Maori subtext in Grace's fiction. Conversely, he adheres to an essentialist notion of Maoriness and keeps on expressing his expectations of what Maori fiction *should* be like (more intensively mythical or social realist or militant) rather than see what is in her work, as his final criticism of *Mutuwhenua* shows:

> Grace's desire to bring Pakeha and Maori close together, to avoid stirring up old prejudices or resentments, put constraints also upon her characterisation of the hero and heroine in *Mutuwhenua*.... By renouncing *unique qualities* of Maori life as subject matter, by avoiding scenes of tension or aspects of discrimination (a word that never occurs in her fiction), Grace considerably narrows the range of what she can write about.[74] (my emphasis)

Maori life is amply explored both in *Mutuwhenua* and in Grace's stories, and what Beston takes for deference to the Pakeha is actually a problematic approach to the condition of Maori in the present, rather than a mere application of abstract postulates about Maoriness.

Norman Simms concentrates on Grace's language, dividing *Waiariki* into three categories of short stories: 'Maori tales' (those written with English words but following Maori syntax and thought patterns); 'Macaronic tales' (those which contain a high frequency of Maori words and suggest in their syntax an impression of Maori thought-patterns); and 'English tales' (those which show a more integrated approach, 'in which there is no sense of disturbing English syntax beyond its normal bounds and the experience of Maoriness is made to flow through the narrative shape of a European story').[75] Needless to say, Simms soon announces that Grace's work will ultimately be judged in the stories of the last kind, as if the others were not worth literary consideration. His comment is critical even for the 'English tales': 'much more remains to be done before the boundaries of the short-story as evolved for the European experience are adjusted fully to accommodate the Maori experience.'[76]

In Simms' view, the Maori world should be conveyed through the short story without undermining its basic aesthetic and narrative principles. The efficacy of Grace's use of language is therefore evaluated according to the degree of its conformity to or assimilation into standardised Western models. 'Toki', 'Huria's Rock' and 'At the River', belonging to the first group, are considered little more than experiments, interesting only from a technical point of view. The 'liberties taken from normal English syntax and thought patterns' are equated with 'mere annoyance' that one feels when 'reading a poor translation'[77] and a passage from 'At the River' is reported in both its original form and a corrected version in 'proper English', as though Grace could not master her own language.

In her seminal book on Aboriginal and Maori writing, *The Circle and the Spiral*, Eva Rask Knudsen underscores how the indigenous roots of non-Western texts are rarely examined by the critics. Indigenous literature in English is a domain apart that needs a willing and conscious effort on the part of scholars, not only to move away from Western rationalist premises and critical orthodoxies, but to acquire some knowledge of the specific culture and understand its subtexts. She therefore argues that all forms of Western criticism, even the postcolonial one, tend to become 'assimilative and unconsciously eurocentric'[78] as long as the less accessible layers of an indigenous text are not uncovered:

> Postcolonial theory — despite the fact that it has liberated non-European literature written in English from an outdated universalising form of criticism — is by no means always emancipating; its attempts to homogenise the postcolonial world vis-à-vis Europe may seem inadequate or perhaps even unfortunate to the indigenous writer or reader.[79]

Labels such as 'post-modernist', 'post-structuralist' or 'magic realist' — all of which originated in the Western academy — are often applied by virtue of apparent affinities to fields that are in reality worlds apart, and tend to recolonise indigenous cultures. Indigenous writers may be keen to escape the particular centre offered in search of other positions more in tune with their creative sensibilities. Rask Knudsen suggests that the best way to study indigenous writing is to take an 'indigenised' reading, that is 'the outsider's attempt to read with an understanding of the indigenous perspective'.[80] This implies historical, anthropological and ethnological knowledge on the part of the critics, which necessarily fills in the cultural gap and allows them to move from an 'outside-in' to a more localised perspective. This is the approach that will be used in the following close analyses of works by Ihimaera and Grace.

5 | Witi Ihimaera and Patricia Grace: Early Writing

Several common themes recur throughout Ihimaera's and Grace's early production. Although their mode and approach were different, they had in common the search for a 'frame', which also characterises their later novels. The first and last story in both *Pounamu, Pounamu* and *Waiariki* deal with a similar theme and setting, functioning as a sort of symbolic container to the others. In 'A Game of Cards' and 'Tangi', which open and close Ihimaera's first collection, an urbanised young man goes back to his family village to see a dying relative or to pay homage to a dead one. In both stories, memories of the past mingle with the present, offering a representation of the spirit of Maoritanga and reminding the young man of his bond with it. The two deceased somehow come to represent a larger system of values that risks dissolution, a world that is disappearing. In Grace's *Waiariki* the first and last story, 'A Way of Talking' and 'Parade', show a young woman returning home from the city to stay with her family for a while. The focus is on the protagonists' reactions, and the new light in which the community and culture appear to them. Distance and the immersion in a new environment have given them new consciousness and sharper instruments to interpret the reality they see. While focusing on the two young women's new ways of seeing, however, the stories also show the Maori sense of family and community, and their cultural background.

Many of the following themes resonate as a background echo across all their fiction, regardless of the subject matter:

1. Evoking a paradigmatic world where humans, nature and inanimate objects interact and are all attributed spiritual qualities. The account of dreams, premonitions and extraordinary events is seen as the characters' ability to communicate with and participate in a larger spiritual reality.
2. The importance of communal spirit and whanau (family) as foundational traits of Maori identity, endangered by Western individualism and the dominant model of nuclear family.
3. The human race's bond with and respect for nature, which entails an environmentally conscious attitude and anticipates contemporary environmentalism.
4. The treatment of time that reflects not only the modernist difference between chronological and mental time but also the existence of the wider time of myth and eternity, which encompasses both.
5. Representing dual lives: the amphibious or hybrid state that especially characterises younger generations bestriding two worlds.
6. The setting up of 'primary oppositions' in the present world: old/new, rural/urban, past/present, wisdom/know-how, conservation/exploitation, whanau/individual, Maori/Pakeha.[1]
7. The transitional nature of most stories, with characters departing from whanau for the city or their returns home for brief periods such as holidays or ceremonies.

Ihimaera's *Tangi* and *Whanau* still belong to the so-called pastoral period insofar as they celebrate the values of Maoritanga. In *Tangi*, Tama Mahana, a young man working in Wellington, attends his father's funeral in the village of Waituhi. The exploration of his grief sets in motion a series of reminiscences about his rural childhood and the poignant intensity of tangihanga (funerals) brings him back to the core of Maori culture, reminding him of his responsibilities towards his family. Tama's personal experience is connected to a larger mythical dimension too, which constitutes the outer frame of the novel. *Whanau* is the account of one day in Waituhi. According to Corballis and Garrett, in Ihimaera's fiction Waituhi becomes a sort of '"objective correlative" to the ethos that binds the tangata whenua [people of the land] together'[2] and will be the setting of many other works. Through the picture of its inhabitants, Ihimaera recreates the spirit of a Maori rural community, and explores the difficulty, especially for younger generations, of finding a balance between modernity and tradition within the dominant Pakeha system. *Whanau* introduces issues of race relations that will be later developed in *The New Net Goes Fishing*. Waituhi becomes the frame connecting and containing all the characters.

Grace apparently started exploring race relations in her novel *Mutuwhenua*, which tells about an interracial marriage between a Maori girl and a young Pakeha man, but she actually focuses on the girl's dilemma, her 'tension of displacement'[3] rather than on a real confrontation between races. Like *Waiariki*, *Mutuwhenua* aims at showing 'who the Maori are', exploring the roots of their culture, and is included in the pastoral tradition.

As for Ihimaera's and Grace's language, their English often reflects the rhythm and grammatical structures of te reo Maori and is interspersed with numerous Maori words, in relation not only to rituals and customs that have no English correspondents but also to semantic fields outside of European culture. There is an evident musical quality about their writing, typical of storytelling and songs, partly explained as the inheritance of Maori oral literature. This phase of experimentation with language and form, however, is definitely more marked in Grace than in Ihimaera, who tends to conform more to the traditional Western canon. Their use of language will be analysed in detail in a later chapter.

Pounamu, Pounamu: the foundation of a paradigmatic textual world

Pounamu, Pounamu celebrates the traditional values of Maori rural life and also the forces threatening them. The order of the stories shows the passage from an idyllic and nostalgic tone to an increasingly darker view, suggesting the author's concern for the future of Maori culture. Corballis and Garrett support Alistair Fox's contention that the turning point of the collection occurs in the fourth short story, 'Fire on Greenstone'.[4] They note Ihimaera's frequent use of a double strand of narrative, meant to contrast the present, factual reality with the past and timeless mental processes (as in 'The Other Side of the Fence'), or two different types of past: a factual one, expressed with the simple past tense, and a ritual one, expressed with the habitual past tense 'she would do' or 'he used to go' (as in 'The Child').[5]

Arguably, the use of the latter applies to many stories, mingling the time of objective reality with the time of subjective past memories, which convey the 'emotional landscape' Ihimaera wants to preserve. An indigenised reading suggests that this narrative technique also serves another purpose: the subjective memory of the past is always connected to a collective dimension of communal participation, shared values and symbols, drawing on a sort of collective unconscious. The habitual past tense underlines a ritual dimension almost out of time, conveying an idea of long-standing traditions and depicting the single character as a manifestation of his community. This is reinforced by the presence of a 'frame' — the first and last story — symbolically suggesting the connection of the parts to the whole.

Another characteristic of the collection is the reiteration of characters, names, places and objects: a typical mode of Ihimaera's writing that will extend to other works. Apart from the omnipresent village of Waituhi, the same families and characters are found in many different stories (and later novels), suggesting the author's will to create links between his works as parts of a greater whole. The representation of a paradigmatic world is therefore reflected in the creation of a corresponding textual world. Stories never appear self-contained, but continue in other short stories and novels. If there are discrepancies — details about the same characters that do not always fit consistently — they may be interpreted as the author's concern to construct of 'a sense of community' rather than the representation of individuals; 'Ihimaera discourages us from focusing closely on the characters as individuals. Instead, he obliges us to focus on the community, which stays the same while its individuals change.'[6]

The first two stories, 'A Game of Cards' and 'Beginning of the Tournament', celebrate 'the irrepressible spirit of the Maori community'.[7] In the former, the pleasure of staying together is exemplified by Nanny Miro's passion for card playing and the depiction of the ritual that took place at her home many times: 'The sitting room would be crowded with the kuias [old women], all puffing clouds of smoke, dressed in their clothes, laughing and cackling and gossiping about who was pregnant — and relishing all the juicy bits too!' (PP 2).[8] On the night of Nanny Miro's death all the whanau gathers to play the last game with her. Maka Heta, her card-mate and rival, performs her tricks, cheating as usual. The whole community joins too:

> The old ladies sat around the bed, playing. Everybody else decided
> to play cards too, to keep Nanny company. The men played poker
> in the kitchen and sitting room. The kids played snap in the other
> bedrooms. The house was overflowed with card players, even onto
> the lawn outside Nanny's window, where she could see ...' (PP 4–5)

Moving from past memories to main narrative is marked by the switch from the habitual past tense to past simple, and by the translation of the Maori word kuia into 'old ladies'. Nanny Miro is the custodian of the whanau's heritage and past. Her place, evoked in the narrator's childhood memories, is defined as a 'treasure house, glistening with sports trophies and photographs, pieces of carvings and greenstone, and feather cloaks hanging from the walls' (PP 2).

In 'Beginning of the Tournament' the community, again, is the protagonist. The Maori hockey tournament is depicted as a fun fair, where people get together to have a good time. Ihimaera's portrayal of the makeshift organisation and the participants' disregard of manners, rules and form is hilarious. Set in a paddock among browsing cows, the two improbable teams include kids who have never played before and grandmothers holding walking sticks in one hand and hockey sticks in the other. Cheating is permitted as long as it favours a team that did not win the year before, according to a redistributive sense of justice, as the protagonist tries to explain to his horrified Pakeha friend, Jerry. In celebrating 'the irrepressible spirit' of the Maori community, Ihimaera echoes the view that Sargeson and Finlayson had previously expressed, that Maori show a deep respect for social instinct and have kept their spontaneity and humanity intact. If Sargeson and Finlayson stressed this point to criticise the spiritual dryness of Pakeha society, Ihimaera emphasises the preservation of communal spirit as an important trait of Maori identity.

'The Makutu on Mrs Jones' is centred on the traditional belief in makutu or magic spells. The protagonist is forced, by his wife, into cutting his long toenails, a trivial act that reminds the man he must dispose of his nail clippings carefully, since 'Maori people believe that if a person gets a bit of you — it might be some hair, a hanky, even a piece of toenail — he'll be able to put a spell on you' (PP 15). A flashback takes him to his boyhood when Hohepa, an ugly old tohunga, put a makutu on the emancipated Pakeha widow Mrs Jones, which led her to marry the man. The tone of the story is a mix of mystery and comedy. Ihimaera may be playing with the imaginative mind of a boy that saw Mr Hohepa as 'three in one: Dracula, Frankenstein and the Werewolf' (PP 17). Yet at the end of the story the grown-up narrator confirms his trust in makutu by hiding his bits of toenails. Ihimaera seems to be purposely ambiguous and leave space for different interpretations, but a Maori reading would support the makutu thesis. This is strengthened by the fact that the story of Hohepa's makutu on Mrs Jones makes frequent use of the habitual past, taking it into the territory of Maori rituals and heritage.[9]

'Fire on Greenstone' tells about the fire that destroyed Nanny Miro's homestead some time after her death. All the taonga are lost, including the whakapapa (genealogy) book and a piece of greenstone that had always exerted an irresistible attraction on the narrator as a young boy. The experience is mentioned in the 'habitual past', as a ritual:

> I used to like to hold it to the sun and look into it, and feel the
> soft luminous glow flooding around me. And I used to whisper to
> myself, 'Pounamu ... pounamu ... pounamu ...', and almost hear
> the emerald water rushing over the clay from where the greenstone
> had come. (PP 38)

The destruction of the taonga appears as an ominous sign for the destiny of Maori, a pessimistic vein that continues in 'The Whale', as we will see later. In another story, 'The Gathering of the Whakapapa' from *The New Net Goes Fishing*, we will learn that the greenstone actually survived the fire.

'Fire on Greenstone' is a crucial story. First of all it focalises the central image of the collection, the pounamu or greenstone of the title, a stone invested with high symbolic as well as historical value for Maori. Many myth cycles have narrated how greenstone came to Aotearoa/New Zealand from Hawaiki with the first ancestors, and it was of tremendous practical importance for Maori before the advent of iron tools. It stands as a symbol of the Maori race in the collection for this very reason. Secondly, it inaugurates the reiterative mode typical of Ihimaera's writing, as already mentioned.

'The Other Side of the Fence' is the only story of this collection depicting close interracial relations in the city. It juxtaposes two sets of neighbours, the Pakeha Simmons and the Maori Heremaia families, and their two different lifestyles. Ihimaera avoids stereotypes by highlighting virtues and vices on both sides, but he also contrasts 'the assumptions and perceptions inherent in both cultures'[10] with particular reference to the notions of privacy and property. The relationship between Jack Simmons and the Heremaia children is explanatory. The children are described as a bunch of amusing pests, irresistibly funny, but so intrusive that 'the fence might as well not exist' (PP 46). The boundary between stealing and borrowing is not clear to them, and they have a penchant for cheating and imaginative lying. Even when they behave with the best of intentions, as is the case for Jimmy, the most sensitive and reserved of the children, they end up causing trouble. For all Jack's efforts to understand, the cultural gap is insurmountable, leading to a state of 'amicable warfare', of 'treaties signed and treaties broken' (PP 49), a clear allusion to the Treaty of Waitangi. The story could also be read as a microcosm within the wider scene of New Zealand domestic history. The insistence on images of enclosure in relation to the Simmonses is reminiscent of Frank Sargeson's representation of the cramped puritanical world in *I Saw in My Dream*: the locked hen-house, the fence, the wire-netting around the goldfish pond. Unlike Sargeson's characters the Simmonses are liberal people inclined to self-criticism, nevertheless they feel the need to trace borders, and exist within rigid schemes. The communal and flexible spirit of the Heremaias is perceived as trespass and abuse, as demonstrated by Jack's comment 'the quicker Maoris adjusted to European life the better' (PP 52). Ojinmah contends that in 'The Other Side of the Fence' Ihimaera is giving a recipe for biculturalism. Elsewhere in the collection he celebrates Maori traditions and values, but in this story he seems to suggest that Maori have some adjustments to make if they want to live in urban areas with dominant Pakeha residency.[11] The theme of bicultural integration, which is different from assimilation, will be further developed in the novel *Whanau*. Following Ihimaera's reiterative mode, the Heremaias will be the protagonists of another short story in *The New Net Goes Fishing*, centred on Jimmy's education.

'In Search of the Emerald City' is a typical transitional story, dealing with Matiu's family moving from Waituhi to Wellington, the Emerald City. Emerald becomes the symbol of city life, flashy and illusory, as opposed to the solid beauty of the greenstone that stands for rural life. The title also refers to the Emerald City in L. Frank Baum's story *The Wizard of Oz*, narrating the quest of four characters (just as for Matiu, his father, mother and sister) to a fabulous place presided over by a magician whom they believe is able to make all their dreams come true. This is precisely what Matiu's father expects from Wellington: 'Plenty jobs, plenty money' (PP 65). Matiu's saga will continue in two more stories, 'Yellow Brick Road' and 'Return from Oz', which begin and conclude *The New Net Goes Fishing*. 'In Search of the Emerald City' is imbued with the melancholy that all emigrants feel on leaving their familiar life behind, amidst all the doubts that accompany making such a decision. Matiu's father still believes in his turangawaewae, as his externalised wish to be buried in Waituhi shows. He will actually move back to Waituhi when an old man, as narrated in 'Return from Oz'. For the younger generation, however, keeping the bond with their origin seems much more difficult.

In 'One Summer Morning' rural life is seen through the eyes of a teenager, Hema, impatient to be a man and resentful of all the chores he has to do. The routine of a small farm is not sentimentalised but presented in all its dreariness and toughness. In an ironic and self-mocking tone, Ihimaera describes adolescent restlessness and problems: Hema's discovery of sex and growing interest in girls; his concern for his physical look, which starts his verbal fights with the mirror; his desire for independence, marked by his final request to his father for long trousers. Like Netta in Hilliard's *Maori Girl* he defines his village (a reiterated Waituhi) as a 'dump' and dreams of 'neat city apartments' (PP 72). The passages about the rhythm of farm work, especially those on shearing, evoke an image of traditional Maori rural life that will be later developed in *Bulibasha: King of the Gypsies*. Discussion by Hema's parents about his long pants, in Maori so that neither Hema nor his sister Georgina can understand, exemplifies the condition of people suspended between two worlds.

Another child, this time probably younger than Hema, is together with his grandmother the co-protagonist of 'The Child'. Strong bonds between grandchildren and their 'nannies' (a term used for female elders in general) are frequent in Ihimaera's and Grace's stories. The structure of extended families favoured close ties between different generations, and whangai was a relatively common practice whereby the young were sometimes raised as the children of grandparents or other relatives.

At the end of Grace's *Mutuwhenua*, for example, the protagonist decides to leave her newborn baby to her mother. The story is fully narrated in the habitual past tense ('she would hold up a sea shell', 'I would help her'), evoking a sense of ritual implied by the protagonists' walking or playing games together, and the rhythm of a paradigmatic timeless world. This is changed into a simple past when the old woman dies: 'One day, my Nanny, she wasn't home when I got back from school.... I looked down to the beach. My Nanny, she was lying there...' (PP 113). 'The Child' depicts a world of warm relationships and caring for elders, which makes the inevitability of their death more natural and easier to accept. It typifies an attitude of respect and consideration towards them that, as shown in *The Carpathians*, Frame regrets is missing in Pakeha society. Nanny's death on the beach evokes the closing of a circle, the return of the body to its natural shrine.

'The Whale' is the most pessimistic story in *Pounamu, Pounamu*, insofar as there seems to be no hope for Maori culture to survive. The story begins 'in the darkness of the meeting house' where an old man has retreated 'because it is the only thing remaining in his dying world' (PP 115). Personifications of nature are frequent in Ihimaera's fiction, aimed at representing the bond between humans and the world around them, as will be seen especially in *Tangi*. The personification of the meeting house that appears in this story is a topos of Maori culture. The wharenui represents the living body of an ancestor, as the old man teaches Hera, one of the few mokopuna interested in Maori culture:

> The head is at the top of the meeting house, above the entrance. That is called the koruru. His arms are the maihi, the boards sloping down from the koruru to form the roof. See the tahuhu, ridgepole? That long beam running from the front to the back along the roof? That is the backbone. The rafters, the heke, they are the ribs. And where we are standing, this is the heart of the house. Can you hear it beating? (PP 116)

The heartbeat is weaker now, however, because the semi-deserted village is breaking apart. Many young people have moved to the city and the picture of those few who still live there, partying and drinking in one of the houses, prefigures some of the characters in *Whanau*. They stay because they have nowhere else to go and have probably already failed in the Pakeha world. This takes us back to Finlayson's exploration of Maori youth's predicament and his vision of an unheroic present as opposed to an heroic mythical past. Images of neglect, decay and death pervade the story: the dissolution of communal spirit is symbolised by the houses 'clustered close together, but closed to one another' (PP 121). The last image of the story, 'a whale, stranded in the breakwater, ... already stripped of flesh by the falling gulls'

(PP 122) is the ultimate sign of death. As Corballis and Garrett note, 'the man has become the dying whale', [12] since in their claws the gulls 'clasp his shouted words' (PP 122) as well as whale flesh. In 'The Whale', Ihimaera uses two images that will be later developed in *The Whale Rider*: the story of the ancestor Paikea, founder of the village, who came to Aotearoa riding a whale; and the image of stranded whales, used to symbolise the disruption of the bond between humans and nature.

The most salient aspect of 'Tangi' is Ihimaera's treatment of time. Its structure will be reproduced and enlarged in the novel bearing the same title. There are basically three alternating narrative strands, separated by double spacing and corresponding to three different times: the present time of the funeral ceremony, narrated in a sort of interior monologue from the moment the narrator, Tama, arrives at the marae to the moment he confronts his father's corpse; the time of Tama's recent memories, when he received the bad news in Wellington; and the time of Tama's earlier memories, going back to his childhood and to Nanny Puti's death. The latter memories are italicised to differentiate them from the more recent ones.

The question of time is a crucial one for Ihimaera and Maori writing in general. In the previous stories the use of the habitual past tense aimed at recreating the atmosphere of a Maori community, and focused on those rituals or repeated actions that embody traditional Maori values and spirit. Myth looms large in Maori works, although Ihimaera's early short stories only refer to it indirectly. The above-mentioned quotation from p. 38 of 'Fire on Greenstone', for example, evokes numerous mythical accounts about the origin of this stone that associate it with a fish. As stated in the *Reed Book of Maori Mythology*, 'the pounamu was originally a fish, who, naturally vexed at being unceremoniously taken out of the water transformed itself into a stone'.[13] Such references cannot be completely understood by readers who are unfamiliar with Maori mythology. Some didactic accounts of Maori myths are given by the old man to his niece in 'The Whale', including the story of Paikea riding the whale. In 'Tangi' the time of myth is expressed in an eternal present by the first narrative strand, the tangi ceremony, throughout the protagonist's slow approach to Rongopai, the meeting house where his father's body lies. Far from his new life in Wellington, Tama is slowly absorbed into a wider ritual dimension, preparing him for the encounter with other members of his community, with his father's body and with death itself. Since the community is made not only of the living members but also of the dead, symbolically represented in the carvings of the meeting house, Tama's ritual entrance into the marae marks his entrance into the world of myth as well.

The other two strands interspersed with the mythical one can be seen as 'two sets of memories which occupy Tama's mind as he copes with the ordeal of the tangi'.[14] The second strand, dealing with Tama's recent past in Wellington, illustrates a different way of looking at grief. Tama conforms to Pakeha ways here: on learning the bad news his grief is contained and reserved as opposed to his whole-hearted abandonment in the first strand. Strand three revives images of Tama's father when he was alive, the sense of protection he gave Tama when confronted with the reality of his nanny's death. Tama's gradual identification with the rituals and traditions of his people during the tangi seems to be a positive sign for all urbanised Maori; recovering their roots is possible but must necessarily pass through an emotional dimension.

The importance of *Pounamu, Pounamu* lies in it being not only the first book offering an unmediated Maori world view but also as the forge on which most of Ihimaera's future works were formed. It laid the basis of all the major themes developed later by the writer and the foundation of his 'paradigmatic textual world' that will extend up to the present with *The Rope of Man* (2005).

Tangi, or spiralling back into the future

As already mentioned, *Tangi* enlarges and develops the themes and narrative technique of the short story bearing the same name. The novel returns to Tama Mahana, who learns about his father Rongo's death while at work in Wellington, attends his funeral in Waituhi near Gisborne, then goes back to the capital after reassuring his family that he will move back to look after them, as he had promised his father. It is divided into 32 numbered chapters grouped into nine unnumbered sections, preceded by an authorial epigraph or poetical foreword, and followed by an epilogue that corresponds to the tenth section. The epigraph evokes the Maori cosmogonic myth of Rangitane and Papatuanuku, setting the mythological frame that contains the whole work. It acts as a sort of manifesto of the author's concerns, illustrating the form (a poetic drama in prose) and content of the novel, and ends with the Maori formula 'Haere mai, haere mai, haere mai' ('Come forward, welcome').

The epigraph is reminiscent of a karanga, the call chanted by women on the marae as the first expression of welcome from the tangata whenua (people of the land or hosts) to the manuhiri (visitors). The marae is not simply the place where people meet, but also has a spiritual importance:

> It is the family home of generations that have gone before. It is the standing place of the present generation and will be the standing place for the generations to come…. It is the place where I have the right to stand before others and speak as I feel…. Maori who have no marae have no turangawaewae (standing place). They do not have the right and privilege of standing and speaking. They do not belong.[15]

The karanga is a welcome for the living, generally ending with the expression 'Haere mai' repeated three times, as in the epigraph. It also summons the spirits of the dead, who may be represented here by reference to the primeval parents, Rangi and Papa. The reader is therefore likened to a visitor and welcomed to a textual marae symbolising the Maori world.

The 32 chapters of the novel can be divided into two types (A and B) according to the temporal and spatial direction of Tama's travel. With a few exceptions, they alternate throughout all the book. Type A is set in the present, after the funeral when Tama is travelling from Gisborne back to Wellington by train. Type B is set in the recent past, on the day he received the bad news in his office, and is marked by his movement by plane from Wellington to Gisborne, then by car to Waituhi, and finally on foot to the marae into the meeting house where his father's body lies. The novel, starting with a type A chapter, opens at Gisborne railway station, with a reference to the circularity of time:

> This is where it ends and begins. Here on the railway station, Gisborne, waiting for the train to Wellington. Here begins the first step into the future, the first step from the past. I am alone now. (TA 1)

The opening underscores the Maori notion of time, which sees human beings advancing into the future with their eyes facing the past. At this point Tama has already undergone the ordeal of the tangi, as a rite of passage, and has retrieved the bond with his Maori roots. All type A chapters are interspersed with memories of Tama's childhood and the wanderings of the Mahanas from one place to another. These chapters illustrate what Corballis and Garrett call 'the social level' of the novel, that is, 'the story of one representative Maori family making its way in a world more and more dominated by the materialistic values of the Pakeha.'[16] Tama's parents began their married life as itinerant workers, doing contract farm labouring. After a great deal of hard work and careful saving, they managed to purchase a house in Gisborne and finally fulfilled their dream of owning a farm in Waituhi, their home village.

Type B chapters narrate Tama's reaction on receiving the news from his sister Ripeka, his colleagues' condolences, his rush first home and then to the airport driven by his sympathetic boss, Mr Ralston; then the flight to Gisborne, the encounter with his other sister Mere and her husband, who drive him to Waituhi, and finally the tangi ceremony up to the time of the burial on the afternoon of the third day. Type B chapters are also interspersed with Tama's thoughts, but they are generally more emotional and intimate than those in A chapters, evoking the figure of his father and events and conversations involving only the two of them.

Tama often addresses his father or engages in imaginary dialogues with him as if Rongo's figure was the leading thread of his interior monologue, which constitutes the whole novel written in the first person. The expression 'E pa' often marks this thread and becomes a sort of refrain:

See, e pa? These are not tears; they are only drops of rain falling.
My heart throbs not with grief, but with aroha. And arms reach up
with love, not pain for you. See? I smile now.
I am calm, e pa. (TA 54)
E... pa. You have gone from me and I am sad. (TA 144)

Every section is characterised by a significant stage in Tama's spiritual and physical journey, either towards Wellington or towards Gisborne. In the first section (TA 0-32), all A chapters are set at Gisborne station where Tama is surrounded by the warmth of his family, while the B ones are in the Pakeha world in Wellington and marked by the formal participation of his colleagues to his grief. The A-B chapter structure conveys the sense of an after and a before: on one hand Tama's achievement of adulthood and the recovery of his Maori identity as a result of his initiation in the tangi ritual, on the other his previous immaturity, unconsciousness and amphibious state. The section finishes with an A chapter. This is the first of the three exceptions to the alternated pattern of A-B types, as the next section begins with an A type again, but in doing so the author seems to underline the beginning of a new phase for Tama: the passage from the reassuring protection of his family to his profound loneliness on the train, which will raise the memories of his past life. The formal break in structure comes to symbolise an emotional and physical rupture in the protagonist's life as well.

In the second section (TA 33–54), A chapters narrate Tama's train journey back to Wellington lost in the solitude of his thoughts. The B chapters also narrate the passage from a collective dimension (his office, his colleagues) to solitude (his drive to his Wellington apartment with Mr Ralston, and his loneliness there).

In the third section (TA 55–74) — and in the following sections up to the two final ones, where A and B chapters merge — all A chapters are set on the train and depict Tama's past life through his memories. The B chapters follow Tama's spiritual/physical journey back to his roots, marked by his natural association of the airport name 'Rongotai' with the name of the Waituhi meeting house 'Rongopai', and by the casual encounter with his cousin Kopua at the airport, which stresses the Maori values of aroha and the importance of family bonds. Kopua assures his presence at the tangi and gives Tama some money to contribute to the expenses.

In the fourth section (TA 75–106), while memories flow longer and more intensely in the A chapters, occupying all of Tama's mind (as shown by the second exception to the general pattern with two consecutive A chapters), B chapters follow Tama's flight. The conversation with the Pakeha lady sitting next to him, who is going to see her first newborn grandchild, increases the poignancy of Tama's grief and loneliness: unlike him, the lady is travelling towards a new life. This episode could also foreshadow Tama's own rebirth after the tangi.

The fifth section (TA 107–132), consisting of only two chapters, is central. A long A chapter narrates the end of the family's wanderings, their settling down in their own farm in Waituhi, and their excitement and pride at fulfilling their dream. It also offers Tama's emotional picture of the village, 'his Eden' (TA 115), and of its meeting house: 'the place of the heart' and the centre of his universe, like his father (TA 115). Waituhi is found in the B chapter as well, which describes Tama's arrival there. Past and present mingle in Waituhi, which is also the centre of attraction for Tama's consciousness, representing his father, his home and his identity.

The third exception to the A-B alternation is in the sixth section (133–55), made up of a single long B chapter. All attention is focused on the rituals of the tangi up to Tama's encounter with his father's body. The importance of the moment, for Tama and in the novel's structure, is evident by the length of the chapter and its position as the only one in the section.

Section seven (TA 157–83) is made up of two chapters. The A chapter goes back to the time when Tama left Waituhi and moved to Wellington, to his 'aimless' and 'selfish' life in the city (TA 160) where he 'would be lonely even on a crowded street' (TA 160). Yet he became accustomed to this, and did not want to leave even when his father called him back. The B chapter continues narrating the tangi.

In the remaining two sections — the eighth section (including chapters 30 and 31) and ninth section (including only chapter 32) — the two strands merge into the story of the funeral ceremony. These chapters do not respect the division between type A and B. Accounts of the tangi had previously always occupied the type B chapters, where the time-spatial co-ordinates were 'recent past' and 'movement towards Waituhi', but in chapters 30 and 32 it becomes part of Tama's memories on the train back to Wellington (type A chapters). Chapter 31 is the memory of a short dialogue between Tama and Rongo, in which Tama promises to look after the family in case of his father's death. The epilogue or tenth section is entirely occupied by the evocation of the final stage of the tangi.

As the novel advances the chapters become longer, even as each section is comprised of gradually fewer chapters. The first section includes 15 chapters; the second and third sections have four chapters each; the fourth section has five chapters; and from the fifth onward each section includes only one or two chapters. The ninth section includes only one chapter and the tenth only the Epilogue. In formal terms, the story seems to develop according to a principle of contraction and expansion.

Moreover, the opposite spatial directions alternating in the story (from Waituhi to Wellington and from Wellington to Waituhi) recall the 'notion of moving on towards the point of departure',[17] also found in Maori cosmogony. Finally, the different temporal strands (present, recent past and far past) merge in the eternal dimension of the tangi, where life and death meet, a site governed by the time of myth. All these elements — development through contraction/expansion, movement forward to the place one came from, [18] use of the eternal time of myth — draw on the traditional Maori world view and are visually represented by the koru or spiral, an icon of Maori art. Comparing Aboriginal and Maori arts, Rask Knudsen argues that the Maori:

> conceptualize their world as revolving; it is 'a world that moves forward to the place it came from.' But while the circular and the linear alternate in Aboriginal iconography, in Māori visual art the two movements are integrated in the *koru* (the spiral), its most significant icon. The koru design denotes eternity and reflects a perspective on space similar to what is found in Aboriginal art: the world inhabited — and the artistic vision of it — embraces not one centre, but a multitude of centres. In visualising the principles of expansion and contraction, the spiral is a symbol of the Māori notion of moving on towards the point of departure. The spiral has no natural beginning or end, no uniform centre and periphery; these are in fact interchangeable — they 'flow into each other' as they do indeed in the composition of Māori carvings, where each ancestral image swirls and loops into the next.[19]

The spiral structure will also be found in Ihimaera's novel *The Matriarch* and in many of Grace's novels.

Mythological references are numerous in *Tangi* and constitute the outer frame that encompasses the story: a sort of 'mythscape', which contains and unites 'landscapes' and 'mindscapes', using Rask Knudsen's words.[20] The cosmogonic account of the epigraph is repeated in a more complete form on p. 26, and again at the very end of the last chapter.

> My mother was the Earth, my father was the Sky.
> They were Rangitane and Papatuanuku, the first parents, who clasped each other so tightly that there was no day. Their children were born into darkness. They lived among the shadows of their mother's breasts and thighs and groped in blindness among the long black strands of her hair.
> Until the time of separation and the dawning of the first day. (TA 26 and 204)

The parallel between Tama's parents and the primeval parents is reinforced at many points. In the train, he thinks of Rongo death directly in mythical terms:

My father was the Sky. He held dominion over night and day. He was both sun and moon, keeping constant watch over his children. Every day he arose to keep Papatuanuku warm. Every night he cast his wistful light upon her. Sometimes he wept and the dew of his tears fell softly upon her. She, to console him, grew beautiful with crops and fruit and flowers. And often she would rise with the mist from the hills and reach out to brush his sorrow away. (TA 52)

In the next lines, however, Tama says that while the primeval children, who were gods, wanted the separation of their parents to see the world of light, his separation from Rongo brings him only darkness. Here Tama is giving voice to his grief and fear for the future, but he is also rewriting the mythical account, producing a sort of variant. In doing so he behaves mythically, using Maori collective knowledge to express his personal experience and finding a place for it in the framework of a mythical system. The same interrelation between identity and myth is explained by Rongo to Tama in one of the flashbacks, when the child asks his father: 'E pa, what is a Maori?' (TA 48). Rongo's answer is the enumeration of the seven legendary canoes that brought the first Maori from Hawaiki to Aotearoa, which takes us back to the notion of subjectivity formed within a discourse that stresses the importance of ancestry (see chapter 1).

Natural elements also partake of the same world as human beings. Parallels between humans and natural elements are countless in *Tangi* and can be grouped into three main categories:

1. Definitions of humans as natural elements.
2. Personifications of nature.
3. Projections of one's feelings into natural images.

Most of these are repeated in various forms throughout the novel. The use of similar parallels in traditional oral literature is confirmed by the numerous waiata sung at the tangi, reported in Maori and translated into English, and which include many natural metaphors and similes.

An example of the first group is the simile between Tama's father and a kauri (native tree), 'E pa, you were a giant Kauri giving shelter to your family. One day, I too will be a Kauri.' (TA 29), which is repeated when Tama meets his mother at the funeral: 'Hold her closely, hold her tightly. Her body trembles with fear. And you must be a giant Kauri, spreading wide its sheltering branches' (TA 150). Several lines of a waiata describe the dead as an anchor and the living as shipwrecked people: 'Our anchor is gone and we/are cast adrift, at the/mercy of the sea …' (TA 147). A typical personification of nature is found in the repeated formula, 'It always rains when a Maori dies … because the wailing makes the sky sad' (TA 90). In a childhood episode 'the meeting house must have been very angry with us sometimes because we liked sliding along the floor' (TA 81), and in a waiata the tides take part in the tangi lamenting: 'Listen to the tides/Lamenting as they flow/Surging sullenly by/the Headland at Turanga' (TA 146). The third group is exemplified by Tama's gradual reaction to the news of his father's death, which are all expressed with natural metaphors. On hearing that there is a phone call for him from Waituhi, he feels 'a warm stream' flowing in his body. His sister's voice fills him with 'a flood of happiness', but then he notices her silence and 'a cold stream begins to seep into the warm flood'. His sister's voice 'breaks and driftwood splinters float in small eddies'. She begins to weep 'scattering the stream with a rain of tears' and a 'cold wind suddenly swirls across the waves' (TA 3). When Tama learns about Rongo's death he has a sort of vision, the canoe metaphor, which will be employed using variants several times in the book: 'And look: there is a small canoe adrift on the waves, the cascading sea, amid the falling rain' (TA 4).[21] The image of the canoe also emerges in a waiata: 'Through the spray of my glistening/tears, I see you, my father./ I weep, for the carved prow/sinks beneath the sea' (TA 153). Here the canoe image is a metaphor not for a feeling (loneliness or endurance), but for his father's end.

According to Jean-Pierre Durix's reading, *Tangi* has 'the splendour of a regressive dream but fails to take into account the inevitability of history'.[22] He stresses two continual shifts within the novel. The first is 'from an uncertain or anguishing present to a reassuring past'.[23] Therefore, Durix says, nothing is said about the negative aspects of the past, which is idealised. He also notices the typical transition from a 'he (or she) was' to a 'so I must be too' that sets the past as a model without which no positive step can be taken. The second shift is from wish to myth. An example he gives is Tama's desire to make time move faster, so that the ordeal of the tangi can be over and his grief too. In other points Tama wishes he could stop the clock, and go back to the time his father was alive. This recalls the demi-god Maui, who captured the sun in order to slow its race across the sky, giving longer days to the world of men. By resorting to myth as a way to endure hardship, Durix argues, Tama can avail himself of 'the immense possibilities opened by [its] imaginary power'.[24] Like Maui, Tama searches for immortality and the links he creates between myth and anguishing events of the present are a way to provide 'a cultural explanation of death'.[25] Durix also underlines that Ihimaera's picture of Maori society is one where the fusion between 'I' and 'you' is almost complete ('your heart is my heart'), and humanity seems intimately linked with the elements ('it always rains when a Maori dies'). While Durix's essay underscores all the most important points of the novel, providing a thorough representation of the Maori world view, his ultimate definition of it as 'a pure and imaginative vision of an idyllic past but also a very static one' and 'a regressive dream',[26] seems to be biased by a Eurocentric perspective. Durix's final lines, expressing his hope that Ihimaera's next novel in progress (*The Matriarch*) 'may well show the emergence of a different attitude towards the past',[27] confirm his lack of understanding of the Maori view of time.

Durix's reading can be called, to use Rask Knudsen's words, a 'Maorist' view. Rask Knudsen underlines how 'Aboriginalist and Maorist' views of indigenous cultures tend to depict them as 'static and unchanging'. On the contrary, she argues that:

> one finds, in both Aboriginal and Māori literature, a strong focus on movement, transformation and passage as integral aspects of the indigenous world-views and notion of creativity. The most explicitly literary expression of this dynamic power is found in the common theme of initiation or *rite de passage*. It evokes the ritual themes of symbolic death and rebirth and the breakdown of the cosmos into chaos, from which both the mind of the initiate and the order of the world will be reassembled.[28]

In later works, Ihimaera did not show the different attitude looked for by Durix. *Tangi* focuses on a rite of passage, by means of which those values and traditions that are endangered by the advance of Western progress are retrieved. It develops, as oral poetry, by means of repetitions, refrains, similes and metaphoric imagery. It gives a visual representation of a paradigmatic society — in its spiral form, treatment of time, reiterations of formulas and images, the search for links between parts and whole, the human world and nature, myth and history — and does not imply a view on race relations. As Corballis states, 'it is an in-depth study of Maori ways.'[29]

Ihimaera's approach becomes more political in *Whanau* and *The New Net Goes Fishing* up to *The Matriarch*, but these values and their underlying aesthetics are reaffirmed. The relationship between myth and history will be expounded in *The Matriarch*, with an attendant indigenous treatment of time. The power of imagination as an enabling force, to be preserved together with communion with nature, is a major theme in *The Whale Rider*. The perception of the world of *Tangi* as static is biased by a different notion of progress and dynamism. Most critics wonder whether Tama will actually come back to Waituhi or not.[30] Ihimaera's answer is found in his recent new version of *Tangi*, *The Rope of Man*, which confirms his will to represent the Maori paradigmatic reality (a cyclic and ordered cosmos) through the construction of a paradigmatic textual world (a fictional universe where the characters and places are reiterated in different stories and novels).

Whanau: an apology for bicultural integration

If *Tangi* focused on the growing consciousness of Maori identity in a single character, *Whanau* pictures the growing consciousness of a whole community. The novel depicts one Sunday in the life of Waituhi's inhabitants, including several well-known characters — Rongo Mahana and his wife Huia, Nanny Miro and her card game partner Maka — and some unknown. As in *Tangi*, Ihimaera's foreword introduces the subject of the book ('"*Whanau*" means *Family*, and *Whanau* is about/the extended family life of a rural Maori/community.'), functioning as a karanga ('Haere mai, come and meet them') that welcomes the reader into the novel and into the village, and establishes the novel's purpose ('Together they are *Family*, written both with/anger and with love — aroha — in the hope that/the values of that life will never be lost'). The inclusion of 'anger' in the writer's moods highlights the less lyrical and more problematic tone of this work.

The third-person narrative develops as a passage from a situation of disorder to one of reconstituted order. In chapter 1, members of the whanau are coming back to Waituhi from a wedding reception. It is four o'clock in the morning and Charlie Whatu is driving his truck. His wife is sitting next to him in the front seat, together with old Maka and a sleeping baby. All the other passengers are jammed on the back of the truck, drunk or sleeping. Hine Ropiho, her husband Jack, her son Boy Boy, Sam Walker, Mattie Jones, Joe, Sonny Whatu and others form a loud bunch of debauched people playing the guitar, singing, joking, getting sick and swearing. These characters, transported as goods, are actually the whanau's burden, no-hopers, people who stay in the village because they have failed and there is nowhere else to go. Although the narrator had announced eleven adults and three children on the back of the truck, not all are identified. This creates a trompe l'oeil effect, the sense that 'there is a greater number of people than those specifically named' and that 'the whole is greater than the parts'.[31] The community of Waituhi is the most important 'character' and is the focus of the book, but this image of corruption at the very beginning underlines its problems rather than celebrate its virtues.

The role of Waituhi as the central character is confirmed in chapter 2, which is completely devoted to the village. Its crisis, however, is reinforced by the emphasis on an external point of view, that of a stranger or tourist who could not help but notice its neglect and dereliction. Local people would likewise be surprised to find a stranger on the bus to Waituhi. The village is 'a backwater place and there is no reason why it should be here except this: the Whanau A Kai, the family of Kai, an ancestor, are the tangata whenua. They are the children of this land' (WH 7). But their number is small now and their representatives — the debauched in the first chapter and the two girls trying to sneak into their own houses unnoticed in chapter 3 — convey a sense of decay in a whole system. Janey Whatu and Hana Walker, Charlie's daughter and Sam's sister, feel trapped and dream of escaping. Throughout the novel they become the symbol of younger generations of Maori bored by the monotony of rural existence and irresistibly attracted by the possibilities offered by urban centres, like Netta in Hilliard's *Maori Girl*.

This gloomy view is reinforced in chapter 4, which contrasts the greatness of the past — the 'dreamtime before we were stripped of our dignity', before the Pakeha arrived and 'a way of life changed' (WH 16) — to the 'shame and poverty of the present' (WH 17). The breaking apart of communal life and family aroha is due to a broken bond with the land, which is partly sold off and insufficient for the sustenance of all its children, and the materialism of the dominating Western system that has created new needs for Maori. As Ojinmah points out, the family is 'the first casualty of both the new wave of individualism which Maori children are embracing and the deprivation of the "stress-absorbing" system of manaakitanga in the urban environment.' The word whanau is used by Ihimaera to symbolise 'Maoridom in microcosm'.[32]

A hint of hope is given by a sort of proverb that functions as a link with the next chapter, where the long gallery of characters that constitutes the novel begins: 'But when times move onward, always something is left behind' (WH 17). From chapter 5 the novel develops as snapshots of each family unit with no real plot, up to chapter 23 where all the whanau gets together for an emergency: the search, in the rainy night, for two runaways, Nanny Paora and his great-grandchild Pene. Until that point, the book provides an extensive cross-section of different attitudes towards the whanau, its values and traditions, among relatives of different ages. The narrator passes from house to house and scene to scene like a camera changing its focus and setting. Yet the passage from one chapter to the next is always linked to the whole in many ways: by references to other members of the whanau, who are seen therefore from different perspectives; by the gossiping of the kuia (old women) Maka and Mere; and by everybody watching everybody else, which actually constitutes the spirit of the clan. Nothing passes unnoticed, secrets cannot be kept, and children are constantly watched over by community members, who follow their wanderings from place to place, as Ojinmah points out.[33]

Reckless young people, liberated from the community's surveillance and going astray in urban areas, will be the subject of short stories in *The New Net Goes Fishing*, but here in the whanau they are kept under control by the 'collective eye'. The kite that Teria and Rawiri Mahana's children are playing with is another symbolic element to exemplify the links between the parts and the whole. It is noticed by many characters soaring and falling, and offers views of the reality below as in a vertical pan shot on film: 'Slowly the kite falls back to earth. Below is the village. The houses still look small from this height and the people even smaller' (WH 129).

In his monograph on the development of Ihimaera's political vision, Ojinmah groups *Whanau's* characters into four categories, according to their degree of biculturalism. They include:

1. Characters who can fit in neither world, Pakeha or Maori.
2. Characters who fit only in the Maori world and feel alienated in the Pakeha one.
3. Characters who reject Maori values and embrace Pakeha life.
4. Biculturally integrated characters.

Ihimaera considered biculturalism as the only possible solution for Maori to avoid the abysses of separatism and assimilation. A truly bicultural Maori is anybody who can 'effectively integrate his or her dual — Maori and Pakeha — heritage without feeling a stranger to either world'.[34] Of course, Ihimaera believes the same integration should occur to Pakeha as well.

Characters such as Mattie Jones, Jack Ropiho and Sam Walker belong to the first category. Each of them has already had a chance in the Pakeha world and failed. They consider Waituhi a prison, a 'nothing place' and a 'nowhere place' (WH 6). They are no-hopers who stay in Waituhi because there is nowhere else for them to go. As Ojinmah underlines, 'while these characters are not prepared to commit themselves to Maori society with its attendant obligations, they are nevertheless willing to benefit from that society's open-handed generosity.'[35] Sam, for example, is living in a tin shack in his Auntie Maka's backyard. He concluded his city experience with a two-year sentence in jail, like Peta in Finlayson's 'New Year', for bashing a taxi driver over the head. Sam's failure disgraced his father, Hepa, and raised tensions between them. In spite of this the community, as a larger encompassing body, takes charge of conflicts within the family.

Miro Mananui, Rongo Mahana and Charlie Whatu belong to the second group, made of people who fit in the Maori world only. They represent the older generation, which has never questioned its roots and whose identity is solidly bound to the earth. The core of their Maoriness is intact and they have accommodated Pakeha ways uneasily. Miro tenaciously believes in the importance of the annual Maori hockey tournament, as a moment of communal aggregation. Fearing she is too old and sick to look after the organisation as usual, she asks Rongo to take care of it. As we saw in *Pounamu, Pounamu*, she is the custodian of the village's treasures and continues fighting to keep the land of the whanau together, refusing to sell. Though Rongo is living in the city suburbs now, he and his wife 'could never break the emotional link between them and the village' (WH 48). On that Sunday, Rongo has come to Waituhi for the harvest, but he has found nobody else in the fields. The same thing happened on the day of the family planting. In the past every family who had left the village would come back on communal occasions like these. Rongo realises that times are changing: people working in the Pakeha urban world cannot afford days off, not only for communal activities but also for a funeral. He holds on to the old ways nevertheless, and identifies with the land. The same applies to Charlie Whatu who, while weeding the paddock around the meeting house with his son Andrew, does not feel time passing:

> After long apprenticeship on the land, Dad works with a freedom
> and fluidity of movement beautiful to see. At his own pace he
> works, each action measured to that pace. Time does not control
> him; he does not seem aware of time. He has lived his life at his
> own pace. (WH 120)

People like Rongo and Charlie Whatu, however, have encouraged their children to succeed in a Pakeha world dominated by the logic of money, speaking to them in English and paying for their education. Rongo's eldest son, Tama, works in Wellington (as in *Tangi*) and Charlie's son, Andrew, is studying for his admission to university. While Charlie is self-confident in his identity as Maori, Andrew lives in an amphibious condition:

> But I don't know who I am, Andrew says. Sometimes I'm Maori,
> sometimes I'm Pakeha, sometimes I'm half and half. You just don't
> understand Dad. (WH 68)

If a character such as Hana Walker, mentioned at the beginning of the novel, represents the third category Ojinmah illustrates — the restless young generation, disillusioned with rural existence and uncritically embracing the Pakeha world — then Andrew is a typical representative of Ojinmah's fourth category, which illustrates Ihimaera's notion of biculturalism. He may have doubts about who he really is but this amphibious state, acquired through education, is the way leading to bicultural integration. It can be defined a 'hybrid' condition, in Bhabha's words, or a 'composite' one, as Rask Knudsen prefers: a 'term embracing creativity as part of its intrinsic meaning', in contrast to Bhabha's 'inappropriately sterile synonym'.[36] Andrew poses questions about his identity. He feels 'caught in between, a Maori forcing himself against the values of the Pakeha world' (WH 67). However, he is moving forward, not renouncing his Maori roots but consciously reformulating his identity in a new context. Andrew is successfully going on with his studies and will probably make it in the Pakeha world. Even so, he tenderly loves his father (WH 98) and, like him, feels proud of their meeting house. The image of father and son working together to clean up the paddock around the wharenui exemplifies a balanced attitude towards tradition and modernity, confirmed by Andrew's final thought: 'A meeting house, it should never be locked' (WH 130). Andrew is the new Maori man, an example of composite identity that creatively reformulates the idea of being Maori in the present.

The same applies to Hepa Walker, another character included in Ojinmah's fourth group. Hepa is a man who holds a position of prominence in both Maori and Pakeha society and firmly believes that the problem with the Maori is more social than racial. In his view the salvation for Maori people lies in education and in their moving upward from working class to middle class. Hepa is not 'a brown Pakeha'. Ihimaera clarifies: 'It isn't as logical as people think, to assume that if you walk into a Pakeha life you walk away from Maori life.... No, Hepa Walker continues to be proud of his Maori blood' (WH 36), probably alluding to his own personal experience. He is the character that most embodies Ihimaera's belief in a pacific integration between the races, testified by his aversion to the belligerent attitudes of some young radicals who, in Hepa's view, promote discrimination and ill-feeling between Maori and Pakeha (WH 92).

Hepa also refers to the Maori as a warrior race, who these days do not need taiaha and mere, only 'the warrior tenacity ... to master the skills of the Pakeha life' (WH 37). This seems to foreshadow Alan Duff's point in *Once Were Warriors*, about indigenous responsibility in redressing the problems affecting Maori,[37] though Ihimaera never takes this discourse to its extreme consequences. Later in the book, Hepa is led to admit that 'perhaps warrior anger as much as warrior strength and tenacity is needed these days' (WH 93). Hepa Walker's perplexity coincides with Ihimaera's, and is probably what led him to his retreat from the literary scene for ten years, after the publication of *The New Net Goes Fishing*. Andrew and Hepa seem to be the most positive figures of the novel, however, educated and skilled in Pakeha ways and at the same time tied to Maoritanga and respectful of its intrinsic principles. They represent a composite person where the adjective 'composite' underlies richness instead of lack, affirmation instead of submission, activity instead of passivity, evolutionary dynamism instead of static essentialism.

After offering a picture of the complexity inherent in the idea of Maori identity in the modern world, Ihimaera ends his novel seeking a sense of unity and order, as shown by the whanau's collective search for Pene and Nanny Paora. The child has run away with his great-grandfather to prevent his Aunt Rosie from taking the old man away from him to a hospital or rest home. With the exception of Jack Ropiho (who becomes the symbol of irretrievable no-hopers) the event seems to be a collective, albeit minor, rite of passage, reinforcing to various degrees the characters' sense of belonging to the community and increasing their consciousness of its importance. The final lines describing the village asleep against the background of a reassuring mythical image is an optimistic sign that a redefined Maori identity can be asserted in a changing modern world:

> The moon brings peace to the land and peace to the people of the land. Rangitane, the Sky Father, ceases his struggle to clasp the Earth Mother, Papatuanuku. His tears diminish, he ceases to sigh. Papatuanuku folds the village and her children into her warmth, the warmth of Mother Earth. No matter if they love her or not, they are still her children and she will love them and protect them until, until …
> The village sleeps.
> Rongopai, the painted meeting house, still holds up the sky. (WH 173)

The suspension after 'until' is ambiguous. It might foreshadow an environmental concern: until mother earth has enough strength to do it, until she is alive. Or it could refer to the openness of myth, with its innumerable versions and retellings. The last comforting line about Rongopai, which 'still holds up the sky', marks an unquestionable hope in the future.

Ihimaera probes into the effects of Western individualism and 'progress' on Maori identity in *Whanau*. Some of his issues had already been explored by Finlayson and Hilliard, but while Finlayson posed questions without answers, Hilliard's shrewd vision anticipated the position Ihimaera is taking here and will be developed in later works. The survival of Maori does not lie in an essentialist return to a pristine past, but rather in a continuity that implies renewal and takes the present into account. This can be connected to Parry's and Hall's notion of nativism as an imaginative rediscovery of culture and heritage, suggesting a reconsideration of the present that values the past. It also alludes to an attitude of openness to mutual exchange and incorporating what the Western world of the present has to offer, foregrounded by Grace's observation: 'It's not sticking to the old ways that's important … but it's being us, using all the knowledge our way. Everything new belongs to us too.'[38]

'A Way of Talking': language experimentation in Grace's *Waiariki*

Waiariki narrates episodes in the life of a wide range of characters of different ages and gender. Each short story sets a point of view, reinforced by the first-person narration that Grace uses in all but one, 'The Dream', which is in the third person. As Pearson notes, memory plays an important part in her short fiction, in which 'the distinctions between a short story and meditative reminiscence' are often blurred.[39] The sense of a lost past in contrast with a problematic present emerges as a leading thread, a feature that characterised Ihimaera's *Pounamu, Pounamu* as well. Unlike Ihimaera's tendency to elegy and lyricism, however, Grace's mode is less emotional and more sober. She works on subtleties and shades instead of Ihimaera's brighter and more definite colours. As Nunns contends, she gives the reader an insight into a sense of psychic difference, 'of what it feels like to identify yourself as a Maori rather than as a member of any other group'.[40]

Another difference between the two authors is that there is no reiteration of characters in Grace's fiction; each work presents a distinct perspective, issue and setting (the only exception is the cycle of the so-called 'Mereana stories' in *The Dream Sleepers*, which were originally meant to form a novel).[41] Yet we find a set of natural images, mythical references and symbols cutting across her works and forming a subtext, which explains the characters' motives and connects them to a wider context of traditional knowledge. Grace does not build a paradigmatic textual world like Ihimaera, nevertheless her characters belong to the same world and share the same assumptions. Furthermore, Grace's narrative is more engaged in linguistic experimentation, showing her desire 'to write about a variety of ideas in a variety of ways'.[42] In her interview with Jane McRae, Grace underlines the fascination that the 'word', both written and oral, has always exerted on her:

> I remember being very interested in the written word and I read indiscriminately — words and sentences from the Weetbix packet, advertisements on trams, comics (we had a steady diet of these), library books and books that I received for my birthday....
> I am influenced by everything, including all forms of speech, whether it's conversation, stories, waiata, whaikorero, tauparapara, haka, chanting, Latin plainsong, radio and television commercials and programmes, news bulletins, talks, readings, lectures, sermons — it doesn't matter what. I'm used to listening, interested in the rhythms of speech and employ these rhythms in my work.[43]

The language used by Grace originates from her characters, from who they are and the way their stories develop. She describes her approach to writing as a sort of organic growth that shuns precise planning or outlines, but works on a 'natural progression' from one stage to another, starting from the idea of a character. Even the choice of genre is subject to this organic development and it 'depends a lot on the idea, though sometimes when beginning a piece of work, I am not sure whether it will be a short story or a novel.'[44]

Writing is likened by Grace to carving and weaving: 'A writer, like a carver, seeks to reveal what is within. A writer, like a weaver, selects the strands and works them together.'[45] Each short story (or novel) is therefore a self-standing unit, organically developed around a central core. But what links *Waiariki's* stories into a coherent volume is 'Grace's concern with Maori ways of understanding the world',[46] bit by bit, showing aspects and snippets of different people. In this sense Grace's fiction can be described as 'paradigmatic', like Ihimaera's, because it shows textually the 'integrated cosmos' of Maori, to use Rangi Walker's words.[47]

The importance of language is implied in the title of the first short story 'A Way of Talking'. Rose, 'the *kamakama* one of the family, and the one with brains' (WA 1), comes back home from Auckland, where she is studying at university, for her sister's wedding (kamakama means 'full of spirits'). The story is narrated by Rose's sister, the one with less brains but 'more sense'. When they visit Jane Frazer, the affable Pakeha tailor who is making the bride's dress, Rose soon notices the woman's unconsciously contemptuous way of referring to the Maori labourers working for her husband: 'He's been down the road getting the Maoris for scrub cutting' (WA 3). Mrs Frazer defines the workers as a racial category, without allowing them any individuality. They are 'othered' — that is, 'homogenised into a collective they' in Pratt's words[48] — a process typical of the coloniser's attempt to define the colonised as an abstract entity of pre-given traits and customs. By doing so, the former identifies the latter as the object of power, devoid of any agency or subjectivity, and reinforces the sense of 'self' as subject. In the context of this story Mrs Frazer's statement externalises her unexpressed will to put some distance between 'her' and 'them', and entails an implicit sense of superiority, which Grace subtly dismantles in two ways: by depicting Jane as a narrow-minded, middle-class provincial woman, in contrast to the highly educated and emancipated Rose; and by Rose's reaction, uttered in a high, deliberately 'Pakehafied' register that undermines Jane's certainties:

'Don't they have names?'

'What. Who?' Jane was surprised and her face was getting pink.

'The people from down the road whom your husband is

employing to cut the scrub.' Rose the stink thing, she was talking all Pakehafied. (WA 3)

While Rose's sharp comment first embarrasses her accommodating sister, the narrator comes to understand how useful Rose's reactive role is because it stigmatises prejudiced behaviours that would otherwise go unnoticed ('And how can the likes of Jane know when we go round pretending all is well?' [WA 5]).

Another reactive young woman is the protagonist of the last story of the collection, 'Parade', who returns from the city to her family in a rural area to participate in the celebrations for the carnival. The narrator feels a heaviness of spirit that she cannot explain at first, since she is at ease in the warmth of her family, but she later identifies an ability to look at her community from the outside and see how Pakeha view them. She feels uncomfortable in front of the Pakeha public clapping and cheering at them as if they were clowns in a circus, animals at the zoo or stuffed birds in a museum. Besides, she can see beyond the shallow friendliness of the authorities, who seem to remember and co-operate with the Maori community only once a year to put on the colourful spectacle for tourists. She feels angry at the condescension of her relatives as well. Like Rose in the previous story, the protagonist of 'Parade' cannot be silent and feels compelled to speak out, finally discovering that the elders are as aware of the patronising attitude as she is, yet they are proud of their traditions and believe it is the Maori duty 'to show the others who we are' (WA 88). Playing and singing traditional tunes or performing haka and action songs are not done for the benefit of a Pakeha audience only. It is instead a proud affirmation of their own identity and culture, grounded on the oral transmission of such rituals, music and songs. Grace will underline this in *Tu*, dealing with the Italian campaign of the Maori Battalion during the Second World War; Maori soldiers find the same attitude to music and songs in Italian culture, which becomes a major bond between them and the local population. In the end the protagonist of 'Parade' understands the elders' point and joins the performance with a renewed spirit.

The two stories, beginning and closing the collection, function as complements in showing a future direction for Maori. On one hand they should be agents of their destiny, taking responsibility for their rights and speaking out against stereotypes and prejudice. On the other they should preserve their traditions, which constitute their identity. It is no accident that the final image depicts the protagonist of 'Parade' reunited with her land and people, in a sort of ritual where nature, present and past, family and ancestors, reality and myth physically converge in her body, giving her new strength. This scene is followed by an untranslated chant in Maori, which closes the collection. Grace's message is not dissimilar from Ihimaera's: a moderate but steady stance that the future of Aotearoa/ New Zealand lies in the acknowledgement and respect of their dual heritage, and that literature and all artistic expressions can contribute to the development of a better understanding between minority groups and the dominant culture.

The other short stories of the collection add to the picture of the Maori world and its values. The elders' point of view is provided in 'At the River', 'Huria's Rock' and 'Transition'. The Maori value system appears in an unmediated form here via the elders. In 'At the River', an old woman is waiting for her husband, children and grandchildren at a camp by the river. The whole family is there for the annual eel fishing, which according to custom takes place at night. When the woman sees their torches in the distance, slowly coming back from the river, however, she already knows what has happened. A 'dream of death' had appeared to her and the morepork had flown above her head: these premonitory signs had announced her husband's death. The story narrates the community preparing for eel fishing, discussing old wisdom and new methods. The young do not want to follow the old ways and make fun of the elders, while the elders reproach them for their lack of respect. The whole story, narrated by the old woman as a stream of consciousness — and therefore presumed to be translated from Maori — is suggestive of a different rhythm and syntax from standard English. This composite language is what gives the story its flavour of the past, adding to the representation of the elders' vision, where present actions are connected to an ordered framework of traditions and wisdom, and using speech that makes frequent use of proverbs or sayings. The old woman's reproach to her grandchildren for their derisive remarks is: 'Enough to roll on the ground and punch each other, but the talk needs to stay in the mouth' (WA 14). When she suggests that the old man should stay with her at the tent, he answers: 'Always these hands have fetched the food for the stomach. The eels taste sweeter when the body has worked in fetching' (WA 12). Unusual word order (WO) and verb omissions (VO) in the narration signal a shift into the old woman's time and space co-ordinates, embodied in her language, as will be explored in chapter 8. The following quotations are complete sentences:

Happy they went with the gun. [WO] (WA 12)

> To the tent to rest after they had gone to the river, and while asleep the dream came. [VO] (WA 11)

The final contributing factor to the elders' vision is the old woman's reaction to her husband's death. The young are contrite for their previous mocking behaviour, but their grandma comforts them, because in the dream her husband appeared smiling 'with his hand on heart' (WA 11), and told her it was his time to go. The old man's passing away belongs to the natural course of life. The 'integrated cosmos' provides the explanation needed to-bear the inevitability of death and the sorrow it leaves in the living.

'Huria's Rock' follows a similar pattern. A man is looking after his baby grandchild sleeping in a tent on the beach, while all the family collect agar from the sea in the same place where the old man's wife Huria had drowned some time before. Another traditional Maori occupation is described and another premonitory sign is revealed to an elder. Huria's apparition is a warning that the child's life is in danger, and when its mother rushes back, called by the old man, she finds a dangerous spider on the child's blanket. As in the previous story, 'Huria's Rock' is narrated through the old man's stream of consciousness, which expresses the elders' world. The language used by Grace again reflects a marked influence of te Reo:

> Young days then I, and the leg without a stick to help it. Two good legs then, and a back strong. [VO+WO] (WA 48)

> Died here, my wife, when we last came to this place. [WO] (WA 49)

> To the rock then I, calling her name. [VO] (WA 49)

The central theme of 'Transition' is the bond between an elder and her land. An old woman, stricken with partial palsy, does not want to move with her family to the city, since she wants to die in the place she was born. They finally decide not to leave and to stay with her, showing the traditional Maori respect and care towards elders. Her stream of consciousness, employing the elders' language again, expresses the woman's gratitude to her relatives for their affection and her concern for their future.

The three stories typify how in Maori literature, the natural landscape — whether bush, the sea or a more generic land — is never seen in frightening or hostile terms, as it often was in Pakeha fiction. For settlers, the bush was a menace associated with irrational forces and the primitive other, as we saw in the literature of the colonial period. Land was an enemy to be tamed, as critically shown in Sargeson's *I Saw in My Dream* and in Finlayson's works. Conversely, in Grace's writing and Maori literature in general, humans are never frightened by nature, nor do they compete with the land. Rather they are a part of nature, and manifest respect and gratitude for its gifts. In the first two stories the supernatural is also treated as a normal part of life — there is nothing frightening or disquieting about it. Apparitions and premonitory signs belong to and are explained by the integrated cosmos of the Maori view. The supernatural is therefore tied to an ordered and comprehensible world, which differs remarkably from colonial literature where the supernatural was charged with dangerous and mysterious attributes, serving to stress the distance between the familiar, ordered rational world of the European and the strange, threatening irrationality of the Maori other. Furthermore, it takes us back to the Maori notion of the supernatural as 'literally true', in Barrowman's words, and its interrelation with Maori religious beliefs.

'Holiday', 'Waiariki' and 'Valley' mainly focus on children's experiences. 'Holiday' is the account from a girl's point of view of her annual summer holiday at her grandparents' home in the countryside. The cheerful communality of the extended family is reminiscent of Ihimaera's 'A Game of Cards' and 'Beginning of the Tournament'. It is a life of close family ties, human warmth, good spirits and outdoor physical games, probably inspired by Grace's own childhood experience among her father's whanau. The girl's change of name from Lynette to Atareta — the way her nanny calls her because of her resemblance to Auntie Atareta living in the South Island — seems to mark her natural passage into the Maori rural world, reinforced by the high frequency of Maori words included in the dialogues. The story has the freshness and immediacy of a school composition, and there is nothing nostalgic or sentimental about it.

By contrast, nostalgia is the main theme of 'Waiariki', where childhood is seen from the eyes of an adult regretting change and acknowledging its inevitability. The protagonist takes his family for a holiday to the place where he grew up but, as Nunns says, 'even the word "holiday" seems startling and a measure of the change that has occurred. His family are almost like tourists; their experience is far removed from the absolute involvement in the lifestyle that characterised his own childhood.'[49] When collecting kai moana (seafood) the man does not dare to tell his children of the rite he used to perform with his brothers to propitiate a good catch, that is to mimi (urinate) on their kits and then wash them with saltwater. On returning with half-filled kits, although the man rationally recognises 'several reasons, all of them scientific, why the shellfish beds are depleted' (WA 41), he cannot help feeling deep regret for not having performed his rite; 'The custom has come to symbolise a vanished way of life.'[50] Interestingly, as in Ihimaera's short stories, subjective memories of a past world and the present reality constitute two separate narrative strands, employing the habitual past tense and the more objective simple past respectively.

'Valley' explores a whole year in a rural school community from the eyes of an attentive teacher. Divided into four sections and subtitled by the seasons, it charts the children's growing self-assurance from an initial sense of displacement to the cheerful atmosphere of Auction Day, which closes the school year. The children learn about the world around them by following the natural progression of the seasons: watching caterpillars turning into butterflies in summer, checking the changing colours of tree leaves in autumn, feeding starving birds in winter, and planting seeds in spring. They create poems and drawings about their experiences, and mould clay into plants and animals. As Pearson notes, 'there is an awareness of weather, light, the seasons, always the movement and sound of children, ... of growth and death, and these are contained in a mood of contented acceptance.'[51] The external and internal worlds form a continuum, exemplified by the death of a teacher, which occurs in the winter section against a background of barren trees, cold wind and rainy sky (recalling *Tangi*, 'it always rains when a Maori dies'), as though the natural world appears to join in the mourning. Although the narration uses standard English and the pupils and teacher are never explicitly qualified as Maori, some of their names and most of their speech identify them as such. The teacher describes a boy's hair, sticking straight up on his head, as a 'kina' or sea urchin (WA 53), and when the teacher's baby wets himself, Samuel screams, 'Hey! You fullas little brother, he done a mimi. Na!' (WA 52),[52] which is unequivocally Maori English.

Two more stories are worth analysis for their Maori aesthetic in particular. One is 'Toki', which recalls a piece of oral narrative poetry and shares a timeless atmosphere. Language plays an important role and is again a composite English, owing much to Maori in terms of word order, sentence structure and syntax. The story tells of a fishing competition between Toki, a stranger, a 'boaster from the north', and the local fisherman who is the narrator. The contest is triggered by the attention that Toki arouses in the narrator's sweetheart. Numerous repetitions and refrains stress the oral quality of the story, as its opening reveals:

> From the north he came, Toki, in his young day. Ah yes. A boaster
> this one, Toki the fisherman.
> 'They are all there, the fish', he said. 'In the waters of the north.
> The tamure, the tarakihi, the moki, and the hapuku. And Toki,
> he has the line and the hand for all of them,' Toki from the north,
> Toki the fisherman. (WA 7)

The local fisherman will win the competition thanks to his knowledge of sea currents. His sweetheart will be reclaimed, the boaster unmasked and order re-established in the community.

The other story, 'And So I Go', is reminiscent of elegiac oral poetry. It is structured as a dialogue between the narrator, who is migrating, and a voice (in italics in the text), a sort of chorus representing his community, which does not want to let him go. His departure is necessary to 'learn new ways' and provide a future for the generations to come. This is a typical transitional story, reminiscent of Ihimaera's 'In Search of the Emerald City', but the mode is completely different. In a highly poetic prose, the exchanges between narrator and community evoke a whole world of warm ties among people and natural elements. The sea, the hills, the soil are addressed as human beings. The emotional landscape that constitutes Maori life emerges from deep within a community that is preoccupied by what the man is going to lose in his new life:

> And when you go our brother as you say you must will you be warm?
> Will you know love? Will an old woman kiss your face and cry warm
> tears because of who you are? Will children take your hands and say
> your name? In your new life our brother will you sing? (WA 45)

Interestingly, just as in 'Parade', singing is signalled as an identity trait, mentioned among the man's sentimental and communal bonds and equated with the love of relatives and family, a theme that will be developed in the novel *Tu*. The narrator is conscious of what he is leaving behind, but also of the renewal that must take place for his people's survival. The Maori holistic vision is forcefully evoked in the list of the things he will miss, starting with human affection, continuing with natural affection and ending in myth. Its structure is characteristic of ancient creation chants that are often deployed in Maori oratory:

> The warmth and love I take from here with me and return for their
> renewal when I can. It is not a place of loving where I go, not the
> same as love that we have known.
> No love fire there to warm one's self beside
> No love warmth
> Blood warmth
> Wood and tree warmth
> Skin on skin warmth
> Tear warmth
> Rain warmth
> Earth warmth

> Breath warmth
> Child warmth
> Warmth of sunned stones
> Warmth of sunned water
> Sunned sand
> Sand ripple
> Water ripple
> Ripple Sky
> (Sky Earth
> Earth Sky
> And our beginning) (WA 45)

In creation chants the birth of the cosmos is recounted as an evolution from an original nothingness, seen 'as the realm of potential waiting and pressing for its own fulfilment',[53] into the world of light and the beginning of life. The passage from one stage to another is an evolutionary progress that each element undergoes, assuming many forms. Similarly, the items on Grace's list are chained to one another in an organic but reversed order; not from myth to man, but from man to myth. The same word, concept or image (warmth/sunned/ripple) presents itself in different forms (Rain warmth, Earth warmth, Breath warmth) and evolves in this backward process toward the origins by connecting itself to the word or image in the next line or stage (Sunned sand/Sand ripple/Water ripple/Ripple sky). Here is an example of an ancient creation chant, illustrating the development of night into its numerous guises:

> The world became fruitful
> It dwelt with the feeble glimmering
> It brought forth night
> The great night, the long night
> The lowest night, the loftiest night
> The black night, the intensely dark night
> The night not to be touched, the night not to be seen
> The night not to be possessed
> The night of death.[54]

By enumerating all affective, natural and mythical components of Maori life and structuring them in a poetic form reminiscent of an oral chant, the narrator of 'And So I Go' offers a distinctive Maori view of the migrant's sense of lack and sorrow. In its content, the whole story is a poetic metaphor representing the condition of a minority group that must adjust to a dominant culture. In its style, it reveals the adjustment of a European genre to a Maori aesthetic, which so often characterises Patricia Grace's works.

A symbolic Maori dilemma: *Mutuwhenua*

If Grace's *Mutuwhenua* can be seen as a race relations novel, insofar as it includes the story of an inter-racial couple, a more careful reading shows that its focus is essentially on the protagonist, Ripeka, and on the forces acting upon her and driving her in two seemingly opposite directions. *Mutuwhenua* is a study of that amphibious condition that characterises young Maori and explored by Ihimaera in the characters of Andrew Whatu in *Whanau*, Tama in *Tangi* and, briefly, with the old man's niece Hera in 'The Whale'. Critics have often stressed that Ripeka's Pakeha husband, Graeme, is not a fully depicted character,[55] but Grace did not intend the novel to be his story. It is Ripeka's, as she argued in an interview:

> I am aware of some criticism of my non-Maori characters. Graeme isn't a fully drawn-out character. I didn't mean him to be because the story is mainly Ripeka's. The developers as well as the placard-bearers in *Potiki* have not been fully developed because it is not their story, even though they are part of it.[56]

The protagonist's upbringing as an only child by lovingly over-protective parents, within the wider context of an extended family, deeply marks her belonging to the Maori world. Yet the pull of Pakeha culture is too strong, as her voluntary change of name signals. She has been given two names by her family: Ripeka, after her grandmother, and Ngaio, after the ngaio tree that was planted at her birth, according to Maori custom (as we saw in Finlayson's 'The Totara Tree'). An analogy between human beings and trees is developed throughout the book, offering a symbolic subtext to the characters' behaviour and attitudes. At the end of primary school, which coincides also with her passage from childhood into adolescence and puberty, Ripeka renames herself Linda: 'I gave myself another name, Linda, certain that this was the beginning of a new, different life for me' (MU 24). After that new christening, Linda tries to be the person that her new name evokes. Her falling in love with a Pakeha guy, their marriage and subsequent suburban life outside the boundaries of her well-known and reassuring world all pertain to this new self. But Linda has not taken into account her 'essential nature',[57] which will be the cause of her profound crisis now she is far away in a strange city.

What Grace emphasises is not so much a difference pertaining to social background or lifestyles. Ripeka's initial anxieties derive from a typically adolescent insecurity — her fear of not being accepted or appearing inadequate — even though, to her surprise, Graeme's parents and house are very much like hers. Grace foregrounds a more profound difference, which pertains to the ontological grounds of Maori culture and is exemplified by the central episode of the greenstone patu. When Ripeka was nine, she, her cousins and a Pakeha councilman's son found an odd-shaped stone in the streambed on her grandfather's land. The Pakeha soon recognised that the stone was very old and valuable. The reaction of Maori and Pakeha to the discovery was quite different. The councilman merely viewed the object in terms of its economic value, while Ripeka's grandfather wanted to return it 'to the hills' (MU 7). They both realised that the patu had probably been buried with the body of an ancestor and so was tapu (sacred), and that a river flood had carried it away. But the councilman supported his son's claim that he alone had found the stone, put it in his car, and proposed a business agreement: '"It was my boy who found it," he kept saying. "But it's your land. There's something in it for everyone"' (MU 7). Finally, following the grandfather's whispered instructions, Ripeka's cousin removed the stone and hid it. Later they would bury it in a deep gully under layers of earth and rock. These events deeply affect Ripeka's perception of who she is and where she belongs: 'Because of my belief in the rightness of what had been done with the stone, my clear knowledge at nine years of age of the rightness (to me), I can never move away from who I am. Not completely, even though I have wanted to, often' (MU 9).

Ripeka knows she cannot share with Graeme the deep significance of this episode, later explained simply by her mother: 'You can't steal from the dead without harming the living' (MU 151). Neither could she share it with her Pakeha primary school mate Margaret. The conversation that takes place between the two girls — Margaret talking of her violin, Ripeka of her stone — is a sequence of alternated remarks that convey each girl's thoughts or emotions about her own object, but produce no communication. Anderson also notices that the conversation points to a number of similarities between the violin and the stone, 'yet each is so much a representative artifact of the opposing culture that these similarities act to emphasise the immense differences between the two and, by extension, between the Maori and the *pakeha* worlds. Ripeka now becomes aware for the first time that her Maoriness sets her apart from people like Margaret.'[58] Nonetheless, she is irresistibly attracted to Graeme and the Pakeha world.

The awareness that 'in some things there can be no bridge to understanding' (MU 121) is the book's central theme and this becomes

Ripeka's dilemma too, together with her fear that such a cultural gap may alienate Graeme's affection for her, as she says: 'I don't know him; he doesn't know me. Love is what you know' (MU 134). The difficulty of bridging differences appears again at the end of the book when, now pregnant and living in the city, Ripeka is affected by terrifying dreams of a tattooed woman who haunts her every time she falls asleep, reclaiming her and her unborn child. Ripeka comes to feel that the house where they are living is unsafe for her, and falls prey to depression and physical exhaustion that threaten the well-being of her and her baby. Although Graeme is a good and caring husband, her fear that he cannot understand makes her reluctant to speak to him and worsens the situation. The answer comes in a letter from her mother who, after consulting Nanny Ripeka, explains that 'these are old matters'. The house has probably been built on a burial place and 'should be left to those who were there first' (MU 129). Supported by her parents, Ripeka finally finds the strength to open her heart to Graeme and they move to another house.

The novel subtly explores cultural differences entirely from a Maori viewpoint. When Ripeka finally externalises to Graeme what was in her that was 'buried and unchangeable and significant' (MU 137), and her feeling that a part of her belongs to 'a different time' (MU 136), she finds a lovingly and totally comprehensive partner who accepts the fact he might not fully understand what he does not know but, nevertheless, trusts her: 'You're the one to know you are right and it's not for me to question what you know' (MU 137). Graeme is open to the possibility that another approach to reality can exist, based on other ontological grounds.

Like *Waiariki*, *Mutuwhenua*'s purpose is to 'show others who we are'. The character of Graeme may be only partly realised or as Nunns argues, 'defined more by what he lacks in Maori terms than by what he is',[59] but the objective of the novel is to show a Maori perspective on subjects of importance to Maori, as Grace herself confirms:

> Cross-cultural decisions are always tough for someone. Most often it's the Maori people who have to go across the gap. In *Mutuwhenua* the Pakeha person is in the position that the Maori usually occupies, but Graeme realises that 'even with differences you can be open to knowing' and Linda feels that he will trust her.[60]

It is this principle that underlies Ripeka's final decision to have her newborn baby fostered by her mother, when she learns that her father died almost simultaneously with the baby's birth. This ending has puzzled many Pakeha readers and critics, since the decision is made by Ripeka only, confident that Graeme will understand.[61] An indigenised reading, however, provides a better understanding. As Anderson argues, Ripeka's choice:

> comes as a shock to most readers unfamiliar with Pacific Island cultures and with the custom of giving a child to a relative who needs or will need the child for psychological or physical support, but it is quite common among the Maori: 'Adopting children was common practice. It was, however, limited to relatives, being used to revive relationships weakened by distance and to keep warm rights of inheritance.' Ripeka is also aware that her son can only remain a Maori if he is taught the old ways — if he has links to the land.'[62]

This is confirmed by the author herself in McRae's interview, when she mentions that unlike Pakeha, Maori readers do not have difficulty with the way *Mutuwhenua* ends. According to Grace:

> There wasn't any issue to resolve. Linda behaved correctly because she did not go away and leave her mother without a family. Also she was giving her child the privilege of being brought up with elders and of living on his own turangawaewae.[63]

In exploring the dilemma of a Maori woman bestriding two worlds and in highlighting the inalienable constituents of her identity, Grace's stance becomes implicitly political, insofar as she does not try to mediate between different ontological grounds. An indigenised reading leads to an interpretation far removed from Beston's argument that Grace's desire not to hurt anyone, especially the Pakeha public, makes her transfer the problems in Ripeka's marriage from the personal sphere to 'Linda's racial unconscious alone'.[64] Beston is implicitly devaluing the importance of a racial unconscious, while Grace acknowledges its determinant influence in directing and affirming Ripeka's agency.

Finally, Grace uses certain mythical or natural images in the book to trace a symbolic subtext, which cuts across her works and draws on traditional knowledge. As already mentioned, Ripeka's other given name is Ngaio, after the tree that was planted at her birth. The narrator explains that a ngaio tree has a 'peaceful appearance' from some distance, but when you get closer to it 'you discover the pained twisting of its limbs and the scarring on the patterned skin' (MU 1). Ripeka's turmoil and interior oscillations are exemplified by its shape. Next to it is a ti kouka or cabbage tree, brought down from the bush when her father was a small boy. The ti kouka is his tree. On the last page, after her father's death, Ripeka plants another ti kouka for her son, the same tree as her father's because the little boy is going to take his place in the family. Both ngaio and ti kouka are sheltered by the big macrocarpa, a centenarian tree with thick, heavy roots that spread wide and deep. The macrocarpa stands for the ancestors and for Maoritanga, protecting the other two smaller trees from the strong wind and the sun's ferocity. Without the macrocarpa's strength, they 'would not have taken root and flourished' (MU 2).

The ngaio tree is connected to another subtext, the legend of Rona, which concludes the novel. Rona's image is employed, here as in *Potiki*, to symbolise a person whose roots are shallow and who is easily taken astray. According to this legend, on a night of Rakaunui (full moon) Rona went to the spring to fill her calabashes, but the moon suddenly became obscured by a passing cloud and Rona tripped, cursing the moon. Hearing this, the moon came down and snatched her up. Rona caught at the branch of a ngaio, but the tree was uprooted and taken to the sky with her. At full moon she can be seen on its surface, still clutching the tree and her calabashes (MU 154). In the last lines of the book, Ripeka evokes Rakaunui and the story of Rona, tracing an analogy between herself and the mythical heroine. This is reinforced by the two episodes about Graeme's gradual entry into her family, which both occur at Rakaunui: the weekend at the beach seashell fishing and the Easter weekend. Graeme 'snatches' Ripeka from her world just as the moon does Rona. The legend comes to symbolise Ripeka's predicament and her fear of being uprooted. In *Potiki* Roimata feels in danger of floating away and becoming a 'sky dweller'[65] like Rona, and for this reason she marries Hemi, a man who is solidly bound to the earth. On the other hand, Ripeka's marriage to a Pakeha undermines her stability.

'Mutuwhenua' means 'the phase when the moon is invisible', a concept foregrounded by the subtitle 'The Moon Sleeps' (often omitted in recent editions). In the novel, different phases of the moon accompany narrated events, symbolising new stages in the story. At full moon, the family goes seashell fishing, following the good tide. That is the time when Graeme becomes a member of Ripeka's family. He practices kina diving, collects mussels according to traditional Maori methods aimed at avoiding the depletion of the seabed, and listens to talks about sacred hills that must be defended by future generations. This episode is an important step in his approach to Maori culture, probably affecting his later openness to a different set of values. The full moon is a positive symbol of growth, change and development. At Mutuwhenua or new moon, on the contrary, Ripeka is on her grandmother's veranda, prey to doubts and confusion around what the old lady has told her (she strongly objects to her marrying a Pakeha). The absence of moonlight is a metaphor for darkness, confusion, a standstill. The title thus refers to Ripeka's amphibious condition and to her dilemma in mediating her essential nature and the pull of the dominant culture.

Parallels between people and trees that we find in *Mutuwhenua* can be connected to a customary ritual and a legendary figure, Rona, and continue in another text, *Potiki*. Rona's image becomes a symbol of all 'sky people', who are an inspiration for other characters such as Mata in *Cousins* (1992). In Grace's works the notion of sky dwellers or sky people recurs and is the subject of her collection *The Sky People*. There is a unifying thread in Grace's works, drawing on myth, natural parallels and legends, which constitutes a subtext and connects characters and events to a mythical or racial collective unconscious. The final message of the novel advocates biculturalism as opposed to assimilation — the possible coexistence of different cultures through equality and mutual respect — and the importance of holding to one's identity. As Grace says, Ripeka 'can leave her place of birth and family behind, but she takes her roots, her treasures, with her.'[66]

Strategies of Resistance: Radicalisation in the 1980s

The works of the pastoral period did not constitute an overtly political act, nevertheless they signalled a remarkable change in Anglocentric New Zealand literature. Maori critic Powhiri Rika-Heke sees them as 'subtle but powerful critiques of the effects of colonisation and the colonising culture, as well as a defence of the indigenous one, embodying a specifically Maori sense of being.'[1] In previous chapters, the close reading of early fiction from Ihimaera and Grace according to an indigenised perspective foregrounded the foundational principles of their world views, as well as stressing the appropriation of European genres that necessarily took place in the process of textualising their heritage and experiences. Later on, these two writers became more consciously political, focusing on the difficulty of race relations in urban contexts and the injustices resulting from colonisation. Three major 'evils' were stigmatised:

1. Faults in the Eurocentric education system, causing dropouts among Maori students and the attendant social consequences such as a general proletarisation of the indigenous minority and widespread criminality among their youth.
2. Conscious repression of Maori language by increasingly dominant English speakers.
3. Alienation of tribal land.

Ihimaera's and Grace's radicalisation coincided with the rise of Maori political activism, as we saw in chapter 4. Yet whether or not Maori literature is overtly political, its subversive power lies mainly in writing back — to paraphrase Rushdie — to those Western texts that formed the dominant discourse; in other words, in the way Maori writers consciously used strategies that ensured texts were transmitted the way Maori wanted them to be. Among the most common examples, Rika-Heke describes how incorporating aspects of oral literature into writing and the inclusion of te Reo helped to emphasise its place as a living language together with English. The most frequently employed strategy, however, was 'to overcode the central meaning with ritual, spiritual or mythological references to Maori culture,'[2] an approach reflected in the oral qualities and spiral structure of Ihimaera's *Tangi* and in the focus on Maori spirituality in Grace's *Mutuwhenua*. This strategy was foreshadowed in many earlier stories, such as Ihimaera's 'Tangi' and 'The Whale' and Grace's 'At the River', 'Huria's Rock' and 'Transition'. The accommodation of the Western canon to the Maori view, history and mythology is a political act itself, as Rika-Heke argues:

> What characterises this kind of writing is not simply the introducing of the history of colonial oppression, but the struggle for control of the word. Writing retains the seeds of self-regeneration and the power to create and recreate the world.[3]

Rika-Heke suggests that the main challenge to hegemony — the authorised version of the dominant group — is 'control of the word', which leads to 'the creation of the world', providing a figurative, indigenous answer to the Marxist-based postcolonial notion of the text as ideological discourse (see chapter 1).

This chapter will analyse examples of overtly political denunciation in the writing of Ihimaera and Grace, as well as the continuation of subtler strategies to undermine the monocentric view of imperial power, which reach their climax in Ihimaera's *The Matriarch* and in Grace's *Potiki*. In these two major works, political stances and appropriation of the Western canon mix into a composite indigenous literary text, which recreates a 'world' through the 'word'.

The construction of a paradigmatic world that is contained within a frame, which had characterised Ihimaera's *Pounamu, Pounamu*, continues in *The New Net Goes Fishing*. The title of this collection evokes a whakatau a ki (Maori proverb), printed in the frontispiece, which figuratively stresses a turning point in the author's way of dealing with Maori preoccupations, his emphasis on the present and on the necessity of renewal:

Ka pu te ruka, ka hao te rangatahi
The old net is cast aside, the new net goes fishing.
A new generation takes the place of the old ...

The first and last short story, which are both centred on the protagonist (Matiu) of 'In Search of the Emerald City', constitute its frame. 'Yellow Brick Road', opening the collection, is the account of his family's car journey on the day they move from Waituhi to Wellington. If Matiu's previous story was imbued with melancholy, this one is tinted with sombre colours. The title refers to Baum's *The Wizard of Oz*, where four protagonists 'follow the yellow brick road' leading to the fabulous 'Emerald City', but in Ihimaera's story the road is instead made yellow only by the headlights of the many cars rushing past. It is pouring down, nobody helps them when they run out of petrol, and Matiu's father is soon involved in an argument with a Pakeha driver, who addresses them with racist epithets: 'You Maoris are all the same. Dumb bloody horis'[4] (NN 5). These signs allude ominously to the conflicting urban reality that will be illustrated further in the book. The collection ends with 'Return from Oz', which is set 20 years later and reiterates the reference to Baum's story. Matiu is by now a successful lawyer, married to a Pakeha, and father of a young child, Christopher, who is as excited to leave for Waituhi as Matiu had been 20 years before migrating to Wellington. But the family is not moving this time, only driving Matiu's father to the village. Recently widowed and ageing, the old man wants to spend the rest of his life in Waituhi and be buried there together with his wife. Matiu represents the Maori who has made it in the Pakeha world and is a symbol of Ihimaera's advocated biculturalism — meaning a bicultural integration and not assimilation — that implies the acceptance of a dual heritage: Pakeha and Maori.[5]

There are many aspects of the story that add up to a vision of society where Maori heritage is not dead, but actually co-habits with Pakeha blood and culture: Matiu's loving attentions towards his father; Christopher's affectionate care for his grandfather and his interest in the stories he learns from the old man; the fact that the child can answer in Maori to him; finally, the respect of all the family (including Matiu's Pakeha wife) for Maori traditions, exemplified by the prayer and waiata recited in Maori by the grandfather before departure. 'Return from Oz' seems to indicate the path Aotearoa/New Zealand could take to achieve a more peaceful future condition, by respecting the dual soul of the country. In spite of this, a shade is cast: Matiu's sister, Roha, does not show up to say goodbye to her father. Matiu and Roha come to symbolise contrasting models of urbanised Maori: the biculturally integrated one and the one who has been assimilated into Western individualism.

Roha is the last of a series of characters and images in the collection that point to how Maori values have come under severe strain in the city. As Ojinmah notes, 'Ihimaera in *The New Net Goes Fishing* analyses the break-up of the family unit and the loss of the community spirit and solidarity on which the culture had hitherto depended and by which it had always been sustained.'[6] The first ones to pay for this condition are children and teenagers, who are easy prey to criminal gangs, drinking and drugs, and grow up as socially marginalised underdogs, doomed to be part of a disempowered Maori proletariat. This issue, foreshadowed by Finlayson and Hilliard, is explored by Ihimaera in several stories, including 'Big Brother, Little Sister', 'The Kids Downstairs', and 'Passing Time'. In 'Big Brother, Little Sister', two children are the victims of violent and neglectful adults who have become individualistic and place their own gratification above family responsibilities. They run away but, on reaching Wellington railway station and walking through an indifferent and chaotic city, realise that the only home they have is, ultimately, their disrupted family. 'The Kids Downstairs' depicts five Maori teenagers with no dreams or plans for their future, living off the earnings of the only one of them working and spending their time partying, boozing and smoking. They are befriended by the couple upstairs — a middle-class Maori civil servant, Rangi, and his Pakeha wife, Susan, a librarian — who act as normative elder siblings. But the 'not to worry'[7] philosophy prevails and, in the end, when the working girl decides to move out, the group splits and leaves the apartment. Ojinmah notes that 'they are content to drift on the brink of society, neither part of the society, nor outside it. In Ihimaera's view, these characters are too rootless and too unconcerned about their future to be biculturally integrated.'[8] The story also shows the degeneration of traditional communal spirit in urban contexts, turned into a parasitic, hopeless, hand-to-mouth lifestyle. The same attitude is found in 'Passing Time', where a gang of teenagers spend their days at the railway station harassing strangers and waiting for the police to arrive. This is basically a game for the youths — a way to pass their time — and the crucial question posed by the story is: 'Passing time between what?' (NN 66).

Grace poses similar questions in 'The Dream Sleepers' and 'Letters from Whetu', from *The Dream Sleepers*. In the first story she exemplifies the disruption of family bonds by describing the daily routines of members of urban working-class families, who end up never meeting. The first shift comes on at three in the morning, the second at five, the third (mainly students) at seven. The 'three o'clockers' and 'five o'clockers' are the ones who never get to dreaming because they are always woken up so early; the only 'dream sleepers', therefore, are the young. This implication sounds ironic, as there seems to be no space for dreams in their dull days at school. In the second story, the narrator writes to a friend that she hardly ever sees the members of her family: 'Anyway he's [Dad is] so busy and on so many committees — marae committee, P.T.A., Tu Tangata, District Council — and Mum's almost as bad.' (DS 34).

If the hope of success in Pakeha society for Maori youth lies in achieving school qualifications, both writers question the validity of an education system based on subjects, knowledge and teaching methods that do not take into account the specificity of their students and are meant to enforce assimilation into the dominant culture. In her article 'Politics and Literature' published in 1985, Miriama Evans argued that:

> Maori readers have been besieged from early childhood with literature patterned by often unintelligible symbols of another culture.... The result of Maori children having been continually bombarded with irrelevant, extraneous, reading material is a population that chooses not to read.
>
> There are overt signs that contradict the popular beliefs that Maori population won't read, let alone buy books. Spiral's distributor has been astounded by orders of *the bone people* for small Maori settlements way off the beaten book seller's track.[9]

Evans' reference to the importance of culturally relevant texts for a junior reading public can be extended to adult readers as well. This validates the argument of text as ideological discourse dealt with in chapter 1, and underlines the crucial role of Maori writing not only in the cultural domain but also in the educational one, with its attendant consequences for the advancement of Maori in New Zealand society. Evans' comment also provides a subtext to Ihimaera's and Grace's pages about the alienation of Maori students at school and their predicament in successfully completing their studies. Ihimaera's 'Catching Up' tells about Jimmy Heremaia (one of the children in 'The Other Side of the Fence') and his long, troubled education. Thanks to his parents' tenacious support, which reinforced his self-esteem and motivations — and despite the discouraging influence of Pakeha teachers — Jimmy finally ends up with a bachelor of arts degree. But at his graduation day ceremony Jimmy realises that he does not understand a single word of what an old relative tells him in Maori: 'He had won, but he had also lost' (NN 62). In 'The Dream Sleepers', the time spent in the classroom is devoid of any significance for Maori students. The reader follows the stream of their thoughts aroused by the teachers' words or by schoolwork, their observations of the world outside the windows, and their side activities such as drawing a snake coiling around a schoolmate's arm (which engross them far more than the educational content). Their assignments include, ironically, copying out a section from the textbook entitled 'Our Heritage', which shows 'all the things that have been handed down to us by the people of Ancient Greece' (DS 8). The gap between school and students' interests is stressed by the continual shift from the formality of the teachers' English to the students' hybridised version of it, mocking the 'authorised version' of the language and responding using the imperfect rhymes of a song, as this example illustrates:

> 'So there you are. Your address, top right-hand corner. Business address — "The Personnel Officer, New World Supermarket", etcetera — below on the left... .'
> 'Buy a bigga block cheese... .'
> 'Then below that, "Dear Sir"... .'
> 'How a-are ya?'
> 'Then you start... .'
> 'I'm all ri-ight.'
> 'All right, no more nonsense, get on with it. Pele you shouldn't be wearing that hat in class should you?'
> 'Sir he can't help it his sister gave him a Kojak.'
> 'There's still plenty of hair on his head.'
> 'She gave him a kina.' (DS 6–7)[10]

Experimenting with language and narrative form is one of Grace's most self-evident acts of resistance to the dominant canon. As Evans underlines:

> Publishers and their authors have shown a colonial bias which refers back to an English tradition for comparison of standards. The criteria for acceptance has worked against Maori writers who have sought to incorporate bilingualism and to integrate Maori and European traditions.[11]

Referring to Simms' article (analysed in chapter 4), Evans also mentions that Grace was 'challenged for her experiments with language in *Waiariki* and that Keri Hulme's novel *the bone people* was rejected by several publishing houses as simply "too unorthodox".'[12] 'Letters from Whetu' is another story revolving around language and form experimentation. It consists of four letters written by a girl, Whetu o te Moana (Star of the sea), to her friends at different periods of her school day 'as part of [her] anti-boredom campaign' (DS 39). Whetu is the only Maori student left in Sixth Form (Year 12); all her friends have dropped out or are repeating lower forms. Her hilarious letters are mocking reports about the lecturing styles and idiosyncrasies of various teachers, yet they also express her feelings about what is really important in her life: in particular, the day spent at the seaside with her friends, and a song they are collectively composing. Teachers are described as show performers. Ms Fisher is 'sort of poised like an old ballet dancer', while lecturing on Katherine Mansfield (DS 29). The maths teacher resembles a clown needing 'a foot drum and some side cymbals' to complete his performance (DS 33). Whetu's letters are pieces of creative writing that include a few verses and a final song.

The most creative part of the story, however, is Whetu's language, which is a mix of Maori English expressions (in a juvenile version faithfully reproducing oral jargon) and abbreviations that anticipate those used in text messages of modern cellular telephones. Sentences like 'Gotta go', 'Howzat?', 'It wuz tanfastic [sic] bowling around in those breakers', 'Well I Dunno' and 'Inaminnit' belong to the first group. The second group includes 'mthmtcl' (mathematical), 'srfbrd' (surfboard), 'wrkng' (working), 'wknd' (weekend) and '4' (for). Importantly, Whetu claims her right to reinvent English throughout her letters, as seen in her play on the words 'yous' (a typical 'mistake' of Maori English) and 'use':

> I sometimes do a bit of a stir with Fisher, like I say 'yous' instead of 'you' (pl.). It always sends her PURPLE. The other day I wrote it in my essay and she had a BLUE fit. She scratched it out in RED and wrote me a double interlined note — 'I have told you many times before that there is no such word as "yous" (I wonder if it hurt her to write it). Please do not use (yous heh heh) it again.' So I wrote a triple underlined note underneath — 'How can I yous it if it does not exist?' (DS 29)

Whetu is basically criticising the authorised version of English imposed by the colonial centre, questioning the authority of grammar rules taught at school and, indirectly, advocating Maori rights to appropriate English to their own usage. Another example is her political pun on 'heart': 'She [her teacher] knows her K.M. off by heart, bless her HART (Halt All Racist Tours), punctuation and all' (DS 30).[13]

The Dream Sleepers is divided into two parts. The first and last story of Part One could be considered a frame to all the others, reporting the point of view of young ('The Dream Sleepers') and of old ('Journey') urbanised Maori.

Part Two is a standalone series of episodes about the same characters, passing from childhood to adolescence.[14] Two further episodes of the saga, 'Boiling' and 'The Urupa', are included in the later collections *The Sky People* and *Electric City*. Since Part Two essentially revolves around childhood life in a rural extended family, whose values have been already analysed, those stories will not be examined in detail. Nevertheless it is worth mentioning that Grace's insight into child psychology is remarkable, as was previously noticed with 'Holiday' and 'Valley'. Her accounts of childhood can be considered as a Maori counterpart to Mansfield's 'Sun and Moon', 'Prelude', 'The Garden Party' and 'At the Bay'.

Two stories by Ihimaera that carry an overtly political message on race relations are 'Clenched Fist' and its sequel 'Tent on the Home Ground' from *The New Net Goes Fishing*. Corballis and Garrett include them among the 'barely-disguised sociological treatises which exist merely for the sake of their "message" and do not really warrant literary investigation'.[15] Such a trenchant comment is clearly not shared by the Nigerian critic Ojinmah, whose perspective instead emphasises the social role of writers, following Chinua Achebe's lesson.[16] Consequently he views the stories as a significant step in Ihimaera's gradual radicalisation and hence worthy of analysis. These contrasting positions raise the question: according to which cultural and critical criteria should indigenous works be judged? Moreover, can a critic's concerns determine what an indigenous work should be about? As argued in chapter 4, Maori writing poses formal challenges to critical orthodoxies. If the straightforward polemical nature of Ihimaera's aforementioned stories was considered a flaw by Pakeha mainstream criticism, it was not recognised as such by an indigenous critic from another postcolonial country. An indigenised reading allows the critic to vocalise indigenous concerns and be open to new composite forms, as we will see in the next chapter in relation to *The Matriarch* and *The Dream Swimmer*.

'Clenched Fist' and 'Tent on the Home Ground' explore divergent views on the solution to racial problems in Aotearoa/New Zealand: the moderate one, embodied by a white-collar, middle-class Maori, George; and the separatist one, represented by radical Api. Both stories follow a similar pattern. Although George's milder position seems well founded, the polemical force of Api's arguments ends up instilling doubts that make him see racial problems in a new light. In 'Clenched Fist', George mocks Api's use of imported Afro-American terms and expressions that, in his view, do not apply to the New Zealand context, such as 'white racist system', 'white regime', and 'blacks' used to define the Maori. Api reproaches him for being 'tamed', 'caged', 'sold out to the Pakeha' and an 'Uncle Tom' (NN 38–39). If for Api the only solution is to 'fight back', 'protest', and 'be political', George's attitude recalls that of

Hepa Walker in *Whanau*: 'Get back our Maoritanga, yes. But don't divide us in the process ... You protest your way, Api, I'll protest mine' (NN 41). George's convictions, however, are shaken at the very end of the story, when he sees a Maori woman almost run over by a car at an intersection and then insulted with a racist epithet: 'Get back you black bitch' (NN 42). 'Tent on the Home Ground' opens at a pub where George is celebrating the promotion of one of his Pakeha colleagues. Api's arrival triggers an argument, since he provocatively suggests that the 'white system' allows only Pakeha to occupy positions of power. Api's extreme statements annoy George's Pakeha colleagues, so much so that one of them finally comments: 'The black bastard ... He'll never win'. Later on, George will join Api in the tent pitched in front of Parliament to protest against Pakeha encroachment on Maori land.

Both stories have an open ending and do not offer a recipe for racial conflicts. Yet, as Ojinmah underlines, in the end 'George ponders if Api and his friends are right in their advocacy for separatism'.[17] This reflects Ihimaera's dilemma. George's doubts are counterbalanced in 'A Sense of Belonging' (included in the 'sociological treatises' by Corballis and Garrett), where a Pakeha bank manager takes sides with a Maori teller, humiliated by the racist behaviour of a Pakeha customer who refuses to be served by her. But in 'Masques and Roses', Ihimaera subtly describes a Pakeha mother's uneasiness about facing the reality that her daughter is dating a Maori boy. The woman does not want to admit the reason for her frustration, which she vents on a vase of roses, arranging and rearranging them.

While offering a range of different points of view on race relations, *The New Net Goes Fishing* also conveys Ihimaera's growing uncertainty about whether or not biculturalism can be achieved peacefully. Roha's behaviour in the last story 'Return from Oz', for example, marks her as a character who symbolises the impending danger of assimilation and loss of Maori identity. The story that probably best summarises Ihimaera's dilemma is 'Truth of the Matter', which presents four different versions of the same incident: the assault and robbery of a Pakeha taxi driver by two young Maori. Each version is apparently convincing, but ultimately none can be trusted. The taxi driver pictures the incident as a premeditated act of racial violence and expresses the white conservative view that the only way to cope with young Maori criminality is to enforce strict laws. His reaction embodies the Pakeha fear of the other, exemplified by his description of the two Maori as 'apes', 'just animals', 'filthy', and 'starved for sex'.

One of the two Maori offers an entirely contrary version, where the assault is depicted as a reaction to racial discrimination. In his view the taxi driver was aggressive, provocative and racially biased, and also tried to cheat them on the fare. The account of the other Maori, relating the incident to his father, pictures the taxi driver as a good man and puts all the blame on his mate and on the fact that they had no money to pay. The fourth version is from a bystander, a girl supposedly under the effect of drugs or alcohol, who transforms the event into an aesthetic experience. 'Truth of the Matter' is a central story because it embodies the spirit of the collection. First, it denounces a situation but openly renounces the search for a solution, like most of the other stories characterised by open endings. Second, it challenges the existence of an objective reality, implying that history is always subject to the point of view and is therefore a story. The first aspect reflects Ihimaera's growing concern about his position, which led to his ten-year self-imposed embargo on writing after *The New Net Goes Fishing*. The second aspect suggests his resolution ten years later, when he wrote *The Matriarch* and gave his indigenous perspective on New Zealand history (see chapter 7).

As for Grace, her most overtly political story in *The Dream Sleepers* is 'Journey', where she contrasts Maori and Pakeha concepts of 'land' and 'development', an issue furthered in *Potiki*. As Sargeson and Finlayson underlined, to Pakeha the land is something to submit and bend to their will; the relationship is fundamentally monetary and economic. On the other hand, Maori have a spiritual bond with nature in general, and with ancestral land in particular. The protagonist of 'Journey', an old man travelling to Wellington to arrange for his land to be subdivided, reflects this point of view. The subdivision is necessary so that his nieces and nephews can build their own houses and stay on the land. During his train journey, his stream of consciousness foreshadows the inevitable clash of views that will occur in the Wellington office. He thinks the land has been violated in the name of progress. The train is running on a strip of land that used to be submerged by the sea, a place where he used to collect pipi, but 'they pushed a hill down over it and shot the railway line across to make more room for cars … Funny people putting their trains across the sea.' (DS 53). The old man passes through tunnels, sees machines further slicing hills and comments:

> Funny people these pakehas, had to chop up everything … But people had to have houses, and ways of getting from one place to another. And anyway who was right up there helping the pakeha to get rid of things — the Maori of course, riding those big machines. (DS 55)

This passage underlines a point that will become crucial in *Potiki*: Maori constitute the labour force of the Pakeha and are partly responsible for the damage done to the environment. The old man cannot fully understand Pakeha ways, nevertheless his sentence 'but people had to have houses', reiterated throughout the story, emphasises a priority for Maori and Pakeha alike: construction responds to the needs of an increasing population. In the City Planning Department, however, he is faced with incomprehensible Pakeha bureaucracy and a notion of development that is alien to him. His land is part of a 'development area', which means that it cannot be subdivided, nor can its owners obtain permission to build. Only the city administration is able to buy it and improve it, and in exchange they promise to give the Maori community equivalent land or monetary compensation. Two major problems arise: first, according to the Maori there is no adequate compensation for loss of ancestral land or turangawaewae; second, the business is very likely to be a public speculation, in other words the land will be purchased as underutilised or waste land, developed and likely resold at a considerably higher price. The administration showed a similar attitude when it had 'resited' an urupa (cemetery) to build the new motorway, as the old man notices on the train: 'That's where they'd bulldozed all the bones and put in the new motorway … Your leg bone, my arm bone, someone else's bunch of teeth and fingers, someone else's head, funny people. Glad he didn't have any of his whanaungas [relatives] underground in that place' (DS 57). The old man's mission inevitably fails and, once back home, he bitterly asks his relatives that he be cremated on his death because 'no one's going to mess about with me when I'm gone' (DS 66).[18]

Grace's denunciation of land speculation continues forcefully in *Potiki*. If in 'Journey' the administration was subtly pushing a Maori community out of their land, in *Potiki* private developers (evocatively renamed 'Dollarman') try every possible way, legal and illegal, to force them to sell. 'Journey' poses the question without giving an answer; the resolution is found in the ampler scope of a novel and implies a defensive fighting back. The community turns down Dollarman's millionaire offer for the land on which their urupa and wharenui stand, which would have given good access to the neighbouring site that was under development. The result is that the community vegetable gardens and urupa are flooded on the first rainy day. They soon discover that the course of a nearby creek was deliberately dammed and channels were built in order to make the water flow on to their land. Later on, the wharenui is set on fire and almost entirely destroyed. The community does not react after either incident, but patiently rearranges what has been disrupted, supported by other families and tribes who come to help clean and rebuild. Police investigations prove useless and the community has to move on or else starve. The aroha of friendly people and the communal reconstruction effort strengthen their spirit and their convictions, as some point out: 'The ground is still the same ground … The dead are still dead … and the living are still on two feet'.[19] Their priest remembers that 'wrongness comes back to the wrongmaker' (PO 141). The philosophy of acceptance, exemplified by the repeated sentence 'All that we need is still here,' prevails.

Yet among the younger generations something is stirring and rises after the ultimate offence is perpetrated by the developers. Toko, the last born or potiki of the family, is killed by a bomb set off at the entrance of the new wharenui. Tangimoana — Hemi and Roimata's eldest daughter and Toko's sister — is a law student at university and represents a new, reactive and activist attitude of Maori, reminiscent of the young radicals that puzzled Hepa Walker in *Whanau* and Api in 'Clenched Fist'. Once she realises that clinging to the old ways is not enough, Tangimoana accuses the Maori labourers who are working for Dollarman of being as guilty as he is and incites them to rebellion. The workers react as cunningly as Dollarman before them; one night, during the three-day tangi in which the workers are also participating, the developers' new structures are mysteriously blown up, their road destroyed and their machines driven into the sea. The police do not find a single witness among those at the tangi.

Potiki is probably Grace's most political work. It reflects the rise of activism in the mid-seventies and it forcefully incites Maori to take their destiny into their hands. Her radicalisation lies not only in the content of the book, but also in its form, as will be seen in the next chapter.

Rewriting History, Rewriting the Novel

Pakeha historian Michael King explains in his introduction to *Nga iwi o te motu: 1000 years of Maori history* (1997) that he departed writing about Maori history in the mid-1980s, because the Maori Renaissance seemed to herald the birth of a home-grown school of historical studies. He justified the publication of the book by stating that 'there is still no single-volume overview of Maori history and Maori-Pakeha relations based on professional research and readily available to general readers and students.'[1] The issue at stake is that the Maori Renaissance had not fostered any comprehensive work of Maori history even to the present day. One reply to King's point can be found in an article by Witi Ihimaera that appeared in the *Journal of New Zealand Literature* within a long section entitled 'A Symposium on Historical Fiction'. In his introduction to the 'Symposium', Lawrence Jones points out that all the contributors — with the exception of Ihimaera — are working within the rationalistic European assumption about history and, whether or not they agree on the issues debated, they can be contained in a single tradition.[2] On the other hand, Ihimaera's different perspective is declared from the very beginning and lies in the answer to the questions he poses: 'What is history and who owns it?'. 'On the first question,' he says, 'the Maori definition of history would be one that includes myth. On the second, the Maori view would be that nobody owns history or should be able to copyright it.'[3] The Western concept of history, based on factual evidence and the search for objectivity, is therefore subverted.

Like many other indigenous writers, Ihimaera contests the authority of an official and univocal 'History', suggesting that there can be many histories, within or outside the Maori framework.[4] These are histories but also stories, as they imply fictionalisation and are always subject to being told from a specific point of view. The term 'copyright' seems purposely to allude to the connection between history and fiction. As well as questioning the validity of the rationalistic view, he endorses an approach that includes myth as its essential assumption. Furthermore, as Keown underlines, the Maori attitude to history is 'a dynamic process which is articulated and rearticulated from various individual and tribal perspectives',[5] an attitude reflected in Grace's use of multiple narrators in some of her novels (*Potiki* and *Baby No-Eyes*, for example), which release 'semiotic reverberations which militate against any sense of a unitary, centralised form of representative authority'.[6] Likewise, Ihimaera's deliberate mix of historical and fictional events in *The Matriarch* and *The Dream Swimmer*[7] aims to erase the boundary between fact and fiction.

His re-writing of some of Mansfield's short stories from a Maori viewpoint in *Dear Miss Mansfield* (1989) follows the same logic, challenging univocal representations of reality. His version of Mansfield's 'How Pearl Button Was Kidnapped' entitled 'The Affectionate Kidnappers', for example, depicts the episode as a big misunderstanding. The two Maori women knew Pearl because they had already done some cleaning work for her mother. When Mrs Button appeared at the window, they made signs to indicate they were bringing her daughter with them to the marae. But Mrs Button thought they were just asking for directions. In fact, at the end of the story we learn that she did not remember the two women at all because 'she couldn't tell one Maori apart from another'.[8] Despite the two women's good intentions, the inflexible Pakeha law will charge them with kidnapping.

This new formula has further entailed a reconsideration of 'History' which questions the supremacy of fact over fiction, stresses the importance of the point of view in recording events, and seeks to reclaim what has been denied by two centuries of European domination. The object of this chapter is to show how the novel has been chosen in contemporary Maori literature as a privileged site to discuss Maori history and how the authors have managed to push this genre into new territories, drawing away from the Western canon and shaping new indigenous forms.

The historical frame turns into a spiral

After the 1980s, the subject matter of Grace's novels became increasingly concerned with contemporary issues relevant to Maori in New Zealand society. *Potiki* (1986) tells of a rural community holding on to the old ways and traditions, but at the same time defending itself against the attacks of modernity. *Baby No-Eyes* (1998) reformulates the notion of family in a modern urban context, exploring the conditions of young urban Maori and of solo parents. The protagonist, Te Paania, is a single mother living in the city with a son, Tawera. The bond with the whanau is kept alive through her great aunt, Gran Kura, who goes to live with Te Paania to tend to her when Tawera is born. The neighbours Dave and Mahaki, a homosexual couple, become part of the small community, which anticipates a theme dealt with by Ihimaera in *The Uncle's Story*. The novel weaves many strands into the story, including Mahaki's fight to get back the ancestral land of his people, unjustly confiscated by the city council. Another is about an invisible member of the family: the 'Baby No-Eyes' of the title. Baby is Te Paania's elder daughter, killed in a car accident while still in her mother's womb. Her little body disappears in the hospital, later to be found in a waste bin without her eyes, which have been removed for unspecified reasons and without Te Paania's authorisation. Baby No-Eyes becomes a real presence in Tawera's life: his sister, playmate and shadow. The predicament of Baby's body leads Te Paania to become involved in a movement against any unauthorised experimentation on aborted foetuses, and to speak out against genetic engineering that does not consider the values of indigenous people.

Set in a rural environment on the East Coast in 1999, the novel *Dogside Story* (2001) explores the life of the Dogside community, its population reduced to a minimum for lack of jobs and the exodus of its members to urban areas. One plot strand shows how locals discover a fraud that had been devised by a con-artist who was renting campsites on their land to tourists wanting to be the first in the world to see the dawn of the New Millennium.[9] The community manages to run the business themselves in order to finance the building of a new wharekai (dining hall). Elsewhere the novel focuses on the degradation and conflict inside the community, describing various evils affecting Maoridom such as alcohol and drug abuse, and child neglect, as forcefully portrayed in the works of Alan Duff. Unlike Duff, however, Grace emphasises her trust in the possibility of Maori overcoming these problems by confronting them within 'the safety of Maori institutional contexts'.[10] The growing self-awareness within Rua, the protagonist, leads the community to assume their own responsibilities.

Each story in the novels draws on events that relate to contemporary New Zealand history or that actually occurred (the fate of the unborn baby in *Baby No-Eyes* was inspired by an incident recorded in the media). Another common feature of these works is the continual interweaving of past and present in the story, as well as in the narrative structure. Both *Potiki* and *Dogside Story* possess an explicit mythical or legendary frame, which introduces and interacts with the events of the community, tracing the origins of its members and giving them a meaning for being there at that particular time and in that particular place. As in the earlier works by Grace and Ihimaera, the construction of a frame seems to fit with their need to connect single episodes or stories to an encompassing whole. A mythical frame cuts across all their works, constituting a subtext or a sort of collective racial unconscious, which links their characters to a world that is one and the same.

Potiki opens with a carver working on a poupou (carved post) in the meeting house at some indefinite time. He cannot finish his work because he does not know yet who is the latest offspring of the genealogy of gods and ancestors he is carving, which represents the history of the whanau. His incomplete work is somehow like a prophecy of the coming of a new hero. The carving is completed at the end of the novel — a history completed by a story — only after the community pinpoints that the missing part of the figure is Toko, who died in an explosion (as mentioned in the previous chapter). Toko is the potiki of the family, which means the youngest child but is also part of the name for the demigod Maui.[11] The analogy between Toko and Mauipotiki is supported by many similarities, including their premature birth on the shores of a beach, being last born in their families, and catching a big fish as a major achievement in their lives. Their deaths are also similar and occur on passing through a door: for Toko, the meeting house door; for Maui, the vagina of Hine-nui-te-Po, goddess of the underworld.[12] Toko is a special child whose physical frailty is compensated for by his wisdom and foresight, and his death is like a sacrificial offering, giving the community new strength to fight back against the developers.

Dogside Story begins with a legendary frame too. The introductory chapter narrates how the Dogside community was founded and named, foreshadowing events and themes of the novel. The rivalry between two sisters, Ngarua and Maraenohonoho, leads to the division of the original group. The object of their dispute is their elder brother's canoe, left to them after his death, but the true reason is the sisters' unnatural love for him and consequent jealousy towards each other. One night Ngarua succeeds in distracting her sister, snatches the canoe and paddles to the south side of the bay, a wild area frequented by pig hunters. The canoe, struck by a piece of driftwood launched by Maraenohonoho, eventually sinks, but Ngarua manages to go ashore and decides to settle there. Later, at low tide, she is joined by others as well as by many dogs, thinking there is a pig hunt on. The south side, with all its mongrel dogs, is then renamed Dogside. The Southsiders become known as the adventurers, 'movers, changers, seekers' (DO 11), symbolising an attitude towards life where enterprise and action prevail to the detriment of morals and traditions. Northsiders, by contrast, are 'the stayers, the originals' (DO 11); their community is renamed Godside. As guardians of traditions and order, they lack imagination and tend to passivity. As the novel develops, subsequent events feed back to the legendary frame. Overturning the Millennium Business to their advantage confirms the enterprising spirit of Ngarua's descendants, and the nature of the sisters' love for their brother is reflected in Rua's personal story. The turning point occurs when he reveals that young Kid is the fruit of a juvenile love game with his half-sister. Conflicts that arise inside the community — over Kid's custody, the unwillingness of elders to face their own responsibilities, and the amorality of the Dogsiders in general — all seem to be part of Ngarua's inheritance.

In both novels, myth and legendary past intertwine with the story in the present, affecting the characters' choices and explaining their motivations. While advancing towards their future, the characters simultaneously move back towards their past. The frame or 'mythscape'[13] starting both novels mixes with the story in a spiral structure, giving a textual representation of the Maori notion of history or 'a world that moves forward to the place it came from'.[14] As in *Tangi*, the spiral denotes eternity and reflects a perspective on space embracing not one but a multitude of centres, both in the world and in artistic representation:

> In visualising the principles of expansion and contraction, the spiral is a symbol of the Maori notion of moving towards the point of departure. The spiral has no natural beginning or end, no uniform centre and periphery; these are in fact interchangeable — they flow into each other as they do indeed in the composition of Maori carvings, where an ancestral image swirls and loops into the next.[15]

The spiral informs the narrative structure of Grace's novels. At the end of *Potiki*, the poupou in the ancestral house is completed by the image of Toko, the embodiment of Maui. This symbolises reinforcement of the bond that the whanau has with its origins, a link with the past necessary to construct the future, the closing of a circle that is a new beginning. The final chapters of *Dogside Story* are also set in the meeting house, the place where past and present join, the repository of talk and stories. Here the final confrontation between the members of the community takes place. Uncomfortable truths come out, old wounds are healed and the community reconstitutes itself into a new whole, rediscovering what good has come from Ngarua's inheritance: 'Ngarua took matters into her hands. After that it became a rivalry cloaked in story, part of who we all are because Ngarua freed us' (DO 290).

The Maori world of the past is described in *Baby No-Eyes* in the chapters narrated by Gran Kura, interspersed among the other stories set in the present. Gran Kura draws upon the memories of her childhood or events reported to her. She is the living book of the whanau, the repository of its history and its stories, which must be passed on according to the oral tradition. Her own education is told in chapter 4 and depicts a repressive school whose objective was to erase the identity of Maori children through the suppression of their native language. This picture contrasts with the present, as narrated in chapter 17, showing how the system has changed: Paania can choose a bilingual school for her son, one with an educational project aimed at the preservation of Maori identity and heritage. We come to know, through Gran Kura's voice, about the convention of arranged marriages for couples of high rank (to reinforce kinship between allied hapu [BN 159]), and how Maori were decimated by the influenza epidemic (BN 179). She also goes back to the first trading between Maori and Pakeha settlers, and explains how the land passed gradually from the former to the latter, as a result of exchanges between two cultures with entirely different notions of land. In her words, Pakeha:

> believed a man could own land in the same way as he owned his coat. He believed that he, one person, could possess land and everything on that land by taking a signature from someone who didn't own that land in that way. Or he believed he could take land by drawing lines on paper. (BN 112)

When the Treaty of Waitangi was signed, the situation did not improve:

> Pakeha were now arriving in shiploads from across the sea and had been promised land by the settler government. And although some Maori had sold land, or given land to Pakeha, it was not enough for them. They wanted more land, they wanted the best land, they wanted all the land.
>
> So now this new government became the biggest stealer of land making more and more laws to steal by. (BN 113)

Conflict over land led in time to war: a different kind of war because it was 'fighting without season' (BN 114). A whole world marked by the rhythm of nature — the changing seasons, the harvests, the fishing or hunting periods — which also ruled over war and peace, collapsed. As in her chapters about school, Gran Kura's account of the land issue is the premise to a story in the present: Mahaki and his people are struggling to regain their confiscated land. Like the frame in the other novels, Gran Kura's chapters provide an historical spiral, intertwining with and encompassing the story strands of the present.

The bond between history and myth is underlined in the prologue and epilogue of the novel, the chronological beginning and ending of a story that lasts about 20 years. *Baby No-Eyes* begins with Tawera's perception of the world from his mother's womb and ends with him as an art student, reading books in order to find what lies 'between the lines of history' (BN 291) and to express 'the unsaid matters of history' (BN 292). He is 'seeking out its missing pages' in the belief that 'this can be one of the journeys that will help him to be an artist' (BN 291). Allusions to things beyond or behind the factual reality are frequent. First, the point of view of an unborn baby in the prologue leads us to a pre-world in a pre-time: the space and time of myth. Then in the epilogue we are told that Tawera's paintings cannot be completed because there is always something missing, a section that lacks the appropriate colours or signs. An epiphany enables him to complete them. Reading the words 'Try Opposite' (BN 293) written on a wall, he understands he must not complete what he has realistically painted, but enlarge the missing space of his works, which he purposely calls 'Te Kore', or the Void (BN 293). Te Kore is the beginning of Maori genesis, the 'nothingness' from which all creation starts. The unsaid events of history that Tawera seeks must embrace myth too. His mission as an artist, like the carver in *Potiki*, is to link present and past, real and supernatural, history and myth; the representational function of Maori art and the social role of the Maori artist pose not only political claims but also convey an indigenous perspective. Their histories will always include myth.

By recounting events that belong to the Maori present and past, and in tracing their bond with myth in a spiral structure, Grace's novels provide a Maori view of history in both their narrative form and contents. In *Potiki* and *Baby No-Eyes* this is reinforced by Grace's use of multiple narrators. Each chapter in both novels is narrated alternately from the point of view of one character, whose name entitles that chapter. Most stories are told in the first person and by the most relevant characters: in *Potiki*, by Roimata and Toki; in *Baby No-Eyes* by Gran Kura, Te Paania and Tawera. Other chapters use a third-person narrator, but the implied point of view is that of the person mentioned in the title, generally a minor character. Examples of third person narratives in *Potiki* are the chapters named after Hemi, Dollarman and even The Urupa (cemetery), which is personified. In *Baby No-Eyes*, third-person narratives are used only in the chapters on Mahaki's secondary story. Plots in both novels develop as a jigsaw puzzle, each piece adding to the complete picture and representing a different point of view. The overall story of each book is therefore composed of many interlinked stories, as well as by many narrative perspectives, which may be read as an assertion of the notion of history as an essentially fictionalised story and consequently subject to multiple interpretations. An indigenised reading, however, allows the critic to go deeper and read them as 'a performative and communal enunciative act',[16] to use Keown's words, which recalls the transmission of knowledge in Maori oral culture and represents the ritual of whaikorero (oratory), where different orators speak in turn on the marae articulating individual points of view on the same subject.[17] Grace appropriates the novel and adapts it to forms belonging to Maori tradition and culture. It is a composite genre, mingling written word and oral enunciation, fact and fiction, story and history, myth and reality, and reflecting a specific Maori aesthetic.

Stories of history

Witi Ihimaera's *The Matriarch* and its sequel, *The Dream Swimmer* (1997), deal explicitly with a Maori view of history. Both are centred on the quest of Tama, the protagonist, to fulfil his destiny as a leader of the Mahana clan. This involves a journey back to the time when his grandmother, Artemis Riripeti Pere, 'the matriarch', was alive. Tama was chosen by Artemis to carry on the mission of recovering land that once belonged to his people and gradually passed into Pakeha hands. For this reason the matriarch attended to Tama's education, to hand down to him the ancient lore, history and genealogies of the iwi as well as her mana. Artemis had herself inherited this role and mission from her great grand-uncle Wi Pere Halbert,[18] an historical figure who was an early member of Parliament. Wi Pere, Artemis and Tama share a common destiny by the manner of their birth: each was born with their left eye swimming in blood and their hands around their own necks. This image, repeatedly used in both novels, symbolises the condition of Maori compelled to fight a bloody war against an enemy who has disrupted the equilibrium of their world, dividing them into opposing factions and depriving them of their land, language and traditions. If *The Matriarch* revolves round the figure of grandmother Artemis, the sequel leads the reader to unravel the personality and past secrets of another key figure in Tama's life: his mother Tiana, the 'dream swimmer'. Tiana belongs to the people of Te Tira Maka, who lived in Aotearoa before Maori migrated there from the land of Hawaiki. Nobody knows where Te Tira Maka came from, all that was said was that they 'had swum in their dreams' (TD 159). Following Maori beliefs in the reality of supernatural events, Ihimaera tells about Tiana's extraordinary powers, which enable her to travel through space and time in her dreams. Artemis and Tiana are the main figures affecting Tama's personality and destiny: uncommon women, doomed to act as opposing and conflicting forces.

The Matriarch opens with an account of the Creation, from the times of Te Kore (the Void) and Te Po (the Night) up to the advent of life, gods and men, as told to Tama by his grandmother (TM 2). Like Grace, Ihimaera binds history and story with a mythical past. He purposely erases the barrier between reality and imagination by making Tama say that the stories of all families are jungles that mingle fact and fiction, and that the matriarch was the one who turned his life 'into fiction from fact' (TM 1). Ihimaera frequently employs extensive references to Western classical myth and culture as well. In *The Matriarch* Tiana's way of staring at people — 'that fixed staring look of hers' (TM 41) — is compared to the look of the Sphinx (TM 41 and 403) and then to Medusa (TM 44 and 126). Her voice recalls the hiss of a basilisk (TM 126). She is described as having 'an Achilles toe rather than an Achilles heel' (TM 52). In *The Dream Swimmer* Tama's village is likened to Delphi and Venice, as one of those places in the world where 'the boundaries between past and future, living and dead, are so fine that you can read the pattern of destiny' (TD 22). The first name of the matriarch, Artemis, alludes to the goddess worshipped in Asia Minor and in Greece, and later in Rome under the name of Diana. She was thought of as the Great Mother, with power over wild beasts, fertility, childbirth, the moon and hunting (TD 237). All these characteristics apply to Tama's grandmother, who is called Te Matua, which means 'the Mother' or 'the Matriarch' (TD 48).

As Joanne Tompkins notes, indigenous writers often draw on Western myths that have circumscribed their education. Ihimaera's implicit message is that if Western myths are worthy of allusion, then Maori myths deserve serious consideration too. Besides, acknowledging that indigenous myths cannot be accepted as the only truth prevents 'charges of reverse exclusivity or ethnocentrism.'[19] Ultimately, his choice demonstrates that Maori notions of history (which include myths) are applied consistently. Western myths are as true to him as are Maori myths.

The Matriarch and *The Dream Swimmer* have a similar structure, defined by Tompkins as 'historiographic metafiction'. They interweave many stories, moving back and forth from past to present, from fictional to historical characters, from myth to real events. In both works, Tama's quest in the present day is the primary narrative that keeps the other strands together. The second narrative is Tama's recollection — part memory and part witness report — of Artemis' story, which begins in *The Matriarch* and continues, intertwined with Tiana's story, in *The Dream Swimmer*. The third narrative covers the general history of the Mahana clan: from the landing of the *Takitimu* canoe in the mythical past, to the historical sections devoted to real people or events connected with the family such as, in *The Matriarch*, the rebel-prophet Te Kooti[20], the Matawhero Retaliation[21] and Wi Pere Halbert; in *The Dream Swimmer*, the Spanish influenza epidemic,[22] Te Kooti's successor Rua Kenana, and Rastafarian chief Chris Campbell. [23] The story of these characters and events is supported by historical sources such as newspaper articles, parliamentary records, radio interviews, memoirs of witnesses and direct reports. Interestingly, one of them concerning Rua Kenana is an anecdote passed by Wi Pere to a man called Te Haa Ihimaera Smiler Jnr (TD 136).

Tompkins points out that the mixture of Maori myth and documented Pakeha history offers a much more complete interpretation of New Zealand history.[24] In recording historical events, however, Tama openly acknowledges that the writing of history is subject to alteration and distortion. His frequent metafictional asides remind the reader that the entire novel offers just a version of history — that is, a story.[25] Before describing the killing of Te Kooti's followers at Ngatapa by the colonial forces, he says: 'I picture it this way' (TM 177), and one of Chris Campbell's speeches is prefaced with the sentence 'I like to think this is what he said to his brothers' (TD 217).

By reporting documented historical events, Ihimaera claims his right to represent the Maori point of view. In *The Matriarch* the notorious episode of the Land Wars generally known as the Matawhero Massacre is purposely called 'Retaliation' to foreground its causes. Te Kooti's cold-blooded slaughter of 63 people — including Pakeha settlers, government officers and Maori loyalists — is defined here as 'his first positive act of war' (TM 176), a war he had not sought and was forced to fight. The Matawhero Retaliation is recounted with a cold detachment. Ihimaera avoids any emotional involvement for an episode that he defines as violent and cruel. Tama further emphasises the Maori point of view by directly addressing the Pakeha reader: 'Yes, Pakeha, you remember Matawhero. Let me remind you of the murders at Ngatapa' (TM 177). Talking about the Treaty of Waitangi he expounds both Pakeha and Maori views, concluding: 'For most assuredly *you*, Pakeha, began taking the land from us as you were signing your worthless Treaty. You, Pakeha, began taking away our culture' (TM 73–74). A whole section of Act 4 in *The Matriarch* is devised as a faithful record of Wi Pere's speeches from the parliamentary Hansard reports. Addressing the House in forceful and direct language, he criticised the government's land policy, stressing over and over again the inadequacy of European laws for Maori and demanding the right for Maori to make their own laws through native committees. In *The Dream Swimmer*, the account of the influenza epidemic in the area around Gisborne is given through the 'Watson Chronicles', a journal kept by the charge nurse Victoria Anne Watson, who helped the matriarch to run a camp hospital in her village (TD 40–46).

The two novels incorporate a variety of literary forms in a way that seems alien to the Western canon. The perception of something different, unusual, distant pervades the critical response to *The Matriarch*, summarised by the opening sentence of Michael King's review of the novel: 'It is a large baffling book'. King describes the novel as 'impressive ... for its sweep, magnitude and courage' and 'immensely important' for its exploration of Pakeha-Maori relations and rejection of stereotypes. Yet he continues, 'Ihimaera's vision is not sufficiently penetrative to unify the many disparate parts into a single work of imagination.'[26] Prentice notices that other two reviews responded similarly to *The Matriarch*.[27] Elizabeth Caffin argued that 'What is missing in a novel of undoubted power is a single confident artistic vision ... [This] is less a novel than a fictional performance.'[28] C.K. Stead identified the failure of the novel in the vertiginous oscillations of tone and voice: 'The tone swings back and forth between the grandiose and the banal. All this puts a great strain on any sense of artistic unity.'[29] While most critics recognise the power and courage of the book, they lament the lack of unity in imagination, in artistic vision, in tone and voice. To these critics the novel does not seem to have a centre. Prentice therefore poses the question: 'According to which cultural and critical criteria is unity sought?'[30]

The lack of centre lamented by the reviewers recalls the Maori notion of history symbolised by the spiral: a space embracing not one centre but a multitude of centres, moving toward and away from the point of entry and departure, without beginning or end, denoting eternity. As Trevor James writes:

> Ihimaera draws upon a primal dimension of Maori mythology and locates the spiralling of time and consciousness, the co-inherence and mutual interaction of past and present, within Maori spirituality. This pattern then absorbs the subsequent narratives and time schemes.[31]

The Matriarch most deliberately articulates a way of seeing the world that is distinctively Maori. Interestingly, the spiral image that had already been employed in *The Matriarch* to describe certain aspects of Maori culture — Tama's process of learning (TM 109) or the patterns painted inside the meeting house (TM 191), for instance — becomes more frequent in *The Dream Swimmer* and is applied to a wider range of experiences. 'No matter how my life might spiral outwards, this was the umbilical that connected me to the centre' (TD 50), Tama says of the bond with his family. An episode of intimacy between Tama and his wife is thus expressed: 'Regan and I had been talking and fighting and laughing and arguing. Spiralling downwards. Spiralling upwards. Spiralling' (TD 53). The image of the spiral is then used explicitly to define the Maori sense of history: 'The old people say "Te torino haere whakamua, whakamuri", that the past and the present are together in the same spiral' (TD 415). Ihimaera explains his spiral narrative structure in one of Tama's metafictional asides:

> In the English novel tradition the novelist takes life and shapes it into fiction according to structural, narrative, stylistic and other dictates of the convention from a beginning through a middle towards a single ending. In *our* tradition life takes the novelist and forces him or her to accept the tribal, holistic, exponential and organic nature of our narratives. In our tradition one story stimulates recollection of another and another and another. For us, there can never be only one story or one ending. All tribal cultures know that the one great truth to our narratives is that they do not end. They go on and on, an unending spiral going forward and returning in a balance of constant tension. (TD 313)

His response to the critics' bafflement is two-fold. Ten years after the publication of *The Matriarch,* Ihimaera confirmed his aesthetic choices through *The Dream Swimmer.* He also openly claimed the right of indigenous writers to shape the novel so that it can conform to their spiritual world, sensibility and sense of history.

If Western written histories are grounded on assumptions that are incompatible with an indigenous view of the world, the novel has proved effectual to convey it, even as it had to be reshaped in order to conform to Maori spirituality and aesthetic principles. In the process, an existing European genre has been counter-colonised and turned to serve non-European purposes.[32] By using literature to present a specifically Maori view of the world and of New Zealand history, Grace and Ihimaera challenged the established narratives of the colonisers. They claimed their right to include myth in history and to use a traditionally realistic genre in order to express it. They underlined the existence of different points of view, that is, of many histories which were also stories and necessarily subject to fictionalisation. In Salman Rushdie's words, 'the Empire has written back to the centre'.

8 | Language as a Site of Resistance

In 2000, *Landfall* asked prominent figures in Aotearoa/New Zealand's cultural arena to identify one key event of the twentieth century that stood out for them in their field of competence (in literature, sport, economics and so on). Ihimaera signalled the Maori Language Petition of 14 September 1972 and explained that the event 'became a knot with which to tie the past to the present, an early warning call to what was happening to our language and, by implication, our literature.' He further emphasised the political valence of language by adding:

> Literature is language. Maori literature is Maori politics. For Maori, literature whether in English or in Maori is a Waitangi issue, a Treaty issue, a sovereignty issue ... When Maori history is writ large, it is my opinion that 1972 will become regarded as one of those seminal years when Maori — and Pacific and other indigenous peoples as well — began to Strike Back.[1]

Ihimaera's belief that the survival of te Reo is a political issue underlines the crucial function of language as a medium of power within postcolonial countries. While Maori were fighting for official recognition of their own language, Maori writers were enacting other strategies of resistance to the language of the colonisers, synthesised by what the authors of *The Empire*

Writes Back define as processes involving the 'abrogation' of the privilege of English and the 'appropriation' of the language of the centre. Abrogation is 'the refusal of the categories of the imperial culture, its aesthetic, its illusory standard of normative or "correct" usage, and its assumption of a traditional and fixed meaning "inscribed" in the words.'[2] Appropriation is the process by which the imperial language is adopted as a tool, remoulded to new usages and 'utilized in various ways to express widely differing cultural experiences.'[3] Ashcroft, Griffiths and Tiffin have further distinguished between the 'standard' British English inherited from the empire and the various 'englishes' into which the dominant language has been transformed in postcolonial countries.[4]

Holmes, Stubbe and Marra argue that language is an important means of indexing social identities, pinpointing salient features of sociolinguistic norms associated with Maori New Zealanders. Their study, based on evidence accumulated over ten years, focuses on the way in which Maori people make use of 'sociolinguistic and sociopragmatic resources to index their distinctive ethnicity, and in some cases to indicate their dissatisfaction with or resistance to the dominant societal norms'.[5] Three particular features of spoken Maori English have been identified:

1. A distinctive prosodic pattern labelled as 'syllable-timed' English.
2. The pragmatic tag 'eh'.
3. A considerable number of Maori lexical terms.

On the first point, Maori English (ME) is characterised by a distinctive 'syllable-timed' rhythm, which distinguishes it from the more 'stress-timed' Pakeha English (PE). A syllable-timed rhythm has a tendency to pronounce small grammatical words in unstressed positions with full vowels more often than is customary in PE, and reflects the influence of the Maori language, where vowels are regularly pronounced and consonant clusters are not used.

The Maori language consists of ten consonant phonemes and five vowel phonemes, which were transcribed into a written alphabet by missionaries in the nineteenth century. The complete Maori alphabet is therefore made of fifteen letters: *a, e, h, i, k, m, n, ng, o, p, r, t, u, w, wh*.[6] The consonants are pronounced as in English, with the addition of the digraphs *ng* for /ŋ/ (as in 'singer') and *wh* for /f/ (as in 'far'). In some regions, the digraph *wh* is also heard as 'wh' in 'whale'. The pronunciation of the five vowels is regular and similar to Italian.[7] Combinations of identical vowels result in a phonetically long vowel (generally, but not always, marked with a macron or a double vowel),[8] and most combinations of a vowel and a second vowel of equal or greater closure result in a phonetic diphthong. Maori does not admit final consonants or consonant clusters — that is, consonants in Maori occur only one at a time, and all syllables end in vowels. This led, in the case of loanwords from English, to considerable phonological adaptations such as the transliteration of 'Robinson Crusoe' into 'Ropitini Kuruho', or 'ice-cream' as 'aihikirīmi'.[9] As Gordon and Deverson noted, 'Maori has often been remarked upon as an aesthetically pleasing language to the ear, so much so that Edward Morris in the nineteenth century called it "the Italian of the south".'[10]

Due to its phonology Maori is mora-timed,[11] a rhythmic pattern more akin to syllable timing than to stress timing. Holmes' study of ME found that a syllable-timed rhythm tended to occur more often in the speech of those with proficiency in speaking te Reo. More importantly, the levels of this distinctive pattern were significantly higher in the speech of Maori, whether they were proficient or not in the Maori language, than in the speech of Pakeha. This suggests therefore that language serves as a marker of Maori ethnic identity. It could also explain why soldiers from the Maori Battalion who fought in the Italian Campaign in the Second World War found it easy to learn Italian, as Grace reports in her novel *Tu*. Not only is the pronunciation of vowels similar in Maori and Italian, but the latter is also syllable-timed and therefore closer to the Maori rhythmic pattern than stress-timed English.[12] Interestingly, Grace mentions that the main linguistic medium of Maori soldiers in Italy was either Maori or Italian after a while. English had become a 'forgotten language'.[13] The contact with a foreign language possessing similar rhythmic patterns and, importantly, that was not associated with the dominant power, reinforced the soldiers' appreciation and use of their native tongue.

The second salient feature in ME is the use of the tag 'eh', described as 'an addressee-oriented pragmatic device'[14] generally located at the end of a sentence. It is roughly equivalent to 'you know' or to an English question tag, and is a form used to maintain or establish solidarity or a connection between speaker and listener. Systematic use can also signal a distinctive ethnicity. Holmes indicates that the frequency index for 'eh' in Maori speakers was almost three times higher than for Pakeha speakers. This may reflect the fact that it functions in English in a way similar to the particle 'ne' in Maori. Both 'ne' and 'eh' (spelt 'ay' in early works) appear frequently in the fiction of Ihimaera and Grace.[15] The former is used when a character is supposedly a Maori L1 speaker, and often follows a Maori sentence or phrase. The latter is utilised by Maori characters who are English L1 speakers. The influence of te reo on the English language is more obviously marked in Maori L1 speakers (typically elders in the present day or middle-aged people from the 1940s and 1950s, as in Grace's *Tu* or Ihimaera's *Bulibasha*).

In *Bulibasha*, Simeon's illiterate mother has just learned the English alphabet and tries to interpret her son's school report. Although she is made to speak English in most of the novel, she uses Maori and *ne* in this crucial scene, showing her progress in reading:

> 'P, Biology. Pass *ne*? Ka Pai, kotahi P.'
> She held both my fists up in the air and made me put one finger
> up from the right fist. She read the next line.
> 'P, English. Pass *ne* ra? Kapai, e rua P.'
> Another finger up, right fist. Next line.
> 'F, Geography. Aue, he raruraru! E rua P, kotahi F.'
> One finger up, but left fist. Next line. (my emphases)[16]

In 'The Dream', Grace's characters are also supposedly Maori L1 speakers and frequently code-switch between English and Maori. Here, they are placing their bets on horses following a dream one of them had:

> 'Pai, Good dream *ne*?' said Haua. (WA 21, my emphasis)

Later on, 'ne' instead completes a Maori phrase:

> 'Ho! A good start. Ka pai ne?' (WA 22, my emphasis)[17]

In Ihimaera's *Tangi* (first excerpt) and in 'Passing Time' (second excerpt) the characters are supposedly English L1 speakers and use 'ay' in the same way as 'ne':

> – All right , she said. Me and Mere, we sleep in that other room.
> No spiders in there, ay. (TA 111)

> – The cops want us to move on but we won't. So they've sent for
> reinforcements. Two of them can't handle us, ay. (NN 67)

The use of 'ne' or 'ay' signals the distinctive ethnic identity of the characters. It also shows how the Maori language has been incorporated in English, and how the dominant language has been appropriated and moulded to express a sociolinguistic function (the maintenance or establishment of solidarity or the connection between speaker and listener) which is proper of the minority language.

The third salient feature of ME identified by Holmes et al. is the deployment of Maori lexical terms, which is considerably more frequent and draws on a broader vocabulary than in PE. Using a relatively high proportion of Maori words serves not only to mark solidarity but also 'carries very strong positive affect, much more than would be the case if the same meanings had been expressed in English.'[18] Code-switching is arguably the most widespread strategy employed through speech or in writing to signal ethnicity or to appropriate the dominant language. Gordon and Deverson underline that there is no clear dividing line between 'borrowing' and 'code-switching', that is, 'combining elements of two different languages or moving from one language into the other and back again, within the same utterance.'[19] They also note that the lexical intake from Maori into New Zealand English was extensive in the early nineteenth century, but that it was 'Pakeha-driven'; Maori was 'little more than a passive partner in the linguistic exchange,'[20] perhaps explained by the reality that it was convenient for explorers and settlers to adopt indigenous names for certain aspects of their new environment. The initial impact that te reo had on New Zealand English was confined to three fields: traditional Maori society and customs; native flora and fauna; and proper names, especially place names. Since the motivation for borrowing lay with the colonisers — who needed to take whichever names the donor language could provide — this kind of borrowing can be defined as 'receiver-oriented'. It served the needs of the English-speaking newcomers. Gordon and Deverson point out that the recent flow of Maori loanwords, which started with the Maori Renaissance, may be conversely described as 'donor-oriented',[21] since the initiative has come chiefly from the Maori side. Maori words have been introduced and given wider currency by Maori writers and speakers in the course of making their voices heard. As a result, they are now encountered more frequently in the media, in articles, reports, public statements and notices.[22]

From a Pakeha perspective, borrowings are naturalised words that have achieved the status of permanent acquisitions, whereas code-switching is the irruption of unknown foreign words that need explaining. For Maori, they both end up being strategies of counter-colonisation of the dominant language and an assertion of the indigenous point of view. Yet, while borrowings have been legitimised by the dominant centre, code-switching responds to the needs of the minority language. By this process, Maori writers introduced culturally relevant Maori words into English, challenging the prohibition against using the indigenous language that had been enacted in classrooms — as related in their fiction.[23] Code-switching allows the writer to deploy not only words or phrases but whole sentences, as the above example from *Bulibasha* shows. Furthermore, it forces non-Maori readers 'to make the same efforts in respect of Maori culture that Maori have been obliged to make in respect of European culture.'[24]

Gordon and Williams identify three types of literary code-switching: 'extrinsic', when the usage of foreign words merely supplies local colour (as in the case of Hercule Poirot's French phrases in Agatha Christie's detective stories); 'organic', when the introduced material is translated or explicated in the new context so as not to alienate the reader; and 'political', when 'the object is to discomfort the reader by confronting him or her with an apparently uncrossable cultural boundary'.[25] Code-switching is never extrinsic in the fiction of Grace and Ihimaera; it is organic in their early productions and becomes increasingly political. No glossaries appear in Ihimaera's works, although early fictions tended to elucidate Maori words within the text itself.[26] On the contrary, Grace includes glossaries in *Waiariki, Mutuwhenua* and *The Dream Sleepers*. If organic code-switching does not want to alienate the reader, its aim nevertheless is to point out that this is not an English book with a few Maori words as decorations or embellishments: it is a Maori book written in English.[27]

In organic code-switching, the Maori words interspersed in the text are mostly related to semantic fields that do not belong to European culture, and are not always able to be translated with a single English term. Frequently used words such as 'aroha' or 'tangi' have a wider meaning than 'love' or 'funeral'. Similarly, 'kuia' (elderly woman) is not easily translatable into English as it represents a category that has a special role in the community.[28] The term evokes a much larger semantic field than the one suggested by 'old/elderly woman', and conveys the mana (prestige and authority) attributed to elders in Maori society. A great deal of code-switching relates to other areas of particular significance in the Maori world, for example family relations, food, spiritual concepts and rituals. Maori words for family relations are more numerous than in English, due to the need to identify figures within extended families. Terms such as tuahine (sister or female cousin of a male), tuakana (elder sibling or cousin of the same sex) and teina (younger sibling or cousin of the same sex) do not find equivalents in most European languages. Spoken ME, as Holmes et al. note, also possesses an abundance of kinship-related terms of address such as 'bro', 'sis', 'cuz', 'nanny', 'aunty' and 'uncle', which derive from cultural norms and are additional ways that ethnic identity may be signalled lexically. Character dialogue by Ihimaera and Grace frequently records this use.

The number of unmediated Maori words increases significantly by the time of Ihimaera's *The Matriarch* and Grace's *Potiki*. Full sentences and passages are included in te reo according to specific narrative needs or characterisation, not merely as solitary terms or phrases. Code-switching becomes more aggressive, assuming a political dimension. During the Wellington hui in *The Matriarch*, for example, karanga and waiata a ringa (action songs) in the powhiri (traditional welcome ceremony) are included without translation:

> Time to start the karanga again. She lifted her voice and together
> with the other women callers, she began to karanga again. 'E Te

Rongowhakaata e Te Aitanga A Mahaki', the caller sang, 'descendant
of Wi Pere, na taku potiki koe i tiki atu i tahu atu o te rangi, i kukume
mai, haere mai, haere mai, haere mai haere mai.' (TM 30)…
… The first action song in the powhiri was followed by a second.
'Ka mate, ka mate, ka ora ka ora.' (TM 30)

Ihimaera implies that readers should know what karanga and powhiri are. He
also incorporates Maori words in English both as nouns and verbs, reproducing
their function in Maori: 'Time to start the karanga again. She lifted her voice and
together with the other women callers, she began to karanga again' (TM 30). He
uses korero (conversation, narrative, to speak) and whaikorero (speech, oratory, to
make a speech) in the same way:

After smoko, while we kids were skinny dipping in the river, he
would korero the problem with the adults. (BU 78)
[A] Maori elder … was preparing to begin his whaikorero. (TM 75)

In *Bulibasha*, the mother is learning to read because she does not want to be cheated
by the Pakeha storekeeper any longer. Literacy becomes an act of appropriation (of
the dominant written language) and emancipation (she can check her own bills
now). Yet while she speaks English throughout most of the novel, in the school
report passage Ihimaera has her use Maori, as though he wanted to stress her Maori
identity and force the reader to know how she felt when she could not understand
the storekeeper's bills. *Potiki* ends with an untranslated waiata (song or poem).
Grace deploys many words in Maori that do not belong to the 'official' list of Maori
loanwords and that would be unknown to non-Maori readers. One of *Potiki*'s
chapters, for example, is titled The Urupa (cemetery) and in *Baby No-Eyes* she makes
Gran Kura (supposedly L1 Maori) use the uncommon terms 'teina' and 'tuakana'
(BN 30). Neither of these words is elucidated or translated.

Williams and Gordon see this type of more politicised code-switching as a
'linguistic means of contesting linguistic and other forms of dominance by writers
speaking for communities in a situation of disadvantage where the resources
of goods and language are unequally divided within society.'[29] If the previously
unthreatening form of code-switching had been 'boundary-levelling', this new type
became 'boundary-marking'.[30] Commenting on Grace's fiction after the 1980s (in
terms that can apply to Ihimaera as well), they argue:

Grace insists that access to the Maori world must be more
linguistically demanding and more politically charged. She uses
Maori language not so much to restrict her novel to a particular
and identifiable readership as to privilege one group of readers at

the expense of another, in the process attempting to reverse an historical relationship of power.[31]

Even so, they continue, while political code-switching serves as a 'boundary-maintaining technique', paradoxically it encourages the inclusion of non-Maori readers, by obliging them to extend their knowledge of the Maori language in order to appreciate full meaning of the text:

> The writing itself — in its form as well as content — is part of the effort to overcome the loss of Maori language that occurred when pre-European life collided with post-contact reality. The writing does not simply reflect the ongoing struggle of people and communities to adapt modernity to their own purposes and priorities, it actively participates in that struggle.[32]

Ihimaera and Grace both confirm the political aim of their later code-switching:

> I never have glossaries, and the reason is that the work has always basically been for a New Zealand audience. What I am saying is if you do not know these words then you are maintaining a monocultural bias in your lives. I could make it easier for you by translating these words and making the sense more accessible. But if you really do want to become bicultural, then you have to begin to do some research of your own and find out these things for yourself. (Ihimaera)[33]

> Writers of small population cultures must have the same freedom as other writers to be true to what they know and true to who they are. I need to be free to write in the way that I judge best for the stories I want to tell. I want my writing to be able to stand with the rest of the writing of the world without encumbrances such as glossaries, italics, footnotes, asides, sentences in brackets, introductory notes, or explanatory paragraphs disguised as plot. ... I use Maori language in my work where I believe it is right and natural to do so, where the people that I've created demand that I do so because the words are their words. I do not italicize because the words are not 'foreign' to me or my characters and are indigenous to my country. (Grace)[34]

The political use of language is not limited to vocabulary but extends to grammar as well, This is definitely more marked in Grace and has characterised her work since she began writing in the 1970s. Ihimaera adjusts English to

Maori grammatical patterns sporadically and only in his dialogues. Grace's adaptation of English, on the other hand, is experimental, utilised extensively within dialogue and applied to the narrative at times, as we saw in the analysis of *Waiariki*. Cases of 'grammatical irregularities' that reflect the impact of Maori language are analysed in the dialogues and narratives that follow.

Distinguishing between mass and count nouns is not necessary when using the Maori language. All common nouns are compatible with plural determiners and with the indefinite article 'he' ('a').[35] Consequently 'a person' and 'some food' would be expressed in the same way: 'he tangata' and 'he kai'. This explains an apparent 'mistake' commonly attributed to Maori characters who use 'a' with mass nouns:

> 'You made a *bread* Mum?' they say.
>
> 'You got any meat? Gee-ee Macky forgot to get us a *meat* for the weekend.' (Grace, 'Holiday', WA 28, my emphases)

Ihimaera follows the same rule in this passage:

> – Auntie, what the heck are you doing in there?
>
> – Making us a *kai*. [food]
>
> – But I already had a *kai*! (Ihimaera, WH 105, my emphases)

Another major difference between Maori and English is the treatment of verbs. Questions in Maori don't have a structural marking, such as inversion or question particles. Direct yes-no questions can take the form of the corresponding statement spoken with a rising final intonation. Yes-no questions that invite agreement may be followed by a universal tag 'ne' or 'ne ra'.[36] There are numerous cases of questions without inversion or auxiliary verbs in the dialogues of both authors:

> – We got enough sticks? (Ihimaera, 'Beginning of the Tournament', PP 11)
>
> – You like this kanga kopiro? (Ihimaera, WH 107)

This is extended also to 'wh-' questions:

> 'How long I got?' he asked. (Grace, 'Boiling', SP 101)[37]
>
> 'Where you going?' (Grace, 'Smoke Rings', WA 80)
>
> 'What you think?' (Grace, 'Valley', WA 62)
>
> – What you say, Dad? (Ihimaera, 'The Escalator', NN 69)

Moreover the phrase, rather than the word, is the basic unit for the description of Maori syntax, as with other Polynesian languages. It is the level at which many categories expressed by inflection in other languages, such as tense, aspect or case, are handled.[38] Tense is indicated by different introductory particles, whereas in English a change of tense is indicated by adding a suffix or auxiliaries, or by altering the verbal stem. Keown gives two simple but clear examples: 's/he goes' in Maori is 'kei te haere ia'[39] (particle marking present tense {kei te}+ verb {haere} + pronoun {ia}), while 's/he went' is 'i haere ia' (particle marking past tense {i} + verb {haere} +pronoun {ia}).[40] This grammatical rule may account for the loss of verbal inflections for person, number and tense in Maori speakers and their frequent omission of verbal auxiliaries. Corresponding forms in standard English are given in square brackets in the following quotations:

> 'We go [we'll go] down to the creek, Ripeka. See [Let's see/we'll see] if we got a eel [sic] in our hinaki.' (Grace, MU 71)

> 'Here's your basket nearly finish [finished],' she said. (Grace, PO 55)

> – Me and your Mum, we been working [have been working] all our lives for you kids. (Ihimaera, TA 80)

> – We taking [are taking] you home, she would tell the shell. We taking [are taking] you home for my mokopuna. (Ihimaera, 'The Child', PP 112)

As Keown observes:

> Within the context of Maori oral narratives, verbal particles marking particular tenses are often replaced by the non-specific verbal particle 'ka', which precedes the verb but has no specific value in itself, merely marking the phrase in which it occurs as verbal. Tense is judged from the context; therefore if a speaker begins a story in the past tense (i + verb), s/he can subsequently mark all subsequent verbs with 'ka' with the tacit understanding that the past sense is being expressed.[41]

This may account for the words of Nanny Ripeka in Grace's *Mutuwhenua*, who starts with a past and then turns to the present tense, although she is referring to the same moment in the past. Here, she is talking about a big eel that got trapped in the hinaki (eel trap):

Took these old hands a long time to get our hinaki up with that big
eel in. Then I have to bang him with a stone so he won't get away.
(MU 70)

In this passage from *Baby No-Eyes* the speaker is talking about old times, but the
only verb in the past in the first one:

There was this old man Hori who talk to me about Anapuke.
Well that hill, that Anapuke, you don't hardly talk about. It's
from the far, old times, when there's only the Maori. (BN 151)

The common expression 'not to worry' for 'don't worry' in Maori English also
reflects Maori grammar. The negation of imperatives in Maori uses the negative
'kaua' followed by the tense-aspect marker 'e' and the infinitive of the verb, as in
'kaua e kōrero!' (don't speak!):

'Not to worry dia [dear], not to worry.' (Grace, 'Parade', WA 89)

– It's so unfair, Susan interrupted.
– Not to worry, Koro laughed. At least we got us a place now
(Ihimaera, 'The Kids Downstairs' (NN 86)

Further incorporations of Maori grammar are evident in Grace in dialogues and
in the first person narration of supposedly L1 Maori speakers. These relate to
word order and, on certain occasions, to the omission of verbs. Unlike English,
a verb in front focus is permitted in statements. One example provided by Lee
is the sentence 'Ka waiata te kotiro i roto i te whare', which means 'The girl is
singing inside the house'. The exact Maori word order, however, is verbal particle
{Ka} + verb {waiata = to sing} + subject {te kotiro = the girl} + complement {i
roto = inside + i te whare = the house}. A literal translation would be 'Sings the
girl inside the house'.[42] Dell Panny mentions that adjectives are also frequently
found as first elements in statements. In 'Valley' a child says 'Cunning that fox'
(WA, 71), which is the direct translation of the Maori sentence 'He murere,
te tauwi ra'. In addition Dell Panny notes that in certain structures Maori
verbs can be implied and are therefore omitted; what appears as an incomplete
sentence in English can be a complete sentence in Maori.[43] In particular the
verb 'to be' and verbs of motion are often implicit in Maori.[44] In the following
excerpts from 'Valley', Grace subverts the standard English word order (WO)
and applies verb omissions (VO):

Different, the father [WO]. Unsmiling. Heavy in build and
mood. (WA 63)

'Too much this [VO],' she explains to me, pointing to her tobacco tin. 'Too much cigarette, too much cough [VO].' (WA 61)

'They're the best stones,' he tells them. 'These old ones that have been used before. From the river these stones [VO].' (WA 62)

Two other stories modifying English syntax are 'Toki' and 'Huria's Rock'. The former, in particular, reads like a piece of oral korero (narrative). The musical quality of the story, narrated in the first person by the protagonist, owes much to grammatical irregularities that appear as a sort of poetic licence to a foreign ear, and were criticised by Norman Simms (see chapter 4). Elements of each story reflect the influence of Maori word order and syntax:

They all spoke then, the old people, of days of fishing, and much advice they gave to we of young days. But sat quietly, I, [WO] to wait for morning ...
To the rock for crayfish they [VO+WO], for it is best bait in these parts.
Next morning then I [VO+WO], with many there early to see me go. Out to the sea [VO] with the day just coming, pulling strong and straight. Around the point, then quickly to the chosen place [VO] to get down my line before sunrise.... Quick to put my bait again [VO] and put it at the bottom of the sea ... The work of a hapuku this, and very excited then I [WO+VO]. (WA 8)

In 'Huria's Rock' the story is told as a stream of consciousness, which reflects the thoughts of a Maori elder. The passage below gives a sense of his 'Maorified' English:

But a sad time that [VO+WO], when last we came to this place. Died here my wife [WO], when we last came. Drowned she [WO], under crayfish rock, now named Huria's rock for her. No more to that rock since then for crayfish [VO] ... To the rock then I [VO+WO], calling her name ... Look now [uninflected verb or UI], to Huria's rock thinking of Huria, and I now see her sitting there on the rock. (WA 49)

Keown describes Grace's strategies as processes of 'linguistic deterritorialisation', since she creates hybridised zones in which English and Maori overlap. 'English is "occupied" and to some extent ordered by Maori grammatical structures'.[45] Furthermore, Keown's analysis of *Baby No-Eyes* demonstrates how Grace shifts 'the narrative mode from what appears to be a conventional first-person "written" narration into the realm of oral immediacy'.[46] This also applies to several of her short stories. 'Toki' and 'And So I Go' (see chapter 5), for example, are deeply informed respectively by korero and by elegiac oral poetry (waiata and creation chants), and could be defined as composite prose pieces intermixing oral immediacy and the written word. Keown uses the following passage from *Baby No-Eyes* to highlight the shift from the written to an oral domain in the same novel. Mahaki's grandfather is speaking in front of the Pakeha council that is investigating his land claim, and he uses the rhetorical devices of whaikorero (oratory), with its emphatic repetitions and references to myth, whakapapa (genealogy) and creation chants:

> 'I come from the ground I tell you. No need to disturb the ancestors to tell you that. I come from the ground and the heavens. I come from the ground and the heavens in the most faraway place. I come from the ground and the heavens in the longest time ago. I come from the ground and the heavens from the place deep felt in my heart, and my tongue come with me. Don't kill our ancestors. Don't kill our childrens [*sic*].'
> Grandfather giving it his best shot, what he believed to be his utmost contribution to their understanding — but the Council didn't have a clue what he was going on about, sitting there like wood. (BN 156)

Keown underscores that the effect the old man has on his audience is estrangement: although they may speak the same language, the old man's words are unintelligible to council staff. Estrangement could very well be what non-Maori readers feel when faced with an 'english', in Ashcroft's words, missing most of its syntactical co-ordinates and with an unconventional narrative form that does not conform to the Western canon.

Gordon and Williams define Grace's linguistic techniques as so radical that even the views of a highly political writer such as Kenyan Ngugi wa Thiong'o seem tame by comparison. Ngugi eventually gave up writing in English and wrote in Kikuyu. By translating his Kikuyu writing into Swahili and then into English he nevertheless made it accessible to as many readers as possible. On the contrary, they argue that '[Grace] has taken the risk of allowing certain groups to be excluded and has enacted in her writing the large dynamics of Maori/Pakeha relations in New Zealand ... [her] novel cannot be expected to be fully understood outside the cultural politics of contemporary New Zealand.'[47]

The extensive use of literary code-switching by Grace and Ihimaera — whether organic or political — and their linguistic techniques (especially the radical ones operated by Grace), are subversive strategies that have helped the filtering of the Maori language into Aotearoa/New Zealand's predominantly monolingual society, and have redeployed English a vehicle to express a specifically Maori sense of the world. At the same time, kohanga reo and kura kaupapa primary schools have supported a new generation of Maori by giving them the opportunity to preserve their indigenous language and make up for the decreasing number of old people able to speak te reo fluently. There is therefore a double front in the struggle against the linguistic monopoly of the imperial centre. For people like Grace and Ihimaera, who grew up when speaking Maori was prohibited in schools and English was considered the only acceptable language, linguistic strategies are a way to make sense of their own 'english' as Maori New Zealanders. They share common objectives in the realms of literature and politics that do not view Aotearoa/New Zealand as a colonial outpost or a European country in the South Pacific, but as a Pacific country blending a dual Polynesian-European heritage in its language, culture and identity. The two adaptations of English employed by these two writers exemplify processes of language abrogation and appropriation that characterise postcolonial literatures. An indigenised reading of linguistic techniques in their fiction illustrates that deviance from the norm is always motivated in cultural or linguistic terms and is grounded in the needs of a minority language to express itself. Crucially, language functions as an identity marker and is an active force in the minority culture's struggle for self-determination.

9 Natural Born Environmentalists

An ecologically conscious attitude is common to indigenous cultures and rooted in their holistic view of reality. Accepting a systemic understanding of nature, indigenous people struggle not only for self-determination (and in some cases, sheer survival) but also to safeguard the environment with which they identify. As environmentalist Paul Hawken states, the indigenous viewpoint blurs the division between human rights and ecology, seeing them as two sides of the same dilemma, since 'the way we harm the earth affects all people and how we treat one another is reflected in how we treat the earth.'[1] Hawken underlines that even today about five thousand indigenous cultures are seeking to protect their homelands, which constitute one-fifth of the land surfaces on earth. In many cases these are 'the least corrupted forests, mountains, and grasslands remaining on earth.'[2] He contends that 'environmentalists and indigenous populations are thus obvious political allies'.[3]

These considerations certainly apply to Maoridom. Danny Keenan quotes Chief Judge Eddie Durie of the Waitangi Tribunal to describe the sense of attachment that Maori have to the land, defining it as 'inherent in the "vastly complex spiritual world through which Maori sought to maintain balance and harmony in his modification of the environment."'[4] Sargeson and Finlayson were particularly attracted to the Maori environmentalist approach — grounded on notions of 'agriculture' as 'culture', and of 'science' as 'observational science' recorded in myths and stories — and advocated the recovery of such values. Their critical depiction of Western capitalist society is centred on the belief that Westerners exploit the planet and each other in equal measure.

There are many examples of ecological consciousness within the fiction of Ihimaera and Grace, frequently connected to myth and legend. Their occurrence often links a respectful attitude to nature to customary practices recorded by common wisdom. Modern development is critiqued in the first pages of *Bulibasha*, for example, when Ihimaera's narrator describes the landscape around the Waipaoa River as losing its epic dimension through a simplification enacted by human engineering:

> Something else happened when human engineers simplified that complex landscape of river bends. With every sculpting movement of bulldozer and grader, they stripped the river of its *mythology*. Engineers control it with scientific and analytical precision, monitoring its rise and fall by computer, taming its wilfulness by the flick of a button. This *simplification* has led to an acceleration of time. The *epic dimension* that existed when you travelled at thirty miles an hour maximum on a twisting, turning road has gone. (BU 11, my emphases)

With *The Whale Rider* (published in 1987 and adapted into an award-winning movie released in 2003), Ihimaera adopts a fictional genre suspended between reality and myth to convey Maori environmental concerns. The protagonist, a young girl named Kahu turns out to be the true heir of the mythical ancestor Kahutia Te Rangi (also known as Paikea), who came to Aotearoa from Hawaiki on the back of a whale and settled at Whangara on the East Coast, where the story is set. The book lends itself to multiple readings, most obviously mythical and feminist. The mythical frame encompassing the story — graphically evidenced by italic text in the prologue and other sections — is a typical mode of Maori writing that constantly evokes the eternal dimension beyond the real. Feminist threads are centred on Kahu's futile efforts to be loved by her great-grandfather, Koro Apirana, the tribal leader who is desperately in search of a male successor. Although in every customary trial for the education of a leader she betters any boy in the village, Kahu is disregarded because she is female. The plot revolves around a theme that recurs frequently in Ihimaera's fiction: the attack on traditional gender relations within a preordained tribal hierarchy. In *The Matriarch* this is evinced by the figure of Artemis Riripeti.

The third major reading is an ecological one, which cuts across both the mythical frame and the main narrative. The mythical frame tells of a time when the human race co-operated with nature, and when all the creatures of earth and sea lived in helpful partnership. This is represented by the kinship between Paikea and the bull whale, a bond that is now broken. Actual events — French nuclear tests conducted at the South Pacific atoll of Mururoa — are also referenced in this frame, and the bull whale laments the death of seven young calves, the contamination of the water by radiation, and the disruption of the herd's primeval migratory route. The main narrative reports the large-scale whale hunting of the past and the whale strandings of the present day, yet also includes Koro's speech to the men of the village on discovering the stranded whales on Whangara beach, in which he yearns for a return to the 'original oneness of the world'[5] that existed before 'man had assumed a cloak of arrogance and set himself up above the Gods', and before 'he divided the world into that half he could believe in and that half he could not believe in. The real and the unreal. The natural and the supernatural. The present and the past. The scientific and the fantastic' (116 WR). His pleas to the people of the village to rescue the bull whale (which will in turn lead the herd) centre on this notion of unity: 'If it lives, we live. If it dies, we die' (117 WR). Reality and myth overlap in the frame and in the main narrative, connecting actual events and ecological concerns to a larger design. Koro's appeal to spiritual and imaginative powers is reminiscent of Finlayson's vocal attack on 'scientific barbarism'.

Kahu will not only guide the whale bull back into the sea but will be able to ride it like Paikea, thereby symbolising the recovery of a unity that had become lost, and reactivating communication between humans and the natural world. Central to the tale is the identification of Kahu as both future chief and the last spear 'which was to flower in the future' (141 WR), as the old mother whale suggests to convince her husband to take Kahu back to the land. On his arrival the ancestor Paikea had thrown out magic spears that turned into birds and fish, populating the earth and sea with his gifts for the new land. But one spear did not want to leave his hand, and Paikea came to understand that this last spear had to flower 'when the people are troubled and it is most needed' (6 WR). Kahu is that spear, the person needed to help a troubled humanity. The story metaphorically alludes to the environmental crisis of a suffering biosphere that can only remain alive if guided by illuminated 'chiefs' (as Kahu is supposed to be) promoting 'oneness', in other words, policies in defence of the Earth and the biodiversity of its ecosystems.

Customary practice and ecological concern also overlap in safeguarding the seabed and foreshore, and among other topics explored by Koro during his wananga (lessons in lore) with the village boys is overfishing: 'for to do so would be to take greedy advantage of Tangaroa [god of the sea] and would bring retribution' (49 WR). The same belief is alluded to in Grace's 'Kahawai' from *Electric City*. A couple decides to 'play truant' from work and go fishing, predicting the presence of a shoal of kahawai (a type of fish) in the bay from seagulls' flight patterns. Referring to the gulls swarming above the fish, the female narrator says: 'But he and I are not a swarm, we are only two of us. One fish each will do.'[6] A similar attitude is found in *Mutuwhenua*, when Ripeka's family spend the weekend seashell fishing at the beach. They collect a quantity of mussels sufficient only to feed themselves and are careful not to take the small ones: 'So they'll always be there' (59 MU). In Ihimaera's 'The Seahorse and the Reef' from *The New Net Goes Fishing*, a father exhorts his children to leave the seahorse they found in the sea to preserve its life and beauty. For all the Maori community's efforts to revere Tangaroa, keeping their bay clean and avoiding the depletion of the seabed, their sanctuary is finally contaminated by an unidentified stream of poisonous waste, probably coming from a nearby factory. Recent debate in Aotearoa/New Zealand concerning customary title of iwi to traditional seafood gathering grounds and access to the foreshore has been of great political significance. Whatever the result, debate has aroused an awareness in the general public that returning coastal land to Maori could promote a shared environmental and cultural patrimony. As the *Listener* remarked in November 2009:

> There is a growing acceptance that Maori should have the right to enjoy, protect and develop their traditional coastal areas — and that this can be done without trammelling the rights of all New Zealanders to enjoy the coastline equally. ... most New Zealanders found the 2003–05 escalation of hostilities disturbing, and in retrospect may well see it as having been unnecessary. There were not, after all, platoons of Maori undertaking paramilitary training in the hills — just a group of disaffected eccentrics. And Maori have found there were not, beside a local minority, legions of Pakeha avid to disrespect ancestral and spiritual claims to the beaches. On the contrary, the coastline's Maori heritage has grown as a source of pride and inspiration to New Zealanders of all races following the foreshore and seabed ructions, which had the handy spin-off of spreading awareness.[7]

Ecologically conscious aspects of Maori culture seem to guarantee, therefore, that the indigenous minority will safeguard a natural patrimony on behalf and in favour of the majority of New Zealanders.

The enormous production of domestic garbage in a globalised material society is the topic of Ihimaera's 'Dustbins', from his 1995 collection *Kingfisher Come Home*. It warns the reader against the extreme consequences of consumerism in the paradoxical final episode of the unwanted newborn baby thrown away into the rubbish-bin as any other useless object. Nuclear threat is explored in his 'Wiwi' (1995) through an original reversal of perspective: New Zealand is conducting nuclear tests in the remote island of Île de la Cité, Paris, raising the disconcerted protest of French 'natives' and governments of nearby 'atolls', including Germany, Belgium, Switzerland, Italy and Spain.[8] Other major environmental themes in Maori fiction are the preservation of the bush and promoting sustainable subsistence agriculture. Earlier, Sargeson, Finlayson and Hilliard had criticised the exploitative attitude of Pakeha toward the land, with the image of landslides symbolising the blindness of the Western approach to natural resources. According to traditional Maori views, logging and deforestation should be reduced to a minimum to avoid soil erosion, landslides and floods, as Ripeka's father suggests in *Mutuwhenua*: "'Leave the trees growing and those places will be all right. Leave them like they are and the creek will be all right too'" (58 MU). The custom of planting a tree for every newborn baby mentioned in the novel (and in Finlayson's 'The Totara Tree') is a typical example of observational science or experiential knowledge recorded in traditional rituals and serving specific customary purposes. After Tawera's birth in *Baby No-Eyes*, Gran Kura comes to live with Te Paania in the city, bringing 'her bag, her oil, a fish and a little tree' (BN 12). Interestingly, this custom has been replicated by environmental associations all over the world, and tree-planting programs are now offered to companies and individuals who want to offset their carbon footprint.

An ideal example of the promotion of subsistence agriculture is offered in *Potiki*. In this novel the Pakeha developers, ironically named 'Dollarman', try to convince a coastal Maori hapu to sell land for an access road to their new tourist facilities. The book sets the scene before Dollarman appears and describes the renewal that is taking place in the community under threat from economic crisis and unemployment. Community members have decided to cling to their land and have re-established gardens using the agricultural knowledge handed down to them by their elders, following a subsistence economy model that allows them to be self-sufficient. When Dollarman comes with a generous offer, they turn it down because they realise it would disrupt their way of life. Starkly different notions of progress are revealed in this passage:

> 'Well now, you've said that the developments here would be of no advantage to you. I'd like to remind you of what I've already said earlier. It's all job-creative. It'll mean work, well-paid work, right on your doorstep, so to speak. And for the area … it'll bring people … progress …'
> 'But you see, we already have jobs, we've got progress …'
> 'I understand, perhaps I'm wrong, that you are mostly unemployed?'

'Everything we need is here. This is where our work is.'
'And progress? Well it's not ... obvious.'
'Not to you. Not in your eyes. But what we're doing is important.
To us. To us that's progress.' (PO 90)

The community claims the right to view progress in terms that are measured not solely by economics but also in affective and cultural terms. This point of difference is reinforced when a Maori spokesman stresses how their quality of life would be impacted if they accepted the agreement, explicitly referring to the environmental impact of the venture:

'I didn't expect you to be so unreasonable ...'
'Unreasonable? Perhaps it is yourself that is being unreasonable if you think we would want pollution of the water out there, if you think we would want crowds of people, people that can afford caviar and who import salmon, coming here and using up the fish ...'
'And jobs ...'
'As we have told you, we have work. You want us to clean your toilets and dig your drains or empty your rubbish bins but we've got more important ...'
'I didn't say ... And I wasn't ... And you are looking back, looking back, all the time.'
'Wrong. We're looking to the future. If we sold out to you what would we be in the future?
'You'd be well off. You could develop land, do anything you want.'
'I tell you if we sold to you we would be dust. Blowing in the wind.' (PO 93)

The spokesman affirms the primacy of 'quality' over 'quantity', 'well-being' over 'well-having', 'the Good' over 'goods', to use Latouche's categories mentioned in chapter 2. He underscores the moral responsibility that his people have for the environment and the generations to come, and how this entails strong implications of cultural identity. Furthermore, any job opportunities that come for Maori from the Western model of progress usually infer some kind of regression, recalling the protagonist of Finlayson's 'Johnny Wairua's Wonderland' who changes from working his own land to being a waged undertaker.

Holly Walker has analysed the evolution of development models proposed in Grace's novels from *Potiki* to *Dogside Story*. To argue her point Walker gives the following definitions of 'post-development approach' and 'participatory development'. Post-development rejects the traditional development discourse outright, seeing it as legitimising and reinforcing Western domination over non-Western cultures. This does not mean the rejection of change and possibility, but rather the awareness that Western development is only one way of seeing the world and is basically grounded on the notion of economic growth. It does not take into consideration factors like resourcefulness, environmental impact or democracy, which could be equally important. Latouche's theory of degrowth belongs to this critical position. Participatory development, on the contrary, is an inflection of traditional development, managed by local communities that possess a large degree of autonomy.[9]

Walker argues that Grace's condemnation of Western development is unequivocal in *Potiki* and that the novelist is taking a 'post-development stance'; in *Dogside Story* she has moved to a concept of 'participatory development', since the Maori community takes over the Millennium Business themselves. The passage is therefore from 'an outright rejection of development as a Western ideology in *Potiki* to a renegotiation of development from a Maori perspective in *Dogside Story*.'[10] This, in Walker's view, reflects the changing political atmosphere characterising the years to which the novels belong: *Potiki* (1986) is imbued with mid-1980s activism and an urge to assert an endangered identity; *Dogside Story* (2001) conveys the political shift to improving socio-economic conditions for Maori. Walker's sharp analysis does not fail to note that the Millennium Business in *Dogside Story* is a one-off venture pursued for a specific purpose (the building of a new wharekai or dining hall); the outcome therefore belongs to yet another category that can be called 'Maori development', appropriating Western tools to further traditional beliefs and cultural values.

The one-off nature of the Millennium Business is evidence, in my opinion, that Grace is encouraging the use of Western models of development not as a rule but as the exception. Renegotiating a development aligned with Maori principles necessitates, above all, respect for the environment and an attitude diametrically opposed to the Western logic of growth for growth's sake. The model implied in *Dogside Story* seems again closer to post-development than to participatory development, insofar as it escapes the logic of profit for profit (the kaupapa is the wharenui), is guided democratically by a communal hui, and has only a limited impact on the environment. The strong objection to the project by Dion, a young community member studying at Victoria University in Wellington, illustrates the wariness of younger generations about Western lifestyles and economic models. Dion advocates a life lived with one's feet on the ground and close to natural surroundings:

> 'People get sad the higher they get off the ground. People with
> the beach and trees around, and a little house flat on the ground
> laugh more. You go and live in a suburb, squeezed in a house or

flat where all the paths and floors are concreted over, then your mouth goes down a bit at the corners and you get a wrinkle on your head.'(149 DO)

'People forget where they belong when they live high up …'(177 DO)

To summarise, the models of development in Ihimaera and Grace lead us in the direction of post-development or degrowth positions, premised on:
1. Rejecting a growth for growth's sake economy that encourages waste, consumerism, despoiling of lands and destruction of eco-systems and bio-diversity.
2. Reducing the consumption of natural resources, not according to a logic of profit but of need, in order to guarantee those resources to the next generations.
3. Relocalising economies to create integrated, self-sufficient and materially responsible societies.
4. Recognising the importance of convivial relationships to fill the void caused by the dominant logic of competition, productivity and profit, which can lead people to compulsive consumerism (or drug/alcohol addiction).

The needs induced by the narrow pursuit of economic growth are self-referential and self-sustaining: they reinforce the system itself.[11] The community spokesman's answer to Dollarman — 'Everything we need is here' — conveys a very different notion of welfare that includes spiritual, material, interpersonal and environmental factors.

Ecological sensitivity and markedly non-Western attitudes to development are cultural traits common across indigenous cultures. Ihimaera has often stressed the kinship between Maori and other indigenous peoples. In *The Dream Swimmer*, protagonist Tamatea is a legal consultant for the United Nations, sent on missions to crisis areas of the world. He reports on the legacies of colonisation among populations like the Yanumani Indians who have been decimated by wholesale gold mining and mercury poisoning in the Amazon rain forest, or the explosive civil wars in Zaire and Rwanda. Recalling Artemis Riripeti's speech at the Wellington hui in 1949, Tamatea echoes the matriarch's remark that the 'Pharaoh' was found not only in Aotearoa/New Zealand but throughout the world:

'What I do care about,' Riripeti continued, 'is that the Pakeha has particular contempt for us, the coloured peoples of the world … Thus, wherever there are coloured people, he has always tried to make us slaves.' (250 TD)

Riripeti enumerates a long list of enslaved indigenous peoples, 'the Great Enslavement of the World' (250 TD), from Africa, Latin America, North America and the Pacific. The Maori predicament is therefore seen as a particular instance of a larger situation: the enemy is not just the single government or local power but a global system that has colonised the Earth, imposing an economy, rules and culture, determining a hierarchy of races and fostering wars to safeguard its privileges. In a later novel by Ihimaera, *The Uncle's Story* (2000), Michael's fight for the recognition of gay rights within traditional culture is threaded into the struggle for self-determination by First Peoples at an Indigenous Arts conference in Ottawa, attended by indigenous peoples from Canada, Mexico, Australia, Iceland, South Africa and the US. Ihimaera increasingly enlarges his political analysis to encompass the entire world. Relating the story of television celebrity Tom Mahana in *The Rope of Man* (2005) allows Ihimaera to include conflicts and violations of human rights, among which the Vietnam War, the Indonesian invasion of East Timor, the killing fields of Pol Pot's rule in Cambodia, pro-democracy demonstrations in Tiananmen Square, and the 1989 Tibet-China crisis. Tom explains that his success as a television reporter comes from his passion, his avoidance of a non-partisan attitude, and his stance in favour of the oppressed, persecuted, invaded and displaced. His attitude likely derives from his membership of a minority culture that has had to fight to see its own rights acknowledged at home.

This ever-enlarging perspective demonstrates that Ihimaera's holistic view is driven, to quote Hawken again, by 'a deep sense of connectedness to the living world'[12], whether natural or man-made. Defending basic rights for the human race and the environment are just two sides of the same dilemma for Maori and indigenous people because 'the way we harm the earth affects all people and how we treat one another is reflected in how we treat the earth.'[13]

10 From Extended Family to Gay Tribe

If the 1970s were characterised by the recovery and assertion of the foundational traits of Maori identity and the 1980s by activism and militant politics, Maori writing from the 1990s onwards reflects an urge to explore the inflections of an identity now reasonably secure and established enough to face the challenges of the present. A comment of Makareta, one of the protagonists of Grace's novel *Cousins*, expresses this position: 'It's not sticking to the old ways that's important ... but it's being us, using all the new knowledge our way. Everything new belongs to us too.'[1] Grace seems to validate Stuart Hall's theory of postcolonial identity (explored in chapter 4) as a question of representation and narrative, subject to changes and dependent on negotiations with historical circumstances. Cultural identity is viewed as a creative act, a continual 'imaginative rediscovery' that redefines itself in contact with changing conditions.[2]

Fiction published since the 1990s has emphasised new Maori men and women, bound to their people and educated in their heritage, who nevertheless subvert customary practices or fixed hierarchies. Their identity draws upon knowledge from both traditional and modern worlds to deal with a changing reality. Hints of this new trend are present in the characters of Andrew Whatu in *Whanau*, Tangimoana in *Potiki* and Tama in *The Matriarch*, each of them problematic young people living in an amphibious state, marked by a deep bond with their origins as well as knowledge of the Pakeha world. This composite condition has made them vulnerable — though at the same time flexible and reactive — in responding to the demands of the world.

Chronologically, the first book exploring this evolution in characterisation is Grace's novel *Cousins* (1992), which deals with the intertwining lives of three cousins — Mata, Missy and Makareta — and juxtaposes the old and new orders in the characters of Grandmother Keita and Makareta. A similar situation is found in *Bulibasha* (1994), where Ihimaera contrasts old and new through Grandfather Tamihana and Simeon (or Himiona, in Maori). Keita and Tamihana embody the defence of an *ancien régime* of rules and behaviours that have to be accepted without question for the good of the people, including arranged marriages (or taumau, primarily motivated by the acquisition of land for the whanau) and the right to rule of the first born and his or her descendants. Makareta is groomed to assume a leadership role, well educated in both Maori and Pakeha heritage and almost idolised by everybody in the family, yet she rejects the imposition of an arranged marriage and leaves the homestead for a life in the city. Simeon, belonging to a minor line of descent entitled to no land of its own[3], is destined only to serve future leaders of the extended family, yet his studies and hard work enable him to challenge Tamihana's patriarchal tyranny. By conforming to the old order, Keita and Tamihana believe they are committing themselves to the good of their whanau, to its economic livelihood and land. Keita's management of the community is a mix of entrepreneurial spirit and mission, as she explains to Missy, who has volunteered to replace her cousin Makareta in the taumau ceremony:

> When I married your grandfather we had seen each other just once, but we had been promised since we were children. We were brought together when I was nineteen. Three months later we were married and it was up to the two of us to make a success of it. We did our best because we had to. It was for the people, and if it went wrong it meant the people were wrong. The people had the responsibility of us. At that time I knew nothing about the land, but I had to learn … Now you have to learn too. (229 CO)

Tamihana has made a profitable marriage with Ramona and, taking advantage of Apirana Ngata's scheme to help Maori farmers, has established a successful business: the largest network of shearing gangs in Poverty Bay, composed entirely of whanau and other kin families. Keita's and Tamihana's perspectives, however, are confined within the boundaries of the hapu and to the interests of each family. Tamihana also demonstrates contempt for learning and formal education, underestimating their importance and mocking Simeon for his good school results. Makareta and Simeon, on the other hand, have broader horizons. Makareta has a career as a nurse and then becomes an activist leader. Simeon's speech at the courthouse as a student shows that, despite his youth, he is able to question the viability of a law system that would find for Pakeha in every case brought by them against Maori. At the end of the novel we are told that he lives in Auckland and has made something of his life (287 BU); we may expect Simeon to have followed a legal career. The importance of an educational background is stressed in both novels: being raised in Maori values as well as achieving high Pakeha academic standards is empowering, to help Maori contribute to society and enable them to change it from within. As Simeon states: 'Grandfather just did not want the world to change. I was a new generation. Somewhere between both lay the reason.' (228 BU)

Old and new orders can also be explored in the approach to illness and medical treatment. Tamihana rejects all medical cures for the cancer that is devastating his body; likewise Joshua 'showed the same stupidity when his waterworks stopped and he couldn't urinate' (259 BU), and refused to see a doctor (though he later did, and was 'fixed'). Uncle Ihaka dies of a swollen appendix at 49, and cousin Haromi dies of breast cancer, refusing mastectomy because 'the body is tapu' and 'the removal of any part of oneself was a heresy' (259 BU). Malady is interpreted as 'a punishment, a retribution for some evil committed when you were younger' (259 BU) in the old paradigm, a perspective that Simeon describes as 'stupidity' at one point. In *Cousins* we are told that Makareta's mother, Polly — another character representing the new order and an inspiration to her daughter — fought fiercely against her cancer, taking 'every treatment with a real hope' (211 CO).

It is important to reinforce that Ihimaera and Grace are not undermining the essential values of Maori culture. They are redefining those values within a new framework. This entails sharing in the ability of modern medical science to save life, for example, yet also implies respecting Maori beliefs of the sacredness of the body and its right to receive customary burial at death. These were denied to the aborted baby in Grace's *Baby No-Eyes*, later found in a hospital waste bin. Since beliefs and values constitute the basis of cultural identity, Maori claim access to 'everything new' but also the right to 'use new knowledge [their] way' (235 CO). An example of this mediation between cultural perspectives is the way Makareta succeeds in pursuing her nursing career in Wellington without abdicating cultural values that prescribe specific rituals in handling the dead. To do this she draws on traditional knowledge, appealing to the teachings of her great-aunt Hinemate, the kuia that raised her:

> When there were things that felt wrong for me — touching the
> dead who were not my own dead to touch, shifting the bed of the
> dead into a ward for the living, handling the linen of the dead and

depositing it with all the other linen without any clearing, preparing the room where someone had died for someone else to come into — she [Kui Hinemate] helped me to have the right karakia to say and to do my own cleansing. They were the customs I had observed so well as I journeyed about with old ones when I was a child, everything that Kui Hinemate and the grandmothers had taught me that would keep me safe during my life. (204 CO)

Lack of cultural identity in *Cousins* brings with it disempowering effects and, ultimately, leads to mental instability, destitution and criminality. The results of 'cultural and emotional deprivation'[4] are embodied in Mata, who must suffer the consequences of her mother's defiance of the old order and her marriage to a Pakeha (instead of Keita's choice). When Mata's mother Anihera dies, her father Albert places her in an orphanage under the legal guardianship of a Pakeha woman and leaves for Britain, depriving Mata not only of love and a family but also of her language, her Maori name and a sense of cultural belonging. As Dell Panny argues: 'The need to belong to whānau, hapū, iwi and the cultural imperative to reciprocate do not involve her, until she is guided out of a mental and emotional void'.[5] Mata is helpless, inadequate and socially inept to the extent of appearing retarded. She is abandoned by an old order that proved as rigid and unforgiving as Keita's words on learning of Anihera's marriage — 'She wasn't their daughter any more, Keita said. This wasn't her home any more.' (55 CO) — until Makareta locates her and brings her back to the whanau.

Makareta's widowed mother Polly also avoided an arranged marriage within the whanau (Keita had wanted her to marry Polly's brother-in-law Aperehama). Instead she left for Wellington 'to do something new' (102 CO) and escape the 'life of waiting and hoping' (109 CO) destined to women of previous generations. Mother and daughter exemplify the novel's central ideas of retrieval and renewal, responding to the powerlessness and degradation among Maori in Wellington by taking charge of the larger problem. Realising that growing up in a warm, caring and well-defined cultural context contributes to individual and collective self-esteem, Makareta conceives of the unemployment, underachievement, criminality and poor health of Maori as a void that must be filled:

They were the beaten, the hollowed-out of our people, the rawakore, the truly disinherited, where nothing substantial was inbuilt and nothing was valued or marvellous — where there was no memory, where the void had been defiled by an inrushing of anger and weeping. (208 CO)

Makareta and Polly join the Land March demonstrators, and Polly opens a kohanga reo in her own house. Makareta will pass on the knowledge of Maori culture and language that she acquired through her education as a leader, working to empower urban Maori who, like Mata, are now dispirited and incapable of asserting themselves.

Simeon's challenge to the old order emancipates his own family and the whole clan, too. Instead of absolute rule imposed by Tamihana, there will be democratic polls (and secret ballots) on decisions relevant to the community. Joshua will find the courage to ask Tamihana for land and will receive some from Grandmother Ramona, and now that she is literate Simeon's mother will be able to check the bills of the Pakeha storekeeper who cheated her.

Another sign of renewal is evident in the notion of family. Two key principles that underlie bonds between whanau and iwi members are those of whanaungatanga (kinship and family responsibility) and manaakitanga (mutual care and respect). Since the 1990s these core values of Maori culture have been extended in novels to non-traditional families or larger groups of people, including Pakeha discarded by their own system. When Polly moves to Wellington, she takes care of her sister Cissie's children while she is in hospital, and acts as their mother after her death from tuberculosis. This family will eventually enlarge to include Alma, the only Pakeha available to rent a house to a Maori. Alma is an extrovert, considered 'mad in the head' (118 CO) because of her love for parrots and becomes 'a lovely grandmother' (131 CO) to Cissie's children, helping Polly look after them, knitting them jerseys and socks. Polly in turn cares for Alma during her final illness and death, becoming the older woman's only beneficiary (together with the parrots). Mata herself applies these values with her only friend from her time at the orphanage, ebullient and anti-conformist Jean, a Pakeha whose son Mata raises for six years. Similarly in *Bulibasha*, a new family is formed that does not conform to conventions. After Tamihana's death, Ramona marries the family enemy Rupeni Poata (actually her first true love) against the will of most of the whanau but with the support of Simeon and his family. Moreover the ethic of kinship and reciprocal care is extended to every Maori in need, those fighting for their land, rights and recognition, as shown in Makareta's commitment to Maori causes.

Reconfiguring whanau and iwi into new forms — unconventional though respectful of foundational values– is found in two different versions in Grace's collection *The Sky People* (1994), and in Ihimaera's *The Uncle's Story* (2000). Grace uses the term 'sky people' to describe all those who are other or unconventional.[6] Roimata explains the risk of becoming a 'sky dweller' in *Potiki* with a mythical metaphor drawing on the legend of Rona, who symbolises a person whose roots are shallow and who is easily taken astray, as we saw in chapter 5. Roimata comments that 'one became a sky dweller by accident, or by way of punishment, not on purpose ... Had [Rona] grasped a more sturdy tree, a more heavily rooted tree, she could perhaps have stood against the anger of the moon' (PO 31). Beyond the mythical reading, the sky people category can be interpreted in terms of mental illness or social isolation, or simply as non-conformists who resist mainstream tastes, attitudes and lifestyles. Grace has elaborated on this concept:

> In *The Sky People*, many of the people are out on the edge, and are connected to the sky in their minds. This can sometimes mean that they are different in their minds through being on the edge of sanity and almost over the edge for one reason or another. Or sometimes 'Sky People' are a little apart from ordinary people through their imagination, their spirituality, or their socialization, and so may not be quite so fixed to the earthly and practical things.[7]

In the story that gives the title to *The Sky People*, Nina is rejected and ostracised by her Maori mother because she is darker than her other children. Grace stigmatises the racist attitudes of Maori who have taken on the view of the colonisers, recalling Finlayson's 'Like the Pakeha'. Nina grows up feeling unworthy and lacking self-esteem, like Mata in *Cousins*. She runs away with another outsider, a funny old tramp who thinks Nina looks like his grandmother. They flee from 'people without faces',[8] looking for 'the eared and eyed' (80 SP) and find these in another unconventional inter-racial family formed by Helene, a Pakeha runaway, her Maori partner Baker and his little daughter Steffy. The three live on the top floor of a disused warehouse, close to the sky, making extravagant clothes and accessories with anything they find from flea markets and rubbish bins. Clearly cast out from society, they harness their non-conformity and use it creatively to reshape the detritus of consumer society into an alternative product that they resell at a stall in the Quay. Their work stands out as a triumph of colours, materials, patterns and shapes of all kinds, and Nina and the old man go into partnership with the enterprising couple. They all speak the same language of imagination. Characters are consequently renamed (Helene turns into 'Jewel' and the old man into 'Skyfinder') and family roles are changed, as Skyfinder pinpoints: "'It's here,' he happily said, 'with a grandmother, a sister, a brother, an angel. It's here, where the birds are, where they come and bring their findings to the sky'" (79 SP). When old Skyfinder dies a big funeral is organised, a colourful mix of traditional and unorthodox rituals. The little community, grounded on an emotional and creative bond outside the conventions of mainstream society, ends up growing a new family and a thriving business, selling their unique products to theatres and shows. This bond declines only when Helene and Baker — now well off and with two more children — move to an ordinary life in suburbia, yet Nina is able to constitute a new family with young Steffy.

The highly figurative language of Nina and Skyfinder, easily decoded by the other members of the community, recalls Janet Frame's characters, who were excluded from mainstream society for being over-imaginative. *The Sky People* is interesting not only because of its equation between Pakeha who do not fit and the indigenous minority who are historically marginalised, but also for their coalition against consumer society, on whose crumbs they thrive. Pakeha and Maori, sharing the same outcast condition, co-operate and establish success in their own terms, in an imaginative reconstruction of discarded objects as much as it does a rediscovery of marginalised identity.

A further reconfiguration of family and cultural identity is offered by *The Uncle's Story*, which establishes the notion of a 'gay tribe' within Maoritanga. The novel aims to redefine a Maori identity for gay men. As in *Cousins* and *Bulibasha*, the book juxtaposes an old and a new symbolic order. The story develops through three generations: Arapeta, the patriarch, embodies the old order. When he discovers that his son Sam is homosexual, Arapeta punishes him with violence and scorn. Sam will be erased from the family's memory after his premature death, and all his belongings will be burned. Sam's younger brother Monty sides with tradition and shares the imposed code of silence. When his own son Michael comes out to the family, Monty reacts according to the old order and ostracises him.

Arapeta recalls *Bulibasha's* Tamihana for his emphasis on virility, bravery and physical prowess as determinant traits of men, and his sexist view of women as the weaker and ultimately inferior gender. According to the traditional Maori view explained in the novel, the mana of a man resides in his fighting power as a warrior and in his reproductive sexuality, which contributes to whakapapa.[9] Connecting man and warrior together with a procreative imperative forms a paradigm seemingly incompatible with homosexuality, which can only be viewed as a temporary aberration. Gays do not belong: they are 'perverts' and 'outcasts' (27 US). The lack of congruence between Maori male identity and gay identity is central to the novel, which poses the question: do you have to choose between being Maori and being gay? Michael, the new man who embodies the new order, answers in the negative.

Ihimaera had already dealt with the difficulty of asserting gay identity within Maori culture in *The Whale Rider* and *Bulibasha*, albeit marginally. In the former, narrator Rawiri poses the ethic of kinship (whanaungatanga) over sexual identity, after he spends some time in Australia and meets his cousin Henare 'wearing a dress' (62 WR). While Kingi, another cousin, tries to avoid Henare, Rawiri addresses him warmly and asserts the right of everybody to live 'the way they wanted to' (62 WR). At the hockey tournament in *Bulibasha* Simeon challenges Tamihana's old order by including Donna, Cindy and Chantelle — transvestite family relations — in his own provocatively named team 'The Waituhi Rebels'. Despite Tamihana's attempts to exclude the transvestites when they unexpectedly get to the final, Simeon stubbornly keeps the same team and they eventually win. His behaviour shows whanaungatanga prevailing over sexual differences. Ihimaera's first major treatment of homosexuality was actually in the novel *Nights in the Gardens of Spain* (1996), although with a Pakeha protagonist: David Munro. Among the social circle in which he moves reference is made to a 'Maori gay tribe' led by the admirable Maori character named The Noble Savage. This alternative iwi becomes central in *The Uncle's Story*.[10]

The plot of *The Uncle's Story* basically intertwines two strands: Michael's discovery of Uncle Sam's story through his diary, rescued from a fire and hidden for many years by his sister Pat until Michael's disclosure to his parents; and Michael's personal quest for reconciliation between identities that appear mutually exclusive. The book steadily blurs the dichotomy inherent in the old order: Sam is both a warrior and a homosexual. Following Arapeta's deeds with the Maori Battalion in the Second World War, Sam volunteered for Vietnam and distinguished himself for his bravery, physical prowess and psychological resistance. In Vietnam he gradually falls in love with another brave warrior, US helicopter pilot Cliff Harper. Arapeta finds out about their relationship when Cliff comes to visit Sam at home and, according to tradition, confronts Cliff in close combat. Arapeta loses; Cliff is younger, stronger and better trained, and he shows Sam that his father is neither an invincible, epic figure who hushes people merely with his rhetoric nor one who 'lifts up the sky' with his back (39 US), not a 'God incarnate' (39 US) but a fallible man. Sam is shown that he could prove himself a better warrior than his father despite his homosexuality. But while Cliff may be invulnerable to Arapeta's charisma, authority and psychic power — he demolishes Arapeta by defining him a 'tyrant' and a 'bully' (253 US) — Sam is not. He is unable to respond in the same way to the old symbolic order because he still believes it to be the only order possible, one inextricably linked with his own identity as Maori. At this point Sam understands Maori and homosexual identities to be incompatible and, after convincing Cliff to leave, submits to a whipping from his father.

It is only while being punished that Sam realises the inherent injustice in the old order and rebels, refusing to repent or to recognise his homosexuality as a sin. He decides to meet Cliff at the airport and fly away with him, but is killed in a car accident. Having been forced to choose between two seemingly irreconcilable identities, Sam finally embraces the homosexual one, but in doing so removes himself from the judgement of his people by leaving the country, as cousin Henare does in *The Whale Rider*. Sam had been ostracised from Maoritanga by Arapeta's ultimate gesture of scorn and repulsion: the patriarch urinates on his son's prostrated body after the whipping. Sam rebels against tradition and is compelled to make a painful choice, but his nephew Michael rebels against having to choose at all, between being Maori or homosexual.

If Sam proves the warrior/homosexual dichotomy to be wrong, Michael and his gay friends prove the fallacy of a second set of opposites: procreative heterosexuality/sterile homosexuality. The book challenges the exclusive right of heterosexuals to procreate, be part of whanau or iwi, and contribute to the continuation of whakapapa. Borne out of a modern conception of tribe and lineage, it gives rise to the notion of a gay tribe, in other words a community that binds together the procreative needs of both heterosexuals and homosexuals, promotes tolerance of sexual practices across a variety of different gender formulations, and erases enforced norms of oppositional identities. A practical example in *The Uncle's Story* is given by Tane Mahuta, an ex-transvestite who founded the first organisation to help gay Maori and Polynesian men during the 1980s AIDS epidemic. As Tane explains to Michael, he has accepted a taumau arranged by his mother, who did not want the family line to die with him. The bride happened to be a mature, open-minded woman aware of Tane's homosexuality as well as her own profound desire to have children. She makes Tane reconsider his abdication of fatherhood, deconstructing enforced notions of gender relationships, sexuality and parenthood:

> 'Just because you're gay, does that mean you can't be a father? I think not. I hope not. You are a fine man and your sexuality has a strength of its own which you can bring to a relationship not only with me but with any children we may have … I admire you for what you do and the courage you have. These are qualities I am looking for in a husband and a father.' (295 US)

Tane is profoundly grateful to his wife for their two sons, and proposes a similar arranged marriage between Michael and Roimata, a lesbian activist who is Michael's best friend. Taumau, a traditional custom, is repurposed for the construction of a gay Maori extended family. Carlos, Michael's partner, and Roimata are willing to accept the arrangement: 'I can share you, Michael, if I have to. Roimata and I have already talked about that. We'll work something out ' (290 US). Fundamental values of Maori culture — the importance of the extended family, of belonging to an iwi and continuing the whakapapa — are in this way preserved. Tane explains further:

> 'Marriage should be an option for gay and Polynesian men and women. With it we can establish a tribe — a tribe based not just on sexual identity but on family. A tribe must have children to survive. It must also have parents, grandmothers and grandfathers. Even though the children may not be gay by practice, they will be gay by

genealogy, through their fathers and mothers. When my children grow up, I want them to think of themselves as belonging to a great new gay family, a wonderful new gay tribe'. (296 US)

Changing the notion of identity into a mutable narrative that can be retold and imaginatively reconstructed means Michael doesn't have to choose between being gay and being Maori. This can be effected within a context of shared values; however, it may be more difficult for people of other cultural backgrounds. Michael's ex-partner Jason, a Pakeha, left him because he felt neglected and not loved enough, interpreting Michael's delay in coming out as a failure to assume his role as an official partner. Raised in a Pakeha nuclear family, Jason underestimates the extent of Michael's cultural dilemma and would probably have considered the notion of gay tribe as aberrant. The condition of homosexual Maori thus appears constrained by two equally alien and disturbing forces: homophobic Maori traditions and the dominant gay Pakeha sub-culture, equally remote from the needs of its own minorities.

Christening the new gay tribe occurs at the tangi of Waka, a young Maori rent boy who has died of AIDS. The tangi becomes the symbol of the reconfiguration of Maori traditions from a gay perspective. Michael, Roimata and Carlos gather a group of Waka's Maori friends — deracinated street kids and transvestites who are themselves entirely ignorant of Maori rituals — and teach the girls to karanga and the boys to haka. Unsure if Waka will be accepted, they all accompany his body to his marae where the boy's grandmother welcomes them, adjusting her karanga to the occasion:

> 'Welcome you strange tribe I see before me! Come forward, you tribe of men who love men and women who love women! Welcome, you brave gay tribe, whom none have seen before! Come! Bring your dead who is also our dead!–
> Our tribe was born that day. (365 US)

Unlike Sam, forbidden by Arapeta to be buried in the family's urupa, Waka is guaranteed the return to his turangawaewae, his belonging and his Maori identity.

The emphasis on evolution and reconstructing identity, as opposed to inert notions of normative rigidity, is further evoked by frequent use of a metaphor for identity as a narrative or history that must be rewritten or retold in order to remain vital. Sam's narrative — his memory and his diary — had been denied and deleted by the old order; his point of view and his words are cancelled by a totalitarian system. Michael, on the contrary, has the confidence to state: 'After all these years of Mum and Dad talking for me, and making up a history for me, it was time I talked for myself' (17 US). Ihimaera claims the right of Maori not only to retell Pakeha history from a Maori point of view, as he did in *The Matriarch* and *The Dream Swimmer*, but to rewrite notions of Maori identity challenging the traditional normative code.

Michael's claim to making his own history affects not only his personal life but also adds to a larger narrative, that of Maori gay men and lesbians in Aotearoa/ New Zealand, and gay indigenous people in the world. At the Ottawa Indigenous Arts Conference, Michael and Roimata challenge the right of the Canadian Council (promoting and subsidising the event) to decide its topics and trends, which in the council's view should stress the achievements of indigenous peoples and a reconciliatory attitude. Instead they present two motions: the first incites indigenous people to become agents of their own history and sovereignty, giving them freedom to enlarge the agenda of the conference. Michael emphasises the need to view culture as dynamic, flexible and open to an imaginative reconstruction:

'We must regain our right to rehabilitate, reconstruct, reaffirm and re-establish our cultures. We must disconnect from the White umbilical ... Although we are minority cultures in the eyes of the White world, we must continue to dream majority dreams.' (326 US)

In the second motion, Michael asks for all gay men and lesbians in traditional indigenous cultures to be recognised. He appeals to the principle that these men and women have always been interlinked with the genealogies of their nations and have contributed to their cause, highlighting how many were given a special social function by remembering the 'people of two spirits' raised to the role of shaman among American Indian culture.

Michael and Roimata's motions are unanimously endorsed. The episode at the conference marks an apex in the process of moving from dependence to independence, from subjection to agency, from being told to telling, and from fixity to renewal.

Cousins, Bulibasha, The Sky People and *The Uncle's Story* seek to redefine Maori identity of the present, distancing it from rigid traditions and stable narratives yet at the same time spiralling back toward core values that are retrieved and then reaffirmed in new forms. This idea informs Stuart Hall's argument that cultural identities are always questions of representations and that they should not be taken literally, but read as narratives subject to change and dependent on historical circumstances. His notion of identity as a continual imaginative rediscovery can be applied vividly to Maori culture.

11 Maori on the World Stage

In these chapters we have followed the course of writing by Grace and Ihimaera from their earliest works up to those of the present day. Analysis of their texts traces an evolution beginning with the recovery of Maori values in the 1970s, to a politically committed literature in the 1980s aimed at asserting Maori self-determination, to an imaginative rediscovery of Maori heritage in the 1990s and early years of the new millennium. This development indicates the constant renewal of Maori coming to terms with present events and, simultaneously, acknowledges that modernity can be accommodated in Maori terms and does not require the abdication of cultural identity. Trends such as these continue in the writers' latest works, which project a Maori vision onto a larger stage, either crossing the boundary of Aotearoa/New Zealand or bringing external or international influences into the Maori world. Ihimaera initiated his own spiralling outwards and inwards in *The Matriarch* and *The Dream Swimmer*, and continued it with *Bulibasha, The Uncle's Story* and *The Rope of Man* (2005). Similarly, Grace broadens her fictional horizons over this time, particularly with her novel *Tu* (2004).

Abrogating boundaries: Ihimaera's Maori as citizens of the world

During an interview with Juniper Ellis in 1998 Ihimaera explored the development of his own writing over the years, as well as the future course it could probably take. He asserted himself as a Maori writer, denying other fashionable 'labels': 'What matters to me is the view from the inside out. I don't consider myself as a postmodern writer, but I know that I am a Maori writer, and this is my world.'[1] Despite acknowledging the importance of listening to 'his own voice', however, he also admits that it 'is not a voice that is pure Maori'[2] and concludes: 'What we are now in is a literature of race relations … Maori literature at its purest is now behind us. Thank God we've got it.'[3] Ihimaera underlines that using English as a linguistic medium has allowed him the freedom to 'ransack' all that has been produced in Western culture from Roman and Greek mythologies to American literature, insofar as English is 'profane', ordinary and common. Being tapu (sacred), on the other hand, the Maori language imposes certain constrictions.[4] In postcolonial terms, Ihimaera is overtly asserting his right to abrogate and appropriate, in relation to both the language and literary genres. His reflections help us to read two major forces acting in his fiction: adhering to a Maori vision and values, which constitute the pillars of his world view; and using Western genres he feels attracted to and that are consciously inflected by his kaupapa or central concerns.

The most evident example of his adherence to a Maori vision is his reiterative mode, which began in his early works and that adds to the construction of a paradigmatic textual world. The recurrence of places and characters affirms the importance of belonging for cultural and emotional self-definition and self-assertion, and the primacy of the community over the individual. None of his books or stories is self-contained, but is completed by stories in his other books. Waituhi is omnipresent from *Pounamu, Pounamu, Tangi* and *Whanau* to *The Matriarch* and *The Dream Swimmer*, in *Bulibasha* and *The Uncle's Story* as well as the new versions of his first three works *Pounamu, Pounamu* (2003), *Whanau II* (2004) and *The Rope of Man* (2005). For all his characters' spiralling outwards to Wellington, Vietnam, London and beyond, Waituhi remains their turangawaewae, their standing place and the centre informing their identities.

Several characters cut across many of his works, and others may have different names but clearly refer to characters of previous books. Certain surnames are repeated and — although they may not always be coherently linked to previously mentioned characters bearing the same surname — they add to the image of an enlarged family and a complex whakapapa. Riripeti, the matriarch, is mentioned in *Bulibasha* as the only one Tamihana 'acknowledged to be above him' (14 BU), despite being a woman. In this novel the genealogy of the Mahana family featuring in *Tangi*, *Whanau* and *The Matriarch* is extended to include Tamihana, introduced as the brother of Ihaka, Riripeti's husband (23 BU). The book is therefore a chronicle of a side branch of the Mahana family, which contributes to the larger saga narrated in *The Matriarch* and its sequel *The Dream Swimmer*. Nani Mini Tupara in *Bulibasha* can claim a literary descent from Nanny Miro Mananui of *Whanau*, as a village kuia and promoter of hockey tournaments. As in *Whanau* there is a Whatu family. Its members work for the Mahana shearing gangs and some of them are married into the Mahanas. Simeon's cousins and best friends are Haromi Whatu and Andrew Whatu. The paradigmatic world continues in *The Uncle's Story*, where the Mahana genealogy is expanded to include Arapeta, as Tamihana's younger brother and grandfather of the narrator (138 US). Tamihana and Arapeta possess the same despotic temperament, virility, physical prowess and sexist attitudes. Uncle Sam is said to have worked in Mahana Number Two gang (139 US). Riripeti is also evoked by Sam, when he finds a tarantula on the battlefields in Vietnam and recognises it a sign of good luck, because spiders were protectors of the Mahanas since the times of Riripeti 'the spider woman of Waituhi' (112 US).

Ihimaera's decision to rewrite his early works in the past decade ascribes to the same paradigmatic logic. *Pounamu, Pounamu, Whanau II* and *The Rope of Man* retell old stories in new ways, taking into account what occurred between the time of their first publishing and the time of their rewriting. This act of reiterative narration itself recalls Maori oral traditions, according to which the same story is recreated in the act of being renarrated and enriched with different perspectives and details. In the preface to *Whanau II* Ihimaera equates writing to carving, and the novel to a wharenui. He states that he is doing what traditional carvers do when they recarve a meeting house, as happened to the meeting house of Poho o Rawiri. Ihimaera's rewriting also allows him to enlarge his earlier stories and connect them to all that he has successively written, adding even more depth to his world.

Pounamu, Pounamu (2003) was written with the political activism of the 1980s in mind, a period that brought important and empowering change to Maori in Aotearoa/New Zealand. The collection also shows the influence of the works Ihimaera wrote in those years — in particular *The Matriarch* and its sequel — with their focus on history, land claims and education issues. His language is profane in the sense he mentioned in his interview: more explicit and informative, mixing different tones and genres. Dialogues are often replaced by narration, aimed at contextualising and explaining. Riripeti reverberates through Nanny Miro in particular (here 'Nani'), with her insistence on recovering lost tribal land and the education of a future leader, as shown in the following passages from 'A Game of Cards' and 'Fire on Greenstone' (they have no equivalents in the previous version):

> 'Here I am, counting on you to get a good education so that you can get the rest of our land back and you're just hopeless, he hoha koe –'⁵

> In this room, surrounded by the past and ancestral memories, Nani Miro had presided over meetings with other elders discussing Treaty matters, the politics of the times and the return of the land. (54 PP03)

Numerous passages on historical or political issues are added in the 2003 version. In 'One Summer Morning' Hema's upbringing is enlarged to include his iwi obligations, which entail his rewriting of the whakapapa burned in Nani Miro's house fire, and supporting Nani Tama in the community's Treaty claim. In 'The Child', the protagonist's beloved Nani is said to have been a follower of Te Kooti and a survivor of the 'Pakeha wars' (145 PP03). She also saved many children from the 1918 epidemic, just like Riripeti in *The Dream Swimmer*. In 'The Other Side of the Fence' the racial conflict has sharper contours. While tracing different notions of ownership between Pakeha and Maori, as in the 1972 story, Jack Simmons overtly appeals to the Treaty to defend his rights:

> Things were different now. The land, its occupants and their possessions no longer belonged to them. It belonged to him, Jack Simmons. His land was like the land bought by settlers after the Treaty of Waitangi. (65 PP03)

The Heremaias use harsher tones too: 'Why don't you go back to where you came from, Jack Simmons? You don't belong here, none of you. We never wanted you here in the first place' (80 PP03).

Whanau II follows the same direction, clearly influenced by the aesthetics and content of *The Matriarch* and *The Dream Swimmer*. The novel includes long expository passages about the history, geography, mythical origin and genealogy of Waituhi, focusing on the New Zealand Wars of the nineteenth century, Te Kooti's deeds, the birth of the Ringatu Church and the construction of the meeting house Rongopai, extending to recent times. Although the novel is told in the third person, the omniscient narrator addresses the readers directly in some historical digressions, as if to underline his place within the community and stress the mix of fiction and fact, story and history. This recalls the metafictional asides of the narrator in *The Matriarch:*

> This is Waituhi. During the time I was a boy, the demographic shock of the rural to urban migration had already diminished the population ...[6]

> We had a distinct and older origin than our allies. We kept ahi kaa since the first settlement of these lands. (23 WH04)

> Listen, and I will sing you the song of Rongopai. (170 WH04)

The reasons behind the community's disruption, the debauchery of its members or the uprooting of its young, can always be traced to historical events. Rongo, mentally answering a question posed by his sister Teria, underlines this in his stream of consciousness:

> 'What *happened* to us? It wasn't supposed to end up this way.'
> What happened? Rongo Mahana felt the question kick him in the solar plexus. Oh sis, what answer do you want? Life happened. The Pakeha happened. After the Land Wars and the Te Kooti Wars, the land was confiscated and the Maori as an automatic underclass happened ...
> You asked what happened, sis? History happened. (133 WH04)

Ihimaera revives the Maori notion of history to include myth, as when Andrew Whatu argues with his teacher about 'what constituted history' (143 WH04). The militant vein is underscored by the narrator's use of Pakeha wars (19 WH04) instead of New Zealand Wars.

Characters are basically identical to their first incarnations with the notable exception of Miro Mananui, who is a reproduction of Riripeti and, like the matriarch, is called the matua. Miro has become the spiritual and political community leader, committed to recovering lost tribal land. She is also a priestess of the Ringatu Church and gifted with second sight and healing powers. As Riripeti did with Tamatea, so Miro has adopted George Karepa and appointed him future leader of the iwi. George eventually renounces this inheritance to pursue a career as a rugby player. Mattie Jones has a larger role in the new story too. Though still a rebellious misfit, her sense of obligation towards Miro — who took her in while she was carrying George's baby — elaborates her character. The narrator defines the relationship between the two women as a bond of 'servitude', like that of Hagar and Sarah in the Bible (157

WH04). Resorting to biblical metaphors was typical of Riripeti's rhetoric, and such allusions also resonate in the sections referring to Miro or in her speech. For example, she calls Mattie 'a Gentile and therefore below [her]' (120 WH04).

What markedly differentiates the new version from the old, however, is the greater degree of historical and political awareness in all the characters. Rongo's thoughts, mentioned above, effectively translate to fighting back. The new novel ends not simply by the spiritual reunion of all iwi (including Jack Ropiho) in the search for Nani Paora and Pene. On Rongo's advice Hepa Walker will raise a topical issue (building restrictions) with the city council, Miro is actively fighting for land rights, and Andrew Whatu has decided to become a lawyer. He may be the future leader that Miro is seeking. Beyond its historical and political emphasis, *Whanau II* constitutes a further step in Ihimaera's construction of an interlinked textual world. Among the many references to *The Matriarch* another link is the figure of Nani Paora, who turns out to be Riripeti's priest, Tamati Kota. There are also explicit allusions to *Bulibasha*. Andrew Whatu is said to have gone to school with Simeon and Haromi (104 WH04), and episodes in Tamihana's life are evoked, including the car races to the one-way bridge (18 WH04) and an act of courage by the old patriarch (20 WH04). The extension of the textual world continues in *The Rope of Man*. Rongo's tangi becomes an occasion to gather the community of Waituhi, including a host of characters inhabiting Ihimaera's previous works. Among the participants are Miro Mananui and her (now) acolyte Mattie Jones, Nani Tama, Maka, Hine Ropiho, Hepa and Sam Walker, Andrew and Charlie Whatu from *Whanau*; Uncle Joshua, Simeon, old Bulibasha (the other name for Tamihana), Aunt Ruth, Aunt Sarah, Uncle Hone from *Bulibasha*; and Tamati Kota from *The Matriarch*.[7] In the course of the novel we also find cousin Michael from *The Uncle's Story* and cousin Tamatea from *The Matriarch* (80 RM), as well as characters from *Tangi*.

As to the second major force acting in Ihimaera's works, his conscious appropriation of Western genres was already evident in his use of Italian melodrama in *The Matriarch* and *The Dream Swimmer*. Judith Dell Panny mentioned how the operatic quotations from Giuseppe Verdi's operas in *The Matriarch* provide a parallel between the Maori struggle to achieve nationhood and retrieve their land, and the nationalistic struggle of the Risorgimento in Italy in the nineteenth century: 'The references [to the Italian context] assist the European reader to proceed from the familiar to the unfamiliar, to see history in a wider context, and to see it from a Maori perspective.'[8] Alistair Fox has analysed their meaning and brings into focus how 'they provide a symbolic subtext that, in combination with elements drawn from Greek myth, helps to shape and intensify the whole fictive representation.'[9] He notes that Ihimaera's use of Verdi excerpts exemplifies the 'appropriation' that theorists have identified as characteristic of postcolonial discourse, which leads to literary and cultural redefinition through the production of hybrid, syncretic texts.[10] But he rightly underlines that Ihimaera's overt inter-textual allusiveness has nothing to do with Homi Bhabha's notion of hybridity as a signifying process involving 'a discourse that is somehow beyond control', arguing that hybridity in *The Matriarch* and *The Dream Swimmer* is intentional, controlled and intellectually well articulated.

The spirit of the Italian Risorgimento is fully evoked by Ihimaera's drawing on the emotional characterisation and sharp opposition between good and evil of Verdian operas, and by blurring the boundary between fact and fiction that characterised the Risorgimento and its most remarkable artistic product, the *melodramma*. Carlotta Sorba contends that Italian melodrama was not only the most popular dramatic and musical genre of this period but became the artistic form that embodied the collective imagery and sensibility of the people.[11] Furthermore, she stresses the complex interrelation between life and art, fact and fiction, which characterised the Risorgimento and *melodramma*, arguing that while Italian political events went on stage, allegorically entering the plots of operas, the aesthetics and ethics of *melodramma* reached out beyond the theatrical world to influence deeply the language, fashion and behaviour of common people and politicians, as though the country had been transformed into one giant stage where patriotic actors performed their struggle for liberation. The interconnection between art and life was a defining characteristic of the Risorgimento, a period in which opera conveyed major historical issues and inflamed the patriotic spirit, while nationalists were dramatising their political ideals according to the aesthetics and ethics of an artistic genre. Sorba views Italian melodrama not only as the product of an age but as an active agent and 'sense producer', following Victor Turner's theory that in a complex culture the performing and narrative arts serve as an 'active and acting' force of the culture itself.[12]

The Matriarch and its sequel owe much to the aesthetics and ethics of Italian melodrama, serving as a sense producer of both fictional story and actual moments of New Zealand history. Italian melodrama not only is present in the quotations from Verdi's operas, interacting with the narrative so as to amplify the protagonists' emotional feelings in various situations. An atmosphere of melodrama escapes from those quotations and pervades the whole works, and as the factual and fictional characters and events intertwine, becomes the link between reality and imagination. New Zealand history and the novel's story are taken onto a stage, amplified and dramatised, endowing their figures with sacredness and symbolism, paralleling the Italian fight for liberation with the Maori nationalist struggle. Every melodramatic ingredient is present in the novel: a Manicheist vision, hypertrophic rhetoric and gestures, and even the use of attire that resembles theatrical costume. Its triangle formula — a convention of melodrama that pits a couple of soprano and tenor against an antagonist, a baritone or mezzo-soprano[13] — forms the basis of complex intertwining subplots in the novels, presenting a heroine (Artemis Riripeti, who has 'a dramatic soprano voice' [368 TM]), a hero (Tamatea) and an antagonist (Artemis' husband Ihaka, or Tamatea's mother Tiana).

The only variation to the melodramatic formula is that Artemis is not a young innocent woman but the young hero's grandmother. Her age is characterised in the dark timbre of her voice as a dramatic soprano.[14] While their relationship can be defined as a physical and spiritual affection there are erotic connotations too, seen in the jealousy aroused in both Ihaka and Tiana. When Artemis does not allow Ihaka into her alcove because little Tamatea is sleeping there, Ihaka's enraged reaction alludes directly to Tamatea as a sexual rival: 'He has taken you away from me, he whose boy-cock is match for that of a full-grown man' (367 TM). Tiana is portrayed in competition with Artemis for primacy in Tamatea's affection, as when she refuses to let Artemis adopt Tamatea and take him away from her, and their confrontation reaches dramatic tones at the Wellington hui when a journalist reports the 'mortal struggle' going on between the two women that is only resolved by Tamatea's intervention (266 TM). Artemis is always depicted as a diva on the stage and compared to Italian opera singer Renata Tebaldi not only for her physical appearance, 'which belies the [same] strength of intellect and beauty', but most of all for the intensity and passion of her voice, conveying her 'imperious' and 'commanding' temper in 'ravishing pianissimo' (13 TM). She shares the 'patrician' features of the Italian singer and a 'madonna smile', emphatic epithets that are repeatedly used for her in the course of the novel, together with those of 'Roman beauty' and 'goddess'. Her position is always in the limelight — literally shining, gleaming, glowing and blazing, or figuratively being the centre of the attention — at family and public events, such as Tamatea's piano concert or the Wellington hui. Her suggestive attire — black dress, veil and pearls threaded through her hair — becomes her costume throughout the novel.

The apotheosis of her theatricality occurs at the Wellington hui. With a dramatic performance, Artemis challenges not only the prime minister but also Maori traditions, which confine the role of women in public meetings to karanga and exclude them from whaikorero:

> Her *voice* was strong and challenging. It seemed to ring out and across the marae, filling the air with its authority and arrogance. The crowd continued to *applaud*. With a *dramatic gesture*, the

matriarch began to stand, climbing into the sky, to receive the acknowledgement of her mana....

('Oh, it was *quite a show*,' the journalist said. 'There's no doubt in my mind whatsoever that your grandmother was *an actress of the first magnitude*. She had us all eating out of her hand ...'). (246 TM, my emphases)

Artemis is not the only melodramatic character of the novel: all the Mahanas are described as opera heroes and heroines and their dramatic roles are judged according to the quality of their performance. Tamatea's Pakeha wife Regan, an external observer, views Tamatea's family as 'so ... so ... Italian. All this Sicilian passion' (19 TM), and she later adds that the whole clan is 'so Italianate' and that they are 'larger than life' (20 TM). The melodramatic traits of the Italian character were noted by Madame de Staël, who defined them as 'a people torn apart by invasions, oppressed by present conditions, but not oblivious of its past greatness'.[15] As Chiappini reports, according to De Staël the opera suited Italian people because it was a projection of all their impulses mortified by their exclusion from active participation in political and civic life, due to the long-standing subjection of the Italian peninsula to foreign powers. The condition of Italians and Maori in the novel is equated not so much with the search of a precise historical parallel as with the dramatisation of a life that results from oppression and foreign colonisation. On the day of their wedding, Uncle Alexis and Aunt Roha are compared to Escamillo and Carmen in Bizet's opera (11 TM). Tamatea's father is described as a 'nobleman' (39 and 58 TM) although lacking the charisma, intelligence and cunning of a leader. He never reaches an heroic stature and remains a second lead in the novel. All the family members are said to have 'patrician' features (216 TM) except for Artemis' husband Ihaka, who becomes Tamatea's principal enemy after Artemis' death. Ihaka appears as a second lead as well, shadowed by Artemis' charisma and beauty. After her death, however, he achieves fulfilment in his role as a villain. Ihaka cannot but be an antagonist because he does not possess the *physique du rôle* of the hero, as Tamatea notes: 'The aging process has not been kind to him. The virility which one associates with a tribal leader has gone from him. The physical presence, that he never had.... Look elsewhere for the patrician features of the family' (216 TM). In *The Dream Swimmer*, Ihaka is described exactly as a bad opera singer, 'a faded Italian baritone who has lost everything except his sense of drama, attempting to convey strength of voice with an instrument that has never been noted for vocality' (400 TD).

Tiana is the other antagonist in the triangle and her character recalls negative heroines such as Amneris in *Aida* or Abigaille in *Nabucco*. While the matriarch's beauty is unquestionable and adds to her charisma, Tiana 'has never been conventionally beautiful' (52 TM). She is never radiant or in the spotlight, rather always in half-shade or in the background like 'a dark star' (402 TM) and must tilt her face for the light to illuminate her: 'My mother had a habit of tilting her face so that the light struck its plane with strength, with resolution' (21 TM). Her character is not fully developed in *The Matriarch*, as it will be in the sequel, but her feeling of 'loving-hate'[16] for Tamatea is already alluded to: the same contrasting feeling that pervades the negative heroines of Verdian opera. Finally, operatic quotations, whether they are sung by a character or inserted in the narrative, always function to provide an emotional equivalent, to offer an amplified explanation for a certain scene or subject — in other words, to dramatise it. Artemis is the only character in *The Matriarch*, who actually sings passages from *Aida* (13, 121, 197), *Don Carlo* (301, 362) and *Otello* (45, 368, 369), which confirms her role as prima donna in the book. The other Verdi excerpts are from *La forza del destino* (51, 55, 62, 392, 415), *Macbeth* (78) and *Un ballo in maschera* (314, 341, 347). All excerpts in *The Dream Swimmer* are from *Aida*.

The operas that enriched *The Matriarch* and its sequel are replaced in *Bulibasha* by action movies. Ihimaera uses cinematic images and references in three ways:

1. Making parallels between characters and movies stars or between episodes of the book and scenes from famous films.
2. Mentioning films that characters have seen.
3. Transforming a scene into a movie script, in Maori with English subtitles.

Simeon's eccentric cousin Haromi (Salomè in Maori) recalls Natalie Wood for her dramatic voice, and her emphatic manners are often described as film performances: 'She subsided in cinematic sobs' (48 BU). Simeon is attracted by Poppy Poata because she reminds him of his favourite actress, Rhonda Fleming in *Serpent of the Nile* (32 BU). The perennial car races between the Mahana and Poata families to be the first to reach the one-way bridge are compared to the air battles in *Twelve O'Clock Battle* starring Gregory Peck (31 BU) and to a 'cavalcade' (30 BU) in typical Western style, but are also suggestive of *Rebel Without a Cause,* a film repeatedly mentioned in the book (48, 119 BU). Vehicles featured in the story regularly draw on the world of Hollywood: Tamihana's De Soto, Matiu's Jaguar, Maaka's Chevrolet, Ruka's Rover, Joshua's Pontiac (26 BU) and Rupeni Poata's Lagonda and Ford (51 BU). The book evokes the irresistible pull of Hollywood on Maori youth in the 1950s. Films are the favourite pastime of Simeon and his cousins during their breaks from school or shearing, and cinematic references help the reader visualise the reality as they see it. Simeon describes the car race scene as a dogfight between foreign troops:

SIMEON E Pa, Hapani rere rangi waka!
(Subtitles: Japanese aircraft at two o'clock, sir!)
JOSHUA Kei whea? Kei whea? Ka, titiro ahau.
(Subtitles: Where? Yes! I see him now!) (73 BU)

Cinematic action pervades the aesthetics of the novel, too, with its emphasis on competitiveness, high performance and goal setting, which add to the driving rhythm of the narrative as though it were an adventure, war or swashbuckler movie. The rivalry between the Mahana and Poata families is inflamed and sustained by numerous challenges, though their central conflict is being competing entrepreneurs in the shearing business. The story includes rugby matches, annual kapa haka competitions, a Maori hockey tournament and the Golden Fleece competition to decide the best shearing gang. While adopting the aesthetics of action movies, Ihimaera also consciously alludes to Sir Apirana Ngata, the pre-eminent Maori politician in the first half of the twentieth century, who promoted a spirit of competition among Maori in order to maintain their mana, and sought to improve and develop Maori culture (203 BU). Ngata is the politician in the novel who granted Tamihana the loan to start his shearing business, as part of an actual scheme to help Maori farmers. Fiction and fact, imaginary and real characters, cinema and history intertwine and overlap to convey the spirit of a period. As in most action movies a dramatic love story is included in the novel — the triangle of Ramona, Tamihana and Rupeni — which explains the reason for the family enmity and provides a final coup de théâtre.

After appropriating Italian melodrama and American cinematography, Ihimaera turns to the genre of television journalism in *The Rope of Man*. The book is divided into two parts: first, the new version of *Tangi* entitled 'Tangi 1973'; second, its follow up entitled 'The Return 2005'. 'Tangi 1973' follows the same structure as its antecedent, with alternating chapters according to the temporal and spatial direction in which Tama is travelling (from Waituhi to Wellington and from Wellington to Waituhi). The 21 chapters are grouped into four numbered parts. The alternation of A and B chapters[17] is regular in the first two parts. However, Part Three includes two exceptions: it starts with a B chapter (11) and has two consecutive B chapters narrating the tangi ceremony (15 and 16). In Part Four the alternation between A and B chapters is abandoned, as there are two chapters of memories (17 and 20) disconnected from the co-ordinates of Tama's journey. The overall structure of 'Tangi 1973' is less evocative and less emotionally intense than the original, no longer 'a poetic drama in prose' like the first *Tangi*, punctuated by the rhythm of Tama's interior monologue, but a narrative mixing elegy and expository prose, memories and historical events, and includes references to Ihimaera's now much larger fictional world. As Anna Rogers mentioned in her review, '*Tangi II* [*sic*] is deliberate, bent on telling and informing, on making sure the reader grasps the sociological and cultural significance of events.'[18] Her criticism that Ihimaera's 'revisionist urge' lessens 'the power of the original by removing its uniqueness' is comprehensible, but easily countered by considering that retelling, as in oral literature, means recreating. Like *Whanau II*, 'Tangi 1973' is a new book indelibly affected by different priorities that arose in a different time, although its tone is generally not as political. Attacks on racial discrimination, land confiscation and Treaty issues are added to 'Tangi 1973' together with a new central concept, which is developed in the second part and gives the book its title. The 'Rope of Man', Te Taura Tangata, symbolises the history of humanity from its origin in the void, Te Kore, through the night, Te Po, up to The World of Light and Gods, Te Ao Marama. At the beginning it was tightly bound with Maori strands, then with the coming of the Pakeha it became frail and almost snapped in the New Zealand Wars. The broad scope of the second part, 'The Return', demonstrates that the rope of man has renewed itself, threading Maori and Pakeha strands together, and is now different but as strong as it used to be.

Tama Mahana did not return to live in Waituhi. He is 52, lives in London and, after a career as a press journalist and TV reporter, has become a successful anchorman for the international network WWN (World Wide News) presenting a weekly one-hour programme entitled *Spaceship Earth*. Set in 2005, 'The Return' allows Ihimaera to continue the account of Tama's life, trace parallels between 1973 and present day Aotearoa/New Zealand, and incorporate previous characters (including some of the 'gay tribe' and others who are said to be dead by now). Tama becomes the quintessence of being Maori in the present global reality. The fact that he has succeeded in his professional life is not as important as the mediation he has attained between modernity, global mobility, world citizenship and the bond with his origins. The metaphor of the astronaut wandering in space while safely tied to his spaceship by a lifeline exemplifies this condition. Tama still belongs to his iwi but his destiny is out in the world, as his mother underlines (315 RM), and renaming himself 'Tom' Mahana symbolises this shift to an international dimension. The values of Maoritanga Tama carries with him deeply inform his job, marked by a focus on the defence of human rights and by his commitment to fight 'man's inhumanity to man' (a sentence frequently used in the novel). Tom says in his final interview:

> Yes, we're all on planet earth, hurtling through space. I like to think that my programme reminds viewers of their humanity. As human beings on our planet, I like to encourage all of us to find the divinity in ourselves, and to nurture and protect it in all our nations so that it can survive any adversity. (319 RM)

Although Tama does not mention environmental issues overtly, his emphasis on survival on the 'planet earth' and the holistic view suggested by 'the divinity in ourselves' implicitly promote ecological consciousness. These issues are explicitly fostered in the book by his son Nathan, who takes on environmental missions all over the world with Greenpeace.

As melodrama and cinema intertwined to form the aesthetic of the previous novels, so the velocity and technological apparatus of broadcasting is introduced with the account of Tama's temporary return to Waituhi, called back to settle a family affair by his mother, who is affected by leukaemia. The narrative mixes an international thread with a home thread: the former includes Tom's memories of past assignments to crisis areas around the world as a TV correspondent, and his current show *Spaceship Earth* broadcast from Auckland with live links from around the world; the latter provides a picture of the changes that have occurred in Waituhi and Aotearoa/New Zealand in the last 30 years. These two intermingling threads come to represent Tama's self: the space in which he is wandering and the spaceship to which he is bound. The frenetic rhythm of his career shapes both his life and the narrative, spiralling out in ever increasing circles throughout a planet that has become a global village scourged by conflict, human rights violations and the migration of the wretched, all recorded by the camera and disclosed to the world. Tom's private life too is affected by his professional whirl, suggested by two failed marriages, and his relationship with his two grown children Holly (living in the US) and Nathan (travelling the world) is affectionate but mediated by modern technology — phone calls and Tom's performances on TV.

The home thread shows the transformations that have occurred in Aotearoa/New Zealand since the 1970s. The rope of man is used again to describe a country where the lives of two peoples have become inextricably entangled, bringing new strength and new possibilities:

> It renewed itself, thickened, matted with strong twisting fibres and was as strong as it had been originally. But it was a different rope. It was different because the Pakeha became added to

the rope, the strands of Pakeha culture entwining with ours,
the blood of the Pakeha joining ours and going into the rope
with our blood. Some people might think that diminished our
strength. I like to think the opposite. (191 RM)

Tama can still remember episodes of racial discrimination from his younger
days. He recalls being excluded from his best friend Michael's birthday party
and dismissed by his girlfriend Rebecca's parents because he was Maori. At the
time the population 'was half Pakeha, half Maori, while now it was 'blended,
laminated' (215 RM), he admits. Tama recognises that '[t]he times of puzzling
dichotomies were gradually receding. Maori and Pakeha were trying to work
out the crucial issues of Waitangi, notably possession and contested spaces, as
we tried to redefine the ways of living together' (215 RM). The conciliatory tone
used by Ihimaera acknowledges a process that is ongoing, prompted by Maori
empowerment, by cutting the economic umbilical cord with Great Britain in
the 1970s, and by the common will to find a distinctive New Zealand identity
together. The family affair for which Huia, Tama's mother, calls him back suggests
this shift in thinking also. Tom helps Huia find a son she had by a Pakeha, the
product of a rape, and that she gave away for adoption. The young man, Eric, is
now mentally ill and institutionalised. Huia finally decides to acknowledge their
blood relationship, despite her daughters' opposition. The rape could be read as a
metaphor for colonisation and Huia's acceptance of Eric into the iwi as weakness
or subjection, nevertheless Huia's act of reconciliation accords with the principle
that the sins of the father must not be visited on the son and actually endorses
Maori values. Eric's heritage cannot be denied him and, although the outcome of
violence, his reconfiguration as whanau reinforces the Maori threads of the rope.

Ihimaera conjugates Maori culture in the modern global world in *The
Rope of Man*. He appropriates television — a global medium par excellence —
and utilises it to convey Maori values on a worldwide basis. He launches the
Maori view beyond the boundaries of Aotearoa/New Zealand by making his
protagonist a citizen of the world and an agent of history, but does not deny his
lifeline to Waituhi, and so for Tama, spiralling out is also spiralling in.

Antipodean affinities

Grace first crossed national boundaries with *Tu*, which deals with the participation
of the Maori Battalion in the Second World War. As the novel recounts, there
were several opponents to Maori participating in the conflict, the most vocal one
probably being Princess Te Puea Herangi, an important figure in Maoridom.[19]

However, the majority of Maori, including Maori politicians and authorities, were in favour on the grounds that it was a way to demonstrate their 'pride of race' (278) to the world and their own country, and thereby to have their rights and full citizenship acknowledged at home. This led to the creation of an all-Maori force within the Second New Zealand Division, the 28th Battalion, whose soldiers saw action in Greece, Crete, North Africa and Italy, suffering extremely heavy losses but gaining a reputation for bravery especially in close-quarter combat.[20]

The war experience of the young protagonist Tu takes place mostly in Italy between August 1943 and December 1945. After over a month at Maadi Camp in Egypt (headquarters of the 2 NZ Division), the 28th Battalion set off for southern Italy along with other Allied troops to free it from German occupation forces. By that point Allied divisions had landed in Sicily, Italian fascist leader Benito Mussolini had been overthrown in an internal coup, and the new Italian military government of General Pietro Badoglio had opened secret negotiations with the Allies, which led to Italy's surrender and withdrawal from the war with the armistice signed on 8 September 1943.[21] A new phase of the war was inaugurated. Nazi Germans, previously allied to Italy, became enemies to be pushed out of the country. Overcome by hunger and poverty, prostrated with the large number of casualties and with the devastation of their houses under heavy bombings, Italians welcomed the Allied troops as liberators from a dictatorial regime whose foreign policy and war strategies had proved ruinous for the country and functioned only to maintain its own power.[22]

Like most Maori, Tu's family pay a very high tribute to the war. Tu is the only male family member to survive the battlefields after the death of his elder brothers, Pita and Rangi. Surprisingly, the pages of his journals offer a picture of Italy that suggests affection and closeness, reflecting accounts given to Grace by Maori returned servicemen and references she found in soldiers' letters from the front.[23] Tu perceives affinities between Maori and Italian cultures that strengthen his sense of belonging and help him reappraise his own heritage, defining a new direction in his life after his return home. Apart from Italian geographical features that often remind the protagonist of the New Zealand landscape, four major cultural affinities are found between Maori and Italians:

1. The central importance of food.
2. The sense of family.
3. Their enjoyment of singing as an emotional and communal experience.
4. Their melodic language, whose flow is similar to that of Maori.

Recognising affinities that pertain to primary needs and especially to the language reinforces Maori soldiers' ethnic identity through a projective process reminiscent of Jung's 'transference'. The Italian Campaign can therefore be interpreted as an act of indigenous appropriation of a Western culture in the service of Maori, working to increase the soldiers' racial self-esteem and prompt the emergence of a new counter-discourse in defence of their own culture at home.

The novel consists of a doubled plot structure. The main narrative, including the events of the Italian Campaign, is told in the first person by Tu through his journals. These chapters alternate with others that employ an omniscient third-person narrator and form the second strand of the book, dealing with the story of the family. Tu is the abbreviation of both Tumatauenga, the Maori god of war, and Te Hokowhitu-a-Tu, the Pioneer Battalion of Maori soldiers of 1914–18 to which his father belonged. Life within a traditional rural community is illustrated, as is the decline of Tu's father, now demented with irreversible neurological damage after being seriously injured and gassed in the First World War. After his death the family migrates to Wellington with the help of an uncle working in Parliament. The second narrative strand also presents a perspective of Aotearoa/New Zealand in the early 1940s as a country where racial discrimination is manifest. Janet Wilson notices that Tu's eldest brother Pita is the character who most perceives the 'subtle forms of marginalisation' enacted by the dominant culture and accepted by Maori leaders. Prejudices end up exoticising and othering the Maori while proclaiming 'well-intentioned beliefs of egalitarianism', as in the episodes of Maori cultural performances at the Wellington Ngati Poneke Club and on the occasion of the Centennial Exhibition to commemorate the Treaty of Waitangi.[24] Pita's growing awareness of the fracture between 'performing' and 'being', epitomised by his perception of himself as a 'performing monkey' (154) and part of a showpiece or a clown act (151), is also fostered by discriminatory laws, as shown by their uncle's comment that 'a Maori woman whose man has died gets only half the pension of a Pakeha widow' (74). When Rangi complains that a Maori boy is 'not allowed in the pubs with the Pakeha and the Chinaman', his mother replies 'Well it's the law'(91), a reference to facts related to Grace by her father, as she explained in an interview.[25]

The dislocation of Maori living in urban environments disrupted the basic tenets of Maori rural culture. As Pita bitterly perceives, traditional Maori values have been turned into empty boxes and lost all symbolic and emotional importance. *Tu* shows how war essentially became an escape from this experience of dislocation and cultural dispersal for a generation of Maori men. Rangi, the most exuberant of the brothers, soon feels trapped between two worlds in Wellington and is among the first Maori to enlist (90). He defies traditional authority (in his reluctance to join the Ngati Poneke Club, for example), rejects the fervent Catholicism of his family, and does not conform to any of the written and unwritten codes regulating the life of Maori in the city. His enlistment is unreflective and instinctual, an escape from restrictions and a way to project his masculine energy. War is an escape for Pita too, who three years later follows his brother's example and flees from the 'mess of himself and what it did to dreams' (38). If Pita is the character who most senses the ambiguity of New Zealand ethnic politics and the erosion of Maori identity, he is unable to articulate a counter-discourse and remains trapped in a paralysing sense of duty, exemplified by his nickname 'Little Father' (51). His over-normative structure causes a disassociation between rationality and instinct, reason and emotion, preventing him from being the agent of his own life. In the end he cannot resist traditional authority, seen in his uncritical Catholicism and his rejection of Jess, the Pakeha girl who had become 'his dream' (38). Unable to deal with dreams or emotions, Pita takes refuge in the more conventional marriage with a Maori girl close to his family, Ani Rose, and in the Maori Battalion.

Seventeen-year-old Tu, destined by his family for law school, enlists without their consent to escape from school, boyhood and boredom (24). But as Wilson remarks, he will succeed in articulating 'the oppositional discourse Pita was unable to',[26] first of all because of the 'strategic survival'[27] enacted by his brothers, who decide that Tu must be maimed in action in order to keep him off the battlefields until the end of the conflict. Secondly, he is able to re-elaborate his experience of war and suffering, retrieving the deep emotional bond with a heritage that Tu's brothers had lost. His interaction with a foreign country dispossessed by war — yet affirming symbols and models deeply rooted in Maori culture — is therefore crucial to the growth of his self-agency and the articulation of a counter-discourse when he is back home.

In his essay *The Healing Tongue*, Peter Beatson devotes a whole chapter to the celebration of food in Maori literature as 'an act of ideological restoration'. He argues that 'one of the things which gives Maori writing a sense of gusto is its celebration of food. This represents a real appetite for and enjoyment of the sheer physicality of existence.'[28] Beatson attributes three main meanings to the celebratory representation of food. The first is a political one: the assertion of their right to gather the food of forest, land and water and the pleasure of eating traditional food are directly connected to the economic and political disputes over the use and distribution of the country's resources. Second, the celebration of food is simultaneously a celebration of the life of the community that collectively gathers and consumes the food. Obviously this contrasts with industrial food economics, which privilege mass production for profit and private consumption within family units. Thirdly, the relish of traditional Maori food produces a 'gastronomic polarisation':[29] food is used as a synecdoche for Maori identity and is set in a binary opposition to Pakeha culture. Beatson's theoretical points are lyrically expressed by Rowley Habib in his poem 'Fish',[30] in which eating fish is invested with both spiritual and sensual attributes. It makes the poet part of a wider design, connecting him to nature and to his ancestors, imparting physical pleasure as well as nourishment. It is the result of specific 'noetics' (ways of knowing), to use Eva Rask Knudsen's words, which have ontological grounds and that produce specific 'poetics' (ways of creating).[31]

Images of collective food gathering and preparation, and shared meals, appear abundantly in Grace's fiction. In 'At the River' from *Waiariki*, the annual eel-fishing is described as a seasonal ritual that brings all the generations of the family together, creating emotional links between them as well as with the elements. In *Potiki* the Tamihanas assert their right to follow the old ways and choose a subsistence economy based on communal gardening and fishing, and sharing the food produced. Graeme's official entry into Linda's family in *Mutuwhenua* occurs when he is invited to spend the weekend at the beach with them collecting mussels and diving for kina. At night they share the fresh seafood with gusto and Uncle Tom parodies the way chefs deal with the Maori delicacy on television, 'arranging' the 'sea-urchins' on a 'washed leaf of lettuce' in the bottom of a 'flash crystal glass' (61 MU). The scene recalls Beatson's notion of gastronomic polarisation, and in fact he cites another passage in the book, when Grace describes 'in mouth-watering (or stomach-heaving) detail the delights of eating fish eyes.'[32] Linda remembers her father's delight in eating fish heads whenever she is far from home and needs reassurance of affection or identity,[33] but a non-Maori reader could react differently to it. In *Tu* we are told how much the soldiers welcomed the food parcels coming from home containing chocolate, puddings, tinned pears and fruit cakes, but also fish and meat cooked in the hangi (earth oven) and titi (mutton bird), whitebait fritters, oysters and shellfish prepared and preserved in fat by their relatives in kerosene tins (95–96). The Maori Battalion Mobile Canteen — a covered truck selling food and beverages purchased by a huge fundraising effort by native school children and their families — becomes the central meeting point for the soldiers in their spare time, connecting them with home and allowing the communal sharing of traditional food (32).

The importance of food for Italians is common knowledge. Montanari traces the relationship back to the etymology of the word *convivio* (banquet or formal dinner), from the Latin *cum vivere* which means 'to live with'. In Italian culture, sitting at the dining table becomes a metaphor for life itself and a symbol of identity, insofar as eating together is equivalent to belonging to the same group of people. A sense of belonging and identity is found not only in the upper classes but among peasants too. In medieval peasant language *vivere a uno pane e a uno vino* (to live on one bread and one wine) is a recurrent idiomatic sentence meaning 'belonging to the same family', and an identical concept is still found in certain Italian dialects where the expression 'getting into one's kitchen' equates with 'getting into one's home'.[34] Sharing food at the same table exemplifies belonging in any Italian community, from the monastic ones (monks are required to eat together in the same refectory) to the community of Roman Catholic believers who share bread and wine — symbolising the body and blood of Jesus Christ — in every mass as part of the liturgy. The importance of food and gastronomy, in all their regional variants, is testified by the numerous references found in works by Latin authors (Horace, Martial, Columella, Marcus Terentius Varro, Cato and Pliny, for instance) and by the vast array of recipe books, the first of which (*Liber de coquina*) dates back to the thirteenth century. Cook books also circulated during periods of dietary restrictions due to war (as in the period between 1940 and 1946), teaching people to make the best of the few resources available and informing the so-called 'war-cuisine'.[35] Possibly the best expression of Italy's strong bond with food is the scarcity, even in today's global world, of fast-food restaurants in Italy; statistics have shown they appeal to only around 3 percent of the total population.[36] Conversely, the success of the Slow Food Movement founded by Carlo Petrini highlights a bond with food that combines sensuality and spirituality, a philosophy synthesised by Alice Waters in her foreword to Petrini's book:

> Slow Food reminds us of the importance of knowing where our food comes from. When we understand the connection between the food on our table and the fields where it grows, our everyday meals can anchor us to nature and the place where we live. And Slow Food reminds us that cooking a meal at home can feed our imaginations and educate ours senses. For the ritual of cooking and eating together constitutes the basic element of family and community life. In short, Slow Food can teach us the things that really matter — compassion, beauty, community, and sensuality — all the best that humans are capable of.[37]

In emphasising the spiritual, sensual and communal values attributed to food by traditional Italian culture, this passage bears striking similarities to both Beatson's analysis of the Maori bond with food and Habib's poem.

The first contacts between Tu and Italians occur in the south of the country, and show a people subdued by poverty, either fleeing or starving. Moved by their plight, Maori soldiers share their rations and food from the Mobile Canteen. In a no man's land devastated by continual bombing and fighting, the soldiers also take advantage of local poultry and pigs, whether they are wandering orphans or belong to a farmer in the neighbourhood fortunate enough to still have them. When Tu spends some time in Florence after its liberation, however, he gets in touch with Italians who live in conditions of gradual normality and the situation is reversed. He makes friends with a young Italian woman, Maddalena, but when Tu talks about the girl he says he 'likes' her (254) while when referring to her family he says, 'I've fallen in love with a family' (254). Among several reasons justifying this love, Tu also mentions his appreciation of their food:

> They're kind, and the food they cook suits me. It's because of Maddalena's family that I feel myself becoming stronger, because of them that I'm able to eat and add a bit of stuff to my bones. There are times when I think of remaining in Italy, in the music of Florence with my new language and new family and Maddalena. I love it here. (254–55)

In this passage Tu explicitly points out his closeness to three aspects of Italian culture: food, family and language. A similar experience occurs to his cousin Anzac, who has fallen in love with a girl living in a house 'stuck up on the ribs of a mountain' (246), and to many other soldiers of the Maori Battalion 'billeted with families they came to love' (246). The Allied army, including the Maori Battalion, had entered Florence after a tough fight lasting many days. They had been welcomed as heroes, showered with flowers and offered fruit and wine. Italian celebrations, like Maori, always include food and the Italian extended family, like the Maori one, is traditionally the propulsive centre of emotional nourishment, identity formation and social regulation, not only in childhood but throughout life.

As Ernesto Galli della Loggia argues, the centrality of family in Italian society is an inalienable trait inherited by the two most powerful forces that have shaped Italian identity: Roman heritage and Christianity.[38] The Roman *familia* (from *famulus*, which means slave) was a large patriarchal structure founded on the cult of the ancestors (*maiores*). It included the *pater familias* — its head, invested with absolute authority — his wife (*uxor*), sons (*liberi*), daughters-in-law (*nurus*) and his slaves. It was part of a larger group or gens, whose members were families related to each other, bearing the same name (*gens Julia*, for instance) and bound together by reciprocity and religious duties towards common ancestors.[39] This structure was culturally reinforced by the gospel, with its symbolic imagery articulated through the figures of 'the Father' and 'his children', and its appeal to brotherhood and reciprocity. The position of the extended family in Italy throughout the centuries is ascribable to the lack of a strong central authority. From the Middle Ages up to the mid-nineteenth century, the fragmentation of the Italian peninsula into a plethora of small states, often under the rule of foreign powers, accentuated the role of the family as the only stable unit of a pre-capitalist society. Galli della Loggia stresses how oligarchies and corporations are the political and economic structures that have most informed Italian society up to the present time. Both are rooted in the same 'logic of aggregation' of a system founded on small groups, bound together by family relations and organising their primacy through alliances and factions. The practice of sharecropping, widespread among peasants up to the twentieth century, was also based on extended family units.[40] Although the persistence of this notion of family is undoubtedly connected to the pre-industrial subsistence economy, it must be remembered that Italy remained an agricultural country until well into the last century and its industrialisation occurred only in the triangle of Turin-Milan-Genoa, a small area in the north.[41] Maori spent most of their time during the Italian Campaign in the south and the centre, still largely a pre-capitalist, agricultural country of villages and small towns, where the extended family still exerted all its possible functions: an economic unit, a social and moral regulator, and an influential network of political alliances. The type of family the soldiers got in touch with in Italy bore many similarities to their own traditional rural communities at home.

Music, the third shared cultural affinity, seems to have been a major medium of communication between Maori and the local population. One of the most moving experiences for Tu comes when he hears an Italian boy singing at Statte (near Taranto), soon after the battalion lands. While waiting for their turn at the barber, the soldiers would sing and play their mouth organs and ukuleles. The barber and his relatives seem to enjoy their tunes and, after a while, a young boy of the family is called in. He clasped his hands in front of him — a typical posture of Italian opera singers — and started singing 'Sul mare luccica l'astro d'argento'. Tu experiences an emotional moment so profound it recalls his ancestral roots, and so intensely that he feels the need to share it with his own family:

> It was like a sound breathed through hollowed bone. I knew it wasn't
> that I wanted to be home, only that I wished the home people could
> be there with us listening to the boy. Their hearts would've expanded
> in their chest as mine did, their throats would've locked as mine did,
> causing tears to run from their eyes.(48)

The song becomes a common tune among the soldiers and is included in the repertoire of their choir (48). Expressing feelings in lyrical form is a common feature among Italian and Maori. In Italy it is epitomised in the tradition of *melodramma*, which reached its climax with Verdi's operas during the Risorgimento, as seen earlier in this chapter. *Melodramma* was a vehicle to convey repressed emotions, which embodied the collective imagery and sensibility of the people and inflamed their patriotic spirit. The operatic quotations that Ihimaera includes in *The Matriarch* and *The Dream Swimmer* not only parallel two nationalist struggles occurring at the same time, but also show the common inclination among Maori and Italians to express emotions musically. Like food, singing can be more generally defined as an assertion of the physicality of emotions, endowed with strong feelings. It reinforces a sense of unity and belonging to a cause, a culture or a people.

In the Maori world, the vocal expression of feelings in music is connected to a body of oral literature, ceremonies, rituals, chants, and rhythmic dances accompanied by the voice, such as the haka. Singing is an assertion of identity and belonging. In a sort of lyric duet, the community of Grace's story 'And So I Go' asks the migrating protagonist:

> And when you go our brother as you say you must will you be warm?
> Will you know love? Will an old woman kiss your face and cry warm
> tears because of who you are? … In your new life our brother will
> you sing?[42]

Singing and playing guitars, ukuleles, and mouth organs were more than just pastimes for Maori soldiers, as Habib's poem 'The Raw Men: For the Maori Battalion' makes clear. While praising the soldiers' undisputed valour on many battlefields, Habib continually returns to their desire to sing and play music:

> With a rifle on one hand and a guitar in the other. That's us –
> And a song ever ready on the tongue. That's us –
> … That's us. The guitars and the song.
> … Always there is singing.
> In the deserts of Egypt there was the singing.
> In the streets of Rome there was the singing.
> Going to the war and returning, there was the singing.
> Always there is the song and the guitars. Above it, beneath it,
> right through it all,
> There is the singing and the dancing and the laughing.[43]

Habib's repetition of 'that's us' and 'always' reinforces singing as a distinctive trait, and this is confirmed by numerous scenes in *Tu*. The Mobile Canteen is the place where soldiers gather to yarn, sing and listen to the radio (32, 137). The soldiers start a choir, which gradually numbers many Italian songs in its repertoire (48, 134). Italian tunes are also included among their 'waiting songs', those sung while waiting for battle (149). In the pauses between actions the men exorcise their fear by singing, as on the Cemetery Ridge near Orsogna (93) or during the attack on Cassino station, where the tune 'Blue smoke goes drifting by' alludes ironically to the smoke wall made by their artillery and gunners (128). Italian melodrama has a great appeal for Maori soldiers too. After listening to the Bari Opera Company's performance of *Tosca*, Tu comes out of the theatre 'floating' and comments that the singing and voices 'just get into your insides — into your mind and into your heart' (249). He is surprised at the vocal way that Italians applaud to show appreciation of the show, but at one of the concerts organised for the soldiers he and the others cheer, clap and call as if they were Italians (216). Interestingly, singing is also the main medium through which Maori soldiers learn Italian: 'In some ways it's an easy language to pick up as the vowel sounds are close to those of our own language. Once you get used to it there's a kind of familiar flow, and plenty of expression to go with it' (213). In one interview Grace confirms that this is exactly what the servicemen of the Maori Battalion believed, as recounted in many of the sources she consulted:

> Often mentioned is the ease with which MB soldiers picked up the pronunciationofItalianbecauseofthevowelsbeingsimilartoMaori. Often mentioned was that Italian people love to sing, just as Maori do too.[44]

Indeed in both Maori and Italian the pronunciation of the five vowels is regular and the vowel sounds are similar.[45] Moreover, Maori does not admit final consonants or consonant clusters. With just a few exceptions, most syllables in Italian end in vowels and few consonant clusters are admitted: the result is its syllable-timed rhythm. Arguably this is much closer to the mora-timed rhythm of the Maori language than the stress-timed English. As we saw previously,[46] a 'syllable-timed' rhythm tends to pronounce small grammatical words in unstressed positions with full vowels. The similarity in syllable structure and rhythm explains the melodic qualities of the two languages and the definition given by the Australian lexicographer Edward Morris in the late nineteenth century of Maori as 'the Italian of the south'.[47] As mentioned in chapter 7, over time the linguistic medium that the soldiers use became either Maori or Italian, as Tu remarks when he joins his unit after his stay in hospital:

> It's true what Anzac told me, the boys are speaking Italian much of the time now. I'm racing to keep up with them. If not speaking Maori we speak Italian, even to each other, as though English has become a forgotten language. But as far as writing is concerned, well English is the only language I've been schooled in. (252)

In exploring the figure of the mutilated warrior that frequently appears in contemporary Maori poetry and painting, Beatson notes how, along with other wounds, his tongue is often removed.[48] Maori language was eroded by the English-speaking education system and by the pervasive force of the dominant language, and habitual violence was done to Maori words and place names, which were mispronounced and made unrecognisable. Teaching the Maori language in schools was forbidden and children were punished when they used it. Grace regularly points to these factors as among the most traumatic experiences for her Maori characters, some of whom end up with mental or physical pathologies as a result, such as Mata in *Cousins* or Gran Kura's little cousin Riripeti in *Baby No-Eyes*. Conversely in *Tu*, the soldiers of the Maori Battalion, by getting in touch with a foreign language whose pronunciation and rhythmic pattern sound familiar to them, are encouraged to speak their own language again.

What happens to Tu in Italy can be figuratively explained, using Jungian terms, as a reappropriation of the 'numinosity' of major cultural symbols through a positive transference with a foreign culture. With numinosity, Jung intends to describe that emotional bridge or energy that transforms an archetype or symbol into more than just a name, a concept or a mere abstraction. It makes it 'living matter'.[49] According to him, cultural symbols 'are important constituents of our mental make-up and vital forces in the building up of human society, and they cannot be eradicated without a serious loss. When they are repressed and neglected, their specific energy disappears into the unconscious with unpredictable consequences.'[50]

Jung contends that the loss of cultural numinosity effects the dissolution and decay of civilisations, and causes neurosis in the individual. This is exactly what Pita has lost — the emotionality of his cultural values — and this is the cause of his disassociation and neurosis. Jung's theory broadens the Freudian notion of transference (a redirection of repressed feelings and impulses of a sexual and Oedipal nature) to encompass a wider projective process in which an activated unconscious starts expressing its deepest affective needs.[51] Transference (literally meaning 'to carry something over from one place to another') is a specific case of projection. It is never a voluntary act but always automatic and spontaneous and, as a rule, is of an emotional nature. It essentially suggests 'a general psychological mechanism that carries over subjective contents of any kind into the objects.'[52] The emotion in the projected contents 'always form a link, a sort of dynamic relationship, between the subject and the object.'[53] Once the transference is dissolved, the projected energy 'falls back' into the subject and 'he is then in possession of the treasure which formerly, in the transference, had simply been wasted.'[54]

In explaining transference, Jung compares it to the spontaneous and unprovoked mechanism of 'love at first sight',[55] although it is not an act of love in the common sense. Tu undergoes a similar process. Italian people, culture, language and the very landscape, by virtue of their affinity with his own heritage and personal experience, activate his unconscious. The closeness he feels with Italy is spontaneous and involuntary, a sort of love at first sight since he is projecting symbols of his own culture that are retrieved and charged with all their numinosity. Tu and the other soldiers are not attracted by Italy per se, but by the projections of their own deeply rooted cultural symbols. It is no accident that while they feel a deep emotional involvement to Mount Cassino (111–12), the old stone towns clung to the hilltops like Orsogna (77), the Pompeii archaeological site (214) and the hills and paddocks of a widely agricultural country (47), they find Rome (and the Vatican) 'overwhelming', 'tiring' and of little appeal for all its cultural wealth (253). Mount Cassino becomes a projection of Taranaki, the old stone towns a projection of their hilltop pa (fortification) sites, Pompeii of a buried village in Whakarewarewa and the hilly cultivated countryside — never too far away from the sea — of their land back home. Rome, conversely, is too crowded, noisy and distant from their culture and transference fails there, to the extent that Tu feels he cannot pray in St Peter's (252), despite his strict Catholic upbringing.

Although Tu is the only one of the brothers spared by the war he comes back physically disabled, mentally unstable and incapable of adapting to the normality of life. The death of his brothers and many relatives and friends leaves an indelible mark on his personality and his equilibrium, yet a new consciousness of the war arises, which informs a counter-discourse. Tu questions whether Maori will ever benefit from the sacrifices of their soldiers, as the Maori authorities and elders had argued: 'We took full part in a war but haven't yet been able to take full part in peace … During our time away the other Kiwi battalions had been more than pleased to have us at their side. These things were quickly forgotten' (279). He realises that the only way to make his life worthwhile is to reveal what he knows, what he has felt and learned, by passing his notebooks to the younger generation: his nephew Benedict (Pita's son, named for the Benedictine Abbey on Mount Cassino) and his niece Rimini (Rangi's daughter, named after the road to Rimini where Rangi died), both born when their fathers were serving at the front. His journals also disclose a family secret regarding Rimini's paternity (Benedict and Rimini are not both Pita's children, as was believed) and trace the correct line of descent so important for Maori identity. Most of all, the pages record the new level of consciousness Tu achieves in Italy, specifically an emotional rediscovery of his Maori heritage.

The message of the notebooks, reiterated by Tu's warm appeal in his final letter to Benedict and Rimini, opposes all wars. Young Maori should not follow their fathers' footsteps — the price was too high to pay — and since each new generation holds the key to the survival of any future generation, Maori should instead value their lives and heritage as treasures. This can happen only if Maori recover the numinosity of their cultural symbols, that is to say, the emotional attachment to their culture that Tu has found in the Italian context.

At the very end of the novel, Tu's desire to bring Rimini and Benedict to Italy in order to see the country and pay homage to their dead implies that he wants them to experience what he has:

> There are places to go to, people to meet, music to listen to. It's a beautiful country, old and eerie. You'll find we haven't been forgotten there in Cassino, Santo Spirito, Tuscany, Florence, Trasimeno, Rimini, all of those places — and not just because we stole the villagers' pigs and chickens. (281)

Tu succeeds in forming a counter-discourse, yet is unable to put the fruits of his Italian experience into practice due to his physical and mental disabilities. Despite this, the lessons he learned have passed to his direct descendants, those who, incidentally, will reach adulthood during the Maori Renaissance of the 1970s. They are the ones who will win the fight for the recognition of indigenous rights at home and revive the emotional attachment to Maori culture through the arts and writing. Set 30 years before the Maori Renaissance, the novel could not allude directly to future events, but from a contemporary perspective a reader can easily see that the Maori participation in the Second World War, and particularly in the Italian Campaign, contributed to bringing forth an awareness of Maoritanga and the assertion of self-determination in the years that followed.

Epilogue

The literary history of Patricia Grace and Witi Ihimaera has mirrored the course of Maori history itself — a history that is also a story subject to a point of view, as the two writers have repeatedly maintained, and therefore destined to be a narrative in literature and beyond. Fictional narrative and real-life narrative have followed a similar route, from the search and assertion of a coherent cultural identity through political activism, and on to a re-definition of that identity in response to problems of the present including the global economy, scientific and technological universalism, and indiscriminate environmental exploitation. Stuart Hall's lesson that old identities should not be taken literally has been put into practice by Maori in their continual exchange with the Pakeha and the wider Western world, which has not affected their essential core but seems, rather, to have enriched and reinforced it in ever-developing forms. Ihimaera's image of 'the rope of man' to describe the new powerful whole formed by Pakeha and Maori in Aotearoa/New Zealand can be set as a model to follow for many other countries in the postcolonial world.

Grace's and Ihimaera's crossing over whanau borders to include wider national and even international horizons evidences the need of Maori (like any other people) to pit themselves against other cultural backgrounds to define their own identity, as seen by Grace's *Tu*. It also shows their will to be part of a larger scene. The global economic and environmental crisis has led to questioning of Western development models. The voice of Maori has become an inflection of the worldwide chorus of indigenous peoples offering old wisdom to face new problems: an alternative discourse on which Western readers should reflect. Indigenous peoples claim 'the right of minorities to dream majority dreams', says Michael in Ihimaera's *The Uncle's Story*. The protagonist of *The Rope of Man*, anchorman Tom Mahana, affirms that belonging to an indigenous minority culture can be seen as a surplus value, because it implies a different sensitivity and perspective, and can help the majority to imagine a future by which we can escape a problematic present, in Hawken's words. So, the voice of Maori now belongs not only to Aotearoa/New Zealand but to the whole world.

Endnotes

Chapter 1

1 Ania Loomba, *Colonialism/Postcolonialism*, Routledge, London/New York 1998: 57.
2 Michel Foucault, *Discipline and Punish: the Birth of the Prison*, Vintage/Random House, New York 1979: 27–28.
3 See Loomba, op. cit.: 20–57.
4 Ibid.: 28–29.
5 See Steve Smith, 'Louis Althusser', in Jon Simons (ed.), *Contemporary Critical Theorists*, Edinburgh University Press, Edinburgh 2004: 51–67.
6 Ibid.: 60. The quoted words are from: Louis Althusser, *For Marx*, Verso, London 1990 [1965]: 235.
7 Ibid.: 61.
8 Ibid.: 63.
9 Patrick Williams, 'Edward Said', in Simons (ed.), op. cit.: 272.
10 See Jon Simons, 'Michel Foucault', in Simons (ed.), op. cit.: 185–86, 188–89.
11 Miguel Mellino, *La critica postcoloniale*, Meltemi, Roma 2005: 67.
12 Edward W. Said, *Orientalism*, Vintage Books, New York 1979. See also Williams, op. cit..
13 Said, op. cit.: 3 and 6–7.
14 Ibid.: 21. Said's quotation is from: Karl Marx, 'The 18th Brumaire of Louis Bonaparte', in Marx, *Surveys from Exile*, Penguin, Harmondsworth 1981.
15 Bill Ashcroft, Gareth Griffiths and Helen Tiffin, *The Empire Writes Back*, Routledge, London/New York 2002 [1989]: 78–82.
16 Tzvetan Todorov, *The Conquest of America: The Question of the Other*, Harper and Row, New York 1982 [1974].
17 Ashcroft et al., op. cit.: 78.
18 Michael King, *Nga iwi o te motu*, Reed, Auckland 2001 [1997]: 18.
19 Ibid.: 8.
20 Witi Ihimaera, 'Bookmarking the Century', *Landfall 199*, 8.1, 2000: 40.
21 Paola Della Valle, 'A Larger Family: Patricia Grace Interviewed by Paola Della Valle', *The Journal of Commonwealth Literature*, 42.1, 2007: 132.
22 Ashcroft et al., op. cit.: 81.
23 King, op. cit.: 33–35.
24 See King, op. cit.: 32: The first article of the treaty 'declared that the "Chiefs of the Confederation of Tribes of New Zealand" […] "cede to her Majesty the

Queen of England absolutely and without reservation all the rights and powers of Sovereignty… over their respective Territories …". Under the second article in English, which in time would become the most contentious, the Queen guaranteed to the chiefs and their tribes "the full exclusive and undisturbed possession of their Lands and Estates Forest Fisheries and other properties…". […] At the same time the chiefs would give exclusive rights to the sale of land to the Queen and her representatives. In the third article the Queen extended to the "Natives of New Zealand Her royal protection and imparts to them all the Rights and Privileges of British Subjects."' The second article was crucial to stopping the activity of private speculators, especially the New Zealand Company, who were buying large amounts of land cheaply from the Maori, with legal or illegal means, to sell them to wealthy British purchasers at higher prices and, with the profits, organise the immigration of labourers who would have to work for some years to buy land for themselves. See also Keith Sinclair, *A History of New Zealand*, Penguin, Auckland 1991 [1959]: 57–69 and 74–77.

25   Jane McRae, 'Māori Literature: A Survey', in Terry Sturm (ed.), *The Oxford History of New Zealand Literature*, Oxford University Press, Oxford 1991: 3.

26   See Loomba, op. cit.: 49.

27   Homi Bhabha, 'Signs Taken for Wonders: Questions of Ambivalence and Authority under a Tree Outside Delhi, May 1817', *Critical Inquiry*, 12. 1, 1985: 150; quoted in Loomba, op. cit.: 177.

28   Ihimaera, op. cit.: 39–41.

29   King, op. cit.: 112.

30   Ihimaera, op. cit.: 40.

31   Eva Rask Knudsen, *The Circle and the Spiral*, Rodopi, Amsterdam/New York 2004: 23–24.

32   McRae, op. cit.: 1.

33   A marae is the open space in front of the ancestral house where public meetings take place and also refers more generally to the complex including the marae atea space, the houses and other parts of the ancestral grounds.

34   See Margaret Orbell, *Waiata: Maori Songs in History*, Reed, Auckland 1991: 1–5.

35   Mana: prestige, authority, psychic force.

36   McRae, op. cit.: 11–13.

37   Ibid.: 9.

38   Ibid.: 5–7.

39   David Daiches, *A Critical History of English Literature*, (3), Secker & Warburg, London 1960: 586–87.

40   McRae, op. cit.: 8. On Grey see also: Michael King, *The Penguin History of New Zealand*, Penguin, Auckland 2003: 199–239; and Sinclair, op. cit.: 80–90.

41   Sinclair, op. cit.: 82.

42   King, op. cit. (2003): 200–201.

43   Ibid.: 201.

44   Sinclair, op. cit.: 83.

45   Ibid.: 82.

46   King, op. cit. (2001): 22.

47   Ibid.: 36.

48   See King, op. cit. (2001): 40–43. The increasing presence of the Europeans created
      a sense of 'Maoriness' in the Maori people and the belief they should unite under
      a king to achieve the same cohesion and confidence that the Europeans had under
      the Crown. In 1858 the first Maori king came to power: the Waikato chief Te
      Wherowhero. He took the name Potatau and established himself at his capital at
      Ngaruawahia. The Europeans viewed this as an act of disloyalty and an attempt
      to prevent land sales. Fighting began in Taranaki, where Government officers
      had bought land from a minor Ati Awa chief not entitled to sell it. By 1863 the
      Waikato War had broken out. messianic movements gained popularity. One of
      them was Pai Marire, also known to the Europeans as Hauhau; its founder was Te
      Ua Haumene. Another was the Ringatu church, founded by the prophet Te Kooti.
      Strongly influenced by the Old Testament, these movements identified the Maori
      people with the Israelites and promised their followers deliverance from European
      domination. The wars were over by 1872, but Pakeha were able to cross the Aukati
      line into the King Country only in 1881. After that, other incidents threatened an
      uneasy peace, which was effective only from the late nineteenth century.

49   Lani Kavika Hunter, *Spirits of New Zealand: Early Pakeha Writings on Maori*, Thesis
      for PhD in English, University of Auckland, 2004: 85–103.

50   Ibid.: 85.

51   The Maori alphabet has ten consonants. They correspond to the actual sounds
      of the oral language. The transliteration of English words or names that did not
      belong to the Maori language follows pre-established rules, according to which the
      English consonant sounds nonexistent in Maori are replaced by others existent. For
      example: 'b', 'd', 'f', 'l' – nonexistent in Maori – become respectively 'p', 't', 'wh/p',
      'r'. Moreover, vowels are always added between consonants and at the end of words.
      This is why the Maori for 'farm' is 'pāmu', for 'letter' is 'reta', for 'bible' is 'paipera'.
      These rules will be explained in detail in chapter 8. See Jenny Lee, *Notes on Patricia
      Grace's Potiki*, Kaiako Publications, Nov. 1990: 39–41.

52   Hiwi and Pat Tauroa, *Te Marae: A Guide to Customs & Protocol*, Reed, Auckland
      1986: 144.

53   Agathe Thornton, *Maori Oral Literature as Seen by a Classicist*, Huia, Wellington
      1999: 33.

54   In Maori mythology, Hawaiki is the island from which Maori originated. Thornton
      states that Te Rangikaheke had met a Hawaiian in Auckland and wanted him to
      take the two manuscripts to his own people in Hawaii to have his work confirmed
      and corrected. He believed, as did some Pakeha scholars, that Hawaiki was not a
      mythical place but a real geographical locality: the Hawaiian Islands. Thornton, op.
      cit.: 34.

55   Ibid.: 50.

56   Ibid.: 50.

57   Ibid.: 56 and 59. Thornton further explains (61) that, like the Maori, the ancient Greeks regarded the past as what lay before them (*prosso*) and the future what lay behind (*opisso*). Their mental orientation was towards the known, the traditional and the customary.

58   Ibid.: 73. A 'doublet' is when the same sorts of events are told twice, but the second time with increased intensity.

59   Ibid.: 72. Thornton explains that in Maori 'the word hika means both "to kindle fire by friction" and "to have sexual intercourse".'

60   Ibid.: 70.

61   On this subject Ranginui Walker has commented that the 'expropriation of knowledge and its transformation from the spoken to the written word is [...] one of many facets of colonisation'. See Roger Robinson & Nelson Wattie (eds), *The Oxford Companion To New Zealand Literature*, Oxford University Press, Oxford/ New York 1998: 53.

62   Lawrence Jones, 'The Novel', in Sturm (ed.), op. cit.: 107 and 109.

63   Lydia Wevers, 'The Short Story', in Sturm (ed.), op. cit.: 203.

64   Quoted in Wevers, op. cit.: 204.

65   Bill Pearson, 'Attitudes to the Maori in Some Pakeha Fiction', in *Fretful Sleepers and Other Essays*, Heinemann Educational Books, Auckland 1974: 48.

66   Jones, op. cit.: 121.

67   Michelle Keown, *Pacific Islands Writing*, Oxford University Press, Oxford 2007: 39–41.

68   Hunter, op. cit.: 162–63.

69   Ibid.: 50–53.

70   Ibid.: 148.

71   Ibid.: 162.

72   A.A. Grace, *Tales of a Dying Race*, Chatto & Windus, London 1901: vi.

73   Ibid.: vii.

74   Jones, op. cit.: 112.

75   Loomba, op. cit.: 152.

76   Keown, op. cit.: 29–35. In particular, she refers to Melville's *Typee* (1846), Loti's *Le Mariage de Loti* (1880) and Gauguin's *Noa Noa* (1890).

77   Loomba, op. cit.: 152–58.

78   Loomba says: 'Sander Gilman shows how nineteenth-century medical and popular discourses progressively intensified the linkages between "blackness", sexuality and femininity by using one to describe the other. [...] Nancy Leys Stepan argues that "So fundamental was the analogy between race and gender (in scientific writing) that the major modes of explanation of racial traits were used to explain sexual traits."' Op. cit.: 160.

79   See A.W. Reed, *Reed Book of Maori Mythology*, Reed, Auckland 2004: 465–69.

80   Hunter, op. cit.: 188.

81   Ibid.: 200.

82   According to the theories of race and racial classification of the nineteenth century,

paternity is genetically dominant, as is the white race. The child born to a white father and a black mother is 7/8 white, but that of a black father and a white mother is only 4/8 white. (Loomba, op. cit.: 119). Consequently, the coupling of a white man and a Maori woman maintains the white racial supremacy; the contrary does not. The nightmare of being absorbed by the other might have been another reason for the absence of romances between Maori men and white women.

83   A.A. Grace, 'Why Castelard Took to the Blanket', op. cit.: 72.

84   Unlike English, in the Maori language the adjective follows the noun. So a Pakeha-Maori is a Pakeha who acts and lives as a Maori, a Maorified Pakeha.

85   Chas. Owen, 'The Disappearance of Letham Crouch', *New Zealand Illustrated Magazine* 4, (July 1901): 777–81. Quoted in Wevers, op. cit.: 206–207.

86   Joseph Conrad, 'Heart of Darkness', *Youth: a Narrative and Two Other Stories*, Blackwood & Sons, London 1902.

87   Pearson, op. cit.: 52.

88   Ibid.: 52–55.

89   Blanche E. Baughan, *Brown Bread From a Colonial Oven*, Whitcombe & Tombs, London 1912.

90   William Baucke [W.B.], *Where the White Man Treads Across the Pathway of the Maori*, Wilson & Horton, Auckland 1905.

91   Pearson, op. cit.: 56.

92   Katherine Mansfield, *Something Childish and Other Stories*, Constable, London 1924 [1910].

93   Ibid.: 15.

94   The women carry flax baskets of ferns; when they reach their place (a 'logroom', probably the ancestral house) there are men on the floor, smoking, with rugs and feather mats round their shoulders; Pearl plays with a green ornament round a woman's neck, probably a tiki, symbol of the demigod Maui.

95   Ihimaera (ed.), 'Introduction', *Where's Waari? A history of the Maori through the short story*, Reed, Auckland 2000: 10.

96   Pearson, op. cit.: 56. The quotation is from J.M. Murry (ed.), *The Journal of Katherine Mansfield*, Constable, London 1954: 29.

Chapter 2

1   See Lawrence Jones, 'Roderick Finlayson, 1904–1992', in *Kōtare 2008*, http://wwwnzetc.org/tm/scholarly/tei-Whi072Kota-t1-g1-t19.html: 1–2.

2   Dennis McEldowney, 'Roderick Finlayson', *Islands*, July 1984, quoted in Jones (2008): 14.

3   See Kai Jensen, *Whole Men*, Auckland University Press, Auckland 1996.

4   Ibid.: 76.

5   W.H. New, 'Frank Sargeson as Social Story-teller', *Landfall* 143, 36.3, 1982: 343.

6   James K. Baxter, 'Back to the Desert', in Helen Shaw (ed.), *The Puritan and the Waif:*

A Symposium of Critical Essays on the Work of Frank Sargeson, typescript, 1954: 8.

7   W.H. New, op. cit.: 344.

8   Frank Sargeson, *The Stories of Frank Sargeson*, Longman Paul, Auckland 1973 [1964]: 15. Quotations from Sargeson's stories, indicated in brackets in the text, are from this edition.

9   Wevers, op. cit.: 227. Wevers says the definition 'third dimension' was used by Sargeson in his article about Sherwood Anderson in *Tomorrow* in 1935. See Wevers, op. cit.: 226.

10   Dan Davin, 'The Narrative Technique of Frank Sargeson', in Shaw (ed.), op. cit.: 57.

11   New, op. cit.: 345.

12   See Baxter, op. cit.: 'In *That Summer* the myth of the lost man who has no place in society and scarcely desires it, is fully developed. One is struck immediately by the similarity of the world-view implied in this story and that which French existentialists have given a philosophical context and some French novelists a voice' (12). Baxter then analyses the similarities and differences of the myth of the lost man in Sargeson and in Camus' *The Outsider* and adds: 'He knows as well as Kafka the landscape of hysteria; and has explored the frozen underside of our well-lighted world of fried steak and football queues, hoping – I believe – to find the backstairs to Heaven' (16).

13   The trilogy of his autobiographies *Once is Enough* (1973), *More than Enough* (1975), and *Never Enough* (1977) was published in one volume, *Sargeson*, in 1981.

14   Jensen, op. cit.: 110.

15   Ibid.: 46–7.

16   H. Winston Rhodes, *Frank Sargeson*, Twayne Publisher, New York 1969: 90.

17   Kai Jensen, 'Holes, Wholeness and Holiness in Frank Sargeson's Writing', *Landfall 173*, 44.1, 1990: 41.

18   The title ironically refers to Kipling's poem 'The White Man's Burden' (1899), which exemplified his role as the bard of the British Empire.

19   In the South Island the number of Maori settlements has always been smaller than in the North Island, even before the white man's arrival. See King, op. cit. (2001): 19 and 51.

20   Elsdon Best (1856–1931), ethnologist, published extensively on traditional Maori lore, life and customs.

21   Paul Hawken, *Blessed Unrest*, Penguin, New York 2008 [2007]: 2.

22   Jensen, op. cit. (1996): 52.

23   Ibid.: 52.

24   Hawken, op. cit.: 98 and 101.

25   Peter Beatson, *The Healing Tongue: Themes in Contemporary Maori Literature*, Studies in New Zealand Art & Society 1, Massey University, Palmerston North 1989: 45.

26   Patricia Grace, *The Dream Sleepers*, Longman Paul, Auckland 1980: 55.

27   James Joyce, *A Portrait of the Artist as a Young Man*, quoted in Rhodes, 'Introduction', in Sargeson, *I Saw in My Dream*, Auckland University Press, Auckland 1974 [1949]: xiii.

28   Sargeson, op. cit. (1974): 3. Further quotations, indicated in brackets, are from this edition.

29   Tarpots: derogatory for Maori; Mr Anderson 'let the maoris use his shed' for shearing: 143.

30   R.A. Copland, *Frank Sargeson*, Oxford University Press, Wellington 1976: 22.

31   'But to think I've had to live all these years stuck away out here, with only those dirty maoris down the road for nearest neighbours. And with my boy growing up. Do you think I could keep him away from that Rangi? [...] Why, there were things about Rangi it wasn't decent to say.': 155–56.

32   'There never would have been any trouble if the maoris had been prohibited from owning land, Mrs Daley said.': 174.

33   'Jerry? He said, answering Mrs Brennan. Jerry is a local tarpot.
      Oh, a maori! Anna said. I love maoris. I wish we'd been here. We could have had him in.': 203.
      'No, Dave said. So far as I'm concerned Cedric's a mystery. ...
      Mrs Brennan said for God's sake tell them who he was, He sounded as if he might be a maori prophet.': 210.

34   See the quotation from *I Saw in My Dream* (112) earlier in the text.

35   Like Sargeson, Finlayson ironically alludes to Kipling's poem, 'The White Man's Burden'.

36   Roderick Finlayson, *Brown Man's Burden*, The Unicorn Press, Auckland 1938: i–ii. References to the text, indicated in brackets with the abbreviation BMB, are to this edition.

37   Finlayson, *Our Life in This Land*, The Griffin Press, Auckland 1940: 4. Further references, indicated in brackets with OL, are to this edition.

38   Bill Pearson, 'Introduction', in Finlayson, *Brown Man's Burden and later stories*, Auckland University Press, Auckland 1973: vii. Further references, indicated in brackets with BML, are to this edition.

39   Hawken, op. cit.: 95. As quoted in Charles C. Mann, *1491: New Revelations of the Americas Before Columbus*, Knopf, New York 2005: 15.

40   Ibid.: 99.

41   Serge Latouche, *La Scommessa della decrescita*, Feltrinelli, Milano 2008 [2006]: 13 and 17. See also Latouche, 'Degrowth Economics', *Le Monde Diplomatique*, November 2004, <http://mondediplo.com/2004/11/14latouche> and 'Would the West actually be happier with less? The world downscaled', *Le Monde Diplomatique*, December 2003, <http://www.hartford-hwp.com/archives/27/081.html>

42   Pearson, op. cit. (1973): x. For Finlayson's biography see also xi–xiv.

43   See Latouche, op. cit. (2003 and 2004).

44   Wevers, op. cit.: 236 (both quotations).

45   'Roderick Finlayson', in Robin Dudding (ed.) *Beginnings. New Zealand Writers Tell How They Began Writing*, Oxford University Press, Wellington 1980: 66.

46   Rome became the capital of the Kingdom of Italy in 1871.

47   See Giuseppe Petronio, *L'attività letteraria in Italia*, Palumbo, Firenze 1991:

707–720. See also G.H. McWilliam, 'Introduction', in Verga, *Cavalleria Rusticana and Other Stories*, Penguin, London 1999.

48   D.H. Lawrence, 'Translator's Preface', in Verga *Cavalleria Rusticana (and other stories)*, Dedalus/Hippocrene, London 1987 [1928]: 13.

49   Verga, *The House by the Medlar Tree*, University of California Press, Berkeley 1964: 4–5. The cycle will never be completed. It includes only the second novel he had planned, *Mastro-don Gesualdo*, also translated by Lawrence and considered as Verga's second masterpiece, and the unfinished third novel *La duchessa di Leyra*.

50   Dudding (ed.), op. cit.: 66.

51   Lawrence, op. cit.: 21.

52   Pearson op. cit. (1973): xix. The quotation is from Dudding (ed.), op. cit.: 65.

53   Luigi Pirandello, *L'Umorismo*, Oscar Mondadori 1992 [1908], Milano: 126.

54   Fiora A. Bassanese, *Understanding Luigi Pirandello*, University of South Carolina Press, Columbia 1997: 29.

55   Ibid.: 29.

56   Pirandello, op. cit.: 133.

57   Pearson, op. cit. (1973): xvii.

58   Verga, *Cavalleria Rusticana*, op. cit. (1987): 42; Finlayson, *In Georgina's Shady Garden*, The Griffin Press, Auckland 1988: 32. Further quotations from this collection are indicated in brackets with GSG.

59   Planting a tree when a child is born is a Maori custom. The tree becomes tapu (sacred).

60   Jones, op. cit. (2008): 12.

61   See for example Ihimaera's 'The Other side of the Fence' or 'Beginning of the Tournament' from *Pounamu, Pounamu*.

62   Wevers, op. cit.: 235–36.

63   Dennis McEldowney, 'Introduction', in Finlayson *Tidal Creek*, Auckland University Press, Auckland 1979: 10. Further quotations from the book, indicated in brackets with TC, are from this edition. He is referring to John Muirhead and his unpublished MA thesis 'The Social Thesis and Prose Fiction of Roderick Finlayson', Massey University, 1971.

64   See Latouche, *In the Wake of the Affluent Society*, Zed Books, London & New Jersey 1993 [1991]: 117, 241–42.

65   McEldowney is quoting from Roderick Finlayson, MS note, 1978.

66   Immanuel Wallerstein, *La retorica del potere*, Fazi, Roma 2007 [2006]: 100–105.

67   McEldowney, op. cit.: 14.

68   Ibid.: 12.

Chapter 3

1   H.W. Rhodes, 'Janet Frame: A Way of Seeing in *The Lagoon and Other Stories*', in Cherry Hankin (ed.), *Critical Essays on the New Zealand Short Story*, Heinemann, Auckland 1982: 115.

2   Ibid.: 112. Rhodes is quoting from Wordsworth's poem 'I Wandered Lonely as a Cloud': 'that inward eye/which is the bliss of solitude.'

3   Elizabeth Alley, 'An Honest Record: An Interview with Janet Frame', *Landfall 178*, 45.2, June 1991: 168.

4   Ihimaera, 'A Maori perspective', in 'A Symposium on Historical Fiction', *The Journal of New Zealand Literature*, (9), 1991: 54.

5   Gorlier's article was written on the occasion of Frame's death. 'Here we see two elements present in her art: verbal invention and the lighting up of the imagination, in such a way as to transform reality, be it human, animal or natural. The result is the meeting between English literary inheritance – Joyce, to name but one – and the decisive contribution of the mythical vision of Maori culture, the New Zealand indigenous population. It was Frame herself who brought this to my attention in a quick meeting and then, a unique privilege, in her response to written questions, which I used for a piece for *La Stampa*.' (Claudio Gorlier, 'Janet Frame: l'ombra del falco', *La Stampa*, 30 January 2004: 25, my translation). In his review of the Italian translation of Frame's *An Autobiography*, Gorlier again highlights the influence of Maori mythology on Frame: 'Frame depicts what she herself defined as the "ordinary", "without characters", without recourse to fiction. Here we find the distinction indicated by Frame between "autobiographical texts" and "autobiography". But in the "ordinary" the "power of words" forcefully introduces itself, with the incessant search and need for that which, after all, was "just a word: fantasy". Therefore, "fiction" claims its rights, permeating, and at the same time overcoming, the quotidian, and, not by chance (the author herself acknowledged it in the interview referred to earlier) this is strongly due to Maori mythology, so important for an entire generation of New Zealand authors, with its spatial-temporal approach, and symbolic and/or magic vocation'(Claudio Gorlier, Review of Janet Frame, *Un angelo alla mia tavola*, Einaudi, Torino 1996, in *L'Indice*, (3), 1997, my translation).

6   Janet Frame, *An Autobiography*, The Women's Press, London 1991 [1989]: 7.

7   Elizabeth Alley, op. cit.: 161.

8   Frame, *Owls Do Cry*, The Women's Press, London 1985 [1961]: 10.

9   Frame, *An Autobiography*, op. cit.: 11–12.

10   Rhodes, op. cit. (1982): 119.

11   Frame, *The Lagoon and Other Stories*, Random Century, Auckland 1990 [1951]: 7. All references to the text, indicated in brackets, are to this edition.

12   Jeanne Delbaere-Garant, 'Janet Frame and the Magic of Words', in Hedwig Bock & Albert Wertheim (eds), *Essays on Contemporary Post-Colonial Fiction*, Max Hueber Verlag, München 1986: 312.

13   Witi Ihimaera, 'Maori Life and Literature: A Sensory Perception', *The Turnbull Library Record*, Wellington New Zealand, 15.2, May 1982: 47.

14   John Beston, 'The Effects of Alienation on the Themes and Characters of Patrick White and Janet Frame', in Daniel Massa (ed.), *Individual and Community in Commonwealth Literature*, Proceedings of the 1978 ACLALS Conference, Old

University Press, Malta 1979: 132–33.

15 Frame, *Faces in the Water*, Virago, London 2009 [1961]: 8. Further references, indicated in brackets, are to this edition.

16 Delbaere-Garant, op. cit.: 313.

17 Frame, *Scented Gardens for the Blind*, George Braziller, New York 1980 [1964]: 31. Further references, indicated in brackets, are to this edition.

18 Antonella Sarti, *Spiritcarvers: Interviews with eighteen writers from New Zealand*, Rodopi, Amsterdam & Atlanta 1998: 46.

19 Janet Frame, *The Carpathians*, George Braziller, New York 1988: 19. All page references to the text, henceforth indicated in brackets, are to this edition.

20 Ibid., in the 'Note' at the beginning of the novel, signed by the fictitious writer of the book: J.H.B. Without page number.

21 Isabella Maria Zoppi, 'Words, Magic, Power: The Memory of the Land in Janet Frame, Derek Walcott and Gabriel Garcia Marquez', *Englishes*, 5. 2, 1998: 42: 'Gravity Star is the name Frame created to describe a quasar, which had been recently discovered at the time she was writing *The Carpathians*. The author herself explained, in an interview with Marion McLeod, that she had utterly invented the legend of the Memory Flower – a hint of magic – but that she had read something about a new galaxy – the realism of sciences and technology. The concept of quasar is of great appeal to Frame, a quasi radio stellar object bearing within itself the concept of *so far*, (really), so full of power, then *so* (apparently) *close*; something which is called a "galaxy" but which is an extragalactic agglomerate of energy still to be observed, studied and understood, but so fascinating and understandable even for the non-initiated.'

22 As previously mentioned, in the Maori language adjectives follow nouns.

23 Zoppi, op. cit.: 42.

24 Ibid.: 45.

25 Ibid.: 48.

26 Ibid.: 52.

27 Anne Salmond, *Hui*, Reed, Auckland 1976 [1975]: 121–22.

28 Zoppi, op. cit.: 52.

29 Peter Beatson, 'Noel Hilliard: The Public and the Private Self', *Sites*.16, Autumn 1988: 110.

30 Lawrence Jones, *Barbed Wire & Mirrors*, University of Otago Press, Dunedin 1990 [1987]: 33.

31 They are all from the collection *Send Somebody Nice* (1976).

32 Beatson, op. cit. (1988): 106.

33 Noel Hilliard, *Maori Girl*, Heinemann, London & Auckland 1971 [1960]: 37. All references to the text, indicated in brackets with MG, are from this edition. References to the other novels, after the first one, will also be indicated in brackets with PJ (*Power of Joy*), MW (*Maori Woman*) and GD (*The Glory and the Dream*).

34 Chris Prentice, 'What *Was* the Maori Renaissance?', in Mark Williams (ed.), *Writing at the Edge of the Universe*, Canterbury University Press, Christchurch 2004: 89.

35 Ibid.: 88–89.
36 Beatson, op. cit. (1988): 110.
37 Jones, op. cit. (1990): 34.
38 Hilliard, *Power of Joy*, Michael Joseph, London 1965:186–87.
39 Hilliard, *The Glory and the Dream*, Heinemann, London 1978: 50.
40 Hilliard, *Maori Woman*, Robert Hale, London 1974: 298.
41 'Yes. You live from day to day. Life is the living of it, what is happening now, in you and all around you. And that's a gift, to live like that. I wish I had it' (239, GD).
42 Jones, op. cit. (1990): 34.
43 Tane is the god of forests.
44 Hilliard, *Selected Stories*, John McIndoe, Dunedin 1977: 106.
45 Ibid.: 104.
46 'Scarf' here means a notch or cut in the tree wood.
47 Agathe Thornton, op. cit.:17–20. The song she analyses is n. 175.

Chapter 4

1 Joseph and Johanna Jones, *New Zealand Fiction*, Twayne Publishers, Boston 1983: 45.
2 Patricia Grace, *Cousins*, University of Hawaii Press, Honolulu 1998 [1992]: 235.
3 Stephen Slemon, 'Post-colonial Critical Theories', in Gregory Castle (ed.), *Postcolonial Discourses: An Anthology*, Blackwell, Oxford and Malden, 2001: 104.
4 This is a general division and does not take into consideration complex postcolonial situations, such as the West Indies or South Africa.
5 Ralph J. Crane, 'Out of the Center: Thoughts on the Post-colonial Literatures of Australia and New Zealand', in Castle (ed.), op. cit.: 393.
6 Ibid.: 392.
7 King, op. cit. (2003): 422.
8 Hunter, op. cit.: 40.
9 Colin James, 'Making a nation is still eluding us', in *New Zealand Herald*, Wednesday, 30 January 2002. The complete article is included in Hunter, op. cit.: 47.
10 King, op. cit. (2003): 416 and 466.
11 Quoted in Slemon, op. cit.: 102.
12 Ashcroft et al., op. cit. (2000): 118 and 130.
13 Crane, op. cit.: 393.
14 Ibid.: 392: '... whereas in countries like India the educated upper classes began at an early stage to write in the language of the colonisers, and to contribute to the body of colonial and postcolonial literatures, this stage only took place much later in Australia and New Zealand, and as a result Aboriginal and Maori literatures in English are largely without that early body of work which sought to mimic the centre at the expense of its own identity.'

15   Ibid.: 394.

16   Gayatri Spivak and Homi Bhabha argue strongly that nativist reconstructions are inevitably subject to the process of natural intermixing that colonialism promoted. Besides, they warned of the dangers of simply reversing the categories of oppressor and oppressed without a critique of the process by which such binary oppositions came into being. See Spivak, 'Can the Subaltern Speak? Speculation on Widow Sacrifice', *Wedge*, Winter/Spring: 120–30; and Bhabha, 'Remembering Fanon: Self, Psyche and the Colonial Condition', in P. Williams and L. Chrisman (eds), *Colonial Discourse and Postcolonial Theory*, Columbia University Press, New York 1994: 112–13.

17   Benita Parry, 'Resistance theory/theorising resistance or two cheers for nativism', in Barker, Hulme and Iversen (eds), *Colonial discourse/postcolonial theory*, Manchester University Press, Manchester and New York 1994: 172.

18   Ibid.: 174. Parry is quoting from Rashmi Bhatnagar, 'Uses and Limits of Foucault: a study of the theme of origins in Edward Said's Orientalism', *Social Scientist*, 158, 1986:5.

19   Ibid.: 174.

20   Ibid.: 179.

21   Stuart Hall, 'Negotiating Caribbean Identities', in Gregory Castle (ed.), op. cit.: 284 and 286.

22   Ibid.: 283.

23   Ibid.: 285.

24   Ibid.: 291.

25   Hall, 'Cultural Identity and Diaspora', in J. Rutherford (ed.), *Identity, Community, Culture, Difference*, London 1990: 223–24. Both quotations in Parry, op. cit.: 175.

26   McRae, op. cit. (1991): 17.

27   Margaret Orbell, 'Introduction', *Contemporary Maori Writing*, Reed, Auckland 1970: 7.

28   Powhiri Wharemarama Rika-Heke, 'Margin or Center? "Let me tell you! In the Land of my Ancestors I am the Centre": Indigenous Writing in Aotearoa', in Radhika Mohanram and Gita Rajan (eds.), *English Postcoloniality: Literatures from Around the World*, Greenwood Press, Westport & London 1996: 153.

29   Ihimaera and Long (eds), *Into the World of Light* , Heinemann, Auckland 1982: 1.

30   Mark Williams, 'Witi Ihimaera and Patricia Grace: the Maori Renaissance', http://www.ucalgary.ca./UofC/eduweb/engl392/492/williams.html: 2.

31   See King, op. cit. (2001): 112.

32   Lee, op. cit.: 18.

33   Williams, op. cit.: 2.

34   Fergus Barrowman, 'Introduction', in *The Picador Book of Contemporary New Zealand Fiction*, Picador, London 1996: xx.

35   Rask Knudsen defines Maoritanga as '"a way of thinking", which loosely translates as a Maori "world-view" or "legacy"'. It refers to 'the experience of being Maori, whereas Maoridom refers to Maori culture as a distinct group, a "nation"'. Op. cit.: 4.

36   Sue Kedgley, *Our Own Country*, Penguin Books, Auckland 1989: 49.

37   Ibid.: 49.

38   Ibid.: 50.

39   Ibid.: 49.

40   Thomas E. Tausky, "'Stories That Show Them Who They Are": An Interview with Patricia Grace', *Australian and New Zealand Studies in Canada*, (6), Fall 1991: 90.

41   Kedgley, op. cit.: 50.

42   Tausky, op. cit.: 91.

43   Dalmatian migrants had been settling in New Zealand since 1857 in search of freedom from oppression by the Austro-Hungarian Empire. Batistich's story 'Roots' (1948) was the first published work in English by a writer of Dalmatian origin. See Robinson & Wattie (eds.), op. cit.: 127. The presence of a large Dalmatian community in New Zealand is also testified by Sargeson's story 'The Making of a New Zealander'.

44   Kedgley, op. cit.: 56.

45   Ihimaera, 'Maori Life and Literature: a Sensory Perception', *The Turnbull Library Record*, 15.1, May 1982: 45–46.

46   Richard Corballis & Simon Garrett, *Introducing Witi Ihimaera*, Longman Paul, Auckland 1984: 9.

47   Ibid.: 9–10.

48   Bill Pearson, 'Witi Ihimaera and Patricia Grace', in Cherry Hankin (ed.), *Critical Essays on the New Zealand Short Story*, Heinemann, Auckland 1982: 166.

49   Corballis and Garrett, op. cit.: 9.

50   Umelo Ojinmah, *Witi Ihimaera: A Changing Vision*, University of Otago Press, Dunedin 1993: 2–3. Ojinmah, reporting J.B. Beston's essay 'Witi Ihimaera, Maori Novelist in a Changing Society', notes that at the time Ihimaera was born (1944) about 85 percent of Maori still lived in rural areas and were mostly agricultural and seasonal workers, like his father. After the Second World War, Maori began to migrate to urban centres. In the early 1970s the ratio of Maori living in the country and the cities was inversed from 60 percent rural and 40 percent urban (1970) to 30 percent rural and 70 percent urban (1975).

51   Ojinmah divides Ihimaera's early production into three phases: pastoral (*Pounamu, Pounamu* and *Tangi*), transitional (*Whanau*) and political (*The New Net Goes Fishing*).

52   Feroza Jussawalla and Reed Way Dasenbrock (eds), *Interviews with Writers of the Post-Colonial World*, University Press of Mississippi, Jackson and London 1992: 225.

53   Ojinmah, op. cit.: 13.

54   Jussawalla and Dasenbrock (eds), op. cit.: 226.

55   Ibid.: 225.

56   Pearson, op. cit. (1982): 167–68.

57   Corballis and Garret, op. cit.: 15 and 35.

58   Ibid.: 33.

59   Ibid.: 64 and 39.

60   Ibid.: 18.
61   Terence Barrow, *An Illustrated Guide to Maori Art*, Reed Methuen, Auckland 1984: 23.
62   Ibid.: 29.
63   Corballis and Garrett, op. cit.: 45.
64   Richard Corballis, 'Witi Ihimaera: Literary Diplomacy', in Paul Sharrad (ed.), *Readings in Pacific Literature*, New Literatures Research Centre, University of Wollongong Printery, Wollongong (Australia) 1993: 110.
65   Pearson, op. cit. (1982): 175. First published in *Landfall* 129, 33.1, 1979.
66   Barrowman, op. cit.: xxiii.
67   Rangi Walker, 'Maori Beliefs: An Integrated Cosmos', in W.T.G. James (ed.), *The Word Within the Word*, University of Waikato 1983 (typescript): 89–90.
68   John B. Beston,' The Fiction of Patricia Grace', *Ariel*, 15.2, April 1984: 41.
69   Ibid.: 41–42.
70   Ibid., 'Grace is aware that the quality of her work alone will not hold the continued interest of her predominantly Pakeha audience: she must make the Maori attractive to the Pakeha': 42. 'Grace is careful to allay Pakeha fears by stressing that the Maori do not threaten the privileges the Pakeha have arrogated unto themselves': 43. 'Grace is careful not to alienate her Pakeha audience by showing her Maori insisting on their rights' : 44.
71   Ibid.: 48.
72   Ibid.: 49.
73   Ibid.: 51 (both quotations).
74   Ibid.: 51–52.
75   Norman Simms, 'A Maori Literature In English. Part I: Prose fiction – Patricia Grace', in *Pacific Moana Quarterly*, 3.2, April 1978: 189.
76   Ibid.: 189.
77   Ibid.: 190.
78   Eva Rask Knudsen, op. cit.: 12.
79   Ibid.: 3.
80   Ibid.: 3.

Chapter 5

1   See Lydia Wevers, 'Short Fiction by Maori Writers', *Commonwealth Essays and Studies*, 16.2, Spring 1994: 27.
2   Corballis and Garrett, op. cit.: 4.
3   William McGaw, '"Another foothold": Exile and Return in Patricia Grace's *Mutuwhenua*', *Australian & New Zealand Studies in Canada*, (6), Fall 1991: 103.
4   Corballis and Garrett, op. cit.: 15–16. They refer to Alistair Fox, 'In Search of the Emerald City: The Short Stories of Witi Ihimaera', *Pilgrims*, (8), 1980: 88–94.
5   Ibid.: 19–21.

6   Ibid.: 36.

7   Ibid.: 16.

8   All references to Ihimaera's and Grace's texts are from these editions and will be indicated in brackets, preceded by the following abbreviations: Witi Ihimaera, *Pounamu, Pounamu*, Heinemann, Auckland 1972 (PP); *Tangi*, Heinemann, Auckland 1984 [1973] (TA); *Whanau*, Heinemann, Auckland 1974 (WH); *The New Net Goes Fishing*, Heinemann, Auckland 1977 (NN). Patricia Grace: *Waiariki*, Longman Paul, Auckland 1975 (WA); *Mutuwhenua*, Penguins, Auckland 1986 [1978] (MU); *The Dream Sleepers*, Longman Paul, Auckland 1980 (DS).

9   'We used to avoid him [Mr Hohepa]. All the kids around the pa avoided him. If we saw him coming down the road, we'd back away. [...] He'd only have to look at us and we'd think: makutu... makutu...' (17); 'There he [Hohepa] would be, sitting on the verandah like a king, acknowledging the service with a grunt and a tap of his tokotoko on the floor' (20).

10   Ojinmah, op.cit.: 17.

11   Ibid.: 20–21.

12   Corballis and Garrett, op. cit.: 22.

13   A.W. Reed, *Reed Book of Maori Mythology*, Reed, Auckland 2004: 333.

14   Corballis and Garrett, op. cit.: 27. See also their analysis of 'Tangi': 23–25.

15   Hiwi and Pat Tauroa, op. cit.: 19.

16   Corballis and Garrett, op. cit.: 32.

17   Rask Knudsen, op. cit.: 24–25.

18   'A world that moves forward to the place it came from': proverb prefacing Michael King (ed.), *Te Ao Hurihuri: the world moves on*, Hicks Smith & Sons, Wellington 1975. Quoted by Rask Knudsen, op. cit.: 24.

19   Rask Knudsen, op. cit: 24–25.

20   Ibid.: 25.

21   The image of a man in a canoe adrift in the sea, suggestive of loneliness, physical danger and endurance, evokes the perilous ocean crossing of the Maori ancestors from Hawaiki.

22   Durix, 'Time in Witi Ihimaera's *Tangi*', *The Journal of New Zealand Literature*, 1, 1983: 111.

23   Ibid.: 104.

24   Ibid.: 105.

25   Ibid.: 106.

26   Ibid.: 111 (both quotations).

27   Ibid.: 111.

28   Rask Knudsen, op. cit.: 25.

29   Corballis, op. cit.: 112.

30   See Durix, op. cit.: 110: 'One may wonder whether Tama will ever come back [to Waituhi].' See Corballis and Garrett, op. cit.: 35: 'That Tama, at the end of the novel, returns to Wellington and does not prepare to live permanently in Waituhi, where he claims to have left his heart, suggests that a rediscovery of a sense of place

by the individual Maori in New Zealand society is a process that is as yet only beginning (and Tama's future urban experience may provide material for a further novel by Ihimaera).'

31 Corballis and Garrett, op. cit.: 38–39.
32 Ojinmah, op. cit.: 31. Manaakitanga means reciprocal assistance to one another.
33 Ibid.: 36.
34 Ibid.: 37.
35 Ibid.: 37.
36 Rask Knudsen, op. cit.: 11.
37 Duff's controversial issue is that the Maori should not lay the blame of their disempowerment on the Pakeha but meet their challenge and compete with them.
38 Grace, *Cousins*, op. cit.: 235.
39 Pearson, op. cit. (1982): 176.
40 Rachel Nunns, 'Doing Her Job: Patricia Grace's Fiction', in Paul Sharrad (ed.), *Readings in Pacific Literature*, New Literatures Research Centre, University of Wollongong, Wollongong 1993: 114.
41 'Kepa', 'The Pictures', 'Drifting', 'Whitebait' and 'Kip'.
42 Jane McRae, 'Patricia Grace/Interviewed by Jane McRae', in Alley and Williams (eds), *In the Same Room*, Auckland University Press, Auckland 1992: 292.
43 Ibid.: 285 and 294–95.
44 Ibid.: 288 (both quotations).
45 Ibid.: 289.
46 Nunns op. cit.: 114–15.
47 Rangi Walker, 'Maori Beliefs: An Integrated Cosmos', in W.T.G. James (ed.), *The Word Within the Word*, (typescript), University of Waikato, 1983: 89.
48 Mary Louise Pratt, 'Scratches on the Face of the Country; or, What Mr Barrow Saw in the Land of the Bushmen', *Critical Inquiry*, 12.1, Autumn 1985: 139.
49 Nunns, op. cit.: 116.
50 Ibid.: 116.
51 Pearson, op. cit. (1982): 178.
52 'Hey, you fellows, little brother has piddled, see!' 'Fullas' is a Maori adaptation of 'fellows'. In Maori 'na' adds emphasis, like 'see'. Judith Dell Panny, *Turning the Eye: Patricia Grace and the Short Story*, Lincoln University Press & Daphne Brasell Associates, Canterbury & Wellington 1997: 42.
53 Knudsen, op. cit.: 3.
54 Ancient chant translated by Rev. Richard Taylor in *Te Ika a Maui*, in Reed, op. cit.: 5–6.
55 See Nunns, op. cit.: 118: 'Graeme never seems a well-realized character.' See Beston, op. cit.: 51: 'Graeme is idealized and, in the process, stripped of individualizing characteristics.'
56 McRae, op. cit. (1992): 291.
57 Nunns, op. cit.: 117.
58 Lauri Anderson, 'Maoriness and the Clash of Cultures in Patricia Grace's *Mutuwhenua*', *World Literature Written in English*, 26.1, Spring 1986: 189. The shape

of a *patu* somehow recalls that of a violin. Ripeka describes it as 'a big tongue'. At one end 'there is a shape curled, like a new fern growing' (MU 23).

59   Nunns, op. cit.: 118.
60   McRae, op. cit. (1992): 291.
61   See Nunns, op. cit.: 118: 'If this novel is simply about what matters to Maoris, to worry about Graeme's feelings is to raise an irrelevant quibble. But if Grace is concerned with relations between races, then it seems to me that she has underestimated the significance that a wanted baby would have for its father.'
62   Anderson, op. cit.: 190. Her quotation is from Alice Joan Metge, *The Maoris of New Zealand*, Routledge and Kegan Paul, London 1967: 28.
63   McRae, op. cit. (1992): 290–91.
64   Beston, op. cit.: 51.
65   P. Grace, *Potiki*, University of Hawai'i Press, Honolulu 1995, [1986]: 31. All references to the text, henceforth indicated in brackets and preceded by PO, are to this edition.
66   Antonella Sarti, 'Patricia Grace', in *Spiritcarvers – Interviews with Eighteen Writers from New Zealand*, Rodopi, Amsterdam and Atlanta 1998: 54.

Chapter 6

1   Rika-Heke, op. cit.: 152–53.
2   Ibid.: 155.
3   Ibid.: 154.
4   'Hori' is a derogatory term for 'Maori'.
5   See Ojinmah, op. cit.: 48.
6   Ibid.: 40.
7   In Maori English, the expression 'don't worry' is often changed into 'not to worry'.
8   Ojinmah, op. cit.: 56.
9   Miriama Evans, 'Politics and Literature' in *Landfall* 153, 39.1, March 1985: 42. She is referring to Keri Hulme's best-selling novel, which won the 1985 Booker Prize.
10   Here, kina (sea urchin) means a very short and spiky haircut. Some lines sound like rap music, using assonance rather than rhyme: 'Dear Sir/How a-are ya/Then you start/I'm all ri-ight'.
11   Evans, op. cit.: 41.
12   Ibid.: 41.
13   K.M. is Katherine Mansfield. HART (Halt All Racist Tours) is the organisation set up in 1969 to oppose sporting contact with South Africa and protest its apartheid policies.
14   Their titles are: 'Kepa', 'The Pictures', 'Drifting', 'Whitebaits' and 'Kip'.
15   Corballis and Garrett, op. cit.: 45.
16   In his foreword, Lawrence Jones pinpoints the influence of the Nigerian writer on his fellow countryman Ojinmah's view of Ihimaera, in particular Achebe's belief that 'literature is representational and that the writer has a social role to play as reality instructor.' Ojinmah, op. cit.: ix.

17   Ibid.: 64.
18   The importance for Maori elders to be buried in their turangawaewae was mentioned in relation to Ihimaera's 'Return from Oz' and Grace's 'Transition'.
19   Grace, *Potiki*, University of Hawai'i Press, Honolulu 1986: 129. Further references to the book are from this edition, indicated in brackets with PO.

Chapter 7

1   Michael King, *Nga iwi o te motu*, Reed, Auckland 2001 [1997]: 5–6.
2   Lawrence Jones, 'A Symposium on Historical Fiction: Introduction', *JNZL*, 9, 1991: 3–9.
3   Ihimaera, 'A Maori Perspective', *JNZL*, 9,1991: 53–54.
4   See Joanne Tompkins, '"It all depends on what story you hear": Historiographic Metafiction and Colin Johnson's *Dr Wooreddy's Prescription for Enduring the Ending of the World* and Witi Ihimaera's *The Matriarch*', *Modern Fiction Studies*, 38. 4, 1990: 484.
5   Keown, 'Maori or English? The Politics of Language in Patricia Grace's *Baby No-Eyes*', op. cit.: 427.
6   Ibid.: 427.
7   Quotations from the texts, indicated in brackets preceded by PO (*Potiki*), BN (*Baby No- Eyes*), DO (*Dogside Story*), TM (*The Matriarch*) and TD (*The Dream Swimmer*), are to these editions: Grace: *Potiki*, op. cit.; *Baby No-Eyes*, The Women's Press, London 1999 [1998]; *Dogside Story*, University of Hawai'i Press, Honolulu 2001. Ihimaera, *The Matriarch*, Reed, Auckland 2003 [1986]; *The Dream Swimmer*, Penguin, Auckland 2005 [1997].
8   Ihimaera, *Dear Miss Mansfield*, Viking, Auckland 1989: 113.
9   The Gisborne area is supposed to be the first place in the world to see the sunrise. For this reason it was inundated with tourists from all over the world on New Year's Eve 1999.
10   Simone Drichel, 'Tough Grace', review in *New Zealand Books*, 11.4, Oct. 2001: 5.
11   The exploits of Mauipotiki (or Maui) form a separate cycle of Maori mythology. After a miraculous birth and upbringing, he snared the sun to give men longer days, tamed fire and fished the North Island of Aotearoa/New Zealand (called Te Ika a Maui; the fish of Maui). He eventually died while attempting to kill the goddess of death, Hine-nui-te-Po. See A.W. Reed, *Reed Book of Maori Mythology*, Reed, Auckland 2004: 117–60.
12   In his attempt to kill the goddess, Maui crept into her vagina while she was asleep, with the intention of crawling through her body and extracting her heart. The birds could hardly contain their excitement, as he disappeared, and laughed. The goddess awoke, closed her legs and killed Maui. See Reed, op. cit.: 143–45. In the Maori world a woman's womb is known as te whare tangata, the house of people, hence the parallel between the door and the female sex organ. See Jenny Lee, *Notes on P. Grace's 'Potiki'*, Kaiako Publications (typescript), 1990: 9.

13   Rask Knudsen, op. cit.: 25.

14   Proverb prefacing Michael King (ed.), *Te Ao Hurihuri: the world moves on*, Hicks
      Smith & Sons, Wellington 1975, quoted by Rask Knudsen, op. cit.: 24.

15   Rask Knudsen, op. cit.: 24–25.

16   Keown, op. cit.: 427.

17   Ibid.: 426.

18   Wi Pere Halbert took the Eastern Maori seat in Parliament in 1883. See King, op.
      cit. (2001): 65.

19   Joanne Tompkins, op. cit.: 490.

20   Te Kooti was a Maori fighting on the government side during the Land Wars.
      Wrongfully arrested in 1865 and deported to the penal settlement in the Chatham
      Islands, he escaped and returned to the North Island to wage the most effective
      guerrilla campaign seen in the country. He was the founder of the Ringatu Church,
      which interwove Maori and Biblical elements, especially from the Old Testament.
      See King, op. cit. (2001): 41–42 and 75.

21   After escaping from the Chathams, Te Kooti and his followers headed for their
      'promised land' in the Urewera Mountains. They had no wish to fight, but were
      intercepted by government forces three times. Then Te Kooti announced he would
      fight against those who were responsible for his exile. He attacked the Matawhero
      settlement on 10 November 1868, killing 63 people, half of them Europeans. See
      Ernest E. Bush, 'Did This Change the Course of History? A centenary of more than
      passing interest …', in *Te Ao Hou*, 64, September 1968, http://teahou.natlib.govt.
      nz/teahou/issue/Mao64TeA/c8.html.

22   The last major epidemic to afflict the Maori population was the Great Flu of
      1918, in which at least 1130 Maori died, a rate 4.5 times greater than that of the
      Europeans. See King, op. cit. (2001): 95.

23   Chris Campbell, known as Kara, was the founder of a sect that incorporated the
      Ringatu religion and the Rastafarian movement. He became famous in the 1970s,
      the great years of Maori protest. See Ihimaera, *The Dream Swimmer*: 214–32.

24   Joanne Tompkins, op. cit.: 488.

25   Ibid.: 492.

26   Michael King, 'A Magnificent New Zealand-Baroque Near-Success', *Metro*, 6.62,
      Aug. 1986: 170.

27   Christine Prentice, 'Nationalism vs. Internationalism? Witi Ihimaera's *The Matriarch*
      and Critical Abjection', *Nationalism vs. Internationalism: (Inter) National Dimensions
      of Literatures in English*, Stauffenburg Verlag, Tübingen 1996: 550.

28   Elizabeth Caffin, 'A Fictional Performance', *NZ Listener*, 16 August 1986: 52.
      Quoted in Prentice, op. cit. (1996): 550.

29   C.K. Stead, *Answering to the Language: Essays on Modern Writers*, Auckland 1989:
      192. Quoted in Prentice, op. cit.: 550.

30   See Prentice, op. cit. (1996): 550.

31   Trevor James, 'Lost Our Birthright Forever? The Maori Writer's Re-invention of
      New Zealand', in *Span*, 24, 1987: 110.

32   Mark Williams, 'Witi Ihimaera and Patricia Grace: The Maori Renaissance', http://
        www.ucalgary.ca/UofC/eduweb/eng392/492williams.html: 2.

Chapter 8

1   Ihimaera, 'Bookmarking the Century' (both quotations), op. cit.: 40–41.
2   Ashcroft et al., op. cit. (2002): 37.
3   Ibid.: 38.
4   Ibid.: 8. They purposely lowercase 'englishes'.
5   Janet Holmes, Maria Stubbe and Meredith Marra, 'Language, Humour and Ethnic
        Identity Marking in New Zealand English', in Christian Mair (ed.), *The Politics of
        English as a World Language*, Rodopi, Amsterdam & New York 2003: 433.
6   See Ray Harlow, *Māori*, Lincom Europa, München & Newcastle 1996: 1–3.
7   Jenny Lee explains the pronunciation of Maori vowels to English speakers in this
        way: *a* as in 'up', *e* as in 'egg', *i* as in 'me', *o* as in 'door', *u* as in 'blue'. Jenny Lee,
        Notes on Patricia Grace's 'Potiki', Kaiako Publications (typescript), November 1990:
        39.
8   The word 'Maori' (pronounced /maaori/), should be spelt 'Maaori' or 'Māori', but
        today most writers tend to use neither the macron nor the double vowels.
9   Other examples are the loans of English names: 'John' is Hone, 'James' is Hemi,
        'Harriet' is Hariata, 'Joseph' is Hohepa, and 'Rose' is Rohe.
10   Elizabeth Gordon and Tony Deverson, *New Zealand English and English in New
        Zealand*, New House Publishers, Auckland 1998: 65. Edward Morris was a
        lexicographer of the University of Melbourne, famous for his seminal study *Austral
        English* (1898).
11   'Mora' is the unit of time or meter equivalent to the ordinary or normal short sound
        or syllable, and is the basic unit in Greek and Latin prosody.
12   With a few exceptions, most syllables in Italian end in vowels. The Italian syllable
        structure is definitely closer to the Maori one than the English syllable structure,
        which also explains the melodic qualities of Italian and Maori.
13   Grace, *Tu*, University of Hawai'i Press, Honolulu 2004: 252.
14   Holmes et al., op. cit.: 436.
15   This can be seen when we compare the 1972 and 2003 editions of *Pounamu,
        Pounamu*. In 'A Game of Cards', we read 'What you think I had all these kids, ay?'
        (1) and ' Sweet, ay?' (2) in 1972. We read 'What you think I had all these kids, eh?'
        (10) and 'Sweet, eh?' (11) in 2003.
16   Ihimaera, *Bulibasha*, Penguin, Auckland 1994: 257. Further quotations, indicated
        in brackets and preceded by BU, are from this edition. The translation of the Maori
        sentences is: 'P Biology. Pass, isn't it? Well done! One P.' […] 'P English. Pass there
        too, isn't it? Good! Two P.' […] 'F, Geography. Alas, some trouble! Two P, one F.'
17   Pai/Ka pai/Kapai: Well done! Good!
18   Holmes et al., op. cit.: 439.
19   Gordon and Deverson, op. cit.: 72.

20   Ibid: 66.

21   Ibid.: 72.

22   Ibid.: 70.

23   English became the only language taught in schools from 1867 onwards. Passages
      on the repressive school system enforcing English language and culture are found in
      Grace's *Potiki* (chapter 5), *Baby No-Eyes* (chapter 4), 'Letters from Whetu' and 'The
      Dream Sleepers' (from *The Dream Sleepers*), and in Ihimaera's 'Catching Up' (from
      The New Net Goes Fishing).

24   Elizabeth Gordon and Mark Williams, 'Raids on the Articulate: Code-Switching,
      Style Switching and Post-Colonial Writing' in *The Journal of Commonwealth
      Literature*, 33.2, 1998: 85–86.

25   Ibid.: 80.

26   The only exception is in the US edition of *The Whale Rider*.

27   This comment was made by Williams and Gordon in relation to Chinua Achebe's
      Things Fall Apart and his inclusion of Ibo elements in the novel, but it can apply to
      Maori literature as well. See Williams and Gordon, op. cit.: 82.

28   See Hiwi and Pat Tauroa, op. cit.: 50–52.

29   Williams and Gordon, op. cit.: 88.

30   Ibid.: 85.

31   Ibid.: 87.

32   Ibid.: 88 (both quotations).

33   Feroza Jussawalla and Reed Way Dasenbrock (eds), *Interviews with Writers of the
      Post-Colonial World*, University Press of Mississippi, Jackson & London 1992: 238.

34   Grace, 'Influences on Writing', in Vilsoni Hereniko and Rob Wilson (eds), *Inside
      Out: Literature, Cultural Politics, and Identity in the New Pacific*, Rowman &
      Littlefield Publishers, Lanham & Oxford 1999: 71–72.

35   See Harlow, op. cit.: 3.

36   Ibid.: 35.

37   Grace, *The Sky People*, Penguin, Auckland 1994. Further quotations from the text,
      indicated in brackets and preceded by SP, are from this edition.

38   Harlow, op. cit.: 11.

39   Maori makes no gender distinction in pronouns. See Harlow, op. cit.: 6.

40   Keown Michelle, 'Maori or English? The Politics of Language in Patricia Grace's
      Baby No-Eyes', in Christian Mair (ed.), *The Politics of Language as a World Language*,
      Rodopi, Amsterdam & New York 2003: 425. See also Dell Panny's analysis of
      'Valley', in Judith Dell Panny, *Turning the Eye: Patricia Grace and the Short Story*,
      Lincoln University Press, Canterbury NZ 1997: 46 and Lee's study of the language
      in *Potiki*, in Lee. op. cit.: 38.

41   Keown, op. cit. (2003): 424.

42   Lee, op. cit.: 38.

43   Dell Panny, op. cit.: 46.

44   Lee, op. cit.: 38. This means that there are particles in the sentence indicating
      motion or the copulative function of 'to be'.

45   Keown, op. cit. (2003): 424.
46   Ibid.: 426.
47   Gordon and Wiliams, op. cit.: 90.

Chapter 9

1   Hawken, op. cit.: 2
2   Ibid.: 102.
3   Ibid.: 113.
4   Danny Keenan, 'Bound to the Land', in E. Pawson and T. Brooking (eds),
      Environmental Histories of New Zealand, Oxford University Press, South Melbourne
      2002: 250.
5   Ihimaera, *The Whale Rider*, Harcourt, Orlando 2003 [1987]: 116. Further
      quotations, indicated in brackets with WR, are from this edition.
6   Grace, *Electric City*, Penguin, Auckland 1987: 78.
7   Editorial, *New Zealand Listener*, 221 (3627), November 14–20, 2009: 5.
8   Ihimaera, 'Wiwi': first published in *Below the Surface*, Vintage, Auckland 1995;
      republished in *Ihimaera: His Best Stories*, Reed, Auckland 2003.
9   Holly Walker, 'Developing Difference: Attitudes towards Maori "Development" in
      Patricia Grace's *Potiki* and *Dogside Story*', *Kunapipi*, 27.12, 2005: 216–18.
10   Ibid.: 223.
11   In this analysis I am using Serge Latouche's critique of Western development,
      expounded in chapter 2.
12   Hawken, op. cit.: 5.
13   Ibid.: 2.

Chapter 10

1   Patricia Grace, *Cousins*, University of Hawai'i Press, Honolulu 1998 [1992]: 235.
      Further references to the text indicated in brackets with CO are to this edition.
2   See Parry, op. cit.: 175. See also Hall, op. cit.: 291.
3   Simeon is the third child of Tamihana's seventh son, Joshua. Being members
      of the community, Joshua's family has a right to live there. But unlike his elder
      brothers, who are entitled to have their own houses, Joshua must live in Tamihana's
      homestead and run it for the patriarch.
4   Judith Dell Panny, 'A Cultural-Historical Reading of Patricia Grace's *Cousins*', Kōtare
      2006, (6), www.nzetc.org/tm/scholarly/tei-Whi06ota-t1-g1-t1.html: 4.
5   Ibid.: 8.
6   Sarti, op. cit: 46.
7   Ibid.: 46.
8   Grace, *The Sky People*, Penguin, Auckland 1994: 71. Further quotations indicated in
      brackets with SP are from this edition.

9   Ihimaera, *The Uncle's Story*, University of Hawai'i Press, Honolulu 2000: 155.
     Further references to the book, indicated in brackets with US, are from this edition.
10   *Nights in the Gardens of Spain* will not be treated in detail since Ihimaera explores
     the theme of homosexuality from a general viewpoint through a Pakeha protagonist.
     The Maori perspective in the novel is offered by a minor character, The Noble
     Savage, who briefly poses issues amply developed later in *The Uncle's Story*.

Chapter 11

1   Juniper Ellis, 'The Singing Word', *The Journal of Commonwealth Literature*, 34.1,
     1999: 176. The interview took place in May 1998.
2   Ibid.: 174.
3   Ibid.: 175.
4   Ibid.: 174–75.
5   Ihimaera, *Pounamu, Pounamu*, Reed, Auckland 2003: 12. Further quotations will be
     indicated in brackets with PP03.
6   Ihimaera, *Whanau II*, Reed, Auckland 2004: 20. Further references will be indicated
     in brackets with WH04.
7   Ihimaera, *The Rope of Man*, Reed, Auckland 2005: 21 and 150–52. Further
     references will be indicated in brackets with RM.
8   Judith Dell Panny, 'Artemis and *The Matriarch*', *The Culture Within: Essays on
     Ihimaera, Grace, Hulme, Tuwhare*, Occasional Paper (3), International Pacific
     College, February 1998: 6.
9   Alistair Fox, 'The Symbolic Function of the Operatic Allusions in Witi Ihimaera's
     The Dream Swimmer', in *Journal of Postcolonial Writing*, 42:1, May 2006: 5.
10   Ibid.: 5. The 'theorists' Fox is referring to are Ashcroft, Griffiths and Tiffin.
11   Carlotta Sorba, 'Il 1848 e la melodrammatizzazione della politica', in Banti and
     Ginsborg (eds.), *Storia d'Italia – Annali 22: Il Risorgimento*, Einaudi, Torino 2007:
     483.
12   Ibid. : 483. Turner articulates his theory by playing on the double meaning of
     the verb 'to act', as both 'doing ordinary things in everyday life' and 'performing
     on a stage or in a temple', and by applying the original etymological meaning of
     'performance', from the old French *parfournir* that signified 'to complete, to bring to
     an end'. 'To perform' means to bring to an end a complex process. Sorba draws on
     Turner, *Dal rito al teatro*, 1982.
13   Simonetta Chiappini, 'La voce della martire. Dagli "evirati cantori" all'eroina
     romantica' in Banti and Ginsborg (eds.), op. cit.: 306–307.
14   According to the timbre of her voice, a soprano can be *leggero* (coloratura soprano),
     lirico (lyrical) or *drammatico* (dramatic). The lighter timbre of a coloratura or lyric
     soprano is more suitable to young heroines.
15   Quoted from De Staël, *Corinna ovvero l'Italia*, 1807, in Chiappini, op. cit.: 290.
16   Fox, op. cit.: 12.

17   See the chapter on *Tangi*.

18   Anna Rogers, 'Revisionist Urges', *New Zealand Books*, 16.4, October 2006: 5.

19   Grace, *Tu*, University of Hawai'i Press, Honolulu 2004: 142. Further references are indicated in brackets. Te Puea Herangi was a descendant of Maori king Potatau. She became active in politics helping the election of Maui Pomare to Parliament in 1911. She was involved in many cultural and humanitarian causes. See Robinson & Wattie (eds), op. cit.: 531.

20   Keown, op. cit. (2007): 101.

21   Megan Hutching (ed.), *A Fair Sort of Battering*, Harper Collins, Auckland 2004: 24.

22   Gianni Oliva, *I vinti e i liberati*, Mondadori, Milano 1994: 6.

23   Della Valle, op. cit.: 131–41.

24   Janet Wilson, 'The Maori at War and Strategic Survival: *Tu* by Patricia Grace', *Hecate*, 34.1 2008: 96–97.

25   'Yes, it was the law. They weren't allowed into pubs over a certain period of years. I know my father wasn't allowed into pubs, but he used to go in anyway. And also there were rules about picture theatres, restaurants and so forth. These weren't laws of the land but requirements in different areas … Maori people were discriminated against in the work place and when it came to accommodation. A Maori widow was given less in her pension than a Pakeha widow.' See Della Valle, op. cit.: 138.

26   Wilson, op. cit.: 97.

27   Ibid.: 93.

28   Beatson, *The Healing Tongue: Themes in Contemporary Maori Literature*, Studies in New Zealand Art & Society 1, Massey University, Palmerston North 1989: 45.

29   Ibid.: 45.

30   Rowley Habib, 'Fish', in M. Orbell (ed.), *Contemporary Maori Writing*, Reed Wellington & Auckland, 1970: 72. 'When I of fish eat; when, with knife and fork/I break the tender segments of flesh within my plate/I feel the pulling back. Strong I feel it;/Pulling me back to my forefathers,/To shores not yet trodden by white men./ It is, then, not a mere eating of the flesh,/A delighting in the sensual taste./It is, for me, more than this: it is a revelation./The sea surges before me, washing upon the shores;/Heaving against jagged rocks; as it did of old./And this sea holds more than just its beauty,/ Its aboundingness. It is something sacred;/It is like a parent to me. For think I then/ That the sea was my forefathers' very existence./This then is what it is when, with knife and fork/ I lift a morsel of fish to my mouth.'

31   Rask Knudsen, op. cit.: 2.

32   Beatson, op. cit.: 45.

33   Grace, *Mutuwhenua*, op. cit.: 38–39.

34   Massimo Montanari, *Il cibo come cultura*, Laterza, Bari 2006: 130–31.

35   Montanari, *La cucina italiana*, Laterza, Bari 2000: 3, 41, xiii.

36   Ibid.: x.

37   Carlo Petrini, *Slow Food: The case for taste*, Columbia University Press, NY 2001: x.

38   Ernesto Galli della Loggia, *L'identità italiana*, Il Mulino, Bologna 1998: 99–100.

39   Angelo Diotti, *Lingua Magistra*, Bruno Mondadori, Milano 2008: 212.

40   Galli della Loggia, op. cit.: 97–98 and 100–102.

41   Paul Ginsborg, *Storia d'Italia: Famiglia, società, Stato*, Einaudi, Torino 1998: 14.

42   Grace, 'And So I Go', in *Waiariki,* op. cit.: 45.

43   Habib, 'The Raw Men: For the Maori Battalion', Orbell (ed.), op. cit.: 70–71.

44   Della Valle, op. cit.: 139.

45   The Maori language has five vowels that are pronounced exactly as in Italian. They
        can be short or long. In the latter, they are generally marked by a macron, as in
        āporo (apple) or pūnu (spoon), although their pronunciation does not change
        remarkably. Maori words always alternate a consonant and a vowel, and finish with a
        vowel as do most Italian words.

46   Holmes, Stubbe and Marra, op. cit.: 433.

47   Gordon and Deverson, op. cit.: 65. Edward Morris was a lexicographer of the
        University of Melbourne, famous for his seminal study *Austral English* (1898).

48   Beatson, op. cit.: 37.

49   C.G. Jung, 'Healing the Split', *The Symbolic Life, The Collected Works of C.G. Jung*
        (18), Princeton University Press, Princeton 1989: 254–57.

50   Ibid.: 253.

51   Jung, 'The Tavistock Lectures: Lecture V', op. cit.: 135–65.

52   Ibid.: 137.

53   Ibid.: 138.

54   Ibid.: 142–43 (both quotations).

55   Ibid.: 143.

Bibliography

Alley, Elizabeth, 'An Honest Record: an interview with Janet Frame', *Landfall* 178, 45.2, June 1991: 154–68.

—— and Mark Willams (eds), *In the Same Room: Conversation with New Zealand Writers*, Auckland University Press: Auckland, 1992.

Anderson, Lauri, 'Maoriness and the Clash of Cultures in Patricia Grace's *Mutuwhenua*', *World Literature Written in English*, 26.1, Spring 1986: 188–90.

Ashcroft, Bill, Gareth Griffiths and Helen Tiffin, *The Empire Writes Back*, second edition, Routledge: London & New York, 2002 [1989].

——, *Post-Colonial Studies: the Key Concepts*, Routledge: London & New York, 2000.

Bardolph, Jacqueline, '"A Way of Talking": A Way of Seeing: the Short Stories of Patricia Grace', *Commonwealth Essays and Studies*, 12.2, Spring 1990: 29–39.

Barker, Francis, Peter Hulme and Margaret Iversen, *Colonial discourse/postcolonial theory*, Manchester University Press: Manchester & New York, 1994.

Barrow, Terence, *An Illustrated Guide to Maori Art*, Reed Methuen: Auckland, 1984.

Barrowman, Fergus (ed.), *The Picador Book of Contemporary New Zealand Fiction*, Picador: London, 1996.

Bassanese, Fiora A., *Understanding Luigi Pirandello*, into University of South Carolina Press: Columbia (SC), 1997.

Baucke, William, *Where the White Man Treads Across the Pathway of the Maori*, Wilson & Horton: Auckland, 1928 [1905].

Baugham, Blanche E., *Brown Bread from a Colonial Oven*, Whitcombe & Tombs: London, 1912.

Beatson, Peter, 'Noel Hilliard: The Public and the Private Self', *Sites*, 18, March 1988: 103–110.

——, *The Healing Tongue: Themes in Contemporary Maori Literature*, Studies in New Zealand Art & Society 1, Sociology Department Massey University: Palmerston North, 1989.

Beston, John, 'The Effects of Alienation on the Themes and Characters of Patrick White and Janet Frame', in Daniel Massa (ed.), *Individual and Community in Commonwealth Literature*, Proceedings of the 1978 ACLALS conference, Old University Press: Malta, 1979: 131–39.

——, 'The Fiction of Patricia Grace', *Ariel*, 15.2, April 1984: 41–53.

Bhabha, Homi K. (ed.), *Nation and Narration*, Routledge: London & New York, 1990.

——, 'Remembering Fanon: Self, Psyche and the Colonial Condition', in P. Williams & L. Chrisman (eds), *Colonial Discourse and Postcolonial Theory*, Columbia University Press: New York, 1994a: 112–23.

——, *The Location of Culture*, Routledge: London, 1994b.

Binney, Judith, 'Maori Oral Narratives, Pakeha Written Texts: Two Forms of Telling History', *New Zealand Journal of History*, 21.1, April 1987: 16–28.

Castle, Gregory (ed.), *Postcolonial Discourse: an Anthology*, Blackwell: Oxford, 2001.

Chiappini, Simonetta, 'La voce del martire. Dagli "evirati cantori" all'eroina romantica', in A.M. Banti and P. Ginsborg (eds), *Storia d'Italia – Annali 22: Il Risorgimento*, Einaudi: Torino, 2007: 289–328.

Conrad, Joseph, 'Heart of Darkness', in *Youth: a Narrative and Two Other Stories*, Blackwood & Sons: London, 1902.

Corballis, Richard, 'Witi Ihimaera: Literary Diplomacy', in Paul Sharrad (ed.), *Readings in Pacific Literature*, New Literatures Research Centre, University of Wollongong: Wollongong (Australia), 1993: 108–113. [First published in *Landfall* 129, 33.1, 1979.]

—— and Simon Garrett, *Introducing Witi Ihimaera*, Longman Paul: Auckland, 1984.

Crane, Ralph J., 'Out of the Center: Thoughts on the Postcolonial Literatures of Australia and New Zealand', in Castle Gregory (ed.), *Postcolonial Discourse: an Anthology*, Blackwell: Oxford, 2001: 389–98.

Daiches, David, *A Critical History of English Literature*, vol. III, Secker & Warburg: London, 1960.

Delbaere-Garant, Jeanne, 'Janet Frame and the Magic of Words', in Hedwig Bock &

Albert Wertheim (eds), *Essays on Contemporary Post-Colonial Fiction*, Max Hueber Verlag: München, 1986.

Della Valle, Paola, 'The Wider Family: Patricia Grace Interviewed by Paola Della Valle', *Journal of Commonwealth Literature*, 42.1, 2007: 131–41.

Dell Panny, Judith, 'A Cultural-Historical Reading of Patricia Grace's *Cousins*', *Kōtare* 2006, (6). http://www.nzetc.org/tm/scholarly/tei-Whi06ota-t1-g1-t1.html

——, 'Artemis and *The Matriarch*', *The Culture Within: Essays on Ihimaera, Grace, Hulme, Tuwhare*, Occasional Paper N.3, International Pacific College, New Zealand, February 1998: 2–9.

——, *Turning the Eye. Patricia Grace and the Short Story*, Lincoln University Press: Canterbury (NZ), 1997.

Diotti, Angelo, *Lingua Magistra*, Bruno Mondadori: Milano, 2008.

Drichel, Simone, 'Tough Grace', *New Zealand Books*, 11.4, October 2001: 4–5.

Duff, Alan, *Once Were Warriors*, Tandem: Auckland, 1990.

Durix, Jean-Pierre, 'The Time in Witi Ihimaera's *Tangi*', *Journal of New Zealand Literature*, 1, 1983: 101–113.

Ellis, Juniper, '"The Singing Word", Witi Ihimaera interviewed by Juniper Ellis', *Journal of Commonwealth Literature*, 34.1, 1999: 169–82.

Evans, Miriama, 'Politics and Maori Literature', *Landfall* 153, 39.1, March 1985: 40–45.

Finlayson, Roderick, *Brown Man's Burden*, Unicorn Press: Auckland, 1938.

——, *Brown Man's Burden and later stories*, Auckland University Press: Auckland, 1973.

——, *In Georgina's Shady Garden*, Griffin Press: Auckland, 1988.

——, *Our Life in This Land*, Griffin Press: Auckland, 1940.

——, *Tidal Creek*, Auckland University Press: Auckland, 1979.

Foucault, Michel, *Discipline and Punish: the Birth of the Prison*, Vintage/Random House: New York, 1979.

Fox, Alistair, 'The Symbolic Function of the Operatic Allusions in Witi Ihimaera's *The Dream Swimmer*', *Journal of Postcolonial Writing*, 42:1: 4–17.

Frame, Janet, *An Autobiography*, The Women's Press: London, 1991 [1989].

——, *Faces in the Water*, Virago: London, 2009 [1961].

——, *Owls Do Cry*, The Women's Press: London, 1985 [1961].

——, *Scented Gardens for the Blind*, George Braziller: New York, 1980 [1964].

——, *The Carpathians*, George Braziller: New York, 1988.

——, *The Lagoon and Other Stories*, Random Century: Auckland, 1990 [1951].

Galli della Loggia, Ernesto, *L'identità italiana*, Il Mulino: Bologna, 1998.

Gaskell, A.P, *The Big Game and Other Stories*, Caxton Press: Christchurch, 1947.

Ginsborg, Paul, *Storia d'Italia: Famiglia, società, Stato*, Einaudi: Torino, 1998: 14.

Gordon, Elizabeth and Tony Deverson, *New Zealand English and English in New Zealand*, New House: Auckland, 1998.

Gorlier, Claudio, 'Janet Frame: l'ombra del falco', *La Stampa*, 30 January 2004: 25.

——, Review of 'J. Frame, *Un angelo alla mia tavola*, Einaudi, Torino 1996', *L'Indice*, (3), 1997.

Grace, Alfred Augustus, *Tales of a Dying Race*, Chatto & Windus: London, 1901.

Grace, Patricia, *Baby No-Eyes*, The Women's Press: London, 1999 [1998].

——, *Cousins*, University of Hawai'i Press: Honolulu, 1998 [1992].

——, *Dogside Story*, University of Hawai'i Press: Honolulu, 2001.

——, *Electric City*, Penguin Books: Auckland, 1987.

——, 'Influences on Writing', in Hereniko and Wilson (eds), *Inside Out: Literature, Cultural Politics, and Identity in the New Pacific*, Rowman & Littlefield: Lanham & Oxford, 1999, 65–73.

——, *Mutuwhenua*, Penguin Books: Auckland, 1994 [1978].

——, *Potiki*, University of Hawai'i Press: Honolulu, 1995 [1986].

——, *Small Holes in the Silence*, Penguin Books: Auckland, 2006.

——, *The Dream Sleepers*, Longman Paul: Auckland, 1980.

——, *The Sky People*, Penguin Books: Auckland, 1994.

——, *Tu*, University of Hawai'i Press: Honolulu, 2004.

——, *Waiariki*, Longman Paul: Auckland, 1975.

Hall, Stuart, 'Negotiating Caribbean Identities', in Gregory Castle (ed.), *Postcolonial Discourse: an Anthology*, Blackwell: Oxford, 2001: 281–92.

Hankin, Cherry, *Critical Essays on the New Zealand Short Story*, Heinemann: Auckland, 1982.

Harlow, Ray, 'Contemporary Māori Language', in McGregor and Williams, *Dirty Silence: Aspects of Language and Literature in New Zealand*, Oxford University Press: Auckland & Oxford, 1991: 29–38.

——, *Māori*, Lincom Europa: München & Newcastle, 1996.

Hawken, Paul, *Blessed Unrest*, Penguin Books: New York, 2008 [2007].

Hereniko, Vilsoni and Rob Wilson (eds), *Inside Out: Literature, Cultural Politics, and Identity in the New Pacific*, Rowman and Littlefield: Lanham & Oxford, 1999.

Hilliard, Noel, *Maori Girl*, Heinemann: London & Auckland, 1960.

——, *Maori Woman*, Robert Hale: London, 1974.

——, *Power of Joy*, Michael Joseph: London, 1965.

——, *Selected Stories*, John McIndoe: Dunedin, 1977.

——, *The Glory and the Dream*, Heinemann: London, 1978.

Holmes, Janet, Maria Stubbe and Meredith Marra, 'Language, Humour and Ethnic Identity Marking in New Zealand English', in Christian Mair (ed.), *The Politics of English as a World Language*, Rodopi: Amsterdam & New York, 2003: 431–55.

Hunter, Lani Kavika, *Spirits of New Zealand: Early Pakeha Writings on Maori*, PhD thesis, University of Auckland, 2004.

Hutching, Megan (ed.), *A Fair Sort of Battering: New Zealand Soldiers Remember the Italian Campaign*, HarperCollins: Auckland, 2004.

Ihimaera, Witi, 'A Maori Perspective', in 'A Symposium on Historical Fiction', *Journal of New Zealand Literature*, 9, 1991: 53–54.

——, 'Bookmarking the Century', *Landfall* 199, 8.1, March 2000: 39–41.

——, *Bulibasha*, Penguin Books: Auckland, 1994.

——, *Dear Miss Mansfield*, Viking: Auckland 1989.

——, *Ihimaera: His Best Stories*, Reed Books: Auckland, 2003.

——, *Kingfisher Come Home*, Secker & Warburg: London, 1995.

——, 'Maori life and literature: a sensory perception', *The Turnbull Library Record*, 15.1, May 1982: 45–55.

——, *Nights in the Gardens of Spain*, Reed: Auckland, 1995.

——, *Pounamu, Pounamu*, Heinemann: Auckland, 1972. Re-published by Reed Books: Auckland, 2003.

——, *Tangi*, Heinemann: Auckland, 1984 [1973].

——, *The Dream Swimmer*, Penguin Books: Auckland, 2005 [1997].

——, *The New Net Goes Fishing*, Heinemann: Auckland, 1977.

——, *The Matriarch*, Reed Books: Auckland, 2003 [1986].

——, *The Rope of Man*, Reed Books: Auckland, 2005.

——, *The Whale Rider* (US edition), Harcourt: Orlando & New York, 2003 [1987].

——, *The Uncle's Story*, University of Hawai'i Press: Honolulu, 2000.

——, *Whanau*, Heinemann: Auckland, 1974.

——, *Whanau II*, Reed Books: Auckland, 2004.

—— (ed.), *Where's Waari?: A History of the Maori through the Short Story*, Reed Books: Auckland, 2000.

——, 'Why I Write', *World Literature Written in English*, 14.1, 1975: 117–19.

——, and D.S. Long (eds), *Into the World of Light*, Heinemann: Auckland, 1982.

James, Trevor, 'Lost Our Birthright Forever? The Maori Writer's Re-invention of New Zealand', *Span*, 24, 1987: 107–121.

James, W.T.G. (ed.), *The Word Within the Word*, University of Waikato (typescript), 1983.

Jannetta, Armando, 'Textual Strategy of Identity Formation in Witi Ihimaera's Fiction', *Commonwealth Essays and Studies*, 12.2, Spring 1990: 17–28.

Jensen, Kai, *Whole Men: The Masculine Tradition in New Zealand Literature*, Auckland University Press: Auckland, 1996.

Jones, Joseph and Johanna, *New Zealand Fiction*, Twayne Publishers: Boston, 1983.

Jones, Lawrence, 'A Symposium on Historical Fiction: Introduction', *Journal of New Zealand Literature*, 9, 1991: 3–9.

——, *Barbed Wire & Mirrors*, University of Otago Press: Dunedin, 1987.

——, 'Roderick Finlayson, 1904–1992', *Kōtare 2008*, Special Issue – Essays in New Zealand Literary Biography Series Two: 'Early Male Prose Writers', <http://wwwnzetc. org/tm/scholarly/tei-Whi072Kota-t1-g1-t19.html>

——, 'The Novel', in Terry Sturm (ed.), *The Oxford History of New Zealand Literature*, Oxford University Press: Auckland, 1991: 107–199.

Jung, C.G., *The Symbolic Life*, in *The Collected Works of C.G. Jung*, (18), Princeton University Press: Princeton, 1989.

Jussawalla, Feroza and Reed Way Dasenbrock (eds), *Interviews with Writers of the Post-Colonial World*, University of Mississippi Press: Jackson & London, 1992: 222–42.

Kedgley, Sue, 'Patricia Grace', in *Our Own Country: Leading New Zealand Women Writers talk about their Writing and Lives*, Penguin Books: Auckland, 1989.

Keenan, Danny, 'Bound to the land', in E. Pawson & T. Brooking (eds), *Environmental Histories of New Zealand*, Oxford University Press: South Melbourne, 2002: 246–60.

Keown, Michelle, 'Maori or English? The Politics of Language in Patricia Grace's *Baby No-Eyes*', in Christian Mair (ed.), *The Politics of English as a World Language*, Rodopi: Amsterdam & New York, 2003: 419–29.

——, *Pacific Islands Writing. The Postcolonial Literatures of Aotearoa/New Zealand and Oceania*, Oxford University Press: Oxford, 2007.

King, Michael, 'A Magnificent New Zealand-Baroque Near-Success', *Metro*, 6.62, August 1986: 170.

——, *Nga Iwi o te Motu: 1000 Years of Maori History*, Reed Books: Auckland, 2001 [1997].

——, *The Penguin History of New Zealand*, Penguin Books: Auckland, 2003.

Köster, Elisabeth, 'Oral and Literacy Patterns in the Novels of Patricia Grace', *Australian & New Zealand Studies in Canada*, 10, December 1993: 87–105.

Latouche, Serge, 'Degrowth Economics', *Le Monde Diplomatique*, http://mondediplo. com/2004/11/14latouche

——, *In the Wake of the Affluent Society: An Exploration of Post-Development*, Zed Books: London & New Jersey, 1993 [1991].

——, *La scommessa della decrescita*, Feltrinelli: Milano, 2008 [2006].

Lee, Jenny, *Notes on Patricia Grace's Potiki*, Kaiako Publications (typescript): November 1990.

Loomba, Ania, *Colonialism/Postcolonialism*, Routledge: London & New York, 1998.

Mair, Christian, *The Politics of English as a World Language: New Horizons in Postcolonial Cultural Studies*, Rodopi: Amsterdam & New York, 2003.

Mansfield, Katherine, *Something Childish and Other Stories*, Constable: London, 1924.

McGaw, William, '"Another Foothold": Exile and Return in Patricia Grace's *Mutuwhenua*', *Australian & New Zealand Studies in Canada*, 6, Fall 1991: 103–11.

McGregor, Graham, and Mark Williams (eds), *Dirty Silence: Aspects of Language and Literature in New Zealand*, Oxford University Press: Auckland & Oxford, 1991.

McRae, Jane, 'Māori Literature: A Survey', in Terry Sturm (ed.), *The Oxford History of New Zealand Literature*, Oxford University Press: Auckland 1991: 1–24.

——, 'Patricia Grace and Complete Communication', *Australian & New Zealand Studies in Canada*, 10, December 1993: 66–86.

——, 'Patricia Grace/Interviewed by Jane McRae', in E. Alley and M. Williams (eds), *In the Same Room. Conversation with New Zealand Writers*, Auckland University Press: Auckland, 1992: 285–96.

McWilliam, G.H., 'Introduction', in Verga, *Cavalleria Rusticana and Other Stories*, Penguin: London, 1999.

Mellino, Miguel, *La Critica Postcoloniale*, Meltemi: Roma, 2005.

Metge, Joan, *The Maoris of New Zealand*, Routledge & Kegan Paul: London, 1976.

Mohanram, Radhika, and Gita Rajan (eds), *English Postcoloniality*, Greenwood Press: Westport (Connecticut) & London, 1996.

Montanari, Massimo, *Il cibo come cultura*, Laterza: Bari, 2006.

——, *La cucina italiana*, Laterza: Bari, 2000.

Murry, John Middleton (ed.), *The Journal of Katherine Mansfield*, Constable: London, 1954.

New, W.H., 'Frank Sargeson as Social Story-teller', *Landfall 143*, 36.3, September 1982: 343–46.

Nunns, Rachel, 'Doing Her Job: Patricia Grace's Fiction', in Paul Sharrad (ed.), *Readings in Pacific Literature*, New Literatures Research Centre, University of Wollongong, Wollongong (Australia), 1993: 114–18.

Ojinmah, Umelo, *Witi Ihimaera: A Changing Vision*, University of Otago Press: Dunedin, 1993.

Oliva, Gianni, *I vinti e i liberati*, Mondadori: Milano, 1994.

Orbell, Margaret (ed.), *Contemporary Maori Writing*, Reed Books: Auckland, 1970.

——, *Waiata: Maori Songs in History*, Reed Books: Auckland, 1991.

Parry, Benita, 'Resistance theory/theorising resistance or two cheers for nativism', in Francis Barker, Peter Hulme and Margaret Iversen (eds), *Colonial discourse/postcolonial theory*, Manchester University Press: Manchester & New York, 1994: 172–96.

Pawson, Eric, and Tom Brooking (eds), *Environmental Histories of New Zealand*, Oxford University Press: South Melbourne, 2002.

Pearson, Bill, 'Attitudes to the Maori in Some Pakeha Fiction', *Fretful Sleepers and Other Essays*, Heinemann Educational Books: Auckland, 1974: 46–71.

—— (ed.), Roderick Finlayson, *Brown Man's Burden and later stories*, Auckland University Press: Auckland, 1973.

——, 'Witi Ihimaera and Patricia Grace', in Cherry Hankin (ed.), *Critical Essays on the New Zealand Short Story*, Heinemann: Auckland, 1982: 166–84.

Petrini, Carlo, *Slow Food: the Case for Taste*, Columbia University Press: New York, 2001.

Petronio, Giuseppe, *L'attività letteraria in Italia*, Palumbo: Firenze, 1991.

Pirandello, Luigi, *L'Umorismo*, Oscar Mondadori: Milano, 1992 [1908].

Pratt, Mary Louise, 'Scratches on the Face of the Country; or What Mr Barrow Saw in the Land of the Bushmen', *Critical Inquiry*, 12.1, Autumn 1985: 138–62.

Prentice, Christine, 'Nationalism vs. Internationalism? Witi Ihimaera's *The Matriarch* and Critical Abjection', *Nationalism vs. Internationalism: (Inter)National Dimensions of Literatures in English*, Stauffenburg Verlag: Tübingen, 1996: 549–55.

——, 'What Was the Maori Renaissance?', in M. Williams (ed.), *Writing at the Edge of the Universe*, Canterbury University Press: Christchurch, 2004: 85–108.

Rask Knudsen, Eva, *The Circle and the Spiral*, Rodopi: Amsterdam & New York, 2004.

Reed, A.W., *Reed Book of Maori Mythology*, Reed Books: Auckland, 2004.

Rhodes, H. Winston, 'Introduction', in Frank Sargeson, *I Saw in My Dream*, Auckland University Press: Auckland, 1974: vii–xix.

——, 'Janet Frame: A Way of Seeing in *The Lagoon and Other Stories*', in Cherry Hankin (ed.), *Critical Essays on the New Zealand Short Story*, Heinemann: Auckland, 1982: 112–31.

——, *New Zealand Fiction Since 1945: A Critical Survey of Recent Novels and Short Stories*, John McIndoe: Dunedin, 1968.

——, 'The Moral Climate of Sargeson's Stories', in H. Shaw (ed.), *The Puritan and the Waif: A Symposium of Critical Essays on the Works of Frank Sargeson*, (typescript) 1954: 29–41. [Printed by H.L. Hofmann: Auckland, 1954.]

Rika-Heke, Powhiri Wharemarama, 'Margin or Center? "Let me tell you! In the Land of my Ancestors I am the Centre": Indigenous Writing in Aotearoa', in R. Mohanram and G. Rajan (eds), *English Postcoloniality*, Greenwood Press: Westport (Connecticut) & London, 1996: 147–63.

Robinson, Roger, and Nelson Wattie (eds), *The Oxford Companion to New Zealand Literature*, Oxford University Press: Melbourne & Oxford, 1998.

Said, W. Edward, *Culture and Imperialism*, Vintage Books: New York, 1994 [1993].

——, *Orientalism*, Vintage Books: New York, 1979 [1978].

Salmond, Anne, *Hui: A Study of Maori Ceremonial Gatherings*, Reed Books: Wellington & London, 1976 [1975].

Sargeson, Frank, *I Saw in My Dream*, Auckland University Press: Auckland, 1974 [1949].

——, *The Stories of Frank Sargeson*, Longman Paul: Auckland, 1973 [1964].

Sarti, Antonella, *Spiritcarvers: Interviews with Eighteen Writers from New Zealand*, Rodopi: Amsterdam & Atlanta (GA), 1998.

Sharrad, Paul, 'Listening to One's Ancestors: An Interview with Witi Ihimaera', *Australian & New Zealand Studies in Canada*, 8, December 1992: 97–105.

——, (ed.), *Readings in Pacific Literature*, New Literatures Research Centre, University of Wollongong: Wollongong (Australia), 1993.

Shaw, Helen (ed.), *The Puritan and the Waif: A Symposium of Critical Essays on the Works of Frank Sargeson*, (typescript) 1954. [Printed by H.L. Hofmann: Auckland, 1954.]

Simms, Norman, 'A Maori Literature in English'; Part I: Prose Fiction – Patricia Grace', *Pacific Moana Quarterly*, 3.2, April 1978: 186–99.

Simons, Jon, 'Michel Foucault', *Contemporary Critical Theorists: from Lacan to Said*, Edinburgh University Press: Edinburgh, 2004: 185–200.

Sinclair, Keith, *A History of New Zealand*, revised edition, Penguin Books: Auckland, 1991 [1969].

Slemon, Stephen, 'Post-Colonial Critical Theories', in Gregory Castle (ed.), *Postcolonial Discourse: an Anthology*, Blackwell: Oxford, 2001: 100–116.

Smith, Steve, 'Louis Althusser', in Simons (ed.), *Contemporary Critical Theorists: from Lacan to Said*, Edinburgh University Press: Edinburgh, 2004: 51–67.

Sorba, Carlotta, 'Il 1848 e la drammatizzazione della politica', in Banti and Ginsborg (eds), *Storia d'Italia – Annali 22: Il Risorgimento*, Einaudi: Torino, 2007: 481–508.

Spivak, Gayatri C., 'Can the Subaltern Speak? Speculations on Widow-Sacrifice', *Wedge*, (7) 8 (Winter/Spring), 1985: 120–30.

Stafford, Don, *Introducing Māori Culture*, Reed Books: Auckland, 1997. [First published as *Tangata Whenua*, Reed Books: Auckland, 1996.]

Sturm, Terry (ed.), *The Oxford History of New Zealand Literature*, Oxford University Press: Auckland, 1991.

Tauroa, Hiwi and Pat, *Te Marae: A Guide to Customs & Protocol*, Reed Books: Auckland, 1986.

Tausky, Thomas E., '"Stories That Show Them Who We Are": An Interview with Patricia Grace', *Australian & New Zealand Studies in Canada*, 6, Fall 1991: 90–102.

Thornton, Agathe, *Maori Oral Literature as Seen by a Classicist*, Huia Publishers: Wellington, 1999.

Todorov, Tzvetan, *The Conquest of America: The Question of the Other*, Harper and Row: New York, 1982 [1974].

Tompkins, Joanne, '"It all depends on what story you hear": Historiographic Metafiction and Colin Johnson's *Dr Wooreddy's Prescription for Enduring the Ending of the World* and Ihimaera's *The Matriarch*', *Modern Fiction Studies*, 38.4, Winter 1990: 483–98.

Verga, Giovanni, *Cavalleria Rusticana and Other Stories*, Penguin: London, 1999.

Walker, Holly, 'Developing Difference: Attitudes towards Maori "Development" in Patricia Grace's *Potiki* and *Dogside Story*', *Kunapipi*, 27.12, 2005: 215–30.

Walker, Rangi, 'Maori Beliefs: An Integrated Cosmos', in W.T.G. James (ed.), *The Word Within the Word*, University of Waikato (typescript), 1983: 89–94.

Wallerstein, Immanuel, *La retorica del potere. Critica dell'universalismo europeo*, Fazi: Roma, 2007. [*European Universalism. The Rhetoric of Power*, New Press: New York, 2006].

Wevers, Lydia, 'Short Fiction by Maori Writers', *Commonwealth Essays and Studies*, 16.2, Spring 1994: 26–33.

——, 'The Short Story', in Terry Sturm (ed.), *The Oxford History of New Zealand Literature*, Oxford University Press: Auckland, 1991: 203–268.

Williams, Mark, 'Interview with Witi Ihimaera', *Landfall*, 45.3, September 1991: 281–97.

——, *Leaving the Highway: Six Contemporary New Zealand Novelists*, Auckland University Press: Auckland, 1990.

—— (ed.), 'Witi Ihimaera and Patricia Grace: The Maori Renaissance', http://www.ucalgary.ca/UofC/eduweb/eng392/492williams.html

——, *Writing at the Edge of the Universe*, (Essays from the 'Creative Writing in New Zealand' conference, University of Canterbury, August 2003), Canterbury University Press: Christchurch, 2004.

—— and E. Gordon, 'Raids on the Articulate: Code-Switching, Style-Shifting and Post-Colonial Writing', *Journal of Commonwealth Literature*, 33.2, 1998: 75–96.

Williams, Patrick, 'Edward Said', in *Contemporary Critical Theorists: from Lacan to Said*, Edinburgh University Press: Edinburgh, 2004: 269–85.

Wilson, Janet, 'The Maori at War and Strategic Survival: *Tu* by Patricia Grace', *Hecate*, 34.1, 2008.

Zoppi, Isabella Maria, 'Words, Magic, Power: The Memory of the Land in Janet Frame, Derek Walcott and Gabriel Garcia Marquez', *Englishes*, 5.2, 1998: 30–55.

Index

illness (Maori attitudes to) 57, 195–96, 198
indigenised reading 101, 106, 109, 142,
    152, 164, 182
indigenous peoples 35, 37, 47, 92–93,
    169, 190–91, 203, 231
Italian Risorgimento 210–14, 226

James, Colin 91
James, Henry 102
James, Trevor 167
Jensen, Kai 28, 31, 32, 36
Johnstone, J.C. 17
Jones, Lawrence 15, 17, 76, 79, 157
Joyce, James 31, 39
Jung, C.G. 220, 228–29

Kafka, Franz 31
Kahukiwa, Robyn 96
Kedgley, Sue 97–98
Keenan, Danny 183
Keown, Michelle 19, 158, 164, 178,
    180–81
King, Michael 7, 11, 12, 31–32, 157, 167
King Movement (Kingitanga) 8, 12, 18
Kirby, Joshua Henry 16
kohanga reo 9, 96, 182, 197
kura kaupapa 9, 96, 182

land
– alienation of tribal holdings 11–12, 54,
    55–56, 90, 96, 125, 145, 162, 164, 166,
    187–88
– in colonial literature 16–17
– in Finlayson 48, 52–53, 54-56, 58–60
– in Sargeson 33–34, 36–37, 41–42
– in Verga 50
– Maori bond with 7, 12, 42, 45, 52,

55–56, 85, 95, 101, 103, 127, 134–35,
    154–55, 162, 183, 194
– Pakeha relations 17, 33–34, 36, 41–43,
    45, 90, 135, 154, 187
– protests 95, 101, 153, 155, 159, 181,
    186, 207–208, 209, 210
Land March 96, 197
Land Wars 166 (see also New Zealand
    Wars)
language
– in Grace and Ihimaera 93, 97, 98,
    101, 105, 109, 131, 133–34, 136, 146,
    150–51, 169–82, 198–99, 206, 207
– in postcolonial theory 5, 7, 8, 9, 93,
    169–70, 181–82, 206
Latouche, Serge 47, 48, 58, 83, 188, 189
Lawrence, D.H. 48–50
Lee, Jenny 179
liminality 8–9, 16, 57, 89, 92
literacy 8, 9–15
Loomba, Ania 3, 18–19
Loti, Pierre 19

Machiavelli, Niccolò 4
magic realism 72, 103, 106
Mansfield, Katherine 24–25, 46, 98, 151,
    152, 158
Maori (origin of the word) 7
Maori language
– alphabet and phonology 170–71, 235
– defence and survival of 9, 74–75, 95, 96,
    146, 169, 181–82, 197
– early texts in 10–15
– repression and loss of 8, 52, 56, 72, 98,
    145, 162, 164, 181–82, 196, 228
– similarity with Italian 171, 219, 224,
    227–28, 229

274

CPSIA information can be obtained
at www.ICGtesting.com
Printed in the USA
LVHW012125140921
697808LV00011BA/263